THE ISLAMIC ART AND ARCHITECTURE

THE ISLAMIC ART AND ARCHITECTURE

Edited by

SIR THOMAS ARNOLD and ALFRED GUILLAUME

Goodword
BOOKS

First published in Oxford 1931
under the title of *The Legacy of Islam*

First published by Goodword Books 2001

GOODWORD BOOKS
1, Nizamuddin West Market,
New Delhi 110 013
Tel. 462 5454, 462 6666
Fax 469 7333, 464 7980
e-mail: skhan@vsnl.com
website: http://www.alrisala.org

Printed in India

PREFACE

*The Legacy of Islam** is a companion volume to *The Legacy of Greece*, *The Legacy of Rome*, *The Legacy of the Middle Ages*, and *The Legacy of Israel.* It seeks to give an account of those elements in the culture of Europe which are derived from the Islamic world. Broadly speaking, the Legacies of Greece and Rome are the legacies of two homogeneous and original cultures, each emanating from a definite geographical centre. The Legacy of the Middle Ages is the legacy of an epoch in the development of western European civilization. The Legacy of Israel is 'the contribution that has come to the sum of human thought from Judaism and from the Jewish view of the world'. The Legacy of Islam is to be understood in a different sense from any of these. It is a provocative title, the meaning of which is only fully explained by the book itself. The nearest parallel is the Legacy of Israel. But whereas it is from the religion of the Jews that the complexion of the Legacy of Israel is derived, in the Legacy of Islam we do not treat of the Legacy of the religion of Muḥammad *quâ* religion: the reader will learn from this book that there is little that is *peculiarly* Islamic in the contributions which Occidental and Oriental Muslims have made to European culture. On the contrary, the legacy has proved least valuable where religion has exerted the strongest influence, as in Muslim Law. But Islam is the fundamental fact which made the Legacy possible. It was under the protection and patronage of the Islamic Empire that the arts and sciences which this book describes flourished.

Arabia is the birthplace of Islam, and the language of Arabia lies behind all that has been written in this book. Islamic and Arabic have often been used as interchangeable terms, and Language and Religion in the great days of the Muslim Caliphate were inseparable. Arabic is the Greek of the Semitic

* The book was first published under the title of *The Legacy of Islam.*

world, and it was a fortunate thing for Islam that its message was delivered at a time when Arabic was potentially at its zenith. Aramaic was a poverty-stricken tongue compared with Arabic, and not even classical Hebrew at its best could rival Arabic in its astonishing elasticity. From its own inner resources it could evolve by autogenous processes the *mot juste* which new arts and new sciences demanded for their intellectual expression.

A fundamental characteristic of the Semitic languages is to have only three consonants to the verb. There are exceptions to this rule in the various languages, but such exceptions are comparatively rare. It follows almost inevitably that compound words to express complex ideas are practically unknown in Arabic. Consequently, it is the more interesting and remarkable that a language which is so circumscribed should be able to cope with all the lore of the Greek world and so seldom give rise to a suspicion that any strain is being put upon its resources.

Arabic is fitted to express relations with more conciseness than the Aryan languages because of the extraordinary flexibility of the verb and noun. Thus, the ideas: break, shatter, try to break, cause to break, allow to be broken, break one another, ask some one to break, pretend to break, are among many variations of the fundamental verbal theme which can, or could, be expressed by vowel changes and consonantal augments without the aid of the supplementary verbs and pronouns which we have to employ in English. The noun, too, has an appropriate form for many diverse things, such as the time and place of an action, bodily defects, diseases, instruments, colours, trades, and so on. One example must suffice. Let us take the root d-w-r, which, in its simplest form, means to turn or revolve (intransitive).

dawwara, to turn a thing round.	*dāwara*, to walk about with some one.
'adāra, to make go round, and so, to control.	*tadawwara*, *istadāra* } to be round in shape.

dawr, turning (noun).
dawrah, one turning.
dawarān, circulation.
duwār, vertigo.
dawwār, pedlar or vagrant.
dawwārah, mariner's compass.
madār, axis.
mudārah, round water-skin.
mudīr, controller.

None of these forms is fortuitous, but is predetermined by the structural genius of the Arabic language.

It will be realized that with such manifold nuances at the disposal of every verb and noun the Arabic language could readily be adapted to express the scientific terminology of the classical world. The Arabs were an observant race. If analytical reasoning was not indigenous to their language they compensated for the lack of it by having a specific name for every different type of thing. A camel of so many years of age, the mother of so many foals, a good trotting beast, a milch camel, and so on, all these had their proper names, a fact which makes an exact and felicitous rendering of Arabic poetry notoriously difficult.

The triliteral root with its ramifications through a thousand forms, each of which has an assonance with the same form of another root, produces a rhythm in Arabic as natural as it is inevitable. When we utter an abstract idea we have no thought of the primitive meaning of the word we employ. 'Association' sits very loosely to *socius* in the mind of the speaker. We have no *socius* nor *ad* in English. But in Arabic the material is never more than faintly obscured beneath the abstract; its presence can always be felt. What in English would be but an indifferent pun at best, is merely etymological consciousness in an Arab, who would perceive at once the nicety of the explanation of *Mene, Mene, tekel upharsin* which is given in Daniel v. 25. The Hebrew of the Old Testament can hardly be said to be free from artificial etymologies which are obviously self-conscious attempts to find a radical justification for names whose primitive significance has been lost. But I do not know of such an extreme example as can be seen in the naive explanation given by an Arabic writer of the name of an ancient chieftain Muzaiqiyā, the little man who tore up (*mazaqa*) his clothes every evening!

Belief in the paramount superiority of the Arabic language is an article of faith among Muslims, and an exact knowledge of its grammar in cultured circles the distinguishing mark of a gentleman. Yet it is a remarkable fact that before the end of the first century of the Hijrah an Umayyad caliph was unable to convey his meaning to the pure-blooded Arabs of the desert. The fact that the chaste language of ancient Arabia is only to be found in the ancient pre-Islamic and early Islamic writers, so far from discouraging attempts to master its intricacies has incited Muslim scholars of all lands to a laborious study of its grammar and rhetoric. Nor are such labours fruitless. If it is profitable for the cultured European to imitate the periods of Cicero, it is also profitable for the Oriental to acquire a discriminating taste for the classics of his own language.[1]

The charm which the Arabic language and Arabic literature never fails to exert on its devotees lies in its unexpectedness, its unaffectedness, and its love of direct speech. Elsewhere in this volume examples will be found of the contributions which the Arabic tongue has made to the languages of Europe. How many words lived only for a day or were slain by the European Renaissance only specialists can say. What, for instance, have the physicians done with the *soda* which once formed the opening discourse of the third book of Avicenna's Qānūn,[2] the *Sermo universalis de Sodâ*? This barbarous transcription stands for *ṣudā'*, headache, and comes appropriately enough from the root *ṣada'a*, to split. Beside this service we owe a great debt to Arabic in the field of Old Testament studies.

[1] Professor Nicholson's *Translations of Eastern Poetry and Prose*, Cambridge, 1922, is invaluable as an indication of the pleasure and profit to be gained from reading Islamic literature.

[2] See further, p. 329.

As soon as Arabic became an imperial language the Jews perceived its close affinity with Hebrew. In the third century of the Hijrah the Jews had imitated the Arabs, or rather, the non-Arab Muslims, and submitted their language to grammatical analysis. The grammar of Rabbi David Qimḥī (died *c.* 1235), which exercised a profound influence on the subsequent study of Hebrew among Christians, borrows a great deal from Arabic sources. His exegesis, which was founded on his Grammar, is frequently to be traced in the Authorized Version of the Old Testament scriptures.

Since the beginning of the nineteenth century there has been constant recourse to Arabic for the explanation of rare words and forms in Hebrew; for Arabic, though more than a thousand years the junior as a literary language, is the senior philologically by countless centuries. Perplexing phenomena in Hebrew can often be explained as solitary and archaic survivals of forms which are frequent and common in the cognate Arabic. Words and idioms whose precise sense had been lost in Jewish tradition, receive a ready and convincing explanation from the same source. Indeed, no serious student of the Old Testament can afford to dispense with a first-hand knowledge of Arabic. The pages of any critical commentary on the Old Testament will illustrate the debt that biblical exegesis owes to Arabic. And the legacy is not yet all spent. When Julius Wellhausen, whose writings still dominate the study of the Old Testament, ceased to write on matters Arabian, the study of Arabic and of Islamic institutions lost the services of a genius. Yet a fair exchange was effected when Ignaz Goldziher forsook Hebrew for Arabic. An outstanding example of what may be done by him who holds the balance true can be seen in the writings of Robertson Smith, whose *Religion of the Semites* is a masterly synthesis of old Arabian and ancient Canaanitish lore.

It is difficult to write calmly of the loss which our book has suffered in the untimely death of my fellow-editor, Sir Thomas

Arnold. He was a personal friend of every contributor, and his death was not only an irreparable loss to Oriental scholarship, but it has left a wound in the hearts of his friends which time alone can heal. His own contribution, a chapter on the Legacy of Islamic Painting, he left unfinished. His knowledge of the subject was unique in England, and it has seemed fitting to print his article, just as he left it, as an appendix to the chapter on Minor Arts, rather than to attempt to add anything to it.[1]

Sir Thomas Arnold and I drew up the plan of the book, and he lived to read most of the articles in proof. Since then Professor Nicholson has been good enough to read every chapter with me, and besides making a number of valuable suggestions has allowed me to consult him on any doubtful matter.

For arranging the illustrations of the volume, apart from the articles on the Minor Arts and Architecture, for which the authors provided their own illustrations, I am indebted to Mr. A. L. P. Norrington, of the Clarendon Press.

It has seemed advisable to confine the scope of this book to the achievements of the past. At the present time Modernism has interrupted the reform movement in the religious world of Islam, while Materialism encroaches daily on the thought and literature of the East. It would be the height of rashness to attempt to forecast the course of events. On the one hand, the past history of Arabic and Islamic institutions displays their extraordinary vitality despite attacks from within and without; on the other hand, many far-reaching innovations have been made in Islamic countries during the last few years. This book may help the observer to estimate the importance of those changes and to pursue them to their outcome with interest and sympathy.

The system of transliteration is that recommended by the Royal Asiatic Society. This system permits certain variations

[1] This course is further justified by the fact that the author had said that the influence of Muslim painting on European painting was negligible.

which will be found from time to time in the different chapters, e.g. the diphthong *ay* may be written *ai* as in Ḥunain (Ḥunayn). Well-known names like Mecca and Caliph and so on have been left in the forms familiar to generations of English readers. The name Muḥammad, on the other hand, is generally written as it is spelt in Arabic.

In a work of this kind in which each chapter is a unity in itself, the same writers and the same subjects must sometimes be discussed more than once. The only alternative is a cross-reference. Occasionally it will be found that the contributors differ in their estimate of the significance of certain phenomena common to East and West. Such differences of opinion have been allowed to stand in order that the reader may see both sides of the question and form his own judgement.

A. G.

CONTENTS

LIST OF ILLUSTRATIONS

SPAIN AND PORTUGAL

THE modern Spanish school of scientific historians is not favourably disposed towards the legacy of Islam. A hundred years ago the importance of 'the Moors in Spain' was unduly exaggerated; to-day the subject is out of fashion among serious workers and apt to be despised by intelligent readers. This attitude may be regrettable, but there are reasons for it, and not all of them are bad reasons. The inaccuracies in Conde's *Historia de la dominación de los árabes en España*, the somewhat unfortunate conclusions reached by Dozy regarding the Cid—conclusions which subsequent research has proved to be fallacious, and lastly the tendency emanating from French and American universities to trace everything, if possible, to a Latin origin, have led Hispanists to regard oriental studies with a certain feeling of distrust, from which not even the solid achievements of an Asín or a Ribera have altogether been able to save them.

Other influences also have been at work, as a result of the social and political conditions of modern Spain. An idea has gained ground that oriental studies, and Islamic solutions for the problems of Spanish history, philology, and art, belong to that romantic but disastrous tradition, which, after a nineteenth century of invasion, civil war, and unrest, ended in the Spanish-American conflict of 1898. The movement for reform and recuperation, begun by 'the generation of 1898' and encouraged by the inspired teaching and blameless life of Francisco Giner, led to the development of that sense of accurate scholarship which is so conspicuously manifest in the work of Professor Menéndez Pidal. Yet it was singularly unfortunate that wherever Pidal turned—to the old ballads, to the poem of the Cid, to the origins of the Spanish language—he found a body of ill-supported assumptions concerning 'Moorish origins', assumptions which had to be cleared away before any real progress could be made.

Menéndez Pidal was so much better equipped than any of his contemporaries that the conclusion was drawn that a Romance philologist must inevitably be more reliable in Spain than an orientalist, and a Romance explanation of any phenomenon in Spanish philology or Spanish art intrinsically more probable than a solution derived from oriental studies. Pidal himself, however, had no illusions as to the value or necessity of the study of Arabic in Spanish philology; and in the first number of the *Revista de Filología Española*, founded by him in 1914, the leading article was by Professor Miguel Asín.

Effects of Islam on political and economic history

Yet there is another line of opposition in Spain to the legacy of Islam: that the Muslims were the cause, directly or indirectly, of all the evils which afterwards befell the country. 'Without Islam' (writes one of the best of the younger Spanish medievalists) 'Spain would have followed the same course as France, Germany, Italy and England; and to judge by what was actually accomplished through the centuries, Spain might have led the way. But it was not to be. Islam conquered the whole of the Peninsula, distorted the destinies of Iberia and allotted to it a different part in the tragi-comedy of history—a role of sacrifice and vigilance, of sentinel and teacher, a role which had enormous importance in the life of Europe, but which proved extremely expensive to Spain.'[1]

The first result of the Muslim conquest of 711 was that Iberian particularism sprang once more to life. All along the mountain chains which cross northern Spain from the Atlantic to the Mediterranean arose nuclei of resistance to the Muslim invaders; and these nuclei became in time the kingdoms of Asturias and Navarre and the 'counties' in the Pyrenees. The

[1] C. Sánchez Albornoz, *España y el Islam*. (*Revista de Occidente*, vii, no. 70, p. 4, April 1929.) The Arabic origin of the famous name (*al-burnusī*, the man with the burnous) will not escape notice.

new states led a separate existence for something like eight centuries, with nothing in common except their faith and the fact that the dialects they spoke had once been a form of Low Latin. They had begun as Christian points of resistance, like the Balkan states, and so they continued. When at length Islam ceased to be a dangerous neighbour, each of the Christian states turned its gaze in a different direction; they fought with one another again and again, and in their isolation created different dialects, different traditions. The most vital of these new kingdoms was the kingdom of Castille; but even that, owing to its prolonged contact with Islam, was some three centuries behindhand in the development of those institutions which are characteristic of medieval Europe. Meanwhile the reconquest advanced southwards, and the Christian kings replenished their resources by the occupation of immense territories inhabited by Muslim agricultural labourers, while their Christian subjects tended to become more and more an exclusive military caste. The economic consequences of the reconquest were disastrous. It was not that the influence of Islam was directly harmful, but it certainly retarded the economic development of the Christian states. Christian Spain revolved for five centuries in the economic orbit of the Islamic South; commerce was monopolized by Muslims and Jews. For nearly four hundred years the Christian kingdoms in Spain used no money except Arabic or French, and for two hundred more the kings of Castille had no gold coinage of their own. Among the 'Old Christians' there was no impulse towards economic activity; the reconquest, whether it was a conscious ideal or not, absorbed all men of action in military adventure. When the reconquest was interrupted, as it was from the middle of the thirteenth century until the fifteenth, the spirit of adventure led Aragon to seek hegemony in Italy and the East, and Portugal to exploration in Africa and the Atlantic, while Castille, having no outlet to the sea, consumed its energies in dynastic quarrels and barons' wars.

The union of Aragon and Castille in the persons of Ferdinand and Isabella, which led to the capitulation of Granada and the end of the *reconquista*, in 1492, coincided with the discovery of America; and this once more drew away, on the greatest adventure in history, the most vigorous part of the Spanish population. The banishment of the Jews, which also took place in that year, had not been unpopular with the 'Old Christians'; but the expulsion of the *Moriscos* (the Spanish Muslims who by one means or another had been converted to Christianity) never had the support of the majority of the Christian inhabitants; and when, at the beginning of the seventeenth century, the country was suddenly deprived of all its skilled workmen and several hundred thousand agricultural labourers by this measure, the decline of Spain was inevitable.

Yet the fact of living in contact with a Muslim people had had at least one advantage. It had created in the small cultivated minorities of the Christian kingdoms a spirit of toleration rare in Europe in the Middle Ages. The French crusaders who had helped Alfonso VIII to win the battle of Las Navas de Tolosa (1212) deserted him in disgust when they saw how mildly he treated the conquered Muslims, while Pedro II of Aragon died fighting for the Albigensian 'heretics', and several monarchs of Castille and Aragon surrounded themselves with learned Moors and Jews. They employed Muslim architects, listened to Muslim musicians, and enjoyed the refinements of Muslim culture. But at the same time the fact of constant 'holy wars' against Islam at length produced an exacerbation of religious sentiment. In no country in Europe did the clergy reach a position of power and influence comparable with that achieved in Spain; and the country came to be governed by an ecclesiastical minority with whom the true interests of Spain took second place: 'Spain sacrificed to Catholicism both liberty of spirit and greatness as a nation.'

'Islam, while it died out in al-Andalus, ended by poisoning Spain.

Ferdinand and Isabella soon fell victims, and with innocent hands administered the draught to their own kingdoms. In the first place they abandoned the traditional toleration of the houses of Castille and Aragon; they allowed themselves to be overruled by the ideas and sentiments of the ecclesiastical minority, and tried to achieve the fusion of their ill-united kingdoms by converting the national unity into a unity which was less political than religious . . . Philip II, urged onward by the ideas which had been imprinted on his mind by the ecclesiastical minority, denaturalized the policy of Ferdinand and Isabella to the limit of intolerance and absurdity; and the prosecution of this line of conduct by the successive Philips ruined in a few generations that marvellous flower of Hispanic thought, the only favourable legacy which Islam had bequeathed.'[1]

Races and Languages in Muslim Spain

Such is the indictment of a modern Spanish historian. Yet it cannot be denied that while Europe lay for the most part in misery and decay, both materially and spiritually, the Spanish Muslims created a splendid civilization and an organized economic life. Muslim Spain played a decisive part in the development of art, science, philosophy, and poetry, and its influence reached even to the highest peaks of the Christian thought of the thirteenth century, to Thomas Aquinas and Dante. Then, if ever, Spain was 'the torch of Europe'.

But who were the torch-bearers? It was formerly the custom to call them 'Moors' or 'Arabs', but such a statement is far too sweeping. The leader of the first successful expedition into Spain, Ṭāriq, was not an Arab but a Berber, and so were a large proportion of his followers: the actual figures given are 300 Arabs and 7,000 Berbers. The forces brought over in the following year, 712, by Mūsā ibn Nuṣair were also a mixed force of Arabs (from different parts of Arabia), Syrians, Copts, and Berbers. Study of ancient records and modern place-names (particularly in the kingdom of Valencia) makes it possible to

[1] *Revista de Occidente*, vol. vii, no. 70, p. 28 (April 1929).

arrive at an approximate tribal distribution of Arabs in Spain, both directly after the invasion and later: and besides their tribal names, the invaders brought their tribal quarrels, which were fought out in Spain with as much bitterness as in the land of their origin. Many families of Christians living in Spain were converted to Islam, and the more important of them, and some who remained Christian, left their names also, with the Arabic prefix *Banū-*, or *Banī-*, 'sons of'.

There was much intermarriage between Muslims and Christians. The son of Mūsā ibn Nuṣair and other leaders of the expedition married into the family of Witiza, the last legitimate king of Visigothic Spain; and throughout the country the mothers of the next generation, whether Muslim or Christian, were all Spanish. The Muslims of succeeding generations preferred the mothers of their children to be those fair-complexioned slaves captured in the north of Spain, rather than, or in addition to, their own womenfolk. Professor Ribera has studied the records of the slave-market at Córdoba at various periods.[1] The purchase of a slave was not so simple a transaction as is often imagined. It had to be concluded in the presence of a notary, and the purposes for which a female slave was required, as well as her capabilities and treatment, were carefully considered. Women enjoyed more freedom and more consideration under the Umayyads in Spain than under the 'Abbāsids of Baghdād; yet it was thought highly desirable that those destined to become the mothers of children in good families should be fair-skinned, and, if possible, Galicians. The result was that, although their descendants bore the names of their ancestors in the male line only, the purity of the Arab race was diminished by crossing with Spanish strains in each successive generation, and the more Arab names a man bore the less Arab blood he had in his veins. It is wrong, therefore, to assume that all Muslims in Spain were Arabs, and all Christians Romans or Goths; that all of these fled

[1] Julián Ribera, *Disertaciones y opúsculos*, vol. i, pp. 17–25. (Madrid, 1928.)

to the north for refuge at the time of the conquest, or that the 'reconquest' was a war lasting eight centuries between the 'Latino-Goths' in the north and the Andalusian 'Arabs' in the south.

From the third or fourth generation after the conquest, most Spanish Muslims were bilingual, both those of Arab descent (by that time a small minority) and those of Spanish Christian origin. Besides Arabic, which was the official language, they used a Romance patois, which was also spoken by the Mozárabes (*musta'rib*, 'Arabized' or 'would-be Arab')—the Christians still living under Muslim rule. Al-Khushanī (Aljoxaní), in his history of the *qāḍīs* of Córdoba,[1] brings out clearly how general the use of this Romance dialect was. It seems to have been used in Córdoba by all classes, even in courts of law and in the royal palace. There were, in fact, four languages in use in Muslim Spain:

(1) Classical Arabic, the language of men of letters;
(2) Colloquial Arabic, the language of administration and government;
(3) Ecclesiastical Latin, a merely ritual language associated with a particular form of worship; and
(4) A Romance dialect, mainly derived from Low Latin, but destined to become (under the name of *Romance castellano* or Spanish) one of the great international languages of the world, by the side of English and Arabic.

It was difficult at first for the illiterate people of Peninsular origin to learn to express themselves in Arabic of any kind; and in the first centuries after the conquest there were many newly-converted Muslims in Spain who were too ignorant of the Arabic language to be instructed in the fundamental laws of Islam.

[1] *Historia de los jueces de Córdoba.* Text, translation, and introduction by Julián Ribera. (Madrid, 1914.)

Even in later times it caused no great surprise when a man who spoke no Arabic was appointed *qāḍī*. 'Abd al-Raḥmān III and his courtiers made jokes and rimes about the odd-sounding words employed by the people.[1] Al-Khushanī relates that there was in Córdoba at that time an old man called Yanair, or Giner—a name which no one at all intimately acquainted with the development of modern Spain can pronounce without emotion. He only spoke in Romance (*al-ʿajamīya* 'the outlandish speech'), but he was so esteemed for his honour and sincerity that his testimony was accepted without question in legal and judicial proceedings. He was much beloved in Córdoba for his virtues and his orthodox professions of the Muslim faith; and one day the officers invited him to give evidence in a case against a certain *qāḍī*. 'The old man replied in *ʿajamīya*: "I do not know him, but I have heard the people say of him that he is a little . . . ." And he used a diminutive of the word in *ʿajamīya*. So when they reported his saying to the Emīr (the mercy of God be upon him!) he was delighted with the man's expression, and said: "There would not have come the like of this word from that honest man, unless it were to be trusted." So he dismissed the *qāḍī* forthwith.'[2]

Mozárabes and Muslim culture

Yet in spite of the fact that many Muslims in Spain were of Spanish origin, and that the Arabic language was by no means universally understood nor spoken very well—even in the ninth century the Arabic of Spain was described by a traveller from the East (al-Muqaddasī) as being 'obscure and difficult to understand'—still the legacy of Islam continued to make progress. If cultivated Mozárabes were bilingual, the majority were illiterate; the few who could read and write preferred to do so in Arabic rather than in Latin. Latin was a clumsy language to write compared with Arabic, and the Latin literature available was of

[1] R. Menéndez Pidal, *Orígenes del Español*, p. 442. (Madrid, 1926.)

[2] J. Ribera, loc. cit., p. 118, and Arabic text, p. 97.

no great interest; so we find a bishop in Córdoba reprimanding his flock not so much for lack of faith as for preferring Arabic poetry and prose to the homilies of the Fathers. Again, the Muslims had introduced paper, and books were more quickly and cheaply produced in Arabic than in Latin.

Córdoba in the tenth century was the most civilized city in Europe, the wonder and admiration of the world, a Vienna among Balkan states. Travellers from the north heard with something like fear of the city which contained 70 libraries and 900 public baths; yet whenever the rulers of León, Navarre or Barcelona needed such things as a surgeon, an architect, a dressmaker or a singing-master, it was to Córdoba that they applied. Queen Tota of Navarre, for instance, brought her son Sancho the Fat to be cured of his corpulence. She was referred to a famous Jewish physician; and not only was the treatment successful, but the government made use of the doctor to negotiate with the Queen an important treaty.

But what most struck the imagination of travellers were the reports of the summer palace of Madīnatu-l-Zahrā, situated about three miles to the west of Córdoba, which even in the sober pages of al-Maqqarī writing long afterwards seems more like a dream-palace of the 'Thousand and one Nights' than a group of buildings of which modern excavators can find little except the drains.[1]

Madīnatu-l-Zahrā was destroyed within fifty years of its completion. But the fall of the Caliphate meant that its culture —or, at any rate, some of it—became available to the conquerors. The tenth century is the period of Muslim city states or 'party-kings' (Ar. *mulūk al-ṭawā'if*, Sp. *reyes de taïfas*); and though Seville under the ʿAbbādite dynasty (e.g. Muʿtamid, the poet) was no less brilliant than Córdoba had been the century before, the Muslim states were now more open to the Christians of the north, and cultural influence spread as their political

[1] R. Velázquez Bosco, *Medina Azzahra y Alamiriya.* (Madrid, 1912.)

power declined. The expansion of Muslim culture to the north was still further encouraged by the emigration of the Mozárabes during the persecution which took place under the Berber dynasties, Almorávides (*al-Murābiṭūn*) and Almohades (*al-Muwaḥḥidūn*), especially between 1090 and 1146. For the first time in Spanish history intolerance had appeared; but it is curious that it should have appeared almost simultaneously in both camps, being introduced by the Berber fanatics in the south and the Cluniac monks in the north. The Mozárabes of Valencia found it impossible to live under the Almorávides; when Jimena abandoned the city in 1102 after the death of the Cid, all the Mozárabes were expatriated to Castille. This mass emigration was followed by others; and under the Almohades (1143) the position of the Mozárabes grew worse. ʿAbd al-Mu'min decreed the expulsion of all Christians and Jews who refused to turn Muslim. It is surprising, however, to find that it is precisely this period of Berber hegemony in Spain (roughly from 1056 to 1269) which includes some of the greatest names in Muslim Spanish culture: al-Bakrī and Idrīsī the geographers and Ibn Zuhr (Avenzoar) the physician lived under the Almorávides; while the succeeding dynasty produced Avempace, Averroes, and Ibn Ṭufayl among philosophers, Ibn ʿArabī of Murcia the mystic, Maimonides the Jewish savant, and Ibn Jubayr the traveller.

The deported Mozárabes had carried with them certain ways of building and styles of dress, certain Muslim customs and expressions (e.g. *quem Deus salvet, cui sit beata requies, que Dios mantenga*),[1] but the legacy of practical Muslim civilization as it had existed in Spain was spread all over the country by the Christian conquests—and by Jewish intermediaries—in the first half of the thirteenth century, which brought large numbers of Muslim craftsmen under Christian rule. The way to Muslim learning had been thrown open to the whole of Europe by the capture of

[1] Menéndez Pidal, loc. cit.

FIG. 1. ALHAMBRA
A gallery in the Court of Lions
Photograph by Arxiv Mas

Toledo (1085), and with the fall of Córdoba (1236) and Seville (1248) it spread rapidly. With the conquest of Granada (1492) the legacy might be said to have come to an end, except for pottery and some of the minor arts.

The Arabic renaissance, which had been preceded by a French renaissance, was followed by the Italian renaissance, and the period of Arabic influence was ended.

Architecture: Mozárabe and Mudéjar

Muslim architecture has been dealt with in another chapter. The periods of the emirate and caliphate are represented by the great mosque of Córdoba (fig. 77); a memorial (one of the very few) of the 'party-kings' are the scanty remains of the Aljafería (al-Jaʿfarīya) at Saragossa. The Almohade period is illustrated by the Giralda tower and the oldest part of the Alcázar (the *patio del yeso*) at Seville; while the art of the Naṣrite dynasty of Granada is represented by the Alhambra (fig. 1) and the Generalife (frontispiece).

There are, however, two other styles, both characteristically Spanish, which deserve attention: the Mozárabic and Mudéjar.

Mozárabic architecture is in some ways a reaction against Islam, but it had to submit to influences from its more powerful and more civilized neighbour in the south. Originating in a style practised in Spain before the invasion of 711, it became the typical style of the Christian kingdoms of the north between that period and the introduction of the Romanesque style towards the end of the eleventh century. As 'a distant outpost of Byzantine art', it shows certain features which appear in Muslim architecture also, such as the paired *ajimez* windows (*al-s̲h̲amās*) and the horseshoe arch. The history of this 'Moorish' arch is a very pretty problem, for it is found not only in Muslim buildings but in Mozárabic churches also. It has been suggested that Christian emigrants from Córdoba, especially monks, brought with them ideas of a higher culture than any known in the north, including new methods of building. The unpretending churches which date from this epoch, though they show certain features of Byzantine origin, betray the influence of Córdoba in the structure of the arch and in the system of vaulting (e.g. San Miguel de Escalada, built by monks expelled from the Muslim capital in 913). Córdoba made the 'Moorish' arch known to the Christians and Muslims alike, but did not originate it, for it undoubtedly existed in Spain before the date of the conquest, and is even found on late Roman tombstones. The Spanish Muslims, however, quickly realized its possibilities, both structural and decorative, and adopted it generally, exaggerating the 'pinch' in the sides and eventually half filling the hollow of the arch. The influence of Córdoba, including the horseshoe arch, is also to be seen in Mozárabic illuminated manuscripts (such as the commentaries of Beatus of Liébana); while other Latin manuscripts are known which actually have marginal notes in Arabic explaining the meaning of the Latin words. But the most original contribution of Córdoba to architecture was the system of vaulting based on intersecting arches and visible intersecting ribs, a system which attacks the main problem of architecture—that of covering space with a roof—in much the same way as the system of Gothic vaulting which developed two centuries later.

The architectural forms developed at Córdoba were carried to Toledo and Saragossa, where they are beautifully exhibited in brickwork. The exquisite 'Cristo de la Luz' at Toledo (fig. 2), originally a Visigothic church, was turned into a mosque at the time of the Muslim occupation, and was restored by a Muslim architect in 980, as is stated in an inscription on the front of the building. Inside, the walls are lined with 'blank arcading'—rows of 'dummy' arches leading nowhere. This is said to be the earliest instance of its use, the next being the cathedrals of Durham (1093, fig. 3) and Norwich (1119). Decorative inter-

Fig. 2. CRISTO DE LA LUZ, TOLEDO

Fig. 3. BLANK ARCADING OF INTERSECTING ARCHES IN DURHAM CATHEDRAL

Fig. 4. MUDÉJAR BRICKWORK

Torre de San Gil, Saragossa

secting arcading became a favourite device with the Muslim workmen after they had submitted to the Christians.

These men, known as Mudéjares (*mudajjanīn*), were the creators of the Spanish national style, perhaps the most characteristically Spanish contribution to the art of Europe, and their work is to be seen all over Spain. But its real home is Toledo. There we find those beautiful brick church-towers with constantly varying courses of blank arcading, the principle of decoration being one of tiers of arches, one above the other in rows, while each story has windows of different form (fig. 4). In Aragon, the Mudéjar towers are separated from the churches, like minarets, and are sometimes decorated with brightly-coloured tiles as well as brickwork. At Teruel, four of the towers are built across the streets, with the traffic going through an arch at the bottom; at Calatayud (*qal'at Ayyūb*) the towers are octagonal.[1] The brick apses of the Mudéjar churches in Toledo are also particularly beautiful examples of brickwork, while the north wall of the older of the two cathedrals at Saragossa is a splendid example of this kind of decoration. Mudéjar workmen were employed all over Spain for the decoration of churches and private houses, e.g. the fantastic courtyard of the Infantado palace at Guadalajara (*wādi-l-ḥijāra*). They were particularly in request for the canopies of tombs, and also for synagogues, as may be seen in the buildings at Toledo now known as 'El Tránsito' and 'Santa María la Blanca'. The Alcázar at Seville was built by Mudéjar workmen for King Pedro the Cruel entirely in the Muslim style, and is still used as a royal residence.

Woodwork, ceramics, textiles, and music

The Mudéjar workmen excelled above all in the minor arts: woodwork, pottery, textiles. The Spanish coffered (*artesonado*) ceilings have no parallel in Europe—if we except that of the

[1] Bernard Bevan, *The Mudéjar Towers of Aragon* (illustrated). 'Apollo', ix, no. 53 (May 1929).

Capella Palatina at Palermo, which is also Muslim work. Their inlaid doors are no less beautiful and individual, and to this day the technical Spanish words of the carpenter's trade are largely Arabic. The various kinds of coloured tiles (*azulejos*), so familiar to-day in Spain and Portugal, are a legacy from the Muslims, as the name implies (see p. 20). After the reconquest the geometrical patterns and inscriptions of earlier times were replaced by pictures, or even by vast frescoes composed of tiles (fig. 5). In Seville, tiles were used for altars, balustrades, fountains (where the water was arranged so as to trickle slowly over the rim of the basin and keep the tiles below it wet and shining); and in public gardens they are used for seats and bookshelves (the free library in a public garden is a peculiarly Spanish institution). In Portugal coloured tiles and tile-pictures are used to an even greater extent: there is a church in Evora, the interior of which is completely covered with blue and white tiles.

The highest level of Mudéjar workmanship was reached in Hispano-Moresque lustre pottery, which, in the eyes of collectors, ranks only below Chinese porcelain. The earliest mention of it is in the eleventh century (Toledo 1066, Córdoba 1068), while Idrīsī describes its being made at Calatayud before 1154. Two other places in Spain, widely separated, were famous for this ware: Málaga and, above all, Manises in the kingdom of Valencia. The earliest existing pieces date from the fourteenth century, though fragments which must have been four hundred years older were found during the excavations of Madīnatu-l-Zahrā. Typical Hispano-Moresque ware has a shimmering metallic golden lustre varying from ruby to mother-of-pearl and greenish yellow. The earliest forms of decoration are Byzantine, but the square Kufic characters were soon introduced for decoration; while later, a favourite inscription was *al-ʿāfiya*, good health (Sp. *alafia*, prosperity, fate, or blessing). This formula was popularly supposed to have been adopted by the potters as a substitute for the sacred name of Allah, so that there might be

Fig. 5. COLOURED TILES IN SPAIN
The Hall of the Ambassadors in the Alcázar

no chance of the piece with that name being broken and the potter consequently losing his soul. The *al-ʿāfiya* is found principally on drug-jars. The Valencian potters, however, invented other schemes of decoration based on the wild bryony (Ar. *al-ghāliba*, Sp. *algalaba*), a plant familiar in their district. Vine-leaves were also employed, and, latterly, heraldic devices (fig. 6), from which it has been proved that Hispano-Moresque pottery was manufactured for popes and cardinals and the greatest families of Spain and Portugal, Italy and France.[1] 'They lack our faith', Cardinal Ximénez remarked of these heretical craftsmen, 'but we lack their works'.

Spanish-Moorish silks were hardly less in demand than Spanish-Moorish pottery. They were particularly treasured in Christian churches; even at Canterbury Cathedral several of the little silk bags which held the seals of documents, dating from 1264 to 1366, were found to be made of pieces of ancient Spanish silk, the patterns being unmistakable and unequalled for their intricacy and fineness of workmanship. The best surviving pieces probably date from the end of the twelfth and beginning of the thirteenth centuries. With the fourteenth century, new designs appeared with still more elaborate interlacings, and these outlasted the Muslim dominion in Spain and are one more manifestation of the Mudéjar art of the fifteenth and sixteenth centuries.

Córdoba became famous for its leather, known as 'Cordovan' or 'Cordwain', so that the Cordwainers' Company, or at least the name, might be considered part of the legacy of Arabia. In later years fine and characteristic work was done by Mudéjar bookbinders. The Muslim-Spanish goldsmiths also achieved renown; and the workers in other metals took no less pains with such things as enamelled and inscribed sword-hilts, as with such every-day objects as iron keys, the wards of which often take the

[1] C. van der Put, in *Spanish Art: Burlington Magazine Monograph* (1927), and separate studies.

form of interlacing letters and words in the square Kufic script to which their shape is admirably adapted.

It is difficult to do justice to the industrial arts of the Spanish Muslims; in music, on the contrary, their influence has probably been exaggerated. The superficial resemblance between popular music heard in the south of Spain and that heard in Morocco and other Muslim countries has led many observers astray. Though in the dances and dance-rhythms there is undoubtedly a relationship between modern Spain and modern Morocco, and although certain melodies in the repertory of musicians at Fez are said to have been brought from Granada, in other music the likeness lies in the manner of performance rather than in the modes and forms of the music itself. There were undoubtedly Muslim musicians at the courts of the medieval kings of Castille and Aragon—their names have been preserved, just as have the names of their colleagues from England or Scotland and other parts of Europe—but in the later medieval period (e.g. that of the Archpriest of Hita) the 'Moors' are more often described as dancers than as players on instruments, though the instrument had in many cases been brought to Spain—and so to Europe—by Muslims: the lute *al-'ūd*, guitar *qītāra* (Gk. κιθάρα), and rebeck or ribible, a favourite instrument with Chaucer, Ar. *rabāb*, Sp. *rabel*, Port. *rabeca*, the last being the ordinary word still used in Portugal for a violin.

There are other instruments in the Peninsula with names derived from Arabic, such as the tambourine (Sp. *pandero*, *pandereta*, coll. Ar. *bandair*); while the 'jingles' round the edge are known in Spain as *sonajas* (Ar. plur. *ṣunūj*; Pers. *ṣanj*). The old Spanish trumpet *añafil* is the Arabic *al-nafīr*; while the word 'fanfare', a piece of music played by several trumpets, is derived by Dr. Farmer from a plural form of *nafīr*—*anfār*. The Spanish bag-pipes *gaita* are the Arabic *al-ghaiṭa* (hautboy), known in West Africa as 'alligator', the nearest English word to the colloquial pronunciation of the Arabic. There is also the old

Spanish instrument known as *albogue*, and *albogón* (Ar. *al-būq*, Lat. *buccinum*). This has long been a mystery; but it has recently been described and illustrated as played to-day in the Basque provinces.[1] Finally (as pointed out in another chapter) the words 'troubadour' and *trobar* are almost certainly of Arabic origin: from *ṭarraba*, to sing, or make music.

During the persecution and gradual expulsion of the Moriscos during the sixteenth century, the Gipsies (who are first reported as landing at Barcelona in 1442) gradually came in and took their place, some even settling down in the abandoned quarters of Granada, and giving up their wandering habits. Though they sometimes plied the trade of tinker or farrier, they had no arts or crafts, and were in every way a bad substitute for the Moriscos; but they gradually became the musicians of the people, performing music which they had heard in the course of their wanderings, but performing it with a dash and fire that was all their own. The manner of performance, which is known to the initiated as a *zambra* (Ar. *zamara*)—and still more, the manners of the audience, breaking in with cries of *Ole! Ole!* (*wallāhi*?)—kept up a likeness to what had been in Muslim times. The guitar-player began alone, playing a long prelude until the spirits of the audience and the other performers were worked up to the proper pitch; and then, when the singer at last entered, he or she would begin with a long *ay!* for the same purpose—to try the voice—or (as was heard as lately as 1922) with a wild wailing *lelí*, *lelí*, which may be nothing else than a memory of the Muslim creed, or perhaps 'my night, my night!'

There is, however, a distinct possibility that European musical theory, like every other branch of learning in medieval Europe, was influenced by Muslim writers.[2] Between the eighth and eleventh centuries many Greek treatises on music were trans-

[1] Rodney Gallop, *A Book of the Basques* (1930), p. 183.

[2] H. G. Farmer, 'Clues for the Arabian influence on European musical theory.' *J.R.A.S.*, Jan. 1925, pp. 61–80.

lated into Arabic, and important original works were written in Arabic by Al-Kindī, Al-Fārābī, Avempace, Avicenna, and others. When students from the north began to visit Toledo, these Arabic works gradually became known in Europe in Latin translations, and it is a curious coincidence that this period (the first half of the twelfth century) is the period in which a new principle appears in northern music—the principle that the notes have an exact time-value or ratio among themselves, instead of the fluid time-value of plain-song.[1] The inventor of this 'measured music' is sometimes stated to have been Franco of Cologne; but he himself speaks of measured music as a thing already in existence, and it seems to have been known to Al-Khalīl as early as the eighth century, as well as to Al-Fārābī (tenth century), who, under the name of Alpharabius, was translated into Latin and widely read among northern musicians. Walter Odington, the greatest musician of the thirteenth century, spoke with enthusiasm of the Arabic masters; and another English musician of the time, a writer on the theory of music, goes so far as to call the new note-values by Arabic names: thus he speaks of 'elmuahym' and 'elmuarifa'.[2]

Medieval music is, at present, a subject in which too much is known about the theory, and too little about the practice; the chapter on the 'Social aspects of music in the Middle Ages' in the introductory volume of *The Oxford History of Music* (1929) broke entirely new ground. Yet the practical value of the system of 'measured music' was immense, for it enabled music to be composed and written down in a legible form for several voices singing together. Such music would probably have been completely unintelligible to 'Alpharabius' and the other Muslim theorists, and they might never have understood that the northern musicians were applying a principle which they themselves had been the first to enunciate. 'Sumer is icumen in',

[1] *Grove's Dictionary of Music and Musicians*, 3rd ed. (1927), art. 'Franco'.

[2] Coussemaker, *Scriptores de musica medii aevi*, i. 339.

the great 'round' for six voices composed about 1240 by a monk of Reading, is in advance of any music of its time; and is in a different world altogether from the songs of the Troubadours and the *Cantigas* of the Spanish king Alfonso the Sage (*c.* 1283) which probably arose under direct Muslim influence.

Arabic words in Spanish and Portuguese

Nothing in Spain gives clearer evidence of the debt to Islam than the Spanish language. Yet here particularly it is important to avoid exaggeration and to estimate as accurately as possible what the debt amounts to. By the time of the Muslim invasion of 711, a Romance dialect was already in process of formation from the Low Latin which had once been spoken in the Peninsula, and it is known to have been used (as we have already seen) by the Christians under Muslim rule, and, as time went on, by numbers of Muslims themselves. A considerable number of Arabic words made their way into this Romance dialect; and the reason is to be found, not so much in the direct borrowing of Arabic words, as that the Spanish dialects themselves were in an uncertain and fluid state while there were Arabic-speaking people in the Peninsula.

The borrowed Arabic words are in most cases nouns, and they are the kinds of objects and ideas which had (and in many cases still have) Arabic names in modern Spanish, e.g. *fonda* hotel (Ar. *funduq*), *tahona* bakery (Ar. *ṭāḥūna* mill), *tarifa* tariff (Ar. *taʿrīf* notice, definition).

As a rule, however, the Arabic word was taken over into Spanish with the Arabic definite article joined to it, and then the Spanish article was added in front of that, e.g. *la alhaja*[1] the jewel (Ar. *al-ḥāja*), *el arroz* the rice (*al-ruzz*), *la acéquia* the canal or dyke (*al-sāqiya*), *el anacalo* the baker's boy (*al-naqqāl* the carrier.) The Spanish words, it need hardly be said, were not

[1] In the sixteenth century the usual form was *el* alhaja.

derived from the classical, written language, but from the colloquial Arabic of Southern Spain; and, in pronunciation, the -l of the article was in certain cases assimilated to the initial consonant of the following word, e.g. *ar-ruzz*, *as-sāqiya*, *an-naqqāl*, but *al-ḥāja*, *al-qubba*, &c. Pedro de Alcalá, the missionary, who in 1505 published two books dealing with the colloquial Arabic of Granada, writes *a dar* the house, *a xems* the sun, *a çoltán* the Sultan, &c. Yet it should not be concluded that every strange-looking Spanish word is of Arabic origin if it begins with al-: *almuerzo* lunch, *alameda* avenue, *alambre* wire, *almendra* almond, are words of undoubted Latin origin; while *albaricoque* apricot, and *albérchigo* one of the numerous varieties of peach, were originally Latin words which have passed through Greek and Arabic before settling down in Spanish.

Nevertheless the fact remains that the Spanish words borrowed from Arabic include some of the commonest objects of daily life:

passage into a house *zaguán*	Ar. *usṭuwán*, Gk. *στοά*
flat roof *azotea*	*al-suṭaiḥa*, dim. of *saṭḥ* roof
awning *toldo*	*ẓulla* canopy
bedroom *alcoba*	*al-qubba* dome
cupboard *alacena*	*al-k̲h̲izāna*, cupboard
shelf *anaquel*	*al-naqqāl* bearer
stand, dais, footstool *tarima*	*ṭarīma*
partition *tabique*	*ṭabaq* layer, surface
carpet or mat *alfombra*	*al-k̲h̲umra* mat of palm-leaves
pillow *almohada*	*al-muk̲h̲adda* pillow
pin *alfiler*	*al-khilāl*
dressing-gown *bata*	*baṭṭa* a coarse garment, lining
overcoat *gabán*	*qabā'* outer garment
builder *albañil*	*al-bannā'*
scaffolding *andamio*	*ad-daʿā'im* pillars, supports
warehouse *almacén*	*al-mak̲h̲zan*
paving-stone *adoquín*	*al-dukkān* shop, stone bench
tar *alquitrán*	*al-qaṭrān*

hire *alquiler*	*al-kirā'*
damage *avería*	*'awār*
to reach, overtake *alcanzar*	*al-kanz* buried treasure
hole in the road *badén.*	*bāṭin* sunk ground
custom-house *aduana*	*al-dīwān*
ticket office (station or theatre) *taquilla*	*ṭāqa*, Gk. θήκη
mayor *alcalde*	*al-qāḍī* judge
executor *albacea*	*al-waṣī* testator, executor
notice, invoice *albarán*	*al-barā'a* document of acquittal
what's-his-name *fulano*	*fulān*
until *hasta*	*ḥattā*

These are common words of every-day use, and the list might have been made longer. Suburbs, village, farm, are all known by Arabic words. The countryman measures his corn by the *fanega* of one and a half bushels (Ar. *fanīqa* a large sack), and divides it into twelve *celemines*, each equivalent to a gallon (Ar. *thamānī*, colloquial *zemenī*, eight), and he has another measure, the *arroba* (*al-rub'a*, fem.) a 'quarter' (of a hundredweight) dry measure, or four gallons liquid. His entire vocabulary concerned with irrigation is Arabic, and so are the names of numerous flowers, fruits, vegetables, shrubs, and trees. Sugar *azúcar* has passed into Spanish, Portuguese, and other European languages through the Arabic *al-sukkar*, Persian *shakar*, and not (as is often stated in Spain) through the Latin *saccharum*; both words are derived ultimately, but by different roads, from the same word in Sanskrit. Again, the word *jarabe* which the traveller in southern Spain sees so often in advertisements is the English 'syrup' (also 'sherbet' and rum 'shrub') derived from the Arabic *sharāb*, drink. *Jarabe* was formerly spelt *xarabe*, the Spanish *x* having been pronounced as *sh* down to the seventeenth century, as it still is in Catalan and Portuguese. It may be surprising to learn that the Spanish-speaking peoples still make use of the Arabic phrase *in shā'llāh*; yet such is the explanation of the common Spanish expression *ojalá*, formerly spelt *oxalá* and then pronounced with the *x* equivalent to *sh*.

Other words borrowed from Arabic,[1] which have survived in literary Spanish, are gradually dropping out under the influence of journalism. Spanish journalism, and particularly Spanish-American journalism, is strongly influenced by Paris, and the so-called 'Latin press' (*prensa latina*) has no love for words which are not immediately intelligible in any Latin country. The most notable modern exception is José Martínez Ruiz—the essayist who has always written under the pen-name of 'Azorín'. No man in Spain is a greater 'Francophil' than he; yet his love for the old Spanish writers, and his early environment—like Professor Ribera he is a native of Valencia, full of Moorish devices for irrigation and the Arabic words and place-names which describe them—led him to use the language with extraordinary richness and variety; while his passion for 'interiors' and his minute and detailed description of common things and his delight in their names make his earlier essays a valuable contribution to the legacy of Arabia in modern Spain.

The really cultivated Spaniard still takes pleasure in words of mixed Spanish-Arabic origin, no less than in those of Spanish-Latin origin which can be traced back to Mozárabic times. The wandering minstrels who recited the 'Poem of my Cid' and the older Spanish ballads, the poems of Gonzalo de Berceo and the Archpriest of Hita, the prose of Alfonso the Sage and Don Juan Manuel—all these drew upon 'a well of Castilian undefiled' which, from its Low Latin origins and Arabic borrowings, had become a possession peculiarly characteristic of the Spanish people. Nevertheless the influence of minds which cannot conceive of

[1] R. Dozy and W. H. Engelmann, *Glossaire des mots espagnols et portugais dérivés de l'arabe*, 2nd ed. (Leyden, 1869); D. L. de Eguilaz, *Glosario etimológico de las palabras españoles de origen oriental* (Granada, 1886); R. Academia Española, *Diccionario de la lengua española*, 15th ed. (Madrid, 1925); K. Lokotsch, *Etymologisches Wörterbuch der europäischen Wörter orientalischen Ursprungs* (Heidelberg, 1927).

any good thing which does not come from Paris is leading to the introduction of colourless Gallicisms in their place. No one in Spain under forty, perhaps, would have taken pleasure in explaining to a foreigner the exact nature of the leather bindings still known by the Berber name of *tafilete*, or have referred to the exactions of the Corunna fish-wives (who seize on the luggage of passengers arriving from America) as an *almojarifazgo*, a kind of customs duty (Ar. *al-mushrif*+Romance suffix *-azgo*, Lat. *-aticum*).

What has been said of the destructive effects of cosmopolitan 'Latin' journalism is no less true of Portuguese. A number of oriental words passed into that language,[1] but they came rather from the Portuguese colonies in India, East Africa, and the Far East than from the Muslim occupation of Portugal. Yet it is curious that some of the Arabic words which have survived there from that time have either died out in Spain, or seem never to have become naturalized there at all. Many of the Spanish words in the foregoing list are also found, under one form or another, in Portugal (e.g. 'until', Sp. *hasta*, Port. *até*; 'warehouse', Sp. *almacén*, Port. *armazem*, &c.) The following common Portuguese words, however, are never used in modern Spain:

Portuguese	*Arabic*
carpet *alcatifa*	*al-qaṭīfa* blanket, velvet
tailor *alfaiate*	*al-k̲h̲ayyāṭ*
custom-house *alfándega*	*al-funduq*
pocket *algibeira*	*al-jaib* (the colloquial *al-jabīra* has returned to Arabic from the Portuguese)
foot-path *azinhaga*	*al-zanqa*, coll. *az-zanāqa*
waste place *sáfara*	*ṣaḥrā'*
harvest *safra*	*iṣfarra* to ripen
and *ceifa*, *aceifa*	*ṣaif* summer
lettuce *alfaça*	*al-k̲h̲ass*
pound weight *arratel*	*al-raṭl*

[1] S. R. Dalgado, *Glosário Luso-asiático*, 2 vols. (Coimbra 1919, 1921).

The word 'baroque' seems to be of Arabic origin, (*burga*, uneven ground) and to have reached Europe through *barroco*, a technical term used by Portuguese pearl-fishers, and dealers in pearls.

Arabic place-names in Spain and Portugal

Place-names are unaffected by journalism, and the map of Spain and Portugal is of extraordinary interest to a student of Arabic. Though some of the names are Arabized forms of older Iberian and Phoenician names, and many are of characteristically mixed origin, Arabic and Romance, they form when taken together a striking demonstration of the mark which the Islamic peoples left on the Peninsula. Mountains and hills, capes and islands, sand-banks, rivers, lakes, and hot springs; plains, fields, woods, gardens, trees, and flowers; caves and mines; colours; and works of man such as farms, villages, towns, markets, mosques, paved roads, bridges, castles, forts, mills, towers, have all become geographical names. Thus *jabal* (mountain) appears in Monte Jabalcuz, in Jabalcón, Jabaloyas, Jabalquinto, Javaleón and the Pico and Sierra de Javalambre; there is also the Sierra de Gibralbin, Gibraleón, Gibralfaro (mountain of the pharos), while Gibraltar (mount Ṭāriq) is named after the Berber chief who led the first successful Muslim expedition into Spain. *Al-kudya* (the hill) appears in the nine or ten places known as Alcudia, as also in Cudia Cremada (Burnt Hill) in Menorca; *al-qūr* (plural of *qāra*, hillock) in Alcor and Alcora; while *al-mudawwar* (round, from *dāra*, turn) is the name of the hill-towns Almodóvar del Rio and Almodóvar del Campo, and others. The port of Almería is named from *al-marīyya* the watch-tower. From *al-manāra* (beacon) are named the heights Cerro de Almenara, Sierra de Almenara, and the harbour Puerto de la Almenara; the Spanish word *almena*, however (battlement), is not *al-manʿa*, but a Latin word *minae* to which the Arabic article has been added; while in Aragon the word *almenar* (*al-manhar*) is connected with irrigation. *Ṭaraf* (cape) has given Trafalgar, *ṭaraf al-ghār*, cape of the cave; *al-jazīra*, the island, appears in Algeciras and Alcira. *Kallā'* anchorage (from *kala'a*, protect) is found separately as Cala (beach), and in combination, such as Cala Barca, Cala Blanca, Cala de San Vicente, Cala Santany, Punta de la Cala, Torre de la Cala Honda, La Caleta. The sand-banks at the mouth of the Ebro are known as Los Alfaques, perhaps from *al-fakk*, jaws.

Ramla, a sandy river-bed, recalls the origin of *La Rambla*, the principal street of Barcelona; but the Arabic word most familiar in Spain in connexion with a river is *wādī*, which in Spanish is spelt *guad*, though still often pronounced with a *w*. Thus we find Guadalquivir, *wādi-l-kabīr*, the great river; Guadalajara, *wādi-l-ḥijāra*, the river of stones, Guadalaviar, *wādi-l-abyaḍ*, the white river; Guadalcázar, *wādi-l-qaṣr*, the river of the fort; Guadalcotón, *wādi-l-quṭn*, the river of cotton, Guadalmedina, *wādi-l-madīna*, the city river; Guadarrama, *wādi-l-ramla*, the sandy river; Guarromān, *wādi-l-rummān*, the river of pomegranates. Others preserve an ancient place-name in an Arabic disguise: e.g. Guadiana, *wādī Anas*; Guadix, *wādī Acci*; Guadalupe, *wādi-l-lubb*, the wolf river (Latin *lupus*). In Portugal the Arabic word has become Odi-, or Ode-; e.g. Odiana (Guadiana), Odivellas, Ribeira de Odelouca, and Odeleite.

Lakes and lagoons in Spain and Portugal have often preserved their Arabic name of *al-buḥaira* (dim. of *baḥr*, sea); thus there are Albuera, Albufera, Albufeira, Albuhera, and Bañalbufar. Reservoirs, ponds, or tanks, *al-birka*, account for Alberca and Alverca; wells or cisterns, *al-jubb*, for Algibe; conduits, *as-sāqiya*, for Acéquia—all of which are common geographical terms in Spain. The Persian *khandaq* is remembered in Laguna de la Janda, Jandula, Jandulilla; it was in the first of these that the greater part of the Visigothic army perished in the decisive victory of Ṭāriq in 711. A familiar place-name is the hot spring, *al-ḥamma*, Alhama.

Woods and thickets have given their Arabic names to

Algaba, *al-ghāba*, and Algaida, *al-ghaiḍa*. Meadows have preserved an Arabic word, *al-marj*, in Almargem (Lisbon), Almárgen (Málaga), Almarcha (La Mancha). Gardens which recall their Arabic origin in their names are Generalife, *jannat-al-ʿarīf*, the garden of the architect or inspector, and Almunia de Doña Godina, *al-munya*, the market garden. Fields of barley, *al-qaṣīl*, have given their names to Alcácer do Sal in Portugal; sunflowers, *al-ʿuṣfur*, to Venta de los Alazores; the tamarisk, *al-ṭarfāʾ*, to Tarfe; the wild olive, *az-zanbūj*, to Azambuja and Zambujeira in Portugal and the Puerta del Acebuche at Zafra. Among colours, a favourite geographical term is Albaida, *al-baiḍā*, the white (fem.), while the Alhambra, *al-ḥamrā*, the red (palace), was the dwelling of *al-Aḥmar*, the red (king).

Familar geographical names are derived from the mine, *al-maʿdin*, Almadén; the farm, *al-qarya*, has given its name to Alcaria do Cume and Alcaria Ruiva in Portugal, and several places named Alquería in Spain; the village, *al-ḍaiʿaʾ* has become the common Peninsular word *aldea*. Medina, Medina del Campo, Medina de Pomar, Medina de Rioseco, Medinaceli, Medina Sidonia, Laguna de Medina show one half of their origin (*madīna*, city) very clearly. The mosque, *masjid*, Mezquita, appears in several names; and the market, *as-sūq*, though officially known as '*el mercado*', is still spoken of by country people as *el azogue* (Port. *azougue*), and survives in a well-known proverb[1] and in the proper names Azoguejo (Segovia), Azuqueca de Henares, and the Zocodover of Toledo: i.e. *sūq-ad-dawābb*, the cattle-market which, in medieval times, was known as the *zoco de las bestias* (*sūq* of the beasts).

Arabic words for fortress have produced many geographical

1 *En el azogue*
Quien mal dice mal oye.
(In the market, he who speaks evil hears evil.)

The common meaning of *azogue*, however, is quicksilver (Ar. *al-zāwūq*, and *az-zauqa*).

names in Spain. From *al-qal'a*, we have Alcalá (de Henares, de Guadaira, de Chisbert, &c.); while without the article this word has given Calatayud, *qal'at Ayyūb*, the castle of Job, Calatanazor, Calatrava, Calatorao. From the diminutive, *al-qulai'a*, comes Alcolea. In the same way *al-qaṣr* (Latin *castrum*?) has produced all the Spanish places named Alcázar, while its diminutive *al-quṣair* gives Alcocer. A fortress, *al-qaṣaba*, makes the Spanish Alcazaba and the Portuguese Alcaçovas. In the same way *al-qanṭara*, the bridge (Gk. κέντρον), has named several points in Spain now known as Alcántara, at which the Muslim conquerors found a Roman bridge. The watch-tower, *al-ṭāli'a*, became, in Spanish, Atalaya; and the name has remained with several places, including Atalayas de Alcalá, while without the article it has given Talayero, Talayuela, Talayuelas. The existence of a paved road, or causeway, probably of Roman origin but called *al-raṣīf* by the Muslim invaders, has given the names Arrecife, Arrizafa, and Ruzafa. The suburbs, *al-rabaḍ*, gave rise to the common Spanish name Arrabal; *al-rābiṭa* on the other hand was 'the hermitage', the place in which one might expect to find a marabout, *murābiṭ*, although the marabout would probably have been armed, and the 'hermitage', a block-house with a vigilant and energetic garrison. The name persists in Arrábida, Rábida, Rápita, Rabeda. The suburbs of a town were also known as *al-barra* and *al-balad*, one of which will account for names such as Albalát, Albalate, Albolote. Towers situated outside the walls are sometimes known as Torres Albarranas, *al-barrānī*; while the name Albarracín commemorates the fact that it was the district of the Berber tribe Banu Razīn. Names beginning *bena-*, *beni-*, *bini-* are extremely common, especially in the province of Valencia and the Balearic Isles: Benadalid, Benalgalbón, Benaguacil, Benajarafe, Benamejí, Benaoján, Benarrabá, Benaudalla; Beniaján, Benicarló, Benicasim, Benifayó, Benigánim, Benimamet; Binacéd, Binisalem, Biniadris, Binicalaf, Binimaymut, Binisafua, Binixerns, and numerous others.

The School of Toledo

Place-names and common words which have survived show how the Spanish language was affected by Arabic at the most tender period of its growth. By the tenth century the whole basis of life throughout Spain was profoundly influenced by Islam: with the capture of Toledo that influence spread to the rest of Europe. Since the destruction of Córdoba by the Berbers at the beginning of the eleventh century, Toledo had gradually become the centre of Muslim learning in Spain, and it maintained that position after the Christian conquest in 1085. The court of Alfonso VI, though nominally Christian, was as much imbued with Muslim civilization as the court of Frederick II at Palermo nearly two hundred years later, and Alfonso proclaimed himself 'Emperor of the two religions'. The schools of Toledo attracted scholars from all parts of Europe, including England and Scotland. Among them were Robert 'the Englishman', Robertus Anglicus, the first translator of the *Qur'ān*, Michael Scot, Daniel Morley, and Adelard of Bath. Their adventures and activities, the shifts and subterfuges to which they resorted in order to obtain Latin translations of the works of Aristotle, Euclid, and other books which were only to be read in Arabic, have been vividly described in another volume of this series,[1] and there is no need to repeat them here.

The greatest contribution of the Muslims in Spain to European thought was (as has been pointed out in another chapter) the work of the philosophers. Though they had adopted the narrowest and most orthodox forms of Muslim theology, they gave free rein to philosophic speculation; and although the Berber rulers—Almorávides and Almohades—were inclined to fanaticism, they not only tolerated the speculations of the philosophers but even encouraged them, with certain reservations, so that the philosophers were left free and unhampered

[1] *The Legacy of Israel*, pp. 204 ff.

in their work of teaching, provided that that teaching was not spread abroad amongst people in general.

The great thinkers of Muslim Spain do not belong to the brilliant age of the Caliphate of Córdoba, but to the ages of political confusion which followed. They rediscovered Greek philosophy, and above all the works of Aristotle. The historians and the dramatists were apparently unknown to them, but they introduced Aristotle to the West centuries before the revival of Greek scholarship which directly preceded the Renaissance and was one of the causes of the Reformation. They seem hardly ever to have known the Greek texts at first hand or to have translated from them directly; their translations were made as a rule from intermediate versions in Syriac; so that an English or Scottish student, if he wished to become further acquainted with the works of Aristotle than was possible from the meagre Latin versions at his disposal, found it convenient to travel to Toledo and learn to read his Greek authors in Arabic. The transmission of Greek learning to the West began at Baghdād, whence it was forwarded by Jewish or Muslim intermediaries to the Muslims in Spain; and thence, by Jewish intermediaries again, it was conveyed to wandering scholars from Christian Europe.

Arabic influences on early Spanish literature

The administrative, economic, and artistic aspects of Muslim civilization in Spain have already been mentioned, while its effects on European literature have been discussed in another chapter. Something more, however, remains to be said concerning the influence of Muslim thought on the literature of Spain.

In the age of heroic poetry (*c.* 1050–1250) the influences are French and Teutonic rather than Arabic. The national epic of Castille, the 'Poem of my Cid', has the form of a *chanson de geste*, though the hero himself was very nearly contemporary with the first minstrel who sang of his doings, and was not (as in the case of Roland) a semi-mythical hero who had perished hundreds of years before. The date of the poem is about 1140, and Ruy Diaz de Bivar, the Cid, died in 1099. His title, of course, is Arabic: *saiyyid* (colloquial *sīd*), lord; and the mixture of languages prevalent at the time could not be better shown than by the usual form under which the Cid was addressed by his men: *Ya mio Cid.* An Arabic-speaking vassal would have said: *Yā sīdī.*

The second period (*c.* 1250–1400) is one in which the chief foreign influence on Spanish literature was Arabic. The gates of oriental learning and story were opened both to Spain and to the whole of Europe by the capture of Toledo (1085), which became a school of translation from oriental languages. As early as 1120 Petrus Alfonsi, a Spanish Jew who was baptized and whose godfather was Alfonso VII, introduced Indian fable into Spain by the celebrated collection of stories known as *Disciplina Clericalis.* The Spanish translation of the 'Indian tales' of *Calila e Dimna* made directly from the Arabic text dates from 1251:[1] it is the earliest attempt at story-telling in the Spanish language. The romance of the Seven Sages (Sindibad or Sendebar) was translated from the Arabic for the Infante Don Fadrique about 1253, under the name of *Libro de los engannos é asayamientos de las mujeres* (Book of the Wiles and Deceptions of Women).[2] From the second half of the thirteenth century, collections of aphorisms and moral tales become numerous in Spain. They include a lost version of the Buddhistic legend of Barlaam and Josaphat, the *Libro de enxemplos por ABC* collected by Clemente Sanchez de Vercial,[3] and the oddly-named *Libro de los gatos*, 'Book of Cats', which is probably a misreading for *Libro de los qẽtos* (*quentos*), 'Book of Stories'—and is derived from an Arabic source through the *Narrationes* of the English monk

[1] Ed. J. Alemany (Madrid, 1915) and A. G. Solalinde (Madrid, 1917).

[2] Ed. D. Comparetti, *Researches respecting the Book of Sindibad* (London, 1882), and A. Bonilla y San Martin (Madrid, 1904).

[3] Ed. A. Morel Fatio, in *Romania* (1888).

Odo of Cheriton.[1] Stories included in these collections are constantly recurring in Spanish literature down to the time of the dramatists of the seventeenth century: the greatest of Spanish plays, *La vida es sueño* (Life 's a Dream), is the story of Christopher Sly in 'The Taming of the Shrew' and 'The Sleeper Wakened' in the 'Thousand and One Nights', and is derived ultimately from Barlaam.

Alfonso the Sage

The greatest apostle of Muslim learning in Christian Spain was Alfonso X, *el Sabio*, king of Castille and León from 1252 to 1284. Under his patronage—and indeed under his immediate supervision—a number of vast works were undertaken, many of them being compiled from Arabic sources, which were made available to him by Jewish assistants.[2] His prose works—and his naive, semi-oriental prose is one of the great delights of medieval Spanish studies—include a code of laws, *Las siete partidas*, which is a mine of curious information on Spanish life and customs of the time; the *Crónica general*, in which chapters 466 to 494 are devoted to a strange life of the Prophet Muḥammad[3]; and the *Grande e general Estoria*, a 'great and general history' on a vast scale which is now in process of being printed for the first time.[4] The astronomical studies of Alfonso the Sage include the famous 'Alfonsine Tables'—a collection of observations taken at Toledo, which were in use throughout Europe for some centuries; he also compiled a *Lapidario*, a treatise on the virtues of precious stones, and a 'Book of Games', *Libro de los juegos*, including dice, backgammon, and several varieties of chess played on boards of different shapes and sizes.

[1] Ed. S. E. Northup, in *Modern Philology* (1908).

[2] *The Legacy of Israel*, pp. 222–5.

[3] R. Menéndez Pidal, *Primera crónica general*, pp. 261–75 (Madrid, 1906), and A. G. Solalinde, *Alfonso X el Sabio: Antología*, i, pp. 152–72 (Madrid, 1921).

[4] Madrid, Centro de Estudios Históricos, vol. i, 1930.

Chess is so characteristic a product of the legacy of Islam that it deserves more than a passing mention. Modern European chess is the direct descendant of an ancient Indian game, adopted by the Persians, handed on by them to the Muslim world, and finally borrowed from Islam by Christian Europe.[1] In most European languages the game is named after the king (Persian *shāh*; medieval Latin *scaci*, chessmen); but the Spanish word *ajedrez* (formerly *axedrez* or *acedrex*), and the Portuguese *xadrez* are derived from the Arabic name for the game itself: *al-s̲h̲aṭranj*, a word borrowed from Persian and ultimately from Sanskrit. Several of the terms still used in chess are Persian: 'checkmate', for instance, *shāh māt*, which does not necessarily signify that 'the king is dead', but that he is dishonoured or defeated.[2] The Castle or Rook is the Spanish *roque*, and the Persian *rukh*—the dreaded 'roc' encountered by Sindbād the Sailor. It has been discovered, however, that this word was in use among the Muslims in Spain for a chariot, and the idea of a chariot seems to explain at once the straight move and devastating power of the Rook in modern chess. In an early set of chessmen, reputed (but only since the seventeenth century) to have belonged to Charlemagne, the Rook is actually a chariot with a man in it; while the triumphal car used in certain religious festivals at Valencia is still known as the *roca*. The Bishop, again, is known in Spain as *el alfil* (Ar. *al-fīl*, the elephant), the French *fou* (when it refers to chess) being a corruption of the same word, and in no way connected with the moves or powers of a dignitary of the church.

Spain provides the earliest certain references to chess in Europe; there are bequests of chessmen in the wills of two members of the family of the Counts of Barcelona, dating from 1008

[1] H. J. R. Murray, *A History of Chess*. (Oxford, 1913.)

[2] 'Check (*xaque*) is a manner of legal affront to the lord; and when they give him *mate*, it is a manner of great dishonour, even as if they should conquer him or kill him.' Alfonso el Sabio, *Libro de los juegos*, fol. 2 b.

Fig. 6. HISPANO-MORESQUE PLATE
with Christian inscription: AVE · MA · RIA · GRA · PLE · NA
Photograph by Arxiv Mas

Fig. 7. CHESS PROBLEM
From the manuscript of Alfonso the Sage (Escorial T. I. 6, fol. 22 *a*) (XIIIth century)

(or 1010) and 1017. The first description of the game in a European language is that of Alfonso the Sage. His book[1] is obviously compiled from Arabic sources and the miniatures usually show players in oriental dress. Sometimes they are accompanied by oriental musicians, while now and then the musicians may be seen having a game by themselves, holding their instruments ready in the left hand, in case they are suddenly called upon to play them (fig. 7). The description of the game given by Alfonso has been found to be not altogether in accordance with Muslim practice, but the problems he gives are almost exclusively Muslim, for the chess-problem is a kind of mental activity which is characteristic of the legacy of Islam to Europe. His pieces, with one exception, are the same as ours. There is no Queen; her place is taken by the piece which Chaucer called the 'Fers' and Alfonso *ell alferza* (*al-firzān*, the counsellor; not *al-faras*, the horseman or knight). The Fers could move one square diagonally; but for his first move he could jump to the third square either diagonally or straight. He is the ancestor of the modern Queen, and the development of his powers in that direction is chiefly due to two Spanish players: Lucena (1497) and Ruy López (1561).

Alfonso X's games of chess on a larger number of squares than usual are of peculiar interest at the present time, when suggestions for improving the game (and reducing the chances of a draw) are being made by such masters as Sr. Capablanca. One of these suggestions is a board of 100 squares instead of the usual 64; while another is a kind of double chess, played on a board with 16 squares at each end and 12 at the sides. It is curious that the name of Alfonso el Sabio has never been mentioned in the discussion of these projects; for he knew of a game played on a board of 100 squares, with two additional pieces (which he calls

[1] J. G. White, *The Spanish Treatise on Chess-Play written by order of King Alfonso the Sage in the year* 1283. Reproduction of the Escurial MS. in 194 phototypic plates. (Leipzig, 1913.)

'judges') on each side, and two additional pawns. A game which interested him more, however, was 'great chess' (*Grande acedrex*), played on a board of 144 squares, with 12 pieces and 12 pawns. Next to the King stood a Gryphon; and then, on each side, came a Cocatrice, a Giraffe, a Unicorn, a Lion, and a Rook. The King moved, as in the modern game, to any adjacent square; and although 'castling' had not yet been invented, he could leap to the third square for the first move. The Gryphon (Sp. *aanca*, Ar. *ʿanqā*) moved one square diagonally and then any number straight. The Cocatrices moved like modern Bishops, though the large board gave them a far greater range and power. The Giraffes had a move resembling that of the modern Knight, except that their leap was longer; for while the Knight moves one square diagonally and two squares straight, the Giraffes moved the one square diagonally and four squares straight. The Unicorns also had a complicated move, and were regarded as the most powerful pieces on the board, after the Gryphon; they began like a Knight and went on like a Bishop, with the proviso that they could not take another piece until the move was completed. The Lion could leap to the fourth square in all directions; while the Rook moved as usual: straight, in any direction. The pawns moved as in the ordinary game: one square forward at a time. They had no right of moving two squares for the first move, but in compensation for that, they started on the fourth row instead of the second, and if they reached the twelfth square of their file and 'queened', they took the rank and powers of the piece on whose file they had started.

Alfonso the Sage has one more connexion with the legacy of Islam to Spain. He was responsible for one of the greatest collections of medieval poetry, the *Cantigas de Santa María*, preserved, with contemporary musical notation, in two manuscripts in the Escurial and one at Madrid. The language of these poems is not Castilian but the Galician dialect of northern Portugal, which, in the thirteenth century, was the language of court poetry in Castille and Aragon as well as Portugal, and continued to be so until Castilian Spanish became sufficiently ductile for refined lyrical expression. The music has been claimed by Professor Ribera to be Andalusian music of Muslim origin, a claim which historians of music are not very ready to admit. Yet many of the instruments shown in the miniatures, and even some of the performers, are obviously of Muslim origin; while the poetic form is peculiar to Muslim Spain, consisting almost entirely of stanzas of the type of the *muwashshaḥ* and *zajal* first employed by Ibn Quzmān (Abencuzmán) and described in another chapter. It has been urged that these poems are of exclusively Christian inspiration, and are therefore unlikely to be tainted with any suspicion of Islamic artifice. But the forms of *muwashshaḥ* and *zajal* developed into the typically Castilian popular verse-form of *villancico* which was extensively used for all kinds of Christian poetry, including Christmas carols; and the subject—the praise of the Virgin Mary—is a logical development of the troubadour's idealization of the lady of the manor; while the poems of the troubadours (as will be found convincingly demonstrated in chapter III) are, in matter, form, and style, closely connected with Arabic idealism and Arabic poetry written in Spain.

Don Juan Manuel and the Archpriest of Hita

The period of translation and compilation from oriental sources represented by the school of Alfonso the Sage was succeeded by a brilliant period of original work, in the prose of the Infante Don Juan Manuel (1282–1349 ?) and the poetry of the Archpriest of Hita (d. before 1351). Both had learnt from Eastern story, not only how to employ fables for teaching a moral lesson, but also how to set them in a suitable framework. In Don Juan Manuel's *Conde Lucanor*,[1] the Count asks the advice

[1] Ed. H. Knust (Leipzig, 1900) and F. J. Sánchez Cantón. (Madrid, 1920.) See also Broadway Translations. (London, 1924.)

of his Councillor, Patronio, on certain questions of life and government, and Patronio replies in each case by telling a story to illustrate the point. The stories have in many cases been traced to an Eastern origin, and on two or three occasions they contain phrases in the colloquial Arabic of the time, written out phonetically in Spanish. The moral tone is uniformly high, and the author, a nephew of Alfonso the Sage, is clearly conscious that by writing he is performing a public duty. Juan Ruiz, Archpriest of Hita, is a man of the people, with no sense of public duty or personal obligation to society and still less with any religious vocation. Yet he is a true poet, among the greatest in the Spanish language. His *Libro de buen amor*[1] ('The Book of True love'—*buen amor* as contrasted with earthly love, *loco amor*) is a satirical autobiography in which he tells with disarming candour the tale of his love-affairs. There is no possibility of an allegorical intention. The love that leads the Archpriest is earthly love, though in lyrics of passionate sincerity he protests his devotion to the Virgin Mary. Not all his desires end in fulfilment; but some of the ladies, e.g. Doña Endrina, are vividly and enchantingly portrayed, and the go-between, Trotaconventos (the direct ancestor of La Celestina and Juliet's nurse), is already one of the great characters in fiction. The Archpriest moved on the margins of society; he ministered to outcasts and wantons, and such despised subjects as musicians and Moorish dancing-girls. He reports conversations and sometimes transcribes answers which were given in Vulgar Arabic. The form of his work is to a certain extent oriental, a framework on which numerous fables and apologues are hung, and the vocabulary is a store-house of words borrowed from Arabic; but the Archpriest also availed himself of subjects borrowed from French and from medieval Latin. He employed every metre known to him in a masterly fashion, not excluding the characteristic *zajal*, with the

[1] Ed. J. Cejador y Frauca, 'Clásicos castellanos', Nos. 14 and 17. (Madrid, 1913.)

thought ever present in his mind that a minstrel might one day sing parts of his book in the street—as indeed is known to have actually happened during the half-century after his death. For a distracted scribe, copying a chronicle in his cell, one day made notes of the performance of a wandering minstrel in the street outside; and the man, in the midst of a string of anecdotes, rhymes, and a somersault or two, was heard to catch the flagging attention of the audience by exclaiming: 'Now we begin from the book of the Archpriest!' [1]

Contemporary with the Infante Don Juan Manuel and the Archpriest of Hita was the author of the earliest Spanish book of chivalry, the *Historia del Cavallero Cifar*,[2] which was probably composed between 1299 and 1335. Like all books of chivalry, it was said to have been taken from a 'Chaldean' (i.e. Arabic) original, and the underlying idea is that of a story in the 'Arabian Nights', though the detail is a strange mixture of the 'Golden Legend', Arthurian romance, and Oriental fable. The name Cifar is Arabic (*safar*, a journey; or *sifāra*, an embassy), so that 'Caballero Cifar' is equivalent to 'Knight-Errant'. His wife is named Grima (*Karīma*, a common name among Muslim women and signifying 'precious thing', 'nobly-born', or 'daughter'). Other Oriental features have been noticed.[3]

Spanish written in Arabic characters

Another contemporary of the Archpriest was the author of the *Poema de Yúçuf*,[4] an anonymous poem based on the legend

[1] R. Menéndez Pidal, *Poesía juglaresca y juglares* (Madrid, 1924), pp. 270–1 and 462–7.

[2] Ed. H. Michelant, *Bibl. des litt. Vereins in Stuttgart*, cxii. (Tübingen, 1872), and C. P. Wagner (Univ. of Michigan, 1929).

[3] A. González Palencia, *Historia de la literatura Arábigo-Española* (Madrid, 1928), pp. 316–17.

[4] Ed. R. Menéndez Pidal. (Madrid, 1902.) [Text in Arabic and Latin characters.]

of Joseph. Its peculiarity is that although the words are Spanish (Aragonese dialect) and the verse-form French, it is written in the Arabic character; and the poem is derived from the *Qur'ān* and other Muslim sources. It is an example of what is known in Spain and Portugal as *literatura aljamiada*, *ʿajama* meaning to speak bad Arabic, whence *ʿajamī* a foreigner, and *al-ʿajamīya* the outlandish language. In Spain it was originally used by Arabic-speaking Spaniards to designate Spanish, and afterwards applied to the writings of the Moriscos who employed the Arabic character for Spanish words. Manuscripts of this kind are fairly numerous. Some time ago a collection was found hidden under the floor of an old house at Almonacid de la Sierra in Aragon, where they must have been placed to keep them out of sight of the 'familiars' of the Inquisition: they are now in the library of the Junta para Ampliación de Estudios at Madrid.[1] They include important legal documents, verses in praise of the Prophet written in *muwashshaḥ* form in the fourteenth century, sermons, legends, stories, and superstitions of the fifteenth and sixteenth centuries; while one of the most instructive manuscripts of the time is a pastoral epistle from the *muftī* of Oran[2] advising the persecuted Moriscos in the century following the conquest of Granada to what extent they should conform to the conquerors, who seemed to regard every decency of Muslim life —even washing—as heresy and therefore a capital offence. The use of the Arabic character, even after the fall of Granada, shows how the conquered Muslim Spaniards clung to the handwriting of their religion, even when they spoke a Romance dialect and were (in many cases) of Christian Spanish descent. The method of transcribing the Spanish sounds in Arabic character offers many points of interest, and is especially valuable as an indication

[1] *MSS. árabes y aljamiados de la Biblioteca de la Junta.* (Madrid, 1912.) See also D. Lopes, *Textos em aljamia portuguesa.* (Lisbon, 1897.)

[2] Pedro Longas, *Vida religiosa de los Moriscos* (Madrid, 1915), pp. 305–7, and *Journ. Asiatique*, t. 210, pp. 1–17 (Jan.–Mar. 1927).

(confirmed by Pedro de Alcalá's transcription into Roman type of the colloquial Arabic of Granada as spoken about 1500), of how the Muslims in Spain pronounced the languages of the country, Spanish and Arabic. The after-effects of Morisco pronunciation are still perceptible to-day.

The pitiful story of the expulsion of the Moriscos need not be repeated here. They were not driven out finally until 1614, so that Arabic was still spoken in the Peninsula during the lifetime of Cervantes, and it could not have struck his contemporaries as fantastic or impossible when, remembering that the romances of chivalry had usually been stated to have been taken from a book in Arabic or 'Chaldean', he declared that the original of *Don Quixote* was the work of a Moor called 'Sidi Hamete ben Engeli', and that it too had originally been written in Arabic.

J. B. TREND.

THE CRUSADES

I

Men have often thought of what may be called the fatalities of history. Among them has always been counted the duel of East and West. Herodotus began his history by asking why they fought, δι' ἣν αἰτίην ἐπολέμησαν ἀλλήλοισι; and our poets still speak to-day of the silent deep disdain of the East for the thundering of Western legions, or celebrate the implacable difference which separates the two for all eternity. The Trojan and the Persian wars of antiquity: the battles of Crassus and Heraclius in Syria: the Crusades and the Ottoman conquests—all seem to make a rhythm and to suggest a regular recurrence. But the duel of East and West is a geographical simplification of a complicated series of historical facts. History is a record of something more than struggles in space; and it is only when we reduce the apparent struggle between 'East' and 'West' into the real struggles, which vary from age to age, between competing churches and races and civilizations, that the story gains point as well as dimension. It is true, indeed, that for a variety of geographical reasons the eastern coast of the Mediterranean, from Constantinople to Alexandria, was for long a vexed region of history. Here, whether by way of the Black Sea, or the Red Sea, or from Beyrout across the desert, Europe touches Asia and the commodities and mysteries of Asia; here, whether in Egypt or Crete, in Jerusalem or Athens, civilizations and religions and philosophies have found their cradle. In such an area many conflicts were bound to arise. Some were economic: some were religious: some were political: some were racial: many were mixed. Each conflict is best understood in itself and its own individuality. One of the greatest is the conflict between the church, the civilization, and the peoples of Western Christianity and the faith, the civilization, and the peoples of Islam. It began, we may say, with the defeat of Heraclius, 'the first of the Crusaders', on the Yarmūk in 636 by the forces of Omar; and who shall give a date to its end? It has at one time been primarily religious, and at another predominantly political: it has been a struggle between different peoples—in the main the Romance and Slavonic on the one side, and the Arab and Turk on the other; but it has always remained a mixed conflict, in which two civilizations have been fundamentally engaged. One of its chapters is the Crusades. That chapter began in 1096: it ended, if we regard it as closed by the loss of the last Christian foothold on the Syrian mainland, in 1291: it lasted, if we look rather to the lingering relics of the old Crusading impulse, till the navigations of the Portuguese and the discoveries of Columbus.

The Crusades have a double aspect. They are, in their original impulse (crossed, it is true, from the first by other strains), a spiritual movement which translated itself into the objective form of a spiritual institution. They are a 'holy war'—a war which, in the theory of the canonists, is not only 'just', but also attains the full measure of consecration; a war which is *res Christiana*, and unites the Christian commonwealth in common hostilities against the arch-enemy of its faith. But the Crusades are also, in their results, the redemption of the Holy Land: they are a projection of the Christian West into the Muslim East: they are the foundation of a Christian State, the 'Latin Kingdom of Jerusalem', camped on the shores of the Levant, and looking eastward to Mosul and Baghdad and southward to Cairo and Egypt. The former is the broader theme: the latter has its particular and peculiar interest. In the Latin Kingdom of Jerusalem the Crusades become specific, and here they show their specific results—the rise of the military orders; the foundation of trading quarters, by the Venetians and Genoese, in the Syrian ports; the growth of trading and missionary connexions with Further Asia. Here (as indeed also in Spain, but here in a way which engaged the general attention of Europe as Spain never did) there was a constant conflict and a permanent contact between Christianity and Islam. It is when the eyes are fixed on the Latin Kingdom that the general background comes most clearly into view (like distant mountains rising above the immediate scene)—the geographical background of the Mediterranean basin: the historical background of the previous centuries of oscillation in that basin between Christian and Muhammadan power.

Geographically we may say that there are two Mediterraneans. There is the Mediterranean of the West, closed on its eastern side by Italy and Sicily, with a sea-passage, some 100 miles wide, between Cape Sorello in the south-west of Sicily and Cape Bon in north-eastern Tunis. There is the Mediterranean of the East, from the eastern shores of Sicily (which again and again in history has been the battle-ground or meeting-place of the two Mediterraneans) to the coasts of Asia Minor and Syria. Two halves of one sea, the eastern and the western Mediterranean became, in classical times, the homes of two civilizations. In the West was Latin civilization; and on this basis, as Christianity triumphed, there arose the Roman Church and the Holy Roman Empire of the West. The East was the home of Hellenistic civilization; and here were developed the Greek Church and the Byzantine Empire. Upon this division there supervened, in the seventh century, the rise of Islam. Spreading with the rapidity of an electric current from its power-house in Mecca, it flashed into Syria; it traversed the whole breadth of north Africa; and then, leaping the Straits of Gibraltar, it ran to the Gates of the Pyrenees. It had fixed itself permanently in both Mediterraneans by the early Middle Ages—on the southern and western shores of the West; on the southern and eastern shores of the East. In both halves of the Mediterranean basin Christianity was engaged in conflicts with it; and these conflicts, even before the Crusades, have already something of the nature of a Crusade. But the peculiarity of the Crusades, when their course began at the end of the eleventh century, is that the Latin Christianity of the West moved over into the East, hitherto secluded from it, and that here it came into contact, on the one hand, and nominally as an ally, with the Greek Church and the Eastern Empire, and on the other, in declared hostility, with the Muhammadans of the East. Perhaps the primary and the most fruitful element in the Crusades is this simple fact of the entry of the West into the East. And yet the simple fact has its complications, for the East into which the West made its entry was itself full of complication. Not only had Latin Christianity to make its terms and settle its relations with the Greek Christianity of Byzantium. Muhammadanism also was divided: the Sunnite Turks, who had established themselves in western Asia from the Black Sea on the north to the Red Sea on the south, were confronted, in the debatable land of Syria, by the Shī'ites of Egypt under the Fāṭimid dynasty; and the Crusading West had to discover, and to use as best it could, an opposition of which it was hardly aware.[1]

Historically, the passage of Latin Christianity overseas to fight against Islam may be regarded as the culmination of a long

[1] The position in A.D. 1096 has some similarities with that in 201 B.C. The Romans, when they began to act in the East, were similarly faced by three powers—the Macedonian Kingdom, which ruled Greece and the northern Aegaean as far as the Bosphorus: the Seleucids of Asia Minor; and the Ptolemaic dynasty in Egypt. On the other hand there were fundamental differences. The Romans came with a readiness to learn and an admiration for everything in Hellenistic culture. Latin Christianity at the end of the eleventh century had a developed culture of its own; and so far as it could learn from the Muhammadan it was able to do so at home, in Spain and Sicily. Moreover the Romans came into a new and different world: the 'Franks' of the eleventh century found in Byzantium something which, though it had pursued a different line of development, was akin to their own traditions. In the issue, as we shall see, they perhaps learned more from the Byzantines than they did from the Muhammadans of Syria and Egypt.

course of hostilities between Christian and Muslim in the western Mediterranean, and this is a large element in the historical background against which we must set the Crusades. By the end of the seventh century the Arabs had mastered the Berbers of northern Africa; and between 711 and 718 the Arabs and Berbers had conquered Spain as far as the Pyrenees. In the course of the ninth century, between 827 and 878 (when Syracuse fell), the Aghlabids of Ḳairawān, in northern Africa, had conquered Sicily; and they also harassed, both by temporary forays and the foundation of robber-states, the south of Italy as far as the Campagna and the Abruzzi. Muslims from Spain raided Provence, northern Italy, and even Switzerland; and Corsica and Sardinia were again and again ravaged by corsairs. Only in Spain and Sicily did the civilization of the Muslim attain any height; but in both of these it flourished, and from both of these it transmitted its influence into France and Italy. The philosophy of Cordova and its great teacher Ibn Rushd (Averroes) penetrated to the University of Paris; Arab villas, Arabic geographers and Arabic poets adorned Palermo under its Norman kings and their successor Frederic II. 'The blessings of culture which were given to the West by its temporary Islamitic elements', it has been said, 'are at least as important as the influence of the East during the time of the Crusades.'[1] But whatever the gifts which it received, the West could not tolerate the occupation of Christian soil by the followers of another faith; and the eleventh century saw a gradual recession of Muslim arms in the western Mediterranean before the advance of the Christians. In Spain, after the death of the great al-Manṣūr in 1002, the small Christian powers of the north—Leon, Castile, Aragon, and Navarre—embarked on a period of expansion. Toledo fell before Alfonso VI of Castile in 1085,[2] and Saragossa was captured by

[1] Professor Becker in the *Cambridge Mediaeval History*, vol. ii, p. 390.

[2] His progress received a serious set-back from the new inroad of the Almoravides in 1086: but the set-back, in the issue, proved to be temporary.

Aragon in 1118. South Italy, torn by disputes between Byzantine governors and Arab raiders, fell into the hands of the Normans during the first half of the eleventh century; and between 1060 and 1090 they had also conquered Sicily. Benedict VIII, about 1016, had instigated the Pisans to the occupation of Sardinia; and with the rise of the Genoese and the Venetians the Muslim corsairs ceased to be the terror of the western Mediterranean. By the end of the eleventh century the Muhammadans held only southern Spain and the north of Africa; and during the twelfth century they were to be attacked by the Normans of Sicily even in their African strongholds. A more consolidated and developed West was making itself master in its own house.

This was the juncture of affairs in the West when the call to the Crusade came from the East. It was a double call, if it was due to a single cause. The pressure of the Seljūḳ Turks—who, beginning as the mercenaries, had become virtually the masters of the Caliphs of Baghdad—had on the one hand, and in Syria, resulted in the capture of Jerusalem from the mild Fāṭimid Caliphs of Cairo (1070), and on the other hand, and in Asia Minor, in the capital defeat of the Byzantine forces at Manzikart (1071). The needs of Jerusalem and the necessities of Byzantium both called aloud to the West; and the First Crusade (1096–99) was an answer to that double call.

The religious habits and the social development of western Europe conspired to produce the answer. The habit of penitentiary pilgrimage for the sake of remission of sins was ancient in the West. Jerusalem—at once the most sacred and the most distant of holy places, and therefore conferring a double grace—had long been the goal of such pilgrimages. The goal was now menaced: the menace must be removed. The Crusade accordingly came as a great armed pilgrimage for the sake of clearing the routes and liberating the goal of future pilgrimages; and it was pilgrim knights who founded, as it was pilgrim knights who came afterwards year by year to maintain, the Kingdom of Jerusalem. The social development of feudalism, under the influence of the Church, was another and parallel cause of the Crusade. The bellicose passion of a military society for private war (*guerra*) had engaged the attention of synods and Popes from the beginning of the eleventh century. At first they attempted to check it by the institutions of the *Pax* and the *Treuga Dei*: later they sought to direct it into the channels of 'just' and 'holy' warfare, partly by consecrating the arms of the knight, in the ceremony of his initiation, to the defence of justice and the remedy of oppression (thus helping to create a new chivalry), and partly again by demanding, as Urban II demanded at Clermont in 1095 in preaching the Crusade, that the fratricidal abuse of private war should be turned into the sanctity of battle against the infidel. The cause of internal peace was thus linked with that of a holy war; and synod on synod enjoined, in the same breath, the cause of the truce of God and that of the Christian Crusade.

So far, the Crusade wears the double aspect of a 'Pilgrim's Progress' and of a 'Holy War'. But it was also something more, or something less, than these. It was, in the first place, a solution of the problem of feudal over-population. The younger sons of the feudal nobility had little prospect at home. It would have fared ill with many of the many descendants of Tancred d'Hauteville, for example, if there had been no founding of a Norman Kingdom of Sicily and a Latin Kingdom of Jerusalem. Such kingdoms were feudal colonies: they provided an outlet for feudal emigrants. In the second place the Crusades afforded a new vent for the commercial ambitions of the growing Italian ports; and the Venetian, Pisan, and Genoese establishments on the Syrian coast, which served as entrepôts for the great routes of Asiatic trade, were no small factor in the history of the Latin settlement. Italian ships accompanied and aided the progress

FIG. 8. THE CRUSADES AS A HOLY WAR
The Norman tympanum at Fordington (Dorset) portraying the intervention of St. George at the battle of Antioch

even of the first Crusade; the help of the Italian towns was a necessity in the war of sieges which led to the subsequent growth of the Kingdom of Jerusalem; Italian transports carried the annual flow of pilgrims; and both for good and for evil the commercial motive was added to the spiritual impulse of the Crusade.

It was these various factors, coupled with the happy opportunity of Muhammadan dissensions in Syria, which enabled Baldwin I and Baldwin II to establish and consolidate the Kingdom of Jerusalem between 1100 and 1131. But the kingdom was hardly established when it began to be menaced with destruction. Christian pressure produced a Muslim reaction. The centre of this reaction was Mosul. Here, among the debris of the Seljūq Empire, which had collapsed into fragments even before the first Crusade began its course, there emerged about 1127 the figure of the atabeg Zangī. He extended his power among his rivals, and in 1144 captured Edessa from the Latins—the first serious set-back to their career. His successor Nūr-al-Dīn (1146–74) was already animated by the religious motive of the counter-crusade (the *jihād*); and during his reign his lieutenants, the Kurd Shīrkūh and Shīrkūh's nephew Saladin (Ṣalāḥ-al-Dīn), brought Egypt under his sway. Menaced both from Mosul and from Cairo, and with the new ardour of the *jihād* ready to meet the waning passion of their own Crusade, the Latins of the Kingdom soon succumbed. In July 1187 they were defeated at Ḥiṭṭīn: in October of the same year Jerusalem capitulated. Saladin had attained 'the goal of his desires, and set free the mosque of Aqṣā, to which Allah once led in the night his servant Mahomet'.

The Third Crusade failed to undo the work of Saladin. The Latins still kept for some time the principalities of Antioch and Tripoli in northern Syria; the emperor Frederic II was able for a brief while (1227–44) to recover, by diplomacy and not by force of arms, the city of Jerusalem; but the Kingdom of Jerusalem had perished. The thirteenth century was full of Crusades; but they were waged, as has been well said, 'everywhere except in Palestine'. They had become uncertain of their goal; and they wandered uncertainly from Constantinople (1202–4) to Egypt (1218–21 and 1249–50) and even to Tunis (1270). The one Crusade which was successful only succeeded in capturing the Christian city of Constantinople, and in dividing the Byzantine Empire, for a time (1204–61), between the French and the Venetians. Constantinople, if it had invoked the Crusades, perished by them; and if it rose again for two centuries of feeble life from 1261 to 1453, it had to leave the French in the Morea, and the Venetians in Crete and the islands of the Archipelago. The First Crusade had been an alliance between French feudalism and the maritime strength of the Italian towns. By the thirteenth century French feudalism was diverted to Greece, and the Venetians and Genoese were founding new entrepôts for Eastern trade in the Crimea and the Sea of Azov. It seemed as if Palestine were left derelict, and the centre of gravity had shifted into the debris of the Eastern Empire.

But a new hope dawned before the middle of the thirteenth century; and a new vicissitude in Asiatic affairs was acclaimed in the West as the promise of better things. A great Mongol Empire, neither Christian nor Muhammadan, had been founded by Jenghiz Khan. It stretched from Pekin on the east to the Dnieper and the Euphrates on the west: the four Khanates, into which it was divided, were each of the dignity of an empire; and the Persian Khanate in particular, with its capital at Tabrīz, was near enough to the eastern Mediterranean to be drawn into its affairs. The Mongols were tolerant: the Nestorian Christians of Asia flourished under their sway; why should they not be converted to Christianity, and why should not the fundamental purpose of the Crusades be realized, after all, on a vastly greater scale than had ever been dreamed before? Envoys came and went: Innocent IV sent John de Pian Carpine on a great journey in 1245, and St. Louis dispatched William of Rubruquis on another in 1250: missions were active, and churches were founded as far afield as China. It was all a dream: no help came to Palestine. For a time Antioch and Tripoli, and the few possessions left to the Latins on the coast of the old Kingdom of Jerusalem, were spared. The successors of Saladin were divided by dissensions; and by the grace of those dissensions the Latins survived. But a new and militant Muhammadanism arose with the Mameluke Sultans of Egypt, who seized the throne of Cairo in 1250. The greatest of these Sultans, Baibars, defeated the one attempt of the Mongol Khanate of Persia to establish a footing in Syria: he established himself in Damascus (1260): he crushed and annexed the principality of Antioch (1268). His successor Ḳalā'ūn conquered and annexed Tripoli (1289); and his son and successor Khalīl captured Acre, the last stronghold of the Latins on the Syrian coast (1291). By the end of the thirteenth century Latin Christianity was entirely expelled from the mainland of Asia.

It survived among the islands. Cyprus, captured from the Greeks by Richard I on the Third Crusade, became under its Lusignan kings the refuge of the Latin feudatories of Palestine. It was here that the feudal jurisprudence of the Assizes of Jerusalem was continued and codified; and the Kingdom of Cyprus survived as an independent state until 1488, when it passed into the hands of Venice.[1] In the same way the Knights Hospitallers, after the final loss of Acre, occupied Rhodes in 1309, and maintained themselves in the island until 1523, when they moved to the west and to Malta. It is in these two islands that some of the finest monuments of the presence of the Latins in the eastern Mediterranean during the Middle Ages still sur-

[1] See Stubbs's two lectures on Cyprus in his Lectures on *Medieval and Modern History*.

vive. While the feudal nobility was thus established in Cyprus and Rhodes, the Venetians held Crete, and a number of islands to the north, as the spoils of the Fourth Crusade; and the Genoese, who had aided in the restoration of the Palaeologi to the throne of Constantinople in 1261, were not only rewarded with the suburb of Pera, but rewarded themselves with the islands of Lesbos and Chios. In this way Latin Christianity kept a hold in the eastern Mediterranean to the close of the Middle Ages; and even if it was confined to the islands, and although its possessions were rather the debris of the Byzantine Empire than conquests wrested from Muslim power, it still waged a war against Islam from its scattered bases, and only abandoned the struggle when the victory of the Ottoman Turks made the eastern Mediterranean into a *mare clausum*. Indeed it was not until 1668 that Candia fell, and Venice lost her last great stronghold in the Levant.

II

What were the results of the long adventure of Western Christianity in the Eastern Mediterranean and of its long contact with the Muhammadans of the East? The question is really double. It is a question, in the first place, of the effects of the Crusades considered simply as a mode of contact between the East and the West—a question of the influence upon the West of factors and impulses derived from the East. It is a question, in the second place, of the effects of the Crusades regarded as a general movement operative in the sphere of Western society—a question of the influence upon that society of a movement which at once sprang from it and reacted strongly upon it. The two questions have been too often confused by historians; and the confusion has produced exaggerations which a distinction might have avoided.

We may take as an example of such exaggerations the passage in Henne-am Rhyn's *Allgemeine Kulturgeschichte* which deals with the Crusades.[1] Here we find the whole development of the Middle Ages ascribed to the Crusades. In the religious sphere they diminished the prestige of the Papacy, irretrievably affected monasticism, and encouraged the growth of heresy. In the social and economic sphere they led to a greater equality of classes, the growth of a free peasantry and of guilds of artisans, and the development of trade and industry. In the field of politics they were followed by the rise of the system of Estates, by a growing centralization of government, and by the appearance of written law and a regular judicial administration. In the great world of culture, philosophy developed its greatest thinkers after the Crusades and the connexion with the Arabs which they brought: even mysticism assumed a scientific character: the study of the ancient languages grew in extent and fertility: historiography and geography acquired a new vigour: a vernacular poetry arose: Gothic architecture succeeded to Romanesque, and a finer taste appeared in sculpture and painting.

Something of the same confusion, the same exaggeration, and the same fallacy of *post hoc ergo propter hoc* appears even in the learned and imposing *Kulturgeschichte der Kreuzzüge* of Hans Prutz.[2] It is a work of massive erudition, but in some respects it is essentially uncritical. In the first place Prutz is apt to write as if the Crusades were the one factor in the development of Europe during the two centuries between 1100 and 1300, and as if all the *causae causantes* of those two hundred years—causes which helped to produce the new Europe of the Age of the Renaissance, the Age of Discovery, and the Age of the Reformation—were compact and contained in that one factor. Actually they were only one factor among many: and the fallacy of the 'single cause' is added to the fallacy of *post hoc ergo propter hoc* when we make

[1] Vol. iii, *Kulturgeschichte des Mittelalters*, Book VII, esp. pp. 498–500.

[2] Berlin, 1883, in five books, of which Book IV (on economic culture) and Book V (on the effects of the Crusades upon the history of culture) deserve especial attention.

them a single and universal explanation. In the second place, though Prutz admits that Spain and Sicily were important vehicles of Arabic influence, he is prone in the issue to forget his own admission, and to make Palestine far the greater and almost the only vehicle. 'In most of the areas of cultural development', he writes, 'we find the first permanent connection of Eastern and Western elements among the Franks (of Palestine), and it is this mixed stock . . . which must be described as the pioneer in the process of mediation between East and West.'[1] Here again we cannot but notice the fallacy of the 'single cause', and the fallacy appears the greater when we remember that the other cause (the mixture of Eastern and Western elements in Spain and in Sicily) was the more potent and penetrating. Finally, it is impossible to escape the impression, in reading Prutz's work, that he has both minimized the culture of the Latin West and exaggerated the culture of the Arabic East, as they stood about 1100, in order to leave a larger scope for the influence of the Crusades, and to provide (as it were) an emptier market for a larger importation than our evidence warrants us in accepting. The Western Europe which was just passing through the great Gregorian age—which was witnessing the growth of thought that culminates in Abelard, the rise of the French communes, the vigour of Norman diffusion and Norman architecture, the industrial and commercial revolution that may be traced at the end of the eleventh century—this was no *tabula rasa*. Nor was the Arabic culture of the East, about the year 1100, in its hey-day. On the contrary, as we shall see, its sun was setting when the Crusades began; and we must always remember that, so far as *Kulturgeschichte* goes, it was a new and growing West which burst upon an old and waning East.

Crusade is a magic word, and magic words may be magnets

[1] P. 452. In justice it must be added that Prutz admits that 'in the sphere of definitely scientific life an essentially different process appears'.

which draw large tracts of irrelevancy into the sphere of their influence. Not everything which happened in Western Europe during the Crusades was connected with them—far less due to them. Even if there had been no Crusade, Western Christianity, in which town-life and trade were rapidly developing during the latter half of the eleventh century, would probably have pushed it commerce into the Eastern Mediterranean. It would have sought to establish itself at the termini of the Eastern caravan routes—on the north coast of the Black Sea, where it might touch the route that went north of the Caspian and west of the Aral Sea to Bokhara and Samarcand; or again in the Syrian ports, from which it might reach Persia and the Persian Gulf, and so touch the sea-route that led past India to China. What the Crusades did was to establish a feudal Syrian State—occupied partly by individual feudatories and partly by the feudal chartered companies of the Templars and Hospitallers—to which the commercial impulse, for a time, particularly attached itself, and in which it created for itself the various 'quarters' occupied by the Venetians, Genoese, and Pisans in the ports along the coast. We have to remember that this commercial impulse was not exclusively tied to these Syrian quarters; that it had also its contacts with Constantinople and the Black Sea; and that after the Fourth Crusade, and during the course of the thirteenth century, these contacts became the richer and the more manifold. But at any rate during the twelfth century, between the First and the Third Crusade, Syria was the particular focus of relations between Christianity and Islam in the Eastern Mediterranean. Here Islam could act upon Western Christianity, partly by its direct impact upon the feudal State and by the repercussions of that impact on the West, and partly by a process of filtration along the routes of commerce. It is this action which we have to study.

But we have to remember, and to repeat, that Islam was also established, and could also act on the West, in Spain and in

Sicily. There was a play of concurrent forces; and though we cannot measure the exact and separate extent of either, we may guess that Islam acted more profoundly on Western Christianity from its bases in Spain and Sicily than it did from its bases in Mosul and Baghdad and Cairo. There are two reasons which support this conjecture. The first is that there was never established in Syria itself the potent influence of a mixture of cultures, such as we find in Sicily under Roger II and Frederic II. The second is that the Latins of Syria were never able to draw on the riches of a Muhammadan culture external but contiguous to themselves, as the Christians of the Western Mediterranean were able to draw on the riches of the culture of Cordova and Muhammadan Spain.

The absence of any mixture of culture, or indeed of any degree of culture of any kind, in the Latin Kingdom of Jerusalem is a striking thing. In Sicily the mixture of stocks—Greek, Norman, Lombard, and Arab-Berber—produced a remarkable mixed civilization. At the court of the Norman kings we not only find Arabic geographers and poets encouraged; we also find a king's chancellor translating for William I the *Phaedo* and *Meno* of Plato, a part of the *Meteorologica* of Aristotle, and the writings of Diogenes Laertius. The court of Frederic II was even more famous. Here, as Dante records in the *De Vulgari Eloquio*, Italian poetry took its beginnings; here the King could concoct, or have concocted for him, knotty questions on the interpretation of Aristotelian philosophy (*Quaestiones Sicilianae*) which still survive in an Arabic manuscript in the Bodleian Library. The Latin Kingdom of Jerusalem was a rude military settlement, without the impulse, or at any rate without the time, for the creation of any achievements of civilization. It was a foreign legion encamped in castles and barracks: it came into no close contact either with the tillers of the soil in the Syrian villages or with the artisans who were busy, then as now, in making carpets and pottery and gold-work in the towns. The Latins were scattered thinly on a narrow littoral, which they had to defend against a vast and dark background of Muhammadanism; and though they might feel that they were in the warmth of Jerusalem, the hearth of their faith and the centre of the round earth (*umbilicus terrae*), they were none the less removed from the great centres of medieval civilization in Rome and Paris.

Nor, if they had the power to draw (and their time was too brief, and their footing too precarious and hostile, for them to do so), was there any neighbouring Muhammadan civilization on which they could draw. The Western Mediterranean had the culture of Arabic Spain before its eyes. Here Ibn Rushd, jurist, physician, and philosopher, was teaching till the end of the twelfth century; here the Jews had come into contact with Arabic philosophy, and Maimonides, under its influence, had attempted to reconcile Aristotle with the Old Testament; and here the Latin Christianity of the West learned, about 1200, a deeper knowledge of Aristotle than it had been able to acquire before from the solitary source of Boethius' translation of the *Organon*. The Mosque Library of Toledo which fell to the Spaniards with their conquest of the city, became a resort of scholars; and the Arabic Aristotle of Spain was one of the sources of the scholasticism of the thirteenth century.[1] Nor was this all. The border-warfare south of the Pyrenees became a theme of poetry; and just as the border-warfare of English and Scots produced our own border-ballads, or the struggle of Greeks and Turks in the Taurus produced Byzantine *chansons de geste*, so the battles of Christian and Paynim in Spain were the theme of the *Song of Roland* and the legend of the Cid Campeador. It was otherwise in the East. Here Arabic philosophy was beginning to wane by the time of the First Crusade; and no native poetry was stimulated by all the border-battles of the twelfth century. The great Ibn Sīnā had died in Hamadān in

[1] Cf. T. J. de Boer, *Geschichte der Philosophie im Islam*, and E. Renan, *Averroes et l'Averroïsme*.

1037; Ghazālī, a sceptic who has been accused of destroying the philosophy which he professed, died in Khurāsān in 1111; in 1150 the Caliph at Baghdad was committing to the flames a philosophical library, and among its contents the writings of Ibn Sīnā himself. In days such as these the Latins of the East were hardly likely to become the scholars of the Muhammadans; nor were they stimulated by the novelty of their surroundings to any original production. No new poetry or art arose in the Holy Land; the minstrels who sang the theme of the Crusades were the minstrels of the West; and if historiography flourished with Fülcher of Chartres or William of Tyre, or law-books were composed by a John of Ibelin or a Philip of Novara, these were the only products which can be celebrated.

In the realm of culture the Latins of the Kingdom thus learned little from Eastern Muhammadanism, and developed little of their own which could influence the West. Indeed it may almost be contended that the chief service of the Crusades to the development of Western civilization was not so much that it brought Latin Christianity into contact with the Muslim East, as that it brought it into relations with the Byzantine Empire and Greek Christianity. Before the First Crusade, the Church and Empire of the West had been separated from the Church and Empire of the East by a gulf of oblivion. Luitprand of Cremona might go on a famous embassy for Otto I to Constantinople in 968; the envoys of Leo IX might appear in Constantinople in 1054; but the relations of East and West were for centuries sparse and infrequent. After 1096 the Comneni are in constant relations with Western powers; after 1204 the Latins are settled in the Eastern Empire. During the thirteenth century the Flemish archbishop of Corinth, William of Moerbeke, and his colleague Henry of Brabant are translating the *Ethics* and *Politics* of Aristotle in collaboration with St. Thomas, and opening for the West another avenue to Greek philosophy than that of Spain. At the end of the fourteenth and during the fifteenth century Byzantine scholars bring to Italy the full wealth of the Greek inheritance, and provide the Italian Renaissance with its material. Constantinople did not lie on the main stream of the Crusades; but it was from Constantinople that the Crusades brought back the richest argosy to the West.

Yet there were ways in which the Crusades, through their direction to Syria, and through the Latin State which they temporarily established there, affected the development of Western Europe. We may appeal, first and foremost, to the evidence of language—to the Western words which flowed into Arabic, and the Arabic words which flowed into Western languages. The borrowed Western words in Arabic are not very numerous. Prutz cites as examples *inbirūr* (imperator), *ḳasṭal* (castellum), *burj* (burgus), and *ghirsh* (grossus). The borrowed Arabic words in Western languages are far more abundant. We need only think of *caravan* and *dragoman*, *jar* and *syrup*, in our own language; and if we turn to the Romance languages of the continent—which borrowed directly, while we, for the most part, only borrowed through them—we shall realize that the list of Western borrowings from the Arabic may readily be increased (witness words such as *douane*, *gabelle*, *felucca*, *chébec*, and the like). But there are obvious philological difficulties in the attribution of these borrowings. Palestine is not the only place, or the age of the Crusades the only time, in which they may have originated. Spain and Sicily are other possible places of borrowing; and long centuries of contact between the West and the Arab-speaking world—both east and west of Suez; both in the way of commerce and in the way of piracy—are other possible times and ways. The West, it is true, still uses Arabic terms of trade, such as *bazaar*,[1] *dinar*, *tariff*, and *zechin*; it still uses Arabic terms of sea-faring, such as *admiral* and *arsenal*; it still uses Arabic terms

[1] The origin is Persian rather than Arabic.

of domestic life, such as *alcove*, *carafe*, *mattress*, and *sofa*, or again *amulet*, *elixir*, *julep*, and *talisman*; it still uses or has used some Arabic terms of music, such as *lute* and *naker*. But before we assign the introduction of such terms to the Crusades we must consult both Arabic and Romance philology, and we must be certain both of the original place and the exact time of the introduction.

The Crusades were a series of wars—wars fought against new enemies, armed with new weapons and following, in some respects, a new technique of war. We should naturally expect to find that they exerted some effect on the development of the art of war in the West. Some writers have held that the 'concentric' castle, of the type which became common in England during the reign of Edward I, was modelled upon the military architecture of the Latin kingdom of Jerusalem, as that in turn was modelled upon the modifications made by the Arabs in the Byzantine forts which they found in Syria. Following this line of argument Prutz suggests that while the general scheme of military defence in Palestine followed the Norman system of castellation (such as we find, for instance, on the Welsh marches and in South Wales), 'Arabic influence may be traced in the disposition of the different parts of the greater fortresses, in the addition of parts unknown to the older military architecture of the West, and in a number of new methods of defence made necessary by the technique of siege tactics developed in the East'.[1] He assigns accordingly to Arabic sources the use of a double line of walls (the essence of the 'concentric' castle) and the erection of an additional tower or keep between the two lines;[2] and he suggests that the famous

[1] *Kulturgeschichte*, p. 194.

[2] An advanced tower of this sort, especially when it is erected over the gate or entrance, is known as a barbican; and it has been suggested that the word may be derived from Arabic (or Persian) words meaning 'house on the wall' or 'gate-house'. (See *N.E.D.*, *sub voce.*)

Château Gaillard built by Richard I in the Vexin shows indisputable traces of Oriental influence. On the other hand it has been contended that the 'concentric' castle was developed in the West, and carried by the Crusaders to the East; and it is at any rate certain that the engineering skill of the adventurous Normans, which showed itself in Western Europe earlier than it did in Palestine, was fully competent to arrive at such a development from its own independent resources. We may assert with more confidence that the Crusades fostered the growth of siege tactics—the use of the art of sapping and mining, the employment of an 'artillery' of mangonels and battering-rams, and possibly the application of various fires and combustibles; though even here the original impulse may be Byzantine rather than Arabic, and the skilled engineer from the Holy Land employed by Frederic I at the siege of Crema in 1159 may have been a disciple not of the Arabs but of the Greeks. The cross-bow is said to have been an Oriental import; the use of mail for the knight and his horse is ascribed to the influence of the Crusades; the wearing of cotton quilts or pads under the armour is attributed to the same origin; and the Frankish knight, at any rate when he was fighting in Palestine, learned to use the Arab *kūfīya* for the protection of head and neck against an eastern sun. The employment of carrier-pigeons to convey military information was a device borrowed from the Arabs, though it must be added that we find it commonly mentioned in the records of Norman Sicily; and it has been suggested that the celebration of victory by illuminations and by the display of hangings and carpets on walls and from windows—natural and indigenous as they may seem to the soil of human emotion—were perhaps borrowed from the same source. The practice of the tournament, which has its affinities with the exercises of the *Jarīd*, was perhaps fostered by the Crusades; and a growing use of armorial bearings may be due to contact with the Saracens in Syria. They certainly used heraldic devices, such as the double eagle, the fleur-de-lis, and the two keys (fig. 10); and many heraldic charges, as well as some of the recognized terms of heraldry (such as azure and possibly gules), spring from this source. It appears to be also due to the Crusades that the rules of armorial bearings became uniform throughout Europe, and that 'the charges and terms and rules of heraldry are identical in all European countries'.

Trade followed in the footsteps of war during the Crusades, and the Italian merchant hurried at the heels of the Frankish knight. It was not only a matter of the products and the wares of Syria; it was also a matter of the products and the wares of India and China and the Spice islands. It is true, and we have already had occasion to mention, that this Eastern trade would have existed, and produced its fruits, even if there had been no Crusades; nor must it be forgotten that Venice had already found her way into the Eastern markets, by way of Byzantium, many years before the beginning of the First Crusade. We cannot therefore ascribe to the Crusades—at any rate we cannot ascribe solely to the Crusades—all the Eastern commodities introduced into western Europe during the Middle Ages, or all the fructification of old trade-routes and markets which followed on that introduction. Equally, however, we cannot deny the great trading impetus which came from the Latin settlement in Syria, with all its native products and manufactures, and with the new access which that settlement gave, on the one hand to the markets of Damascus, and on the other hand (by way of Raḳḳa and the Euphrates) to the markets of Baghdad. In this way we may explain the dissemination of new plants and crops and trees from the Levant to the regions of the Western Mediterranean—sesame and carob, maize and rice, lemons and melons, apricots and shallots.[1] In this way too we may explain the spread into the West of new manufactures and fashions, or

[1] The shallot (French *échalote*) is the *allium Ascalonicum*—the onion from Ascalon.

Fleur-de-lis

Two-headed eagle

Cups

Polo-sticks

FIG. 10. EXAMPLES OF SARACENIC HERALDRY

at any rate the growing vogue of old manufactures and fashions—cottons; muslins from Mosul; baldachins of Baghdad; damasks and damascenes from Damascus; 'sarsenets' or Saracen stuffs; samites and dimities and diapers from Byzantium (ἑξάμιτος, δίμιτος, and δίασπρος); the 'atlas' (Arabic *aṭlas*), a sort of silk-satin manufactured in the East; rugs and carpets and tapestries from the Near East and Central Asia; lacquers; new colours such as carmine and lilac (the words are both Arabic); dyes and drugs and spices and scents, such as alum and aloes, cloves and incense, indigo and sandalwood; articles of dress and of fashion, such as camlets and jupes (from the Arabic *jubbah*), or powders and glass-mirrors; works of art in pottery, glass, gold, silver, and enamel; and even the rosary itself, which is said to have come from the Buddhists of India by way of Syria to western Europe.

This Eastern trade, which the Crusades stimulated if they did not produce, and which in the twelfth century was mainly concentrated in Syria, produced no small effects in the development of trade-routes and the growth of new instruments of credit and finance. The great trade-route of medieval Europe, which ran from Venice over the Brenner to Cologne, and bifurcating there turned to Lübeck on the Baltic or Bruges on the North Sea, was fed by this Eastern trade; and it was along this route, in Lombardy and along the Rhine and in Flanders and Northern France, that medieval towns and medieval guilds clustered most thickly. At the same time a regular system of shipping developed in the Mediterranean, partly for the transport of goods and partly for the conveyance of pilgrims: Venice and Marseilles became its head-quarters, and the military orders joined with lay shipowners and shipping companies in the operation of the system. The financial needs both of a far Eastern trade and of pilgrims and knights travelling and sojourning overseas developed a system of credit-notes; firms of bankers arose (Genoese, Pisan, or Sienese) with branches and business in the Levant; the military orders, and especially the Templars, became banks of deposit and lending. One of the curious monetary results of the Crusades and of the Eastern trade which they encouraged was the striking by the Venetians of *Byzantini Saracenati* in the Holy Land. This was a gold coinage (perhaps the earliest gold coinage struck by the Latins) for the purpose of trade with the Muhammadan *hinterland*; and down to 1249 (when Innocent IV protested) these gold coins bore Arabic inscriptions, with some brief text from the Quran, a reference to the Prophet, and a date calculated from the Hijra. Even in southern France, and as late as the end of the thirteenth century, coins of this character are to be traced.

In building, in the arts and crafts, and in the general framework of daily and domestic life, we may trace some influences that passed from the East to the West during the two centuries of the Crusades. There seems indeed to be little ground for thinking that the Crusades influenced the general architectural development of the West, any more than that they influenced the particular development of the concentric castle. There is no general style of Saracenic architecture. It varied from country to country, according to the type of indigenous building which the conquering Arabs found; and the only uniformity was that of decoration and ornament. The Arabs used a form of pointed arch, but it differed from that of Gothic architecture: they used geometrical designs, because they were forbidden by their religion to copy animal forms, but there is no evidence that their designs influenced the trefoil or cinquefoil of Western Gothic in its geometrical stage.[1] The monuments of ecclesiastical architecture in the Holy Land are almost purely Western in style, and constructed on the rules and according to

[1] Prutz, op. cit., p. 419, conjectures (but he admits that it is conjecture) that Arabic influences may have introduced into the West the horse-shoe arch and the semicircular arch composed of many small arches, and so have helped to create cinquefoil and the various forms of decorated tracery.

Fig. 11. THE ROUND TEMPLE CHURCH AT NORTHAMPTON

the plans of Western building. At the most we can say that local factors induced local variations, as when, for example, the lack of timber in Palestine led to the building of flat roofs to churches, or again when local masons and stone-cutters, naturally imbued with Oriental traditions, introduced some Eastern twist or turn into a building generally constructed on Western lines.[1] Arabesques in mural decoration are of Moorish and not of Eastern origin; and if the Crusades introduced any new elements into the sculpture of the West, these elements were Byzantine rather than Arabic. Painting was not an Arabic art; and the mosaics in the churches of the Holy Land were of Byzantine inspiration. It is in the narrower sphere of the domestic arts and crafts that we may perhaps trace Arabic influence most. In the Kingdom of Jerusalem itself the houses of the magnates might follow the Arabic pattern of courtyard, marbles, fountain, and the murmur of running water; and the internal decoration and furniture might also copy the same model. The importation of Oriental gold-work and jewellery may have influenced the art of design in Italy and especially at Venice; and the ivories, the enamels, the carpets, the tapestries of the East may have exercised a similar influence in the West at large. We may perhaps speak of the 'rebesk' or arabesque fashion in the Middle Ages in the same sense in which we speak of the *chinoiserie* (in wall-papers, lacquers, and furniture) of the eighteenth century. Pilgrims might buy and bring home Arab reliquaries for the keeping of Christian relics; they might wear, and bring back for imitation in Paris, the girdle-purses of the East; or they might bring into the West horns whose blast had once been borne on Syrian echoes.

[1] The round 'Temple' churches (of which there are four in England, and which may also be traced in France, Spain, and Germany) are a deliberate imitation of the church of the Sepulchre and the 'Temple' at Jerusalem—analogous to the 'labyrinths' or 'chemins de Jérusalem' in some Western churches, or the 'Jerusalems' in some of the towns of the Teutonic Order in Prussia.

In the field of science and philosophy it was the Arabs of Spain rather than the Arabs of the East who brought gifts to the Latin West. Some mathematical knowledge may indeed have been imported from the East. Adelard of Bath, who studied the astronomy and geometry of the Arabs, is said to have travelled in Egypt and Asia Minor as well as in Spain during the first half of the twelfth century. Leonardo Fibonacci, the first Christian algebraist, a contemporary of Frederic II, to whom he dedicated his treatise on square numbers, is also recorded as having visited Egypt and Syria. The diffusion of Arabic numerals and arithmetic may have owed something to the lively trade between the Italian ports and Syria. Medicine, like mathematics, was one of the staples of Arabic science; but the home of the staple, and the source of its diffusion, was Spain rather than Syria, and the utmost licence of possible conjecture about Syrian influence is that which would connect the rise of a medical school at Montpellier with the trade between southern France and the Levant. The scholastic philosophy of the thirteenth century, as we have seen, owed no debt directly to the Arabic philosophers of the East. The material which it used, apart from the Christian tradition and the teaching of the fathers, was the Aristotelianism of the Arabs of Spain or the knowledge of Aristotle which it drew directly from Byzantium.[1]

In arts and letters the influence of the Crusades was perhaps deeper and more pervasive. One of their direct results was the study of Oriental languages. This development, however, was due less to the Crusades themselves than to the Asiatic mission which succeeded to the Crusades and was directed to the conversion of the Mongols. It was a Catalan, Raymundus Lullus, who first attempted to promote the development of Oriental

[1] Professor C. H. Haskins remarks, in an article on Arabic Science in Western Europe (printed in *Isis*, vol. vii, p. 3), that 'the Crusades as such had a surprisingly small part in the transmission of Arabic science to Christian Europe'.

studies as the instrument of a pacific Crusade in which the arms should be entirely spiritual. In 1276 he founded a college of friars for the study of Arabic at Miramar; and in 1311, perhaps at his instigation, the Council of Vienne resolved on the creation of chairs of Oriental languages (in Arabic and Tartar) at the Universities of Paris, Louvain, and Salamanca. But his restless and devoted spirit carried him to martyrdom in Tunis in 1314; and little came of his endeavours. The Eastern mission of which he was the eager advocate continued; but it resulted, as we shall see, less in the growth of Oriental studies than in the growth of geographical knowledge.[1]

In the field of literature the Crusades produced a great deal of history, and they were a theme of many Western poets. Among the Western historians of the Crusades are the anonymous Norman who wrote the *Gesta Francorum* and described the First Crusade; Fulcher of Chartres, whose *Historia Hierosolymitana* describes not only the First Crusade, but also the history of the kingdom down to 1127; and above all William the Archbishop of Tyre, whose *History of things done in the parts overseas*, in twenty-three books extending to the year 1183, became, in a French translation, the current staple of the Middle Ages and the chief basis of the story of the Crusades. William of Tyre not only wrote of the deeds of the Latins; he also compiled a *History of the Muhammadan Princes from the appearance of the Prophet*; and though the work is now lost, the traces of it which survive in William of Tripoli's *Tractatus de Statu Saracenorum* (1273) show the extent of its author's understanding of the Arabic world, and attest his insight into the character and genius of Islam. Among Eastern sources proper there is the autobiography of

[1] Professor Haskins (op. cit.), basing his remark on J. K. Wright's *Geographical Lore of the Time of the Crusades*, suggests that 'if the Crusades widened the geographical knowledge of Christian Europe, it was by actual experience, rather than by contact with the writings of Arabic geographers', which were unknown in the West during the Middle Ages.

Usāma ibn Munḳidh, a north Syrian Sheikh, which covers the twelfth century; Ibn al-Athīr's history of the Atabegs; and Bahā-al-Dīn's life of Saladin. But in the West at any rate the story of the Crusade rapidly turned from history to legend. The way had already been shown in the *Song of Roland*, which is the fruit of the play of poetic imagination on the theme of the border-warfare between Christianity and Islam in northern Spain. Early in the history of the Crusades—perhaps during the First Crusade itself—the same play of imagination began to create a legend which ran by the side of the history but departed widely from it.[1] The legend already appears in the *Chanson des Chétifs* (1130) and the *Chanson d'Antioche* (1180): it glorified Peter the Hermit or Godfrey of Bouillon, as the *Song of Roland* had glorified Roland and Oliver: it played at will over the Crusades, throwing its limelight now here, now there, and creating a saga which for centuries usurped the place of reality. It is this saga which came to Tasso, and which in his *Gerusalemme Liberata* he dressed in the conventional heroic dress of the sixteenth century. Nothing shows better how far the Crusades had passed from the heart of Europe. Tasso had wished, says de Sanctis, to write a poem which was seriously heroic, animated by the religious spirit, *possibilmente storico e prossimo al vero o verisimile*. What had he achieved? *Un mondo cavaleresco, fantastico, romanzesco e voluttuoso, che sente la messa e si fa la croce.*[2]

The Crusades, in reality, never became one of the great 'matters' of medieval poetry, like the 'matter' of Charlemagne or the 'matter' of Britain and the Round Table.[3] They affected,

[1] See Von Sybel's *Geschichte des ersten Kreuzzuges*.

[2] De Sanctis, *Storia della Letteratura Italiana*, ii. 161, 168.

[3] Prutz remarks (op. cit., p. 494) that the *gesta* of the early Crusaders, which had once excited an insatiable fund of interest, had already lost that quality by the end of the Crusades. James of Vitry (†1240), the author of a collection of *Exempla* or edifying stories, notices that any other 'matter' was more attractive to writers than the matter of the Crusades.

indeed, those two great themes: Charlemagne was made a Crusader, and sent on voyages to Constantinople and even Jerusalem; the poets of the Arthurian cycle learned to put something of a crusading complexion on their story; and the *Morte d'Arthur* would not have been what it actually was if the Crusades had not filled the Middle Ages. But there is nothing derived from Islam in such influence. It is simply the idea of the fight of faith against unfaith, as the best kind of fight for a fighting age; and this is an idea as old as the fight between Iran and Turan. Islam itself added little to the poetic stock of the Middle Ages, except as the incarnation of unfaith. The author of the *cantefable* of *Aucassin and Nicolette* may have borrowed something from Arabic sources; but if he did, his borrowing is independent of the Crusades.[1] And if again there be any truth in the 'Saracenic' theory, which refers to the East the origin not only of the sonnet, but also of the form of rhymed lyrical verse, that again is independent of the Crusades, and a matter of Sicilian history. It would almost seem as if the story of Troy and the romance of Alexander had given medieval poets their picture of the East even more than the Crusades. One might even hazard the saying that it is not till the days of *Count Robert of Paris* and *The Talisman* that the Crusades became the real stuff of Western romance. But themes and motives derived from the Crusades, if not the Crusades themselves, became a part of the romantic tradition of the Middle Ages. There is the theme of the knight imprisoned in Saracen-land and his rescue by the Saracen princess whose love he has won: there is the *motif* of the wife who after long mourning has abandoned hope of her Crusader husband's return, and is about to marry again when he

[1] Prutz suggests (p. 450) that an Indian cycle of romances (Calila and Dimna) may have been carried by the Crusades to western Europe. He adds that the *trouvères* incorporated Oriental elements into their lays, and were the bridges by which Eastern tales and fables passed to Boccaccio and the Italian novelists.

reappears—alone, or with a Saracen lady. But these are romantic embroideries, and they do not touch the true matter and essence of the Crusades.[1]

III

Apart from the question of the influence which the Muhammadan East exerted in Western Europe through the channel of the Crusades, or through the conduit (if it may so be called) of the Kingdom of Jerusalem, there remains the further and the broader question of the whole general influence of the Crusades themselves, as a movement of Western Europe at large, on the home of their origin and diffusion. That further and broader question lies beyond the limits of our theme; but it may be permissible, by way of an appendix and epilogue, to add some few observations, and, in particular, to draw attention to those general results of the Crusades which affected the relations of East and West.

The Crusades affected the Christian commonwealth of Western Europe in some four ways. In the first place they affected the Church, and particularly the Papacy. In the second place they affected the internal life and economy of each of the several states; and we may trace that effect partly as it shows itself in the action of the Government (the 'State' proper), and partly as it appears in the position of the two secular estates —the nobility and the commonalty, more especially the commonalty of the towns. In the third place, they affected the external relations of the different states; and that effect may be traced both in the changes of their relative weight and importance and in the general development of a concert or system of Europe. Finally, they affected the relations of Europe to the continent of Asia; and in the widening ripples of exploration, from the thirteenth century to the end of the fifteenth, we

[1] It is perhaps worth adding that the music of the West may have been influenced, in some small degree, by that of the East in the epoch of the Crusades.

may trace the successive stages of a movement which the Crusades first set on foot.

The Church and the Papacy

The clergy were an international Estate; and the Pope, the head of the clergy, was a great European figure. An international and European enterprise such as the Crusade seemed naturally destined to come under clerical and papal control, and thereby to exalt the theocratic tendency already implicit in the Gregorian movement. In the idea of Urban II the Pope was to be the generalissimo of the Holy War; the Crusade was to be the foreign policy of the Papacy, conducted at its nod; and a papal legate was to accompany and rule the army of God. In the event this ambition was far from being realized. The secular ambition of lay princes is already prominent, and indeed dominant, in the First Crusade itself; and the foundation of a lay Kingdom of Jerusalem in 1100, in place of the clerical theocracy of which some seem to have dreamed, is itself significant. In the Second and Third Crusades the emperor and the kings of the West, absentees from the First Crusade, play a foremost part; and we shall have occasion to notice how the lay State imposes its own system of taxes for the sustentation of Jerusalem. None the less, and in spite of lay direction and lay diversion (which were nowhere more conspicuous than in the course of the Fourth Crusade), the Crusades remained essentially connected with the Papacy. It was by Popes that they were preached and organized. It was by Popes that they might be directed, not only against the Muslim of the East, but also against the heretic Albigensian in the West itself; and the time even came, in the reign of Frederic II, when they might be launched by a Pope against an offending Emperor. Not only were they a weapon of papal policy: they were also a part of papal finance. If the lay State imposed its Saladin tithe, the Papacy could also levy a tithe of its own; and tenths of ecclesiastical revenues, on the plea of the Crusade, were levied regularly from the clergy after the beginning of the thirteenth century, first by the decree of Councils and then by the Pope's authority, and continued in force in England till the Reformation. As the Crusades added new revenues to the Church, so they also added new orders; and the Templars and the Hospitallers, following a rule based on that of the canons regular, gave to Europe the new spectacle of the warrior-priest who combined the rules of monasticism with the life of a professional soldier.

The mixed character of the military orders admirably illustrates the mixed character of the Crusades, which made them at once papal and anti-papal, clerical and anti-clerical, a support of ecclesiasticism and at the same time a mine beneath its foundations. The Crusades, if they did not remove, at any rate weakened the old clear distinction between sacred and profane, the lay and the clerical, the temporal and the spiritual. They were the consecration of the fighting layman, and in their way they led to the emancipation of the laity. On the Crusade the layman might become something of a priest; and by collaboration with it the lay State might acquire some measure of sanctity. A movement which had proceeded from a temper of otherworldliness, and had been born in an age which seemed set towards theocracy, was thus none the less a contributory force to the development of the lay spirit and the lay power. The day-to-day contact with Muhammadanism in the East—a contact which brought familiarity, and with it the toleration which familiarity can breed—weakened the old opposition of faith and unfaith, just as the Crusades had weakened the distinction between secular and clerical within the bounds of the faith. Not all men in the thirteenth century were of the temper of Frederic II, who used a Saracen army against the Pope, corresponded with Arabic scholars, and negotiated with Muhammadan rulers even when Jerusalem itself was in question. But at any rate scholars showed themselves ready to borrow from Arabic philosophers;

some began to study Arabic; and a new spirit of comprehension arose. There is a difference between St. Louis, the survivor of an earlier age, who would argue with an infidel by plunging his sword into his vitals, and the attitude of the University of Paris which could draw even on Arabic Spain for the *fisica et metafisica* of Aristotle. Scholasticism arose and developed its doctrines independently of the Crusades; but it was only in the new age of comprehension which the Crusades had done something to create that scholasticism could attempt its great task of reconciling the secular wisdom of Aristotle with the received tradition of the Bible and the Church.

The State and the Secular Estates

One of the simplest and clearest results of the Crusades, in the internal life of the States of the West, was the development of a new species of taxation. Taxes had hitherto fallen on land: it is with the Crusades that we get the beginnings of taxes on personal property. Louis VII in 1146 was the first to impose a tax *propter sustentationem terrae Hierosolymitanae*: he repeated it in 1165; and Henry II of England followed his example in 1166, exacting twopence in the pound for that year, and one penny for each of the four next succeeding years, from all classes indifferently, in respect of personal property and income (*catalla et redditus*). In 1184 Philip Augustus and Henry II agreed on the exaction of a similar tax for the next three years in their dominions—though the agreement appears not to have been executed. In 1188, after the fall of Jerusalem, both kings imposed the Saladin tithe. In England, at any rate, the precedent was not forgotten; and in the thirteenth century the tax on *catalla et redditus* is made a current feature of the national system of finance. 'From the needs of the Holy Land', it has been said, 'arises modern taxation'.[1]

[1] Cartellieri, *Philipp II August*, vol II, p. 85. A full account of the development is given p. 5 onwards.

The effects of the Crusades on the secular Estates of the Western Kingdoms are less certain and obvious. It has been said that the Crusades contributed to the dissolution of feudalism and the depression of the baronial Estate. Certainly they drew unquiet spirits away to the East, to find new fiefs in Syria or to become members of the military orders: perhaps, too, they resulted in some sales of property and some disturbance of the validity of titles; but the feudal baronage could still show itself a lively force till the end of the fifteenth century, and the influence of the Crusades on its members is shown less in any disturbance of their status than in the new methods of their warfare, and the greater vogue of the tournament and of heraldry, of which we have already spoken. In the same way the rise of municipal independence has been often ascribed to the Crusades, and the grant of municipal charters has been assigned to the need of crusading lords for ready money. Here again presumption has outrun proof; and we are on safer ground if we simply say that, so far as the Crusades fostered the growth of trade and commerce, they necessarily encouraged the growth of towns. The great Italian ports certainly owed much of their early prosperity to the Crusades; and the inland route of commerce, by which Venetian goods were carried up the Rhine to the Baltic and the North Sea, was also, as we have seen, the route and the focus of the growth of free towns and free guilds.

The External Relations of States and the System of Europe

The Crusades affected the system of Europe, not only by their influence on the Church and its general position, but also by affording a new bond of European unity. After 1096 we may say that the idea of a united Western Europe is expressed not merely in the formal scheme of a Holy Roman Empire, but also in the actual fact of a common Christian Crusade. It is true that the rulers of European States, when they met on a Crusade, met only to disagree; it is true that national differences were accentuated by the national rivalry which accompanied, for example, the Third Crusade. And yet the feeling of a unity of interests and a common cause was never entirely obliterated. There was no common direction from Baghdad, and no call of the Caliphate, to unite the Muslims of the East: at the most there was the *de facto* power of Mosul, and the puritan faith of a Nūr-al-Dīn or the ardour of a Saladin. Western Christianity had its Papacy and the papal direction of a Crusade: it was internationalized, as it were, in a common system of offence against its enemy. The idea of a European Commonwealth—a *res-publica Christiana*, engaged in the *res Christiana* of defence or offence against the Turk—survives through the centuries. A Dutch scholar, Ter Meulen, has written a work entitled *Der Gedanke der internationalen Organisation*, in which he traces the various schemes which, from the time of Dubois (1300) to that of the Abbé de Saint-Pierre and Kant (1800), were directed to the foundation of some scheme of European unity or League of Nations. In almost all the basis adduced is the need of common action against the Turk: in almost all we may trace some relic of the lingering idea of the Crusades.

Meanwhile, during the Crusades and in their course, the balance of European States had been altered. The Byzantine Empire had ceased to weigh in the scales against the Empire of the West. It had fallen in 1204; and if by the end of the thirteenth century there were again Greek Empires in Constantinople and Trebizond, they were only the shadows of a great name. The balance of Europe had come to lie in the West. Among the Western States, France had achieved a predominance; and in its achievement the Crusades had played their part. They had been preached on French soil; they had been waged by French knights; it was France which had produced in St. Louis the perfect type of Crusader. French colonists had settled in the Kingdom of Jerusalem and, when it was lost, in that of Cyprus: they had settled in the Morea and the Duchy of

Athens. 'The noblest chivalry of the world', says a French writer of the fourteenth century, 'is the chivalry of the Morea: as good French is spoken there as in Paris.' The Lingua Franca of the Levant was not 'good French': so far as it had a Latin basis, it derived that basis from the Italian of Venetian and Genoese traders; but if the French language did not survive in the Eastern Mediterranean, the French tradition was never extinguished. The protectorate of the Holy Places, which had been exercised by Charlemagne, was vindicated by Francis I in the sixteenth century; treaty stipulations gave the Latins possession of the grotto of the Nativity and the Holy Sepulchre in Jerusalem; and these stipulations were still active enough in the nineteenth century to be one of the causes of the Crimean War. Even to-day we may count the French mandate in Syria among the legacies of the Crusades.

The Relations of Europe and Asia

It remains, in conclusion, to speak of the new system of relations between Europe and the continent of Asia which was inaugurated by the Crusades. Not only did Europe find in the Crusades a new form of internal union and a new influence on its own inner life: it also gained in their course a new and vastly extended view of the world. This widening of view, with the growth of exploration and of geographical knowledge by which it was accompanied, is the last, as in its sweep it is the greatest, of the results of the Crusades. Already, during the twelfth century, geography was the richer for the pilgrims' guides,[1] with descriptions of routes and of holy places, and for the military reconnaissances of strategical areas (especially of the area between Palestine and Egypt), which were then undertaken. These only touched the coast fringe of Hither Asia; but in the

[1] On the *peregrinatores* see Prutz (op. cit., pp. 470 sqq.), the editions of *Itinera Hierosolymitana* (e.g. in the *Corp. Script. Eccl. Latin.*), and the publications of the Palestine Pilgrims' Text Society.

thirteenth century, as we have already had occasion to notice, exploration and description turned to the whole of Further Asia. The great age of Asiatic discovery, which is parallel, if it is not equal, to the age of American discovery in the sixteenth century, began about 1240 and ended a century later.[1] During that century Asia was loosely united in a Mongol Empire, which stretched from the Crimea and Tabrīz, through Bokhara and Samarcand, to Cambäluc (Pekin) and Kinsai (Hangchow). The Mongols, who kept their old Shamanism, were tolerant of other faiths; if they were not Christians themselves, they yet sheltered in their Empire Christian elements; Christian zeal hoped for their conversion, and commercial ardour sought routes to the fountain-heads of Eastern trade through their dominions. The mission to the Mongols was partly based on the interested calculation that with their conversion the objects of the Crusades might yet be finally achieved, and the Holy Land permanently recovered; but while it was connected with the Crusades it came to transcend their scope. There were those who, like Raymundus Lullus, believed that the mission must supersede the Crusade, and peaceful preaching displace the military expedition; and to such as these the conversion of Asia became an end in itself—a filling of the earth with the knowledge of God as the waters cover the sea. Aided by Mongol tolerance and the presence of Nestorian Christians in Asia, these missionaries went far afield; and in the beginning of the fourteenth century John of Monte Corvino, the founder of the Latin Church in China, became archbishop of Cambaluc with three Franciscans as suffragan bishops. With the mission went the Italian merchant, just as the First Crusade had been accompanied by the mariners of the Italian ports; and not only did the Polos make their great journeys, but (a mark of more solid

[1] See Miss Eileen Power's chapter on 'The opening of the Land Routes to Cathay' in *Travel and Travellers of the Middle Ages*, edited by Professor A. P. Newton.

establishment) a Genoese company navigated the waters of the Caspian Sea, and a Venetian consul was settled in Tabrīz. All the great hope was in the issue dashed; and the prospect of a great mass-conversion of the Mongols, which would have linked a Christian Asia to a Christian Europe and reduced Islam to a small faith encamped in a portion of Spain and a corner of the Levant, dwindled and disappeared. The Khanates of Persia turned to Muhammadanism in 1316; by the middle of the fourteenth century Central Asia had gone the same way; in 1368–70 the native dynasty of the Mings was on the throne and closing China to foreigners; and the end was a recession of Christianity and an extension of Islam which assumed all the greater dimensions with the growth of the power of the Ottoman Turks. But a new hope dawned for the undefeated West; and this new hope was to bring one of the greatest revolutions in history. If the land was shut, why should Christianity not take to the sea? Why should it not navigate to the East, take Muhammadanism in the rear, and, as it were, win Jerusalem *a tergo*? This was the thought of the great navigators, who wore the cross on their breasts and believed in all sincerity that they were labouring in the cause of the recovery of the Holy Land; and if Columbus found the Caribbean Islands instead of Cathay, at any rate we may say that the Spaniards who entered into his labours won a continent for Christianity, and that the West, in ways of which it had never dreamed, at last established the balance in its favour.

If we regard their larger scope, and the long after-swell which followed the original impulse, we shall not regard the Crusades as a failure. Nor did they fail altogether even in their original motive—the defence of a common Christianity against the menace of Islam in the Eastern Mediterranean. We may say, it is true, that the Crusades began with the Seljūq Turks encamped at Nicaea on the confines of Asia, and that they ended with the Ottoman Turks encamped in Europe itself on the Danube. We may say, again, from another point of view, that after nearly five hundred years all ended as it had begun, with a Frankish protectorate of the Holy Places in a territory governed by Muhammadans. But territory is not everything; and if the Crusades did not gain, or even maintain, what can be measured on the map, they gained or maintained other things which are more impalpable, but not less real. They defended Western Christianity during the crucial period of the growth of Western civilization in the Middle Ages; they saved it from any self-centred localism; they gave it breadth—and a vision. 'The people that hath no vision perisheth'; and to the peoples of the Middle Ages the vision of the Crusade—seldom seen steadily, perhaps never seen whole—was none the less a saving ideal.

ERNEST BARKER.

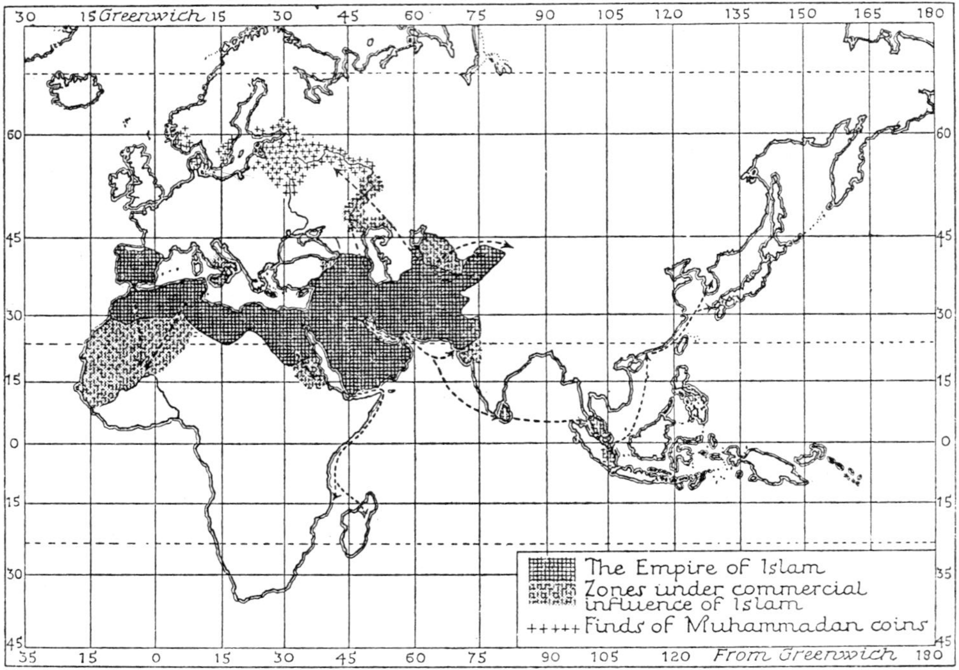

FIG. 12. Map showing the geographical extension of Islamic rule and its commercial influence in the tenth century A.D.

GEOGRAPHY AND COMMERCE

Were we to draw a map of the political condition of Europe, Africa, and western Asia about the middle of the tenth century of our era, we should see that by far the greater part of that 'inhabited world', which the Greeks called the 'oikoumene', was occupied by countries possessed of an Islamic government and an Islamic civilization. They no longer constituted a strict political unity, but they were connected by such strong ties of common religion and culture that their inhabitants—and not only their Muhammadan inhabitants—felt themselves citizens of one vast empire, of which Mecca was the religious, and Baghdād the cultural and political centre. This vast empire had grown in the three foregoing centuries from a series of conquests that started originally from Medina. Arabia was its centre. To the west it comprised Egypt with the entire northern coast of Africa, including the Atlantic coast as far as the Anti-Atlas and, further, nearly the whole of Spain (with the exception of Asturia), and the islands of Sicily and Crete. Sardinia and Cyprus, too, were constantly exposed to Muhammadan attacks; so was also the southern Italian coast, where some towns, like Bari, were actually under Islamic rule, while others, like Amalfi, belonged to its sphere of influence. To the north of Arabia, Syria with Armenia and the south-east of the Caucasus belonged to the permanent possessions of Islam; and, farther to the east, Mesopotamia with 'Irāq, followed by the whole of the territory of modern Persia with Afghanistan. Northward of these countries, again, Transoxania belonged to Islam, including in the west the delta region of Khwārizm, and, in the east, the valley and the mountains of Farghāna. The Indus had been crossed already in the eighth century; the regions on its lower course belonged, with Sind, to the Islamic Empire. Only in the southward direction did the territorial extension of Islam in Africa scarcely exceed the latitude of Aswān in Egypt.

'The length of the Empire of Islam in our days extends from the limits of Farghāna, passing through Khurāsān, al-Jibāl (Media), ʿIrāq and Arabia as far as the coast of Yaman, which is a journey of about four months; its breadth begins from the country of the Rūm (the Byzantine Empire), passing through Syria, Mesopotamia, ʿIrāq, Fārs and Kirmān, as far as the territory of al-Manṣūra on the shore of the sea of Fārs (the Indian Ocean), which is about four months' travelling. In the previous statement of the length of Islam I have omitted the frontier of the Maghrib (northern Africa) and Andalus (Spain), because it is like the sleeve of a garment. To the east and the west of the Maghrib there is no Islam. If one goes, however, beyond Egypt into the country of the Maghrib, the lands of the Sūdān (the Black) lie to the south of the Maghrib and, to its north, the Sea of Rūm (the Mediterranean) and next the territory of Rūm.'

These are the words of the geographer Ibn Ḥauqal, writing about A.D. 975.

Although the regions enumerated above do not coincide at all with, and are even smaller than, the countries now inhabited by a Muhammadan population, the fact that they constituted not only a religious but also a politically powerful block, brought together and kept together by force of arms, enabled them to hold the position of a strong central power in the world then known.

If we consider, on the other hand, the geographical and political conditions of the Christian European world of those days, we immediately realize to what extent in reality the latter must have been dependent on the huge Islamic Empire. To the south the Mediterranean, at that time under the domination of the rulers of the Muhammadan shores, formed an insurmountable barrier; to the east the Byzantine Empire stood face to face with Islam in Armenia; the northern Caucasus and eastern Europe were the home of half-civilized nations that were at least as much under Muhammadan as under Christian influence. Only in the north of Europe the heathen Northmen were at the beginning of their powerful extension, which was largely to contribute, in the twelfth century, to the annihilation of the political and economic hegemony of Islam.

The relative geographical position of the pilgrimage centres of the two rival religions was quite different. Jerusalem, the ideal religious centre of Christian Europe, had since A.D. 638 been under the control of the Muhammadans, but the Muhammadan conquest had not put an end to the pilgrimages undertaken by European Christians to the Holy Sepulchre. The first pilgrims of whose travels accounts have come down to us, were the Frank Arculf (*c.* 680), the Saxon Willibald (*c.* 725) and a certain Bernard, who started *c.* 870 from Rome on a pilgrimage. No doubt they were not the only ones that contributed to the maintenance of knowledge about the countries conquered by Islam. The relations of the Christians in the Byzantine Empire with their co-religionists in Egypt, Syria, and Mesopotamia must have been very important in this respect.

In the Islamic world matters were quite different. Mecca, the centre of pilgrimage, occupied a central geographical position in Islam itself. The pilgrimage or 'ḥajj' to Allah's house was one of the five 'pillars of Islam', according to the Sacred Law, and Muhammadans from all parts of the Islamic Empire met at that place. So the 'ḥajj' became not only a powerful factor in promoting religious unity, but it also materially assisted in strengthening the ties of commerce between all Muhammadan countries, and disseminated among Muhammadans a fairly good knowledge of all parts of their world. To the 'ḥajj' was due the compilation of a number of itineraries, in which the stations and stages of the roads leading from different countries to Mecca were indicated. There was, however, a great ignorance of, and lack of interest in, the non-Muhammadan parts of the known world.

Nearly a millennium has passed since the cultural horizon of

Christian Europe was bounded in nearly all directions by Islam. In the meantime Europe has circumnavigated and pierced the barriers that separated it from the southern and eastern parts of the known world, not to speak of the unknown world. Europe owes much to its own force and initiative, but it has also largely profited by the knowledge and the experience of those who were at one time the masters of the world. Therefore Europe ought to look upon them as its cultural ancestors in the domain of geographical knowledge, of discovery, and of world trade. The influence which Islam has exercised on our modern civilization in these spheres of action can be seen in the many terms of Arabic origin which are to be found in the vocabulary of trade and navigation. The measure of this influence can only be proved by studying the historical development of the domain over which our actual geographical knowledge extends. For modern geography is a science so positive and independent of tradition that it all but excludes the more or less correct views of former ages; I say 'all but', for it is only just to remember the fact that, when Jaubert in 1840 edited his French translation of Idrīsī, it was thought not unlikely that this edition might increase geographical knowledge of the world, and especially of Africa.

The study of the historical influence of our Islamic cultural ancestors on our knowledge of the world is not without its difficulties, because it is not always easy to ascertain how far the geographical knowledge of the Muhammadans was based on personal observation, how far they actually went on their voyages, and what was the extent of their commercial relations. This statement may cause surprise in view of the fact that from the ninth to the fourteenth century a considerable and important geographical literature was produced in Arabic. But what the bulk of this literature has to offer us is only the official science of scholars and literary men. However observant these writers may have been of the regions and peoples which they visited, and with however much interest they may have listened to the travellers and sailors from whom they derived their information, they were still more or less captivated by ideological religious and traditional views, which prevented them from seeing certain facts in their true light, even if their opinion was much less prejudiced than that of the Christian scholars of the 'Dark Ages'. Apart from this official and literary science there was the great naval and geographical experience of seafarers and merchants. The literary men certainly profited by their knowledge, but it appears sometimes from their own writings that the less pretentious traders and navigators were less prejudiced than themselves. Now it is this more humble kind of people whom we must consider as the principal mediators and teachers in the relations between Islam and medieval Europe. The big Arabic geographical works appear to have had practically no immediate influence on medieval geographical views, except in so far as astronomical geography is concerned.

We must not omit, however, to give a survey of the way in which the vast geographical knowledge of the Muhammadans was reflected in Arabic literature. In the first 150 years of Islam geography as a science was certainly not superior to what we observe in the Christian world. Curious opinions are reported, on the authority of contemporaries of the Prophet, concerning the length of the world and its parts, the sources of the Nile, and so on. Among them we meet with the comparison of the world to a bird, whose head is China and whose tail is north Africa. The Qurān itself contains a geographical indication in the twice recurring statement that God has separated the two seas by an insurmountable barrier (xxv. 55; lv. 19, 20). These words are interpreted by the scholars as alluding to the Mediterranean and the Indian Ocean, including the Red Sea, which interpretation is probably correct. There is little doubt that this theory of the two seas is of Persian origin, and its occurrence in the Qurān has elevated the theory to a dogma, which has dominated to a great extent all Muhammadan geographical literature and cartography.

The scientific study of geography in Islam began under Greek influence. One result of the widespread activity in translating Greek works, which, at the beginning of the ninth century—especially in the reign of the Caliph al-Ma'mūn (813–33)—made the Muslims the spiritual heirs of Hellenism, was that they became acquainted with the geographical work of Ptolemy; and Ptolemy's doctrine of the prolongation of the east coast of Africa to the East fitted very well into the theory of the two seas. We possess no early Arabic translation of the text of Ptolemy, but there exists an adaptation of this work, made about 830 by the astronomer al-Khwārizmī; the map which must have accompanied his text is lost. Al-Khwārizmī's longitudes and latitudes go back for the greater part to Ptolemy, but the book gives also the geographical positions of such places as originated after the conquest of Islam. It is not certain if the latter indications are due to new astronomical observations; we only know that the Caliph al-Ma'mūn had ordered the measurement of a geographical degree in the Syrian desert and that the same caliph had caused to be executed by seventy scholars—amongst whom was al-Khwārizmī—an 'image of the earth', of which a description is still extant in a work of rather late date. So we may assume that al-Khwārizmī's book already contained the results of the research of Islamic scholars. It bears, moreover, traces of other influences, such as the division of the inhabited world into seven zones or climates, which does not appear in Ptolemy. Traces of the doctrine of the seven climates are no doubt to be found among Greek scholars, perhaps as early as Eratosthenes. It is probable, however, that this theory of the division of the inhabited world was of Persian-Babylonian origin and this may account for the predominant place it has occupied in much of the geographical literature of the Muhammadans, who were more receptive of Eastern traditions than the Greeks.

But the world image, that had made its entry with Ptolemy into the Muhammadan world, did not accord very well with the idea which the citizens of the new Islamic Empire must necessarily have formed of the world. They had no objection to the spherical form of the earth—then denied by many Christian theologians—neither did they see the necessity of affirming it. This explains the fact that very soon Islamic geography and Islamic astronomy went their own ways. The astronomers, such as al-Farghānī (*c.* 860), al-Battānī (*c.* 900), Ibn Yūnus (*c.* 1000), and the great al-Bīrūnī (*c.* 1030), continued to give geographical tables of longitudes and latitudes, following the division of the seven climates, but they added little or nothing to the actual knowledge of countries. Such knowledge was gained from a description of countries and itineraries, so useful for the administration of the Empire, of which those to Mecca have already been mentioned. Thus, already in the course of the ninth century, several descriptions of countries came into existence under such titles as 'The Book of Countries', or 'The Book of Roads and Kingdoms'. The chief writers of that epoch were Ibn Khurradādhbeh (*c.* 870), al-Ya'qūbī (*c.* 890), Ibn al-Faqīh (*c.* 903), and Ibn Rusta (*c.* 910). In a more or less systematic form they give an administrative and topographical description of the different countries belonging to Islam, in which the itineraries occupy a prominent place. In these works considerable attention is still paid to non-Muhammadan countries, such as the countries and islands in the Far East and also the Byzantine Empire; on the other hand they give a large place to all kinds of legendary stories. To the same period belong the accounts of the sea-captain Sulaimān of Sīrāf of his voyages to India and China.

In the tenth century we observe the development of a literary geographical school, which was to exert a lasting influence on the geographical views of the Muhammadans. The contents of these books are based to a large extent on the earlier works, but they are enriched by the knowledge of Muhammadan countries which had been gained meanwhile; most of the authors of this epoch were travellers themselves. This new school is distinguished from that of the foregoing period, in that it paid very little attention to countries not belonging to Islam, and in its systematic treatment of the geographical matter, accompanied by a number of maps, of which the text is meant to be a description. The first of these maps is a map of the world, circular in form, Mecca being the centre. The world is surrounded by the 'encircling ocean' and from this two gulfs enter the continent, so as to approach very close to one another at one point, the isthmus of Suez. These gulfs are the Mediterranean and the Indian Ocean (the Sea of Rūm and the Sea of Fārs), in accordance with the Quranic tradition. After the map of the world, Arabia is treated as being the centre of the world, and next north Africa, Muhammadan Spain, Egypt, and Syria; this part is completed by the description of the Sea of Rūm. The second part of the geographical description treats of eastern Islam, beginning with Mesopotamia and finishing with Transoxania.

The first author who is said to have composed a geographical treatise of this kind is Abū Zaid al-Balkhī (*d.* 934), who was a famous scholar at the court of the Sāmānid dynasty, the rulers of Khurāsān and Transoxania (822–999). Al-Balkhī stood in high favour with the vizier al-Jaihānī, who is likewise the writer of a voluminous geographical treatise, of which the text is not yet known in Europe. Balkhī's book itself is not preserved either, but some of the principal geographical works are elaborations of the system established by him. These are the books of al-Iṣṭakhrī (*c.* 950) and Ibn Ḥauqal (*c.* 975), and the somewhat more independently composed work of al-Maqdisī (*c.* 985). It is very probable that this geographical school partly inherited

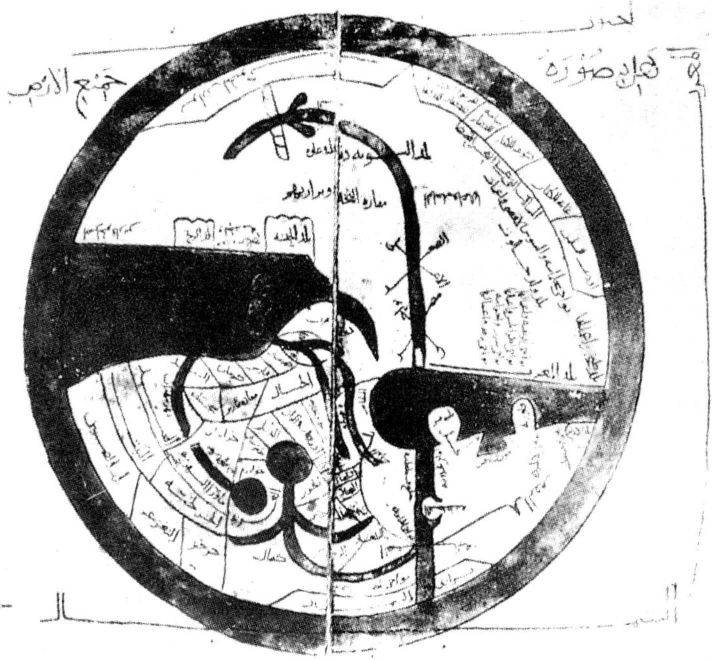

FIG. 13. WORLD-MAP

From a manuscript of Ibn Hauqal (*c.* A. D. 975) copied in the year A. D. 1087

e south is at the top; the big sea to the left is the Indian Ocean, into which flow the ers Indus, Tigris, and Euphrates; the smaller sea to the right is the Mediterranean h, on its north coast, the peninsulas of the Peloponnesus and Calabria. From the th comes the Nile and from the north the entrance of the Black Sea, which was thought to be connected with the Encircling Ocean.

older Persian traditions from the time of the Sāsānids—as appears, for example, from the naming of the Indian Ocean 'the Sea of Fārs'. The maps (fig. 13) certainly show a more exact notion of geographical reality than those which circulated at the same time in Europe, founded chiefly on the world-map of the Spanish monk Beatus (*c.* 730–98). We never find in these Muhammadan maps pictures of men and animals, owing no doubt to the prohibition against the pictorial representation of living beings. The addition of pictures makes most European maps, such as the famous map of Hereford, appear still more fantastic. But, on the other hand, we can observe already in the Islamic maps of the tenth century a tendency to represent the coast-lines and the rivers under conventionalized forms; thus many Iṣṭakhrī maps show the Mediterranean in a circular or elliptical form.

In other works of a geographical nature written at this period only one special region is treated. The best known are the description of the Arabian peninsula by al-Hamdānī and the famous description of India by al-Bīrūnī. Several works of this sort have not come down to us intact, but are known from later compilations, such as the report given by Ibn Faḍlān of the embassy sent in 921 by the Caliph al-Muqtadir to the Volga Bulgarians. A special place is held by the work of al-Masʿūdī. Al-Masʿūdī was a globe-trotter of the Muhammadan world and collected on his travels a large amount of geographical and ethnographical knowledge. He wrote several works, two of which, finished in 956, are preserved. In geographical matters they show a remarkable lack of system, but they are important in that they display the great difference between 'imperial' Islamic geography and the independent geographical notions of travellers and sailors; thus, after giving in one place a survey of the views prevailing among Islamic scholars as to the extension of the Indian Ocean, he cannot help remarking that the seafaring people from the ports on the Persian Gulf, who are well at home in those seas, do not agree at all with the measurements given by the scholars, and that they even claim that those seas have no limits at all in certain directions. This was totally opposed to the prevailing dogma, that the 'Sea of Fārs' was a gulf of the 'encircling ocean', and that it had a rather narrow entrance, like the Mediterranean. Similarly the above-mentioned author al-Maqdisī, while discussing the shape of the Indian Ocean, says that some people represent it as a 'ṭailasān' (a kind of semicircular Persian coat), and other people as a bird, but that after long investigations a certain sheikh, who was one of the experts in the matter, had drawn for him in the sand the shape of this sea. It did not resemble either a 'ṭailasān' or a bird, but was full of irregular forms for gulfs and peninsulas. Al-Mas'ūdī seems to have visited China and to have known a good deal of the east coast of Africa. On the other hand, he seems to have had little grasp of astronomical geography; for we find in one of his books the curious view that in *one* climate all important towns must necessarily lie on the same latitude.

The eleventh century continues, but less brilliantly, on the lines of its predecessor: the best-known author of this time is the Spanish Muhammadan al-Bakrī (wrote *c.* 1067), of whose voluminous work only the part concerning Africa has been edited. Here we find a still more elaborated knowledge of itineraries and especially of the coast-line with its numerous ports and inlets. From about the same time there is an account of the travels of the Persian Nāṣir-i Khusrau, who came from Khurāsān and visited Egypt and Mecca; this man, while showing himself a keen observer, held very erroneous views as to the structure of the world in general.

The eleventh century had witnessed events which were to deal serious blows to the ideal unity of the Islamic world. The eastern half was invaded about 1050 by the Seljūq Turks; while, in the west, the island of Sicily, a good deal of Spain, and even some places on the African coast had been conquered by Christian rulers. At the same time Europe was preparing itself for the Crusades. This was also the time when the exclusiveness of the Islamic world towards the Christian world began to break up. By disintegration it had lost its political strength, which was to reappear, only for a short time, under the hegemony of the same Seljūqs and the Ayyūbids in their fierce struggle against the Crusaders. These events did not affect the prevailing geographical views in Muhammadan literature: only a slight approach towards astronomical geography is perceptible. We find, for example, that in a later extract from Ibn Ḥauqal's geographical treatise of about 1164, the world-map is no longer round, but elliptical, in conformity with the astronomical representation of the inhabited world.

The most brilliant author of this time is al-Idrīsī, formerly called Edrisi. Al-Idrīsī has, more than any other Islamic geographer, a claim on our attention, first because he worked at the court of a Christian ruler, the Norman King Roger II of Sicily (1101–54), at the very meeting-point of the two big cultural areas, and secondly because he long passed for the sole representative of Islamic geographical knowledge. From the study of earlier Arabic geographical texts we know that al-Idrīsī was to a great extent dependent on his predecessors. But the fact that King Roger entrusted the composition of a description of the known world to a Muhammadan scholar indicates clearly how far the superiority of Muhammadan learning was acknowledged at that time.

It is well known that the Norman court of Sicily was half oriental; Roger's desire to have a geography made for him was itself oriental in character. Since olden times it had been considered as the prerogative of great monarchs, such as Alexander the Great and some Persian kings, to have a synopsis made for them of the world that lay at their feet. A similar idea had been at the bottom of the Caliph al-Ma'mūn's geographical interest, and even of the tenth-century geographical school which had started at the court of the Sāmānids. According to al-Idrīsī's preface, King Roger had sent in all directions for information to be incorporated in the book; he had also ordered, just like al-Ma'mūn, the construction of a big world-map. Al-Idrīsī's work, too, contains maps, and the maps are in a way its most important part, as the text is a commentary on them. In the best known of its two editions there are seventy maps (actually in all manuscripts one is lacking), each representing the tenth part of one of the seven climates into which he divides the world after the fashion of the Islamic astronomers. If put together, these seventy maps constitute an oblong quadrangle, much after the Ptolemaean pattern. But the specific Islamic conception of the two big seas is strictly maintained, whereas the details, especially the coast-line of the Mediterranean, answer much better to the reality than any of the previous Islamic maps.

Al-Idrīsī's text shows the author's indebtedness to the earlier geographers, and the work as a whole is a good illustration of the reconciliation between descriptive and astronomical geography. It is doubtful, however, if the result of the measurements of great astronomers, such as al-Bīrūnī, have been used. For in the second, abridged, edition of al-Idrīsī's book, the so-called 'small Idrīsī', we find, in addition to the seven climates, an eighth climate, to the south of the equator. Moreover, the world-map, which in the 'big Idrīsī' precedes the other maps, is round, after the traditional fashion.

It is difficult to believe that al-Idrīsī's work, composed as it was at the chronological and geographical point of contact between the Islamic and the Christian civilizations, remained wholly unknown to Christian scholars in Sicily, Italy, or other Christian countries. At present, however, there is no certain trace of its influence. The first translation known of al-Idrīsī was published in Rome, in 1619, after an incomplete abridgement of the work; the translator did not even know the author's name.

The geographical literature after al-Idrīsī cannot claim any great originality, except the narrations of travellers, which become more numerous about this time. Among the best known are the Spaniard Ibn Jubair, who went in 1192 to Mecca and Mesopotamia; and, more than a century later, Ibn Baṭṭūṭa, a man from Morocco, who journeyed all over the Muhammadan world and farther eastward to Ceylon and the Maldives, visiting also Constantinople; his last travels brought him, in 1353, far into the interior of Africa. Another traveller, who had left a valuable description of this part of the world, about 1250, was Ibn Fāṭima; we do not possess his book, but it was utilized by the author Ibn Saʿīd, about A.D. 1274. The work of this last writer is of great interest, because it treats its subject in the same way as al-Idrīsī and, though less detailed in description, it shows how greatly Muhammadan knowledge of Africa had grown. Moreover, it approaches still closer to astronomical geography in that it gives very exact indications of the geographical position of the principal towns and places. Ibn Saʿīd, again, is one of the chief authorities for Abū'l-Fidā, prince of Ḥamā in Syria. Abū'l-Fidā''s 'Table of Countries' (1327) was, about 100 years ago, the best-known geographical work in Arabic next to al-Idrīsī; it is, however, a rather poor compilation of earlier sources.

A much more valuable compilation, for our purpose, is the big geographical dictionary of Yāqūt (1228); it contains all geographical names in alphabetical order. This work owed its existence as much to biographical as to geographical interest, the compiler's aim being to explain the surnames of well-known people, named after their birthplace or the place where they lived. Another kind of compilation was that of al-Qazwīnī (*c.* 1275). This writer has been styled the Pliny of Arabic literature; he wrote a cosmography and a geography and gave in the latter many curious and fabulous details about the places he mentioned; he has also some information about the German countries. A better and more original geographer was al-Dimashqī (*c.* 1325), although his general tendency is the same as al-Qazwīnī's.

The great number of Islamic geographers after al-Idrīsī shows clearly that the knowledge of geographical matters was still widespread at that epoch, but we can no longer speak of an Islamic school of geographers. After the Mongol invasions the Muhammadan world lost for ever its ideal and even its cultural unity. It is true that by this time the faith of Islam had made new progress—in Asia Minor and Central Asia by Turkish aggression, and in inner Africa by the more peaceful way of trade and preaching. Arabic as well as Persian literature still continues to give us much information about those countries, but the Christian peoples themselves, in the first place the Italians, were already active in travel and discovery. An Egyptian author of the fourteenth century, al-ʿUmarī, quotes a Genoese as his authority in describing Asia Minor. We now find more specialized geographical descriptions of one country and its institutions. Thus the Egypt of the early Mamlūk period was fully described by a series of authors; the best known is al-Maqrīzī's voluminous description of Egypt (*c.* 1420).

As has already been said, literary Islamic geography does not seem to have left much *direct* impression on European thought in the Middle Ages. One of the few proofs of the acceptance of Muhammadan geographical views by Christian writers is the world-map to be found in the *Opus Terrae Sanctae* completed by Marino Sanuto in 1321 and dedicated to the Pope. This map is round, Jerusalem being its centre, and shows clearly the two big seas derived from the ocean and the prolongation of the African coast to the east. Thus this indefatigable reviver of the crusading spirit showed himself one of the few students of the lore of the people he wanted to destroy.

Something has been said already about the geographical work of the Muhammadan astronomers. This had much more direct influence on medieval science in Europe than had geography. Some of their works were translated at an early period, such as the *Zīj* of al-Battānī (wrote *c.* 900), by Plato of Tivoli (*c.* 1150). The chief centre where Christian scholars from all countries became acquainted with Arabic scientific literature was Toledo, after its conquest by Alfonso VII. So far as geography is concerned, these studies contributed in the first place to the keeping alive of the doctrine of the sphericity of the earth, which had been nearly forgotten in the 'Dark Ages' and without which the discovery of America would have been an impossibility. All Islamic astronomers treated geography only in connexion with the determination of the geographical longitude and latitude of a certain number of places, without ever attempting, seemingly, to draw a map. Their tables of longitude and latitude are arranged after the seven climates. Because of the more general character of this science, Christian scholars took a greater interest in it than in purely Muhammadan geography; consequently, in the twelfth century there began to appear astronomical tables in Latin, sometimes accompanied by geographical tables. Some Christian scholars accepted also the division into seven climates. A legacy of still greater importance was the idea that the known hemisphere of the world had a centre or 'world summit', situated at an equal distance from east, west, north, and south. Al-Battānī speaks of this 'cupola of the earth' as an island, but another author of his time (Ibn Rusta) already knows it as the 'cupola of Arīn'. The word *Arīn* is a misreading of the Arabic transliteration of the name of the Indian town Ujjiyaini (Ozene in Ptolemy's geography), where there had been an astronomical observatory, and on the meridian of which town the 'world summit'—originally an Indian conception—was supposed to lie. Like the Muhammadan astronomers, their Christian disciples considered this doctrine of the highest importance; amongst the latter were Adelard of Bath, who translated in 1126 the trigonometrical tables of al-Khwārizmī, Gerard of Cremona (1114–87) and, in the thirteenth century, Roger Bacon and Albertus Magnus. The Arin (or Arim) theory was still later to be found in the *Imago Mundi* of Cardinal Peter of Ailly, published in 1410, and it was from this book that Christopher Columbus learnt the same doctrine, which had developed in the meantime so far as to make Columbus believe that the earth was shaped in the form of a pear, and that, on the western hemisphere, opposite the summit of Arin, there was another centre, much more elevated than the one on the eastern side, so as to form the shape of the lower half of a pear. Thus Islamic geographical theory may claim a share in the discovery of the New World. We find the influence of the same theory in quite another domain. It is highly probable that it induced Dante, whose indebtedness to Muhammadan traditions has been established in many respects, to localize his *Purgatorio*, in the shape of a mountain, in the western hemisphere, by combining with it, in an ingenious way, the ancient Christian belief that the terrestrial paradise was situated in the extreme east of the world, behind the sea (as shown on the different world-maps of Beatus).

Islamic navigation had already reached its widest extent in the ninth century. But, while navigation on the Indian Ocean derived its chief importance from the commercial relations with the non-Islamic coasts of Asia and Africa, commercial navigation in the Mediterranean was limited to the parts under Muhammadan rule, the relations with Christian ports being of a military and predatory character.

The Indian Ocean, consequently, was the only field of great enterprise. Its base was the Persian Gulf, where ports like Sīrāf and Baṣra, with its suburb al-Ubulla, and those on the Omān coast had been, even in pre-Islamic times, very important centres of trade and navigation. The coming of Islam, however, and especially the establishment of its political centre in ʿIrāq, encouraged the spirit of enterprise. About the middle of the tenth century Muhammadan ships had already reached the Chinese town of Khanfu, now Canton. There was then a considerable Islamic colony in that town, which had become an emporium of the trade with China. From here some Muhammadan traders and sailors went even farther north, and it is probable that they knew Corea and Japan. This early commercial prosperity seems to have been brought to an end in 878 by certain disturbances, in which the port of Khanfu was destroyed. From that time regular navigation did not extend farther than a town which the Arabic authors call Kala, famed especially for its tin mines, the position of which must be sought on the western coast of Malacca. Kala was politically dependent on the ruler of Zābaj, which name is the early Arabic rendering of the name Java. But at that time Zābaj stood in the first place for Sumatra, and particularly for the centre of the then flourishing empire of Shrivijaya; with these regions trading connexions existed. It appears from such authors as Ibn Rusta (*c.* 900), Sulaimān (*c.* 850) and his continuator Abū Zaid (*c.* 950) that the Muhammadan navigators were quite at home in those seas, though the texts do not give a very clear account of the sea-routes which were followed. The ships of Islam kept up an equally lively traffic with the ports of Ceylon (Sarandīb) and with the west coast of India; a prosperous Arabic colony inhabited the town of Ṣaimūr in the neighbourhood of Bombay. Daibul, situated in Sind on Muhammadan territory, was an important emporium for these regions. On the eastern coast of Africa—where, on the whole, trade was less important—they reached, in the beginning of the tenth century, the country of Sufāla, known for its gold. This region was on the African coast, opposite Madagascar, and the island itself was known to the Muhammadans as the isle of Wāqwāq. Now the authors knew also another Wāqwāq, which was opposite China, and the description of which seems best to answer to that of Japan. The result was, of course, a fatal confusion in the accounts given in geographical texts, caused, no doubt, by the geographical dogma that the east coast of Africa ran in an eastern direction to reach, somewhere in the neighbourhood of China, the mouth of the 'sea of Fārs'. The knowledge of the sea-captains was not hampered by traditional views, as has been shown; stories of their voyages are very popular in Arabic literature and were soon invested with a romantic hue which has survived in the well-known tales of Sindbād the Sailor in the *Arabian Nights*.

The age-long seafaring tradition which centres in the Persian Gulf prepared the way for the nations that afterwards sailed and ruled those waters: Portuguese, Turks, British, and Dutch. When Vasco de Gama, after his circumnavigation of Africa in 1498, had reached Malindi on the east coast of Africa, it was an Arab pilot that showed him the way to India. According to Portuguese sources, this pilot was in possession of a very good sea-map and of other maritime instruments. Arabic sources of that time also knew the story; they state that the pilot, whom they knew under the name of Aḥmad ibn Mājid, could only be induced to show the way to the Portuguese after having been made drunk. This probably fictitious story shows that the Muhammadans fully realized the far-reaching consequences of the coming of the Portuguese. The same Aḥmad ibn Mājid is also known as the writer of a sailing-manual for the Indian Ocean, the Red Sea, the Persian Gulf, the South China Sea, and the East-Indian archipelago. According to a statement of Sir R. F. Burton it even seems that Ibn Mājid was venerated in the past century on the African coast as the inventor of the compass.

The idea of piercing the isthmus of Suez is ascribed to some of the earlier Abbasid caliphs; it was never realized, however, and since the Crusades such an enterprise was justly considered a great danger to Islam. Islamic navigation in the Mediterranean has therefore always been isolated from that in the Eastern waters: trade in the Mediterranean was restricted to Muhammadan ports. Commercial relations with Christian countries were strongly opposed, both from the Islamic side—as early as the Caliph Omar—and from the Christian side. The result was the decay of the port of Alexandria and the ruin of many other ancient seaports. Now Tunis became the new centre of the considerable traffic between north African and Spanish ports. Towards Christians Muhammadan navigators were often nothing but pirates, but it is only just to say that the same thing is true of Christian navigators.

From the beginning of the Crusades the Mediterranean ceased to be the almost exclusive domain of Islamic navigation. Islam had lost a great part of Spain, the island of Sicily, and its hold on the Italian coast; at the same time the Italian seaports of Genoa and Pisa began to develop. The traveller Ibn Jubair, in 1192, made use of a Christian ship to go from Ceuta to Alexandria. In practice this transition of maritime hegemony was much less violent. It only meant that the Christians, who had navigated before as sailors or slaves under Muslim control, now fully emancipated themselves and sailed and traded on their own account. The modern international maritime vocabulary contains not a few words of Arabic origin, which show the former Muhammadan supremacy on these seas, such words for example as admiral, cable, average, shallop (sloop), barque, and, in the maritime language of the Indian Ocean, monsoon.

Mention has already been made of the compass in connexion with the pilot Ibn Mājid. This man himself supposes in his work that the inventor of the compass was King David. But it cannot even be proved that the Muhammadans were acquainted with this instrument at an earlier date than the Christians. It may be true that the Chinese knew this instrument and its use in the second century and that they transmitted it to the West.

But the first indubitable indication that Islamic sea-captains knew the compass is found in an author of 1282, and this is about the same time that a knowledge of it can be traced in France and Italy. Some terms of oriental but not Arabic provenance in the terminology relating to the compass make it probable that Europe received the knowledge of the qualities of the magnetic needle from the East, but it does not appear that the Muhammadans were the predecessors of the Christians. Their, in many respects, clumsy cartography makes us rather suppose that their ships could sail only in sight of the shore. So it is safer to assume that, even if the Muhammadans knew of the compass earlier than European Christians, their acquaintance with it does not go back beyond 1200 and that, soon after it became known to them, the knowledge of it was passed on to Christian navigators.

The problem connected with the appearance of the first sea-charts of the Mediterranean at the end of the thirteenth century closely resembles the problem of the compass. The oldest known portulan was probably made by the Genoese. The portulans give at once a much more exact image of the position of coasts and islands than all the earlier maps, and their construction was only made possible by the use of the compass. The portulans also show a very detailed design of the coastlines, and these details can hardly have been the work of one generation. Now we need only remember the exact description of the African coast in the work of al-Idrīsī and his predecessors Ibn Ḥauqal and al-Bakrī, to realize that the experience of the Islamic navigators—reflected in the geographical treatises cited above—must have contributed considerably to the composition of those prototypes of modern cartography, the oldest portulans.

By the big water-ways of Mesopotamia the Persian Gulf was linked to Baghdād, the centre of the Islamic Empire. By this means the navigation of the Indian Ocean became the instrument of a world-trade. The great merchants of Baghdād obtained in this way the silks of China and the spices and aromatics of India, different kinds of wood, coco-nuts, muscat-nuts, and the tin of Kala. All these wares found their way from Islamic countries into Europe, then deprived of all direct traffic with those countries. A part of this sea-trade did not enter the Persian Gulf, but brought the products to Aden and the Red-Sea ports of Jedda and al-Qulzum (the ancient Clysma near Suez), and, in the crusading times, to ʿAidhāb, an ancient port for pilgrim caravans which lay about opposite Jedda. From here the occidental part of the Islamic world was supplied. By the same way came also the African products, such as ivory; these were shipped from the Ethiopian seaport of Zailaʿ, opposite Aden.

More typical than navigation of the traffic of Islam is the overland trade by the 'ship of the desert'. Though, long before the appearance of Muhammad, trade caravans had crossed the steppes of Asia and Africa, we are accustomed to associate caravan trade with Islam. Even down to the last few years the Islamic peoples have not been surpassed by western civilization in the means of locomotion in the desert. The recently started motor traffic in the Syrian desert, in Arabia, in Persia, and in the Sahara, some railways in Central Asia, and the recently established air services have begun to follow the immemorial tracks of the camel. In the centuries when the Islamic Empire flourished, caravan traffic was the most common means of travelling and trading between the different Islamic countries, especially the pilgrim caravans to Mecca. At the same time there were some important overland routes that led out of the Empire, first those to India and China, secondly those to southern and central Russia and thirdly the African trade-roads. India and China could also be reached by sea; for this reason the caravan trade was not so important on this side as in other directions. The land-route to India was moreover hampered by the difficult roads in the mountains of Afghanistan. To trade with China it was necessary to pass through the regions occupied by Turkish peoples; the chief Chinese product, silk, was produced, moreover, in Persia at an early period. After the fall of the Sāmānid Empire, in the eleventh century, political conditions became still more unfavourable for the Chinese overland trade. The great revival of the Asian trade routes in the thirteenth century was not the work of Islam, but of the Mongols.

For our knowledge of the extension of Islamic trade influence in a northerly direction we can rely not only on written sources, but also on the enormous number of Muhammadan coins which have been found in different parts of Russia, Finland, Sweden, and Norway, not to mention some isolated finds in the British Isles and in Iceland. On the middle course of the Volga, in the province of Kazan, great quantities of these coins have been found, but these are far surpassed in number by the Arabic coins found in the Baltic provinces. In Scandinavia the chief finds are on the south-western coast of Sweden and the southern point of Norway. The coins belong to the period from the end of the seventh to the beginning of the eleventh century. It is very unlikely that the Islamic merchants themselves advanced so far to the north as these places, for it appears from the written Arabic sources that the country of the Volga Bulgars, on the middle course of that river, was the final goal of their trade expeditions and their embassies; the faith of Islam, too, penetrated as far as those regions at an early date. The route generally followed by trade went from Transoxania to the Delta region of Khwārizm (Khiva) at the mouth of the Oxus; the way up the Volga from its mouth was less usual. The fact, however, that the coins are found over so wide an area is a symptom of cultural influence, and proves that the Muhammadans purchased in the Bulgarian markets a good many wares from the peoples living in the north-west. Amongst these the Scandinavian Russians were the most important. We know from geographical works, principally from al-Maqdisī, what were the wares that the Islamic merchants acquired in this way: 'sables, miniver, ermines, the fur of foxes, beavers, spotted hares, and goats; also wax, arrows, birch bark, high fur caps, fish glue, fish teeth, castoreum, amber, prepared horse hides, honey, hazel nuts, falcons, swords, armour, maple wood, slaves, small and big cattle'. Most of the slaves came from the Slavonic peoples, whose name still bears witness to the role they played in the civilized world and especially the Islamic countries. Another way by which slaves were imported was Spain, whence they came to the Maghrib and Egypt. This last category were chiefly eunuchs destined for the Islamic harems. It is well known that the slaves of different races so imported have contributed not a little to the spreading of Islamic cultural acquisitions in Europe. Apart from this far-reaching Islamic-Bulgarian trade—of which traces have been found also in Germany—there were also commercial relations with the empire of the Khazars, by the Caspian Sea and the mouths of the Volga, where was situated Itil or Atil, the capital of the Khazars. This trade was less important for the exchange of merchandise, but the Khazar Empire, constituting a kind of buffer-state between Islam and the Byzantine Empire, furthered the transmission of many Islamic and oriental products which found their way into Christian countries.

The African overland trade was divided into an eastern and a western area; on both sides the chief import was gold. In the country of the Buja, to the east of Aswān, beyond Islamic territory, lay al-ʿAllāqī, the big trade-centre of the region of the gold mines, famous since ancient Egyptian times. In western Africa an active trade went on with the gold country of Ghāna, the capital of which must have been on the Niger. The Muhammadan merchants from Morocco, Algeria, and Tunisia travelled several months' journey to the south and passed generally through Awdaghosht, an oasis situated fourteen days' journey to the north of Ghāna. As a proof of the importance of trade in those regions the geographer Ibn Ḥauqal (*c.* 975) alleges that he saw in Awdaghosht an I.O.U. (the Arabic word is *ṣakk*, from which the modern word cheque has been derived), for an amount of 42,000 dinars, addressed to a merchant in the town of Sijilmāsa in southern Morocco. It is even said that in the preceding century the volume of trade had been still greater, as there existed then a straight road connexion between the western regions and Egypt, which road had been given up on account of its insecurity.

In later centuries, also, Africa remained a domain where Muhammadan enterprise and missionary zeal could display their activity without competition. The author Ibn Saʿīd, in the thirteenth century, is very well acquainted, through the travels of Ibn Fāṭima, with the Atlantic coast as far as the Senegal (which was thought to be connected with the Niger and even to belong to the same fluvial system as the Nile), and with the negro peoples living round Lake Chad; on the other hand, the Muhammadans never knew the sources of the Nile, for they only repeat the tradition of Ptolemy on this point. Still the Europe of the Renaissance had no information except from Muhammadan sources about the interior of the Dark Continent, for the description of Africa by the christianized Muslim Leo Africanus in 1526 was then, and for long afterwards, almost the only source of knowledge. The value attributed to Idrīsī in the first half of the nineteenth century has already been pointed out.

The trade between Islam and Christian Europe showed at first a sharp contrast with the large commercial development previously described. There was as good as no direct commercial intercourse. What trade there was lay in the hands of Jewish merchants. At that time the Jews were almost exclusively a commercial people and only they could trade freely in both areas of civilization. Ibn Khurradādhbeh relates that Jewish merchants from the south of France crossed the sea to Egypt, traversed on foot the isthmus of Suez, and travelled by ship to India; others went overland from Ceuta to Egypt, and from

Syria to the Indus. They often visited Constantinople also. In this way the Islamic countries received from Europe slaves—of whom mention has already been made—silks (from the Byzantine Empire), furs, and arms, all of which came also by way of Russia. The same traders brought to Europe musk, aloes, camphor, cinnamon, and similar products; the names betray their oriental origin. Other routes by which oriental products could enter Europe were the Empire of the Khazars, between the Caspian region and Byzantium, and the half-barbaric peoples of Russia, that kept up a lively trade with central Europe. On the Byzantine frontier the town of Trebizond was in the tenth century an important emporium for the Islamic-Greek trade. A number of Muhammadan merchants lived there, and the Byzantine government profited largely by the levying of customs. There was also some direct trade on the Spanish border.

So we may speak, in a way, of a state of mutual commercial isolation between the Christian and the Muhammadan world. It is true that since the eighth century Muslim travellers and traders are to be found in Italian towns and in Constantinople, but these relations were only the germ of the lively commercial intercourse that began to develop in the eleventh century, to be interrupted only for a short time in the first period of the Crusades. After the barrier of former ages had broken down, trade itself subsequently became one of the strongest factors in promoting the transmission of cultural values to the European peoples, who, aided by their rulers (as Roger of Sicily) were eagerly seeking to benefit by them.

The manifold ways in which commercial relations led to close co-operation between Muslims and Christians—e.g. in the form of joint partnerships and of commercial treaties—cannot be treated here in detail. The great riches of material culture, which the Islamic world had gathered for nearly five centuries, were poured down upon Europe. These riches consisted not only of Chinese, Indian, and African products, which the enterprising spirit of Islam had fetched from far-distant lands; they were in the first place represented by what the Muhammadan countries themselves yielded of natural and industrial products. Industrial production in Muhammadan countries had developed in a particular way; it was chiefly characterized by being completely under the control of the rulers, by its lack of capital, and by its organization of the craftsmen in guilds. This peculiar form of industrial development proved a great disadvantage to Islam when it came, in later times, into economic competition with European industry; but at the time of Islamic prosperity it had made possible a development of industrial skill which brought the artistic value of the products to an unequalled height. In the first place should be mentioned the products of the textile industry; a number of names, now commonly in use, shows which textiles were originally imported from Islamic countries: muslin (from Mosul), damask (from Damascus), baldachin (originally a stuff made in Baghdād), and other woven stuffs, which bear Arabic or Persian names, like gauze, cotton, satin, &c. The import of oriental rugs is likewise as old as the Middle Ages. It is curious to note, too, that the state robes of the medieval German Emperors bore Arabic inscriptions; they were ordered and executed probably in Sicily, where Islamic art and industry continued for a long time after the Christian reconquest. Natural products, which, by their name, betray their original importation from Muhammadan countries, are fruits like the orange, lemon, and apricot, vegetables such as spinach and artichokes, further saffron, and the now so important aniline. Likewise names of precious stones (lapis lazuli) and of musical instruments (lute, guitar, &c.), though it cannot be proved that the borrowing of these terms goes back directly to commercial intercourse. The same is to be said about so important a material as paper, the fabrication of which Europe learnt from the Muhammadan peoples in the twelfth century.

Finally, our commercial vocabulary itself has preserved some very eloquent proofs of the fact that there was a time when Islamic trade and trade customs exercised a deep influence on the commercial development in Christian countries. In the word 'sterling', for example, is contained the ancient Greek word 'stater', but it has reached the English language only through the medium of Arabic. The word 'traffic' itself probably is to be derived from the Arabic *tafrīq*, which means distribution, and such a well-known word as 'tariff' is nothing but the good Arabic *ta'rīf*, meaning announcement. To the same origin belong the words 'risk', 'tare', 'calibre', and the everyday word 'magazine', from Arabic *makhāzin*, meaning stores (the French 'magasin' is still the common word for shop). The 'cheque' has already been mentioned in the description of the African trade, and the German and Dutch words for the same thing (*Wechsel*, *wissel*) are equally Arabic. So is also the term 'aval'. Next to the knowledge of the bill of exchange the conception of the joint-stock company was acquired by the partnership of Muslim and Christian Italian merchants. Muhammadan mercantile law was based only theoretically on the Sacred Law, derived from the Qurān and the sacred tradition; practically it was governed by a developed system of trade customs, to which the instances cited above bear witness. One of these trade forms was also the feigned bargain called 'mohatra', which word has also passed from Arabic into European languages.

A largely used word like 'douane' is a reminder of the time when regular commercial intercourse had developed in different ports of the Mediterranean. It is well known that this intercourse has also reacted largely on the commercial organization of western nations. The treaties which they concluded with Muhammadan rulers, and the institution of consular representatives in eastern ports, have been important stages in the development of the rules that nowadays govern international trade.

As may be seen from the previous observations, the cultural

gain, which Europe has acquired from the Islamic world in the domain of geography and commerce, is not the fruit of one moment, but is based on the mutual relations that have gone on since the beginning of the eleventh century and were especially lively during the Mongol period in the thirteenth century. Also the fact that Islamic civilization with its accretions has been continued by States such as Turkey, Persia, and Muhammadan peoples in India and the East Indies, has caused many Islamic views and customs to become known and even practised in European countries. But no period shows so clearly the once enormous superiority of the Islamic peoples over the Christian world as the tenth century, when Islam was at the summit of its prosperity and Christian Europe had come to a seemingly hopeless standstill.

J. H. KRAMERS

FIG. 14. A gold coin struck by Offa, King of Mercia (757–96), closely imitating an Arab dīnār. The words 'OFFA REX' are inserted upside down in the Arabic inscription. The coin illustrates the wide influence and distribution of Muslim coinage.

BIBLIOGRAPHY

A. REINAUD, *Introduction Générale à la Géographie des Orientaux*, in Tome I of *Géographie d'Aboulféda*, Paris 1848.

C. SCHOY, *The Geography of the Moslims of the Middle Ages* in *The Geographical Review* (published by the American Geographical Society of New York), 1924, pp. 257–69.

K. MILLER, *Mappae Arabicae*, Vols. I–IV, Stuttgart 1926–9.

Monumenta Geographica Africae et Aegypti, par Youssouf Kamal, Tome III (Époque Arabe), Fasc. 1, 1930. (This publication is the first to enable a complete survey to be made of the extant texts and of the maps, which have been arranged in a strict chronological order. It also makes possible a comparison of the European and the Islamic general geographical knowledge of the time.)

J. Lelewel, *Géographie du Moyen Âge, avec cartes.* 2 vols. Bruxelles, 1852. *Atlas*, Bruxelles 1850.

C. R. Beazley, *The Dawn of Modern Geography*, Vols. I–II. London 1897–1901; Vol. III. Oxford, 1906.

G. Jacob, *Studien in Arabischen Geographen*, Vols. I–IV. Berlin, 1891–2.

Ch. de la Roncière, *La Découverte de l'Afrique au Moyen Âge*, 3 vols. Cairo, 1925–7.

Sir Arnold T. Wilson, *The Persian Gulf.* Oxford, 1928.

G. Ferrand, *Relations de Voyages et textes géographiques arabes, persans et turcs relatifs a l'Extrême-Orient des VIIIe au XVIIIe siècles*, 2 vols. Paris, 1913–14.

A. Heyd, *Histoire du Commerce du Levant au Moyen Âge*, 3 vols. Leipzig, 1885–6.

W. A. Bewes, *The Romance of the Law Merchant*, London, 1923.

L. de Mas Latrie, Historical introduction to *Traités de Paix et de Commerce et Documents divers concernant les relations des Chrétiens avec les Arabes de l'Afrique Septentrionale au Moyen Âge.* Paris, 1866.

al-Muqaddasi, *translated from the Arabic and edited by G. S. A. Ranking and R. F. Azoo*, Vol. I 1–4 (incomplete), Calcutta 1897–1910 (Bibliotheca Indica).

Edrisi, *Géographie traduite de l'Arabe en Français d'après deux mss. de la Bibliothèque du Roi et accompagnée de notes par Amédée Jaubert.* Paris, 1836–40, 2 vols.

C. Barbier de Meynard, *Dictionnaire géographique, historique et littéraire de la Perse et des contrées adjacentes, extrait du Modjem al-Bouldan de Yaqout et complété a l'aide de documents arabes et persans*, Paris, 1861.

Ibn Battuta, *Travels in Asia and Africa, 1325–54; translated and selected by H. A. R. Gibb* (The Broadway Travellers, edited by Sir E. Denison Ross and Eileen Power), London, 1929.

Pierre d'Ailly, *Ymago Mundi*, ed. par Edmond Burn, Tome I, Paris, 1930

ISLAMIC MINOR ARTS AND THEIR INFLUENCE UPON EUROPEAN WORK

When Islam began that dramatic career which, in its Western course, was destined to plant a new form of art in cities overlooking the Atlantic, it set out from regions where art was in a primitive and backward state. Such art as existed in Arabia was either a sterile survival from the remote past, or merely imitative in nature, a reflection from abroad that flickered in places precariously affected by alien progress. Not even in the fertile spots where a settled population prospered, under conditions very different from those that kept the nomads of the desert in stagnant isolation, does any outstanding native art seem ever to have arisen. Islamic art derived its spiritual complexion from Arabia; but its material texture was fashioned elsewhere, in lands where art was a vital force.

In Syria and Egypt Christianity had wrought profound changes in the pagan art current at its inception. Various factors, rooted in the soil or brought in and developed by foreign domination, had been reanimated by a new spirit, and combined to produce a coherent and impressively beautiful art. Beyond the Euphrates and the Tigris another order of things prevailed. Some centuries had elapsed since the Persians, rising against their Parthian overlords, had set up the native Sāsānian dynasty and entered upon a brilliant national revival. Their art, an ancient stock upon which Greek elements current since Alexander's invasion, and later importations from Inner Asia, had been grafted by Iranian genius, was now a vigorous growth characterized by most splendid magnificence. It was amidst these two cultures, mutually hostile and both equally repugnant to the Muslims, that Islamic art came gradually into being.

In the Middle Ages art was first and foremost a religious

expression. We instinctively identify the great orders of medieval art with the creeds that shaped them, for however clearly certain elements in their composition and technical procedure may unite them in common ancestry, they were moulded into distinct entities by religious influences. Christian art was essentially a vehicle for religious edification; its mission was always plainly apparent, clearly expounded with all the subtle resources of picture and symbol in ways as intelligible to the unlettered as to the scholar. But its superb iconography seemed sheer idolatry to the Arabs, who, lacking any artistic tradition, regarded art with suspicion, associating it, like all primitive people, with magic. Moreover, in the first flush of puritanical zeal, luxury was to them specially reprehensible; an outcome of effete infidel levity, it was a snare of the Devil with which the true believer could have no truck. The splendour of Persian art, the very quality that Persian craftsmen were presently to impress so deeply upon Islamic art, was at first as offensive as the heathen abominations it so patently displayed.

Islamic art had its beginnings in the mosque. Here it was born in the full light of day, and bred openly under public tutelage. The first mosques were bare structures without any architectural pretensions, planned solely for prayer and exhortation. Their furniture, when it appeared—for at first there was none—was as simple as could be, and every innovation was subject to rigorous criticism. It is said that the first pulpit set up in Egypt was destroyed by order of the Caliph when the scandal reached his ears, for it raised the preacher in unseemly dignity above his brethren. The first recessed niche built to mark the direction of Mecca was sharply questioned because it recalled too closely the Christian apse, from which, indeed, it was undoubtedly derived. But soon a more sophisticated generation arose to contrast the poverty of the mosque with the richness of the infidel church. In due course the *minbar* and the *miḥrāb* became the chief ornaments in buildings that for skill in design and diversity of decoration count amongst the triumphs of architectural art.

As Islam spread farther afield, contact with alien races enlarged its artistic vision, and, within the restrictions permanently imposed by the creed, produced fresh aspects of the ideal type. Moreover, as it acquired a wider outlook, a new cultural element purely secular in nature began to assert itself at the expense of spiritual supremacy. When alien customs began to infect rulers who were not conspicuous pillars of the faith, the odour of sanctity waxed faint in the palace. Kinds of art not strictly orthodox crept in when cultured sovereigns began to indulge refined tastes for beautiful books, richly figured stuffs, and other such things, fit, perhaps, for a king, but not for a successor to the Prophet. When the ruler's connoisseurship found imitators amongst the nobility and those who aped the manners of their betters a distinct 'Court art' arose, a development not without profit to the craftsman, but grievous to the devout.

Aristocratic seclusion was impossible under the early Caliphs, who enforced social equality as an inviolable principle, holding that every one at his need might seek the presence of the ruler, whose way of life, whose house and its appointments, should be above reproach. It was not until an easy-living governing class began to detach itself from public business that the palace became a place apart, where a new standard of conduct prevailed. That a secular court art was already in being under the Omayyads is shown by some remarkable wall-paintings with finely designed figure subjects, in mixed Hellenistic and Oriental tradition, which still survive in a derelict hunting-lodge in the desert to the east of the Dead Sea,[1] a building thought to have been erected by the Caliph al-Walīd I between the years 712 and 715. Court art was an established tradition when the Abbasids moved the seat of govern-

[1] Coloured drawings of these decorations are reproduced in Alois Musil's *Kusejr 'Amra*. Vienna, 1907.

ment from Damascus to the new city of Baghdād, practically completed in 766. This change of capital marks an epoch in the history of Islamic art, for henceforth Persian influence predominates in its development.

It is not our purpose to follow the growth of Islamic art step by step, but to sketch briefly some of its mature developments; and, concentrating upon certain important products, to trace how they affected contemporary and subsequent progress in Christian Europe. Moreover, we are concerned solely with the minor arts, the work of those craftsmen who, when a building was erected, were called in to furnish it down to the last detail with all the necessities and amenities dictated by the purpose which it was to serve.

The Muslims soon became great builders. Their genius realized definite architectural ideas with acute technical insight. Religious objection to representation of the human form prevented any development of statuary, but as carvers in stone, wood, and other materials they were extremely skilful. Although mural painting seems to have existed from early times, the painting now known is restricted to so-called 'miniature' work, small pictures, illustrations in manuscripts and the like, which, whilst they display masterly technical ability and keen sense of colour, lack certain qualities conspicuous in the best work done under similar conditions in medieval Europe. Master builders of great ability abounded, but we seek in vain for their peers in sculpture and painting.

If, however, with the single exception of architecture, the Muslims failed to equal Western achievement in the fine arts, their success in the arts in which their genius had free play was unparalleled in medieval times. Islam was the direct heir to many ancient craft traditions unknown in the West. In much the same way that Muslim scholars transmitted to posterity a large fund of ancient learning, Muslim artisans preserved, developed, and spread abroad the traditional 'workshop practice' of arts current in the Orient, which had either never penetrated into Europe, or, if known there in former times, had decayed during the period of storm and stress that ushered in the Middle Ages.

In developing anew this ancient skill Islamic art acquired a characteristic so obvious that it may easily be taken as a matter of course and overlooked. Everything, whether made for common or ceremonial use, is lavishly enlivened with ornament, so justly planned and expressed that the patterns seem to be natural growths, like the figurings with which Nature endows living creatures, rather than artificial embellishments. The forms taken by the designs, although definitely exotic, are not so far removed from European tradition as to be inconsistent with it. Their strangeness is attractive and romantic. So dexterously are their component elements unfolded that we are beguiled almost into the belief that beyond their material structure lies some elusive vitality. Such enrichment is no mere space-serving artifice for masking bare forms, but an essential part of fine craftsmanship, without which a work is incomplete. To the contemplative Oriental eye the rhythmic dance of a pattern is as much a recreative necessity as is melody to the Western ear. Ornamental composition had such fascination for Oriental craftsmen that they continually devoted intensive study to its problems, systematizing its practice on lines which modern workers still pursue. The most casual survey of Islamic art will show that ornamental design must be ranked as the outstanding minor art evolved by Muslim genius.

Although religious tenets absolutely forbade Muslim designers to introduce into their work human figures or living creatures, such representations are, as a matter of fact, very commonly found in Islamic ornament. But they are not tolerated by any particular sect, as is sometimes supposed, nor are they under any circumstances allowed in the mosque. Their occurrence at once stamps the objects they decorate as made for secular use. Offences breaking the bounds of a discipline too exacting for universal sufferance, they were passed over by the broad-minded, but were always vexatious to strict spirits, who might at any moment rise in angry protest. In our museums and art collections are many things showing how blatant lapses have been purged by a swift blow or scrape, sure evidence that at some time or other the fervour of rectitude has impelled the hand of reproof.

Another notable feature in Islamic ornament is the use of Arabic inscriptions. A passage from the Qur'ān, an apt verse from a poet, or a phrase of greeting or blessing often runs round a border or frieze, or fills a shaped cartouche. Now and again the name and grandiose titles of a noble owner enrich some valued possession, giving a welcome clue to its date and provenance; facts which are sometimes exactly stated when the master craftsman has added to his work his signature, the name of the city where it was made, and the year of its completion.

Arabic script, the sole Arab contribution to Islamic art, is a universal mark of Muslim dominance or influence wherever it spread. The script in which the Qur'ān was written, it was held sacred throughout Islam, whose scribes vied with one another in perfecting its beautiful characters. Generations of expert calligraphers worked with such success and approval that not only was a fine book a priceless treasure, but the merest scrap of a great master's writing a collector's prize.

European craftsmen gradually became familiar with the semblance of Arabic script, even if they could not read it. Early evidence of this knowledge and ignorance is afforded by a gold coin struck by Offa, king of Mercia (757–96), now in the British Museum (Fig. 14). This closely resembles a Muslim *dīnār*, but has the words 'OFFA REX' inserted upside down in the middle of an Arabic legend, which is so accurately rendered that the date of the original piece (774) and the Muhammadan religious formula it recited are both clearly legible in the copy. This coin had no successor similar in type, but it records how widely the sound currency then being issued from Muslim mints was circulating. In the same museum another instance of Western contact with Muslim work is seen on an Irish bronze-gilt cross of about ninth-century date, which has in the centre a glass paste inscribed with the Arabic phrase *bismi'llāh* in Kufic letters. In neither case can the workers have realized the significance of the strange writing they copied or adopted, for inscriptions so flagrantly Muhammadan could hardly have been set knowingly upon the coinage of a Christian king, or inserted on a sacred emblem.

From this time onward scraps of Arabic lettering, often so crudely rendered as to be illegible scribbles, and ornamental details derived from Muslim sources become increasingly numerous in craftwork wrought in Christian Europe. Pious attraction to the Holy Places, thirst after the learning inherited solely by Islam, commercial enterprise and other such interests, drew many travellers to Muslim lands, whence they returned with trophies of Muslim skill to bear out their tales of Saracenic magnificence.

Amongst the things brought back by wandering scholars who sought in Muslim seats of learning knowledge unknown in their own countries, the astrolabe was a most important acquisition. An astronomical instrument of ancient Greek invention, improved by the Alexandrian geographer Ptolemy, and perfected by the Muslims, the astrolabe came to Europe some time in the tenth century. Its principal use in the East was to determine the hour of prayer and the position of Mecca. But it also served other purposes, like that described in *The Story Told by the Tailor*, where the glib barber delays his exasperated victim whilst he finds with his astrolabe the precise moment auspicious for shaving. Association with astrology gave the astrolabe and those versed in its use a sinister reputation throughout the Middle Ages, when in popular belief astronomy and astrology were synonymous terms. The great tenth-century scholar Gerbert of Auvergne, who became Pope under the name of Sylvester II in 999, was held, from his astronomical learning, to have had dealings with the Devil during his sojourn in Córdoba. In recounting how Gerbert, who 'surpassed Ptolemy in the use of the astrolabe', revived the legitimate mathematical sciences in Gaul, where they had long been in abeyance, William of Malmesbury gives a dark hint of his necromantic skill. An interesting relic of late tenth-century science is preserved at Florence, an astrolabe made for the latitude of Rome, which is thought by some authorities to have belonged to Pope Sylvester.[1]

The earliest dated astrolabe known is at Oxford. Made in 984, it was the joint work of two masters, Aḥmad and Maḥmūd, sons of Ibrāhīm the astrolabist, of Ispahan. Amongst those in the British Museum is an English example dated 1260. Merton College Library possesses the instrument traditionally associated with Chaucer, who wrote a treatise on the astrolabe for his little son.

To mariners the astrolabe was invaluable. Its use for nautical observations continued in the West until the seventeenth century, when it was superseded by new inventions. A fine astrolabe is a beautiful work of art, made and engraved with amazing care and skill in a form that persisted for centuries without material change. One made under the superintendence of Ibrāhīm ibn Saʿīd at Toledo in 1066–7, shown in Fig. 15, may be compared with another (Fig. 16), similar in shape but covered with delicate ornament, the work of a celebrated Persian master, ʿAbdu'l-Ḥamīd, in 1715.

Amongst the many specimens of early Islamic metal-work that have come down to us is a casket in the Cathedral of

[1] See Eduardo Saavedra, 'Note sur un astrolabe arabe'. *Atti del iv. Congresso Internazionale degli Orientalisti*, 1878. Firenze, 1880.

Gerona (Fig. 17), made of wood sheathed with silver-gilt plating heavily patterned in *repoussé* with scrolling foliation. The casket bears an inscription stating that it was the work of two craftsmen, Badr and Ṭarīf, and was made for a courtier of al-Ḥakam II (961–76) to give to the heir-apparent, Hishām, who succeeded his father as Caliph at Córdoba. This is one of the few pieces of silver-work which have survived to our times; but, despite religious objection to the use in this world of the precious metals reserved for the blessed in Paradise, gold and silver plate was by no means prohibited in the Caliphs' palaces.

Egyptian records describe in some detail the gold and silver treasure accumulated by the Fāṭimid Caliphs in Cairo, the bulk of which was dispersed by tumultuous Turkish mercenaries during a rising in 1067. An inventory of the heirlooms hoarded in the palaces since their foundation, transcribed by the historian al-Maqrīzī from early archives still existing in his time, helps us to picture some of the curious luxuries that the court goldsmiths were then contriving. It is a lengthy document, describing with business-like precision items such as gold and silver inkstands, chess-men, parasol-handles, vases for narcissus flowers and violets, golden birds, and trees set with precious stones, in such amazing numbers, that, even if we discount a few hundreds or so from the round thousands freely enumerated by the enthusiastic surveyors, the sceptical cannot remain wholly unimpressed. Moreover, the reputed wealth of the Fāṭimids is amply borne out by a contemporary witness, the Persian traveller Nāṣir-i-Khusrau, who, in 1047, by favour of a palace official, made a tour of the State apartments. He traversed in succession eleven chambers, each more splendid than the last, before entering the twelfth, in which was the throne, a stupendous work made of gold and decorated with scenes of the chase, interspersed with finely wrought inscriptions. Before the throne, which was raised upon three silver steps, was set a wonderful golden trellis of

FIG. 15. ASTROLABE
Toledo. Dated 1066–7. Museo Arqueologico, Madrid

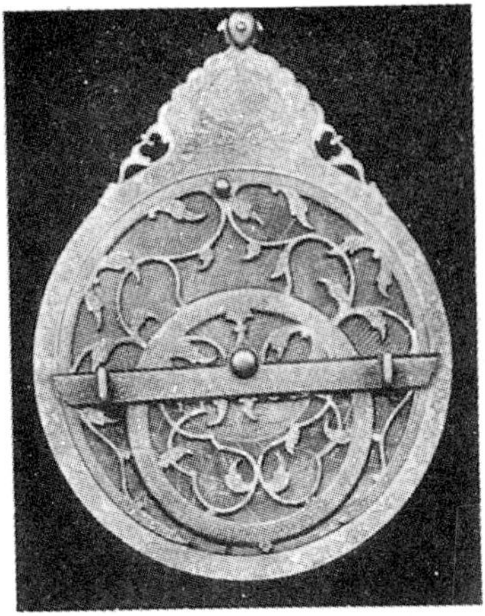

FIG. 16. ASTROLABE
Persian. Dated 1715. Victoria and Albert Museum

FIG. 17. SILVER-GILT CASKET
Córdoba. Xth century. Cathedral of Gerona
Photograph by Arxiv Mas

FIG. 18. BRONZE GRIFFIN IN THE CAMPO SANTO, PISA
Fatimid, XIth century

open-work. Unfortunately its beauty was such that 'it defied description'.[1]

Early Islamic gold- and silver-work has practically disappeared. It is mainly in what survives of the bronze, brass, and copper furniture and utensils used by wealthy Muslims that Islamic metal-work can now be studied. The great bronze griffin (Fig. 18) that stands in the Campo Santo at Pisa is a monumental example of a type more usually represented by small birds and beasts, often parts of fountains, or portable water-vessels, from some of which the later European so-called *aquamaniles* derived their fantastic shapes. The body of this engaging monster—he has all the self-satisfied assurance of a pampered pet—is completely covered with engraved patterns. On the neck and wings in represented a scale-like feathering, and the back bears the semblance of a close-fitting cloth decorated with roundels and edged with an inscription in Kufic characters, which is continued on a band round the chest. On the haunches are pointed panels engraved with lions and falcons within borders of running spirals. The inscription, a verse showering adulation on the possessor, gives no clue to the date or origin of this remarkable piece of bronze-casting, but in all probability it is a relic brought from some Fāṭimid palace of the eleventh century.

Other ways of decorating metal besides raising patterns in relief or engraving them were practised by Muslim craftsmen. They excelled in the art of inlaying designs in gold and silver in bronze or brass; a process performed in several ways, known generally as *damascening*, a term derived from European association of the work with Damascus, where it was certainly practised, although it did not originate there. In the finest and most ancient kind the patterns were incised in the metal ground and the grooves filled in with gold or silver, both sometimes being used on the same object. The brilliance of the design was often

[1] See *Sefer Nameh: Relation du Voyage de Nassiri-Khosau*, translated into French and edited by Charles Schefer. Paris, 1881.

heightened by filling other interstices with a black mastic composition, and in some cases this was the sole method of enrichment.

Muslim inlaid metal-work reached perfection about the middle of the twelfth century, and persisted in great excellence for two hundred years. A typical specimen, one of the finest extant, is a brass ewer in the British Museum (Fig. 19), entirely covered with designs inlaid in silver. The ten-sided body and neck are divided horizontally into zones diversified with variously shaped panels, and every part of the surface is heavily enriched with figure subjects, geometric or floral patterns, and inscriptions. At the base a valance of knotted-work, finishing in tassel-like pendants, completes the design. The little inlaid silver plates that express the figures are exquisitely shaped, and have details such as features of faces, hands, and folded draperies, engraved upon them with minute care. An inscription running round the neck states that the ewer was made by Shujāʿ ibn Hanfar [1] at Mosul in the year 1232.

This ewer is representative of a school supposed to have been centred at Mosul, a city in close touch with ancient and prolific copper-mines, and filled with craftsmen who were renowned for all sorts of artistic products; particularly, as a thirteenth-century writer quoted by M. Reinaud explicitly declares, for the manufacture of copper vessels for table service. But the same technique and similar decoration occur on work earlier in date made in regions to the north and east of Mosul, showing the school to have had Armenian and Persian connexions, which are not yet clearly defined. As the technical processes and some elements in the decoration of the later pieces go back to Hellenistic traditions of the second century, it is not improbable that

[1] The name is so given by M. Reinaud, who first read the inscription in 1828. But a revision by M. Max van Berchem ('Notes d'archéologie arabe', *Journal Asiatique*, XIe série, Paris, 1904) substitutes Manʿah for the paternal name Hanfar.

FIG. 19. BRASS EWER INLAID WITH SILVER

Mosul. Dated 1232. British Museum

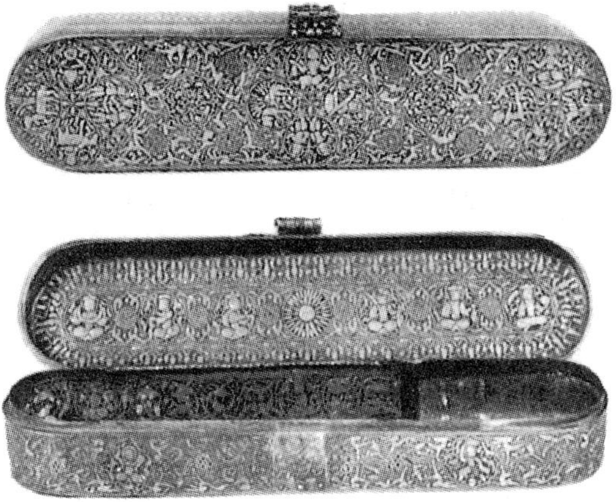

FIG. 20. BRASS WRITING-CASE INLAID WITH SILVER AND GOLD
Mosul School. Dated 1281. British Museum

FIG. 21. BRASS SALVER INLAID WITH SILVER
Venetian. XVth century. Victoria and Albert Museum

Islamic developments originated in a local art current in these regions from remote times.

The influence of this school spread rapidly through Syria to Egypt, a migration accelerated by the Mongol invasion, which laid the cities of Mesopotamia in ruins and dispersed their craftsmen. The capture of Baghdād by Hūlāgū, grandson of Chingīz Khān, and the death of the Caliph Musta'ṣim brought the Abbasid dynasty to an end in 1258.

A writing-case in the British Museum (Fig. 20), made of brass inlaid with silver and gold, bears the name of the master, Maḥmūd ibn Ṣunqur of Baghdād, but it cannot have been made in the city of his fathers, for it is dated 1281, when the sole inhabitants of Baghdād were country folk who had settled amidst its ruins. A most beautiful piece, this writing-case is in design and workmanship scarcely inferior to the ewer. The twelve signs of the Zodiac, grouped in fours in three medallions, are the chief ornaments on the lid, which has, inside, a row of circles containing astronomical devices. The circle in the centre has a rayed human-faced Sun, and in those on either side of it are seated figures representing the Moon, Mercury with pen and script, Venus with a lute, Mars holding a sword and severed head, Jupiter seated like a judge, and Saturn with staff and purse. All are set upon a richly patterned ground, and enclosed by a border of intricate design. This case is a magnificent example of many similar objects which in their original state were fitted with ink-wells, boxes for sand and paste, and oblong cells for reed pens, arranged as shown in Fig. 22.

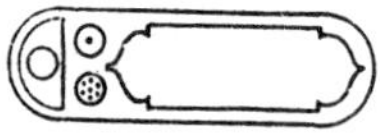

FIG. 22. Plan of internal fittings in writing-cases.

As the inlayer's art spread southwards its decoration changed, and new developments became characteristic of a second school centred in Cairo during the fourteenth century. The medallions placed at intervals in the ornamental bands acquired delicate floral borders, and the inscriptions, from being more or less subsidiary, became the most important features. In Fig. 23 is a typical bordered medallion, a detail from a large basin made for al-Nāṣir Muḥammad ibn Qalā'ūn, Sultan of Egypt, who reigned, with two interruptions, from 1293 to 1341.

These two examples must suffice to give some idea of the many lovely pieces that have come down to us, often in marvellous preservation. Amongst them are ewers and basins, and other shapely vessels which, as is shown by the names and titles incorporated in their ornament, once graced the banquets of sultans and great nobles. Things such as jewel-cases, writing-boxes, candlesticks, perfume-burners, flower-vases and other similar objects of sumptuous domestic use abound in variety and quantity too numerous to specify. During the thirteenth and fourteenth centuries this beautiful inlaid work was much favoured, and fine examples by famous masters were eagerly sought by wealthy nobles, who frequently had pieces specially made for them. In the British and Victoria and Albert Museums are many specimens with interesting historical associations, and several of outstanding excellence unrivalled elsewhere.

FIG. 23. Detail from brass basin inlaid with silver. Egypt. Fourteenth century. British Museum.

At the end of the fourteenth century the art of inlaying was already in decline. The Mongol irruption into Syria and the sack of Damascus by Tīmūr in 1401 wrought havoc in busy centres, and the Ottoman conquest of Egypt in 1517 scattered the few remaining Cairo masters. But whilst it was decaying in its original home, the art was receiving increased attention in Europe, where it was destined to enjoy a brilliant rebirth. In the fifteenth century the Oriental trade established by Italian cities during the Crusades flourished exceedingly. Eastern products became popular in the splendid pageantry of the petty Italian princes, whose workmen adopted them as models and began to emulate their triumphs. In Venice Muslim metal-work inspired native craftsmen so profoundly that a distinct Venetian-Oriental school arose in which Muslim technique and designs were adapted to Italian Renaissance taste. An example of this development is seen in Fig. 21, a brass salver dating from about the middle of the fifteenth century. It is inlaid in silver with an Islamic interlaced knot-pattern that recalls the bold Cairo ornament of earlier times, and has as a central feature a silver shield enamelled with the arms of the Occhi di Cane, a noble Veronese family. Other pieces were modelled upon contemporary Persian work, which was then actually being made in Venice itself by Persian craftsmen settled in that city.

During the thirteenth and fourteenth centuries metal-working had followed in Persia a course similar to that taken by the Mosul school with which it was intimately connected, but its progress was marked by increasing refinement in the shapes of the vessels and certain modifications in their decoration. At the beginning of the second national revival of Persian art, which dates from the rise of the Ṣafavid dynasty in the opening years of the sixteenth century, these changes were fully developed into a new style, in which the inlays were generally reduced to linear patterns or inscriptions, set on grounds covered with minutely chased scrolling patterns. An example of this style is shown in Fig. 24, the top of a bowl-cover signed by Maḥmūd al-Kurdī, a famous Persian master who worked in Venice in the first years of the sixteenth century.

As used by medieval Muslim craftsmen, gold and silver inlaying was in some measure an Oriental counterpart of the enamelled metal-work produced by contemporary European workers, whose *champlevé* process inlaid designs in coloured glass-pastes upon many objects which it was customary for the Muslims to enrich with precious metals by a similar method. Enamelling on metal was certainly practised in the Orient, but examples definitely Islamic are rare. Gold plaques enamelled in colours are mentioned in al-Maqrīzī's inventory of the Fāṭimid treasures, and a metal disk with foliated ornament and an inscription enamelled in *cloisonné*, recovered from the rubbish heaps of Fusṭāṭ and now in the Museum of Arab Art at Cairo, is apparently a relic of this period. But the most important specimen of Muslim enamelled metal-work known is a copper bowl in the Museum Ferdinandeum at Innsbruck, which is decorated in *champlevé* with a central medallion containing a representation of the Ascent of Alexander, surrounded by others filled with mythical beasts, set upon a ground enriched with palm-trees and standing figures. Although Byzantine in style, this bowl bears an inscription showing that it was made for an Ortuqid prince of Mesopotamia, who reigned towards the middle of the twelfth century.

Judging from the few specimens that have come down to us, it would seem that enamelling did not find favour with Muslim metal-workers. It was not until the fifteenth century, when richly enamelled sword-furniture was made in Spain, that the art reappears in Islam; and these examples, like the later enamelled work made for the Mughal Emperors of India, are perhaps rather reflections of foreign fashion than traditional developments.

In enamelling of another kind, the application of coloured glazes to earthenware, the Muslims were from an early period expert masters. Under Islamic rule native potters in Egypt and the Near East revived and developed technical processes and decorative devices which had survived from ancient times in more or less decadent forms. Wall-tiles with beautiful greenish-blue glazed surfaces go back to a very early period in Egypt, and similar work, variously coloured, was used with great effect in the palace of Darius at Susa about 500 B.C. In these regions the art persisted in obscurity until the Arab invasion, when, under

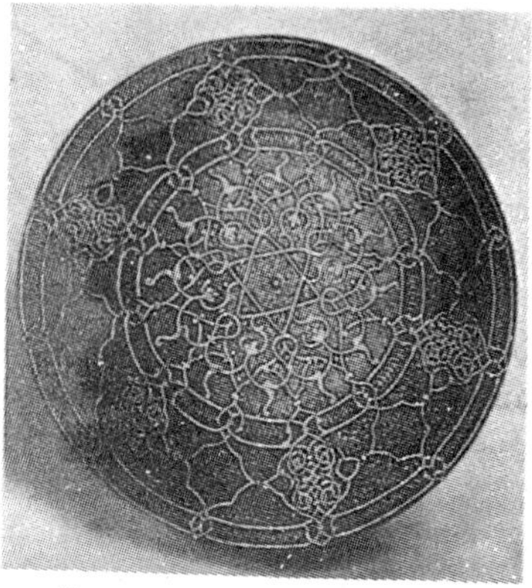

Fig. 24. BRASS BOWL-COVER
inlaid with silver
Made at Venice by a Persian craftsman
Early XVIth century. British Museum

Fig. 25. EARTHENWARE CUP
painted in colours and gold. Ray. XIII
century. Musée du Louvre
Photograph by Archives photographiques, Par

Fig. 26. EARTHENWARE VASE PAINTED IN LUSTRE
Fatimid. XIth century. Musée du Louvre
Photograph by Archives photographiques, Paris

FIG. 27. EARTHENWARE DRUG-JAR

Painted in colours. Sultanabad. XIIIth or XIVth century. Victoria and Albert Museum

Fig. 28. EARTHENWARE DRUG-JAR

Painted in dark blue. Faenza. XVth century. Victoria and Albert Museum

FIG. 29. EARTHENWARE DISH

painted in yellow lustre and blue

Valencia. XVth century. Victoria and Albert Museum

Muslim influence, potters began again to experiment with new technical processes and ornamental schemes.

The early history of Islamic ceramics is as yet unwritten, and although many interesting specimens have been unearthed in recent years, their provenance and chronology are largely matters of conjecture. It is clear that various types spread rapidly throughout the Islamic world from centres situated in Persia, Mesopotamia, Syria, and Egypt, but it is impossible to determine exactly where specific wares originated. So widely were popular kinds scattered that pieces similar in make and design are found on several ancient sites, in places far separate from one another. One or two specimens must serve to show what early Islamic pottery was like.

FIG. 30. Painted earthenware dish. Susa. Ninth century. Musée du Louvre.

A glazed earthenware dish found at Susa (Fig. 30), painted with a poppy-head in bright cobalt blue upon a white ground, is assigned to ninth-century date, as similar pieces have been excavated on the site of a palace at Sāmarrā, built by a son of the Caliph Hārūn al-Rashīd in 836 and abandoned fifty years afterwards. The dish is an early example of the blue and white decorative scheme now so familiar in Western ceramic art, a fashion that came to modern Europe in later times from China. In the ninth century the Abbasid rulers were already importing Chinese wares; characteristic pottery and porcelain made under the T'ang dynasty have been recovered at Sāmarrā, together with pieces which are plainly native imitations of those wares. The realistic design upon the dish belongs to this alien tradition; but the beautiful blue with which it is expressed is an indigenous product, a colour that was eventually exported to China, where it was known as 'Muhammadan blue'. So essential was it to the Chinese for the manufacture of blue and white wares that when, for unknown reasons, the supply occasionally failed, the production of them temporarily ceased. Thus, although the West habitually ascribes 'blue and white china' to the Far East, the typical blue was there associated with Islam. Muslim potters used it with superb effect upon certain wares made at Kutāhia in Asia Minor during the fifteenth and sixteenth centuries.

FIG. 31. Lid of earthenware jar with incised and painted decoration. Persia. Eleventh century. Metropolitan Museum. New York.

Whilst readily absorbing progressive ideas the Muslim potters maintained great originality, very thoroughly welding their acquisitions from abroad into a distinct tradition, in ways clearly shown by many interesting examples. The lid of a jar drawn in Fig. 31 is a piece of so-called *Gabrī* ware, a kind of pottery supposed to have been made by Fire-worshippers, who in certain parts of Persia clung obstinately to their ancient religion long after the Arab conquest. In this the decoration is roughly but expressively drawn by cutting through the thin white clay 'slip', with which the surface is coated, to the brick-red body beneath. The whole is then covered with a transparent glaze, tinted yellow, green, purple, or warm brown, colours in some cases distributed in irresponsible splashes in a way that recalls a contemporary Chinese practice. From the prevalence of Sāsānian motives —such as mounted huntsmen, mythical monsters, and characteristic foliated work—*Gabrī* ware was formerly assigned to the beginning of the Muhammadan era, but as examples have been found inscribed with Kufic letters of eleventh- or twelfth-century style, most of it is now dated from this period. The incised method of drawing, known as *graffito* work, was in common use in China, but did not necessarily originate there, as it also occurs in pre-Islamic Egypt. In the fifteenth century the process was used with great success by Italian potters, who probably derived it from Islamic sources, whence they obtained much of the mature technical knowledge that was so serviceable to them in the revival of the ceramic arts during the Renaissance.

FIG. 32. Earthenware dish painted in lustre. Persia. Tenth century. Musée du Louvre.

In what is termed 'lustred pottery' the Muslims achieved their great triumph. In this the design is painted in a metallic salt on a glazed surface and fixed by firing in smoke in a way that gives it a metallic gleam, which varies in different specimens from a bright copper-red to a greenish-yellow tint, and in some cases throws off brilliant iridescent reflections. Pieces dating from the tenth century have been discovered in the Near East, north Africa, and Spain, showing by their wide diffusion how the ware was esteemed throughout Islam, but leaving its place of origin in doubt. Whether it was first made in Egypt or Persia is still a moot point upon which authorities are somewhat hotly divided. The large vase in Fig. 26 was recovered from the ruins of Fusṭāṭ, and is assumed to be Fāṭimid work of the eleventh century. Fig. 32 is a dish, painted in pale lustre with a sprightly griffin, foliated work, and formalized Kufic lettering, which was found on the site of Ray, or Rhages, an ancient Persian city destroyed by the Mongols in 1220.

Ray was a great centre of ceramic industry, where several characteristic types originated. Its ruins are a mine of lovely specimens. Definitely associated with this city are certain vases and dishes painted in opaque colours—blue, green, red-brown, and purple, touched here and there with gold-leaf upon white or tinted grounds—with figure subjects and formal decoration remarkable for their delicate workmanship, which resemble so closely the paintings in contemporary manuscripts that it would seem that the artists were inspired by them. The cup in Fig. 25, decorated with sphinxes and seated musicians set in shaped panels formed by a series of opposed S-shaped curved lines, is a typical example of this 'miniature' ware, as it is often called, the manufacture of which was at its height when Ray was overwhelmed by the Mongols.

The vase in Fig. 27, painted in turquoise, dark blue, and black, represents a type of pottery made at Sulṭānābād, in Persia, during the thirteenth and fourteenth centuries. A pot so shaped was known to the Italians as an *albarello*, a term perhaps derived from the Arabic *al-barnīya*, denoting a drug-jar. The name shows the purpose that such vessels served in the Orient and the use to which they continued to be put in Italy. In the fifteenth century Italian apothecaries' shops displayed many such pots, filled with drugs and preserves imported from the East. This trade brought westwards the prototypes of the Italian drug-jars in much the same way that Chinese ginger-jars still come to us. In Fig. 28 is seen an Italian development of the Oriental form, an albarello of buff-coloured earthenware painted in dark blue, made at Faenza about the middle of the fifteenth century.

The Italians obtained drug-jars painted in lustre from Valencia, the Islamic centre of this ware in the West, where examples that rank amongst the finest ever made were manufactured, sometimes to the order of foreign purchasers, whose arms were painted upon them. In Fig. 29 is shown a dish decorated in yellow lustre and blue which was made at Valencia late in the

Figs. 33, 34, and 35. EARTHENWARE TILES PAINTED IN COLOURS
Asia Minor. XVIth century. Musée des Arts Décoratifs, Paris

FIG. 36. PANEL OF PAINTED EARTHENWARE TILES
Damascus. XVIth century. Musée des Arts Décoratifs, Paris

fifteenth century for a member of the Degli Agli family of Florence, whose blazon it bears. Spanish lustred pottery inspired Italian emulation so successfully, that in the sixteenth century native potters learned how to illuminate characteristic Renaissance designs with its unfading brilliance in ways that broke definitely with tradition. At Gubbio, a famous centre, worked the great master Giorgio Andreoli, whose golden and ruby lustres remain unsurpassed either in Italy or the Orient.

At the opening of the sixteenth century the old order of ceramic art was everywhere changing; amongst its new manifestations two closely allied types which had been slowly emerging in Asia Minor and Syria flourished in superb magnificence. Made of earthenware coated with a white slip, they are painted under a transparent glaze with designs outlined in black, and coloured vivid green, blue, and dull purple, to which the Asia Minor factories often added a bright tomato-like red. In what was, perhaps, the most interesting development of these wares, they were used as wall-tiles, moulded in squares and painted either with the repeating units of formal patterns or the separate parts of large symmetrical compositions complete in themselves. In Constantinople, Brussa, and other great cities of the Ottoman Empire are many buildings with walls gleaming with this ornate decoration.

The next three examples illustrated are specimens of tile-work decorated with repeating patterns. In the first (Fig. 33) the designer, setting in the middle of each tile a pointed oval device, and repeating one quarter of the same figure in each corner, produces—when a number of tiles are fixed in place—an effect of white bands running in opposed curves from top to base of the space decorated. In contrast to this design the second (Fig. 34), is purely naturalistic, being made up of parallel waved stems bearing alternately vine-leaves and grapes, and almond-blossom. Both these motives, one formal and the other realistic, are combined in the third pattern (Fig. 35), which adds a network of slender acanthus leaves punctuated with acanthus rosettes. Such elaboration of simple themes into complex designs in which apparently incongruous motives are skilfully played off against one another is characteristic of this school, and incidentally we see how methodically Islamic designers were experimenting with decorative ideas. The beautiful panel in Fig. 36 illustrates the second type of tile-decoration, a large set piece, composed as a whole. It is a fine example of Damascus work in the subdued blue, green, and purple scheme that distinguishes Syrian from Turkish wares.

FIG. 37. Painted earthenware bottle. Asia Minor. Sixteenth century. British Museum.

Turkish and Syrian potters used the same technique as in their tiles, and similar kinds of decoration, in beautiful dishes, bowls, vases, and other vessels of various forms. The slender bottle in Fig. 37, ornamented with a strange medley of sphinxes, birds, and beasts, reserved in white on an apple-green ground, is a remarkable example of a distinct type, in which somewhat archaic elements persist. The red touches that enliven the colour-scheme show Turkish origin. Red is not always present on pieces made in Asia Minor, but it is never found in Syrian work.

The most striking decorative elements used in this kind of pottery are undoubtedly the floral forms, such as those displayed so profusely upon the Damascus panel (Fig. 36), where tulips, roses, hyacinths, irises, and almond-blossom issue from two elegant vases in a splendid riot of vigorous growth. The flowers are always drawn with consummate skill, and with such just decorative sense that their naturalism never sinks into mere pictorial representation. It was from Persia that the designers gathered their floral elements and learned how to draw them with such exquisite grace. We have in FIG. 38 a fine piece of Damascus work influenced by Persian models, a jug, decorated with tulips and roses on a blue scale-patterned ground, which for delicate drawing and brilliant colour is a masterpiece of its kind.

FIG. 38. Painted earthenware jug. Damascus. Sixteenth century. Ashmolean Museum, Oxford.

From Persia, largely through Turkish and Syrian channels, Western art obtained certain flowers now commonly cultivated in our gardens, but once known in Europe only from representations of them seen on pottery and porcelain imported from the Islamic East. The tulip was first brought to the West by Busbecq, imperial ambassador to Constantinople, about the middle of the sixteenth century.

In Syria, where excellent native material for glass-manufacture had been exploited in ancient times, the Muslims developed a characteristic style of glass-decoration, seen upon numerous bottles, beakers, vases, and other objects painted with figure subjects and formal ornaments in coloured enamels, and often heightened with gold. Some examples enriched in ways that recall certain kinds of Persian and Mesopotamian pottery are assumed from technical reasons to be the earliest in date. They were, perhaps, the work of Mesopotamian craftsmen who migrated to Syria during the first Mongol invasion, and established there the workshops that flourished so brilliantly throughout the fourteenth century, only to suffer extinction when Tīmūr overran Syria in 1401.

The beaker in Fig. 39, painted with two horizontal inscribed bands, and between them a prince seated upon a throne, with a standing attendant on either side, is a typical composition of late thirteenth-century style, resplendent in red and white enamels and gilding. The beaker must have come to Europe soon after it was made, for it is mounted as a chalice with a broad foot and slender stem of silver-gilt, heavily ornamented in *repoussé* work of French fourteenth-century fashion, being evidently regarded as a thing of great value. Contemporary documents show that Syrian glass was highly prized in Christian Europe at this period. In the inventory of the treasures belonging to Charles V of France in 1397 two entries describe this kind of glass very explicitly, thus: 'Trois potz de voirre ouvré par dehors a ymages à la façon de Damas'; and 'Ung bassin plat de voirre paint à la façon de Damas'. Another Syrian beaker in the British Museum must have been made specially for a Christian, for it bears figures of the Virgin and Child, St. Peter and St. Paul, and an inscription in Latin. In the fifteenth century, Venetian glass-workers, famous throughout Europe since the thirteenth century, turned their attention to Oriental methods, and mastered the process of enamelling so thoroughly that it soon ceased to be a Muslim monopoly. From Venice the art spread to other European centres, and developed new styles. The gaily enamelled spirit-bottles common in the seventeenth and eighteenth centuries are debased descendants of medieval Muslim skill.

Interesting as are the imitations they never rivalled their Oriental prototypes in either beauty of form or spontaneous directness in their ornamentation. Such pieces as the long-necked bottle in Fig. 41 and the delicate bowl and cover in Fig. 42 are typical representatives of Muslim table-glass. The bottle is enamelled with medallions, inscriptions, and foliated work

39

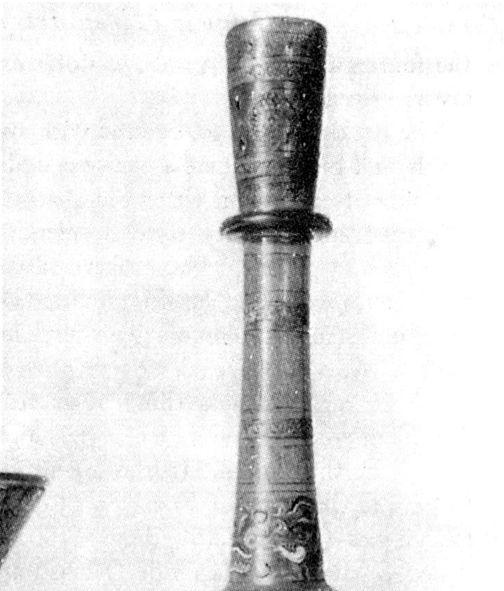

40 41

FIG. 39. ENAMELLED GLASS BEAKER. Syrian. XIIIth century. British Museum

FIG. 40. ENAMELLED GLASS LAMP. Syrian. XIVth century. Musée du Louvre

FIG. 41. ENAMELLED GLASS BOTTLE. Syrian. XIVth century. Musée du Louvre

FIG. 42. ENAMELLED GLASS BOWL AND COVER
Syrian. XIVth century. British Museum

FIG. 43. SILK FABRIC
Baghdād. Late Xth or early XIth century. Colegiata de San Isidoro, Leon
Photograph by Arxiv Mas

disposed in horizontal bands, and it bears the name of an Amīr associated with al-Kāmil Sayfu'l-Dīn Sha'bān, Mamlūk Sultan of Egypt in 1345. The bowl has a similar design, enamelled in green, blue, red, and white, and is gilt in places. This fine piece, of uncommon shape, bears no name, but is inscribed 'Glory to our Lord the Sultan!'

FIG. 44. Enamelled glass lamp. Syria. Fourteenth century. Museum of Arab Art, Cairo.

The most splendid achievements of the Syrian glass-workers were the lamps—or rather lamp-shades, fitted internally with small oil-vessels hooked by wires to the rim—which, suspended by three or more silver or brass chains attached to loops contrived on the body of the lamp, illuminated the gloom of many great mosques with jewel-like radiance. They are generally ornamented with band-work filled with medallions and inscriptions, enlivened with conventional foliage; but in some the whole surface is covered with floral patterning, like a brocaded silk, as in Fig. 44. Another (Fig. 40), is treated in the same way, but bears a shield with the blazon of the donor who dedicated it to some unknown mosque.

Muslim nobles, following an ancient Oriental tradition, often set devices of heraldic character upon their belongings. Their use of such figures influenced the development of Western heraldry which, during the Crusades, evolved into a systematic science with a peculiar nomenclature of its own. In this the technical term for blue, *azure*, is derived from the Persian word denoting the blue stone called lapis lazuli. There are other interesting links between European and Oriental heraldry, such as that curious figure the double-headed eagle which makes its first appearance in remote antiquity on Hittite monuments. It became the badge of the Seljūḳ Sultans early in the twelfth century, and in the fourteenth was adopted as the blazon of the Holy Roman Emperors.

FIG. 45. Muslim heraldic blazons.

Muslim heraldic devices were set upon shields either circular in form, as on the lamp in Fig. 40, or pointed at the base, like the one enamelled on the bottle in Fig. 41. Besides symbolical birds and beasts—such as the eagle, which was fairly common, and the lion, borne by the Mamlūk Sultan Baybars—there were other devices of a different nature, attached to certain court functionaries—the cup-bearer, the polo-master, and various military secretaries of state—by virtue of their offices. In Fig. 45 some of these devices are brought together. The significance of the chalice-like cup and the polo-sticks is obvious, but the meaning of the last figure in the series was long a perplexing question. Once thought to be the sole survival of ancient Egyptian hieroglyphic writing in Islamic art, it is now recognized as a diagrammatic representation of a writing-case, showing the internal fittings as in the plan given in Fig. 22.

The pointed shield on the tall bottle shows how a personal device—an eagle—sometimes accompanied an official badge. Muslim blazons were always brightly coloured if the means by which they were expressed rendered this possible, for a noble's colours were an important part of his arms.

In Persia, Syria, and Egypt the sumptuous textile arts—to which we shall now turn—were already highly developed when the Arabs conquered those countries. In the adjoining provinces of the Byzantine Empire important weaving centres were manufacturing silk fabrics of wonderful richness, and incorporating in their patterns many Sāsānian elements taken over when Christian workers began to emulate their neighbours' skill. Although silken garments had been specifically prohibited by the Prophet, the Muslims not only encouraged existing silk factories but established new ones wherever they went. So shameless and unrestrained was their interest in the forbidden luxury that they rapidly and surely gained a dominating position as leading silk-mercers in the medieval world. This is shown by the names by which many fabrics were known in the Middle Ages, trade terms that in some cases have persisted down to our own times, recording the distant places where certain materials were originally made, or the markets where they were procured. Thus the cloth known in Chaucer's time as 'fustian' came from Fusṭāṭ, the first Muslim capital of Egypt. The stuffs we still call 'damasks' took their name from Damascus, that great trade-centre to which the West referred many things not exclusively made there. Our 'muslin' is the *mussolina* imported by Italian merchants from Mosul. Baghdād, Italianized as 'Baldacco', gave its name to the rich silk fabrics brought thence and also to the silken canopy suspended over the altar in many churches, the 'baldacchino'. In later times dress fabrics from Granada were known as 'grenadines' in European shops, where ladies also bought Persian *tāftah* under the name of 'taffeta'.

The ʿAttābīyah quarter of Baghdād, where dwelt the descendants of ʿAttāb, great-grandson of a companion of the Prophet, was in the twelfth century renowned for a special fabric which, imitated in Spain, was known there as *attabi* silk. France and Italy adopted it as *tabis*, and by this trade name it became popular throughout Europe. In 1661, on October 13

(Lord's Day), Mr. Pepys put on his 'false taby wastecoate with gold lace', all unconscious of the word's ancient history; and in 1786 Miss Burney attended a royal birthday celebration at Windsor attired in a gown of 'lilac tabby', a tint known in Persia as *līlāq* and brought westwards with the flowering shrub of that name. These beautiful watered silks are now out of fashion; but a brown and yellow *attabi* pattern is still worn by our familiar friend the tabby cat.[1]

Although there is in Berlin a scrap that bears the magic name of Hārūn al-Rashīd, silks associated with Baghdād are extremely rare. A fragment preserved in the Colegiata de San Isidoro at Leon (Fig. 43) bears an inscription definitely stating that it was woven at Baghdād, perhaps by a master called Abū Naṣr, a name that appears in the mutilated lettering in a place where the maker's signature might well be put. Woven in red, yellow, black, and white, the design is a characteristic early Islamic pattern of about the end of the tenth century in date, showing birds, beasts, and foliated ornaments inherited from an older tradition set in and around large circular panels. A prominent element, the elephant, probably came from India. This beast occurs on a somewhat earlier Persian silk discovered a few years ago in a village church near Calais, a piece which is now one of the treasures of the Louvre. It is also found on several Byzantine imitations of Persian fabrics, notably on the magnificent silk preserved in the tomb of Charlemagne at Aachen.

In Europe the demand for rich silk textiles increased rapidly as the Oriental trade developed. Finely wrought stuffs came from Muslim countries in such quantity that Western enterprise saw in this lucrative industry a potential source of wealth, and, setting up looms in various centres, began seriously to compete with the Eastern and Spanish factories. It was largely from Sicily, where Muslim invaders had established in the royal palace at Palermo a famous weaving-house—which continued to flourish when the

[1] See G. le Strange, *Baghdad under the Abbasid Caliphate.* Oxford, 1900.

island reverted to Christian rule under the Normans—that the first Italian workers gained their technical knowledge and models for their designs. During the Norman occupation the Sicilian school was reinforced by contact with Byzantine traditions brought in when a number of Greek weavers, captured in a raid into the Aegean seas in 1147, were installed in the palace workshops. At the beginning of the thirteenth century silk-weaving was already the chief industry in several opulent Italian cities, where fabrics, hard to distinguish from the Sicilian stuffs they imitated, were produced and exported in profusion.

In the fourteenth century Italian silks reflected new influences which were then affecting Muslim art. In the blue and white silk fabric brocaded with gold shown in Fig. 46 are seen not only the lions, palmettes, and foliated work, Arabic inscriptions, and other Oriental elements usual in Italian work of this period, but also characteristic Chinese birds. Their appearance in Europe was largely due to events that had brought about great changes in the Far East. In 1280 the nomad Mongols under Kublai Khān, brother of Hūlāgū, who had overthrown the Abbasids in 1258, invaded China, and set up the Yuan dynasty which lasted until 1367. As a result of these conquests a wide stretch of Asia, extending from Persia to the Pacific, was for nearly a century ruled by members of the same Mongol house, a circumstance that led to a remarkable interchange of artistic traditions between eastern and western Asia. In China an imposing Muhammadan population had sprung from colonies planted there during the T'ang dynasty, using, as happened wherever Islam spread, the Arabic language. It included many craftsmen, among whom were silk-weavers, who, working with the skill hereditary in the ancient home of silk-culture, produced at unknown centres fabrics that were prized throughout Islam. Their beautiful stuffs so appealed to their Western brethren that they affected everywhere the development of Muslim textile design, and, through this channel, the textiles of western

Europe. Some superb examples of medieval Chinese workmanship have survived; the most remarkable is, perhaps, a piece preserved at Danzig which must have been specially made for the Mamlūk Sultan al-Nāṣir Muḥammad ibn Qalā'ūn, whose name is woven into the design. In Fig. 47 is shown a silk and gold brocade of Chinese origin, with a pattern composed of phoenixes and palmettes inscribed in Arabic, set in bands between lines of formal ornament, an example of a type from which the bird in the design shown above it might have been derived.

Not only in the Middle Ages but also in later times Oriental silks were often made up into church vestments. The chasuble in Fig. 48 was cut from a Persian fabric of late sixteenth- or early seventeenth-century make, with a pattern by no means suitable for the purpose to which it was put, and one that most certainly would not have been tolerated in a mosque. Its main elements are rows of standing youths attired in court dress, holding cups and wine-bottles. They are set amidst slender trailing stems bearing foliage and flowers of the kind that the Turkish potters were then closely copying; in the interspaces are lively birds posed and drawn in a manner that points to a Chinese origin. The design belongs to a group of similar gay patterns fashionable upon such brocades during the Ṣafavid period. Elaborate examples were even more pictorial in character, showing episodes from romantic histories, such as the meeting of Khusrau and Shīrīn or the woful story of Lailā and Majnūn, and sometimes enriched with veritable landscapes of flowering trees and shrubs wherein roam all sorts of kindly or ferocious beasts, drawn and coloured with irresistible spirit and brilliance.

The pattern on the silk strip used for the orphrey introduces an interesting series of textile designs produced during a period when Turkish and Italian weavers were so actively and successfully imitating each others' stuffs that experts often find it difficult to distinguish fabrics as definitely of European or

Fig. 46. SILK FABRIC

Italian. XIVth century. Victoria and Albert Museum

Fig. 47. SILK FABRIC

Chinese. XIIIth or XIVth century. Victoria and Albert Museum

FIG. 48. CHASUBLE OF PERSIAN BROCADED SILK

XVIth century. Musée des Arts Décoratifs, Paris

The Orphrey is of Turkish (?) silk damask

of Oriental origin. Although late in date and European in appearance, this piece has a Turkish pattern of a type that arose in Asia Minor some time in the fifteenth century. In their simplest forms these patterns are composed of plain or decorated bands running vertically in opposed curves which, uniting at intervals, cover the field with a net-like design. Some examples have more or less elaborated formal ornaments set within the meshes of the net, as in the pattern on the orphrey; whilst in others similar elements spring from the bands at their junctions. The latter plan is followed on the magnificent silk brocade in Fig. 50, with a pattern woven in gold, outlined and touched with cobalt blue, upon a crimson ground. Within the interspaces left by the main system a secondary netting is contrived, from which spring roses, tulip buds, pinks, and narcissus flowers.

FIG. 49. Detail from a woven silk fabric. Italian. Sixteenth century. Museo Nazionale, Florence.

From flower-knops, such as the main element in this design, the Italians evolved the floral elements drawn in Fig. 49, and the very similar one used in the late fifteenth-century velvet shown in Fig. 51. During the sixteenth century European and Turkish weavers, each alternately outdoing their rivals, worked out many intricate variations of the net and knop theme, and gave the rich velvets so fashionable at this period the special type of pattern that became traditionally associated with them. It was a pattern of this kind that William Morris designed for the sumptuous brocaded velvet woven in blue, orange, white, and gold (Fig. 52) which was his sole attempt to revive these costly fabrics.

The carpet, now a universal necessity, came into Europe from the Orient as a luxury reserved for wealthy connoisseurs, who at first regarded it more as a treasure than as a thing of use. Carpets, both with smooth faces like tapestries, and with loose threads knotted into the fabric so as to produce a velvet-like 'pile' surface, are of great antiquity in the East, where they served as sleeping-mats and hangings, as well as coverings for floors. From representations of Oriental rugs in Italian pictures it is known that they came to Europe at least as early as the fourteenth century. In the sixteenth they were regular articles of commerce. It is recorded that in 1521 Cardinal Wolsey, through the good offices of the Venetian ambassador, secured sixty Oriental rugs for his palace at Hampton Court. They probably resembled examples seen in pictures by Holbein, which can be matched by existing carpets made in Asia Minor at that time. At Boughton House, in Northamptonshire, are preserved three pile carpets specially made for Sir Edward Montagu, with his arms and the date, 1584, woven in the border. Of a type known then, as now, as 'Turkey' carpets, they are decorated with shaped ornaments, coloured blue and enlivened with detail in yellow, set upon a red ground.

In the sixteenth century Persian craftsmen carried carpet-weaving to heights never attained before or since, producing with miraculous skill designs unparalleled in beauty. One of these masterpieces, brought from Ardabīl—where it lay for centuries in the mosque of Shaykh Safī the venerated ancestor of the Ṣafavid Shāhs—is now in the Victoria and Albert Museum. Fig. 53 shows a portion of this colossal carpet, which is of most delicate workmanship, being built up of more than thirty million minute knots, 380 to the square inch. In the centre is a large medallion with serrated edges, surrounded by pointed oval panels, all enriched with foliated work in glowing colours. A quarter of the central element is repeated in each corner of the rectangular field, which is of deep blue covered with gay flowers issuing from meandering stems, amidst which two lamps, represented as if suspended in mid-air, form secondary centres

FIG. 50. SILK FABRIC
Asia Minor. XVIth century
Musée des Arts Décoratifs, Paris

FIG. 51. SILK VELVET
Italian. XVIth century
Victoria and Albert Museum

FIG. 52. SILK VELVET
Woven by William Morris in 1884
Victoria and Albert Museum

FIG. 53. PILE CARPET FROM THE MOSQUE AT ARDABIL

Persian. Dated 1540. Victoria and Albert Museum

in the design. The border, bounded by rigid marginal lines, is filled with lobed circles and elongated panels, which, like the plum-coloured ground they ornament, are heavily decorated. In a cartouche at one end is a verse by the poet Ḥāfiẓ; and beneath this is written: 'The work of the slave of the threshold, Maqṣūd of Kāshān, in the year 946' (A.D. 1540). Although many older carpets exist, this one was long the earliest dated example known; in this respect it must now, however, yield pride of place to another very fine Persian carpet, in the Museo Poldi-Pezzoli at Milan, which is stated to have been woven by Ghiyāthu-l-Dīn Jāmiʿ in 1521.

European craftsmen learned how to weave pile-carpets from the Muslims, using at first the traditional Oriental sleight-of-hand, but in later times purely mechanical means. Upon the machine-made carpets and rugs now almost universally in use, designs borrowed from Islamic originals are common, but they are freaks of fashion rather than traditional survivals. It is in their velvet-like texture rather than in their designs that the ancient ancestry of modern carpets is most worthily perpetuated.

When we pass from flat surface decoration to ornament executed in relief we find Muslim carvers and modellers pursuing much the same system of design that governed their practice in other modes of technical expression. The diversity of style to which we are accustomed in European relief work, where sculpturesque and pictorial influences unknown in Muslim countries have become traditional, is absent in Islamic carving and modelling, in which repeating patterns similar to or precisely the same as those used in weaving, inlaying, or painting are generally found. Such patterns were adapted to decorative purposes in ways wholly foreign to European usage. A design that served to enrich the title-page of an illuminated manuscript, or as the pattern of a silk fabric, would be deemed equally suitable for carving in stone upon the exterior of a dome, or the walls of a mosque. The white marble fountain-basin in Fig. 55, dated 1277–8 and inscribed with the name of Muḥammad II, Sultan of Ḥamā—uncle of Abu-l-Fidā the historian—shows how the carver adapted a type of design common to several crafts to his special needs. The scheme is essentially a repeating pattern; its elements might be extended indefinitely either laterally as a border or frieze, or both laterally and vertically as an 'all-over' design. Similar ornament is carved on the long frieze and in the panels of the wooden casing from the tomb of a Shaikh who died in 1216, shown in Fig. 56. One side of this remarkably rich example is at South Kensington, and the rest at Cairo. In carvings of the Fāṭimid period the ground was often sunk very deeply, with almost the effect of pierced work, as in Fig. 54, a panel in the Museum of Arab Art at Cairo. Although made in Sicily, the carved wooden ceiling in Fig. 57 is Fāṭimid in style. Besides showing how effective are such deeply cut panels, it has amongst the leafage in its ornament numerous birds and beasts, features often seen in Fāṭimid work designed for court or secular decoration, in which human figures were also freely used.

FIG. 54. Carved wooden panel. Egypt. Tenth or eleventh century. Museum of Arab Art. Cairo.

This ceiling follows the characteristic method of construction adopted by Islamic carpenters, a system which arose from considerations both practical and decorative. Climatic conditions that rendered wood very liable to shrink and warp, and scarcity of suitable timber, led to panels being reduced to the smallest possible dimensions, and to a corresponding increase in the supporting framework. To secure stability and variety of in-

Fig. 55. MARBLE FOUNTAIN-BASIN

Syrian. Dated 1277–8. Victoria and Albert Museum

Fig. 56. CARVED WOODEN PANELLING FROM A TOMB AT CAIRO

Dated 1216. Victoria and Albert Museum

FIG. 57. CARVED WOODEN CEILING
XIth century. Museo Nazionale, Palermo

FIGS. 58 and 59. DOOR-LEAVES PANELLED WITH CARVED AND INLAID IVORY
Cairo. XVth century. Victoria and Albert Museum

terest in the designs, a strangely elaborate method of assembling small panels was gradually evolved, a scheme that actually expressed by structural means pattern-schemes in which the Muslims took particular delight. Designs made up of various polygonal shapes radiating from stars form a type of ornament that is, perhaps, the most characteristic Islamic contribution to decorative art. In woodwork, which played a great part in developing the type, it finds its most complete expression, but such patterns were used by many craftsmen working in different arts. The designing of them exercised ingenious spirits everywhere throughout Islam, and if in later times they tended to become irritatingly intricate and to degenerate into over-conscious spectacular geometry, their simpler forms were always singularly effective vehicles for displaying the rich colour-schemes in which Muslim genius was so adept.

FIG. 60. Islamic geometrical design.

A pattern of this type is given in Fig. 60, an ingenious arrangement of twelve-pointed stars set within hexagons. This drawing is developed from the outline in Fig. 61, traced from a note made by Mīrzā Akbar, architect to the Shah of Persia at the beginning of the nineteenth century, many of whose working drawings are preserved in the Victoria and Albert Museum. In the original the geometrical setting-out, shown by thin lines in the diagram, is scratched with a pointed tool upon the paper, and the pattern is drawn in ink upon this basis. The method used is instructive, as it probably records an ancient workshop tradition, showing how Oriental designers set about a task which may be tackled in many different ways—as the very considerable literature devoted to these patterns testifies.[1]

In the two door-leaves of fourteenth- and fifteenth-century Egyptian work shown in Figs. 58 and 59 the panels are so small that it has become possible to substitute ivory for wood, and so to gain an effect of surprising richness. In one of them the panels are carved with foliated ornament cut in sharp relief, and in the other they are inlaid with geometrical patterns. Both are probably relics of pulpits similar in design to the one in the Victoria and Albert Museum, which was erected by the Mamlūk Sultan Qā'it Bey (1468–95) in a mosque at Cairo, destroyed in the nineteenth century to make way for a new street.

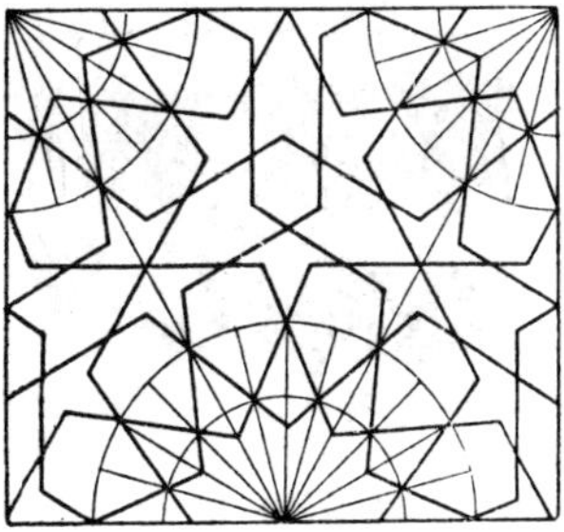

FIG. 61. Structural basis of design in Fig. 60. From a drawing by Mirza Akbar. Persian. Early nineteenth century.

The Muslims produced many beautiful things made partly or wholly of ivory, a substance which they decorated with carved, inlaid, or painted ornament. In the tenth century a school of ivory-carvers centred at Córdoba was working in a style that already proclaims mature experience. Amongst the extant examples of their work is the cylindrical casket in Fig. 62, from the cathedral of Zamora, which is now exhibited in the Museo Arqueológico at Madrid. Around the domed lid runs an inscription stating that it was made in the year 964 for the

[1] M. J. Bourgoin in *Le trait des entrelacs* (Paris, 1879) has analysed some two hundred of these curious designs. Dr. E. H. Hankin (*The Drawing of Geometric Patterns in Saracenic Art*, Calcutta, 1925) has explained with uncanny wizardry some remarkably intricate examples.

FIG. 62. CARVED IVORY CASKET

Córdoba. Dated 964. Museo Arqueológico, Madrid

FIG. 64. PIERCED IVORY BOX

Cairo. (?) XIVth century British Museum

FIG. 63. CARVED IVORY CASKET

Córdoba. Dated 1005. Cathedral of Pamplona

Photograph by Arxiv Mas

Fig. 65. CARVED ROCK-CRYSTAL EWER

Fatimid. Xth century. Treasury of St. Mark's, Venice

Caliph al-Ḥakam II, as a gift to his wife, the mother of prince 'Abd-al-Raḥmān. The finest example of a group that includes several similar objects made in Córdoba at about the same date, it is entirely covered with palmette leafage, peacocks and other birds, and beasts. Other specimens now in London, Paris, and elsewhere, although similar in shape and workmanship, have different ornament, being carved with interlaced lobed circles enclosing figure subjects, like the design upon the rectangular ivory casket in Fig. 63. This piece is the work of several craftsmen, the names of two of them —K͟hayr and 'Ubayda—being legible upon panels they carved. It was made in 1005 for a court functionary whose name and titles are prominently inscribed upon the lid.

FIG. 66. Painted ivory box. 'Siculo-Arabic'. Thirteenth century. Private collection, Paris.

Another type of ivory work is seen in Fig. 64, a circular box with geometrical ornament pierced through the body and flat lid. This is representative of a series thought to have been made in Cairo in the fourteenth century. Dating from the thirteenth century, and rather vaguely described as 'Siculo-Arabic', are a number of plain cylindrical and rectangular ivory boxes painted in colours and gold, with circles filled with knot-work or with figures, beasts and birds, flowers and trees, in a style that recalls illuminated manuscripts. An example decorated with a mounted huntsman, who has a cheetah perched behind him, is shown in Fig. 66.

Ivory caskets, painted, carved, or pierced, were used as jewel-cases, perfume or sweetmeat boxes, and for other similar purposes. They were often, as the inscriptions testify, made specially as gifts. The earliest are amongst the most valuable records of Islamic art in its beginnings. Many have come down to us in wonderful completeness, but judging from the traces of colour still visible on some specimens, it is probable that the carved caskets in their original state were resplendent with colour and gold. Some still retain their metal hinges and clasps, fittings which are interesting examples of a minor branch of the metalworker's art.

As a final specimen of Muslim skill in carving, a remarkable rock-crystal ewer in the Treasury of Saint Mark's, Venice, is given in Fig. 65. This superb work is historically important, for it bears the name of al-'Azīz, the second Fāṭimid Caliph of Egypt, and may well be one of the crystal ewers mentioned in al-Maqrīzī's inventory of the treasures dispersed in 1067, because they had this Caliph's name engraved on them. In workmanship and design it is a worthy memorial of a period that marks an epoch in Islamic art.

Amongst the things in every-day use that owe something of their substance, technique, or design to Islam, our printed books are, perhaps, the most widespread. Although at first sight their connexion with the Orient may appear remote, modern methods of book-production have gained much from medieval Muslim enterprise and skill. It was only in recent times that Islamic literature began to be reproduced by mechanical means, either from type or by lithography, the latter process being specially favoured, as it faithfully preserved the actual work of the scribe, the most honoured of all craftsmen. But although printing was perfected in Europe long before it spread to Muslim countries, it is to the Orient that we owe a substance that was a great, if not the chief, factor in its development. Paper, an ancient Chinese invention, became known to the Muslims when they captured Samarqand in 704, and learned how to make it from Chinese workmen. Its use spread westwards throughout Islam. A considerable number of Arabic manuscripts written on paper date from the ninth century, but it was not imported into Christian Europe until the twelfth, and was still uncommon there in the thirteenth. The first European paper factories were established by the Muslims in Spain and Sicily, whence the manufacture passed into Italy.

When in the fifteenth century book-production was commercialized by the introduction of mechanical apparatus, paper became an essential material in the manufacture of machine-made books, without which printing could hardly have progressed as it did. It is not, however, solely for paper that the modern publisher is indebted to the Muslims. During the fifteenth century, when Venice was so actively absorbing and scattering abroad Islamic fashions in art, books bound in Italian workshops assumed a very Oriental appearance. At this period some volumes took on a peculiarity common in Muslim bindings, the flap that folds over to protect the front edges. This feature still persists in certain bindings made for accountants—such as our bankers' 'pass-books'—and is a memorial of their Oriental descent.

Another innovation inspired by Muslim work was a new method of decorating leather covers. In the Middle Ages European binders often enriched leather covers by impressing devices upon them by means of metal dies, a process that developed effective schemes as the stamps became larger and more elaborate in design, and cleverly devised units giving a wide range of repeating surface patterns and borders came more generally into use. But ornament produced by 'blind tooling', as it is termed, was expressed only in relief until Oriental workers began to enrich stamped designs by filling the sunk parts with gold paint, a practice introduced into Europe by Muslim binders settled in Venice. Towards the end of the fifteenth century this method was supplemented by a new process, in which the gold was permanently fixed by reimpressing the heated tool through gold-leaf. This new departure appears to have originated at Córdoba. In the sixteenth century it was universally used by both Christian and Islamic binders, although the older Oriental way of using gold was never entirely superseded.

The result obtained by the Oriental use of gold is seen in the superb patterns worked on the late fourteenth- or early fifteenth-century binding of which the inside is illustrated in Fig. 67. It is a marvel of clear, delicate design, patiently executed by making an infinite number of impressions with a few simple tools. Fig. 68 shows some other decorative processes used by Oriental binders, methods that go back to times much earlier than the seventeenth century, when this example was made. The crimson leather cover has a central device stamped and enriched with gold; above and beneath it, and in each corner, are shaped panels sunk below the surface and decorated with lace-like ornament cut out of thin white leather and pasted on a black ground. A formal landscape, with trees, birds, and beasts—amongst which is a dragon from the Far East—is painted in gold upon the plain field. The Venetian sixteenth-century cover in Fig. 69 has similar sunk panels and painted decorations obviously imitated from a Persian model.

The Egyptian binding (Fig. 67) has a central pointed oval panel, which is quartered in each corner, and the Persian cover is decorated with a variant of the same scheme, a plan, as we have already seen, common to many crafts. A similar design, with central and corner devices of Muslim origin and linear work of Oriental inspiration, is tooled in gold upon a Venetian cover, dated 1546, shown in Fig. 70; and in Fig. 71 the same arrangement appears in a later German example, although the details are now being modified in accordance with contemporary European fashions.

These four bindings trace roughly the development of certain technical processes that, originating in Muslim lands, found their way into European workshops and brought with them schemes of design and ornamental elements which, with slight

FIG. 67. INSIDE OF LEATHER BOOK-COVER

Cairo. Late XIVth or early XVth century. Victoria and Albert Museum

68

69

70

71

LEATHER BOOK-COVERS

in the Victoria and Albert Museum

FIG. 68. Persian. XVIIth century. FIG. 69. Venetian. XVIth century. Fig. 70. Venetian. Dated 1546. FIG. 71. German. *c.* 1583

changes, have become firmly incorporated in modern practice. The gold tooling and lettering now universal upon fine leather bindings are expressed by means that were perfected by Muslim workers; and when, in the nineteenth century, mechanically produced book-covers began to supplement ancient hand-work, machine-bound books to a great extent merely stereotyped ways of working that hark back to Islamic origins.

The gaily decorated 'marbled' patterns so common upon end-papers, paper covers, and edges of books bound in European workshops during the eighteenth century, were directly derived from Oriental sources. Delicate examples of such patterns occur on strips of paper pasted round the margins of Muslim drawings and specimens of calligraphy mounted during the sixteenth century for connoisseurs whose fastidious taste required elaborately contrived settings for their treasures. Marbled papers were known in England in Bacon's time; he tells us that 'the Turkes have a pretty art of chamoletting of paper, which is not with us in use. They take divers oyled colours, and put them severally (in drops) upon water; and stirre the water lightly, and then wet their paper, (being of some thicknesse,) with it, and the paper will be waved, and veined, like Chamolet or Marble.'

Books bound in the West towards the end of the sixteenth century are found with end-papers brought from the Orient, but it was not until about a century later that European binders began to make them themselves. Hand-made marbled papers are now rarely used, but more or less clumsily reproduced imitations still serve various purposes.

For more than a thousand years Europe has looked upon Islamic art as a thing of wonder; at first largely because it was closely associated with lands deemed the Christian heritage, but later solely by reason of its own intrinsic beauty. Many of its rich products owe their preservation to medieval piety, for not a few have rested secure for ages in churches, where a casket that had served as a Caliph's jewel-case became the repository of sacred relics, perhaps brought in it from the Holy Land wrapped in a scrap of splendid silk cut from a Muslim robe of honour. The awe with which such things were regarded found appropriate meanings for the strange figures and mysterious writings upon them, thought sometimes to be talismans and characters in the tradition of Solomon, or even to date from his time, for in the Middle Ages archaeology was nothing if not romantic. It was only in the last century that the cold light of research dared to throw doubts upon the associations which had long hallowed some remarkable treasures as gifts from Hārūn al-Rashīd to Charlemagne, or as acquired by Saint Louis in the Orient. But whether such things were paraded under false colours or not, their magnificence was real enough. Masterpieces that every craftsman revered, they were always an inspiration to those who devoted themselves to arts neglected in the West.

Intercourse between Christians and Muslims began in times long prior to the Crusades. In Spain Islam was firmly established upon the very frontiers of western Europe, and from the first exercised profound influence upon Christian culture. In Sicily the two religions occupied common ground, while North Africa was wholly ruled by the Muslims, whose ships swept the Mediterranean from end to end.

With the Crusades a new era opened. The half-fabulous magnificence traditionally ascribed to the Saracens became a reality to astonished Christendom. A host drawn from every part of Europe came suddenly into close contact with a social order that in every respect outranged the narrow limits of their experience. In every activity of life the reactions of this impact with alien progress soon became apparent, and in art its results were by no means the least far-reaching. As time went on Italian merchants established direct traffic with Syrian ports, Oriental trade became regularly organized, and all kinds of rare things from Islamic workshops arrived in European markets. These imports met new-found needs, aroused emulation wherever they went, and opened up lines of development either immediately or in subtle ways destined to mature in the future.

During that critical period when the West was emerging from medieval conditions, forces aroused and fostered by religious enthusiasm entered upon another phase of energy centred wholly in commercial activities. In the fifteenth century European craftsmen, impelled by Muslim success in the sumptuous and lucrative arts that had become essential to Renaissance splendour, turned with renewed interest to the Orient. Moved by deeper study of Islamic methods, they reviewed and enlarged their own technical procedure, and in so doing were no longer content to absorb such ornamental elements as came by the way. They began to explore intently Muslim canons of design, and to adapt them in a new spirit to work that was purely European in conception. Not only humble craftsmen, but also outstanding figures like Leonardo da Vinci, experimented with Oriental pattern-work; the design in Fig. 72, developed from a rough sketch in one of his notebooks, records his interest in such studies.

FIG. 72. Islamic design. Developed from a drawing by Leonardo da Vinci. (From *Il Codice Atlantico.*)

These innovations were not always results of direct observation, for early in the sixteenth century a new method of spreading the inspiration came into being, the 'pattern-book', an immediate product of the printing-press. By means of such collections specimens of master designers' researches in the new style became known to those to whom access to original sources was difficult. One of the most interesting pattern-books is the rare volume by Francesco di Pellegrino,[1] whose examples are wholly derived from Islamic models. From this and contemporary pattern-books of the same kind—such as those by Peter Flötner, Virgil Solis, Martinus Petrus, and others—it is instructive to turn to the designs by Holbein, in whose drawings for silversmiths and workers in other crafts Muslim inspirations are skilfully welded into an original style.

In the seventeenth and eighteenth centuries Dutch and English enterprise was reaping the fruits of Vasco da Gama's adventure into the Indies. A new stream of trade flowed in ever increasing volume directly from the Orient, and influenced crafts closely connected with everyday life, which, attracting an increasing demand, were now being organized in ways that foreshadowed modern industrial developments. From Muhammadan Asia came many seemingly insignificant things which, becoming necessities, have found not only European favour but spread throughout the civilized world. Cargoes of cottons and 'chintzes' printed with gaily coloured patterns brought a new vogue in textiles, which, developed in the 'persiennes' of Paris, gave ladies in the time of Queen Anne pretty dress fabrics, and, later, brought wealth to Manchester. New 'shawls', as their name tells us, came from Persia. Certain forms of tea- and coffee-pots, imitated perhaps from Moghul ewers brought back from India by opulent nabobs, were still common on Victorian breakfast tables, and have persisted in modified shapes until to-day.

Ever since the beginnings of Islam, Western piety, learning, commerce, and curiosity have found each something to its taste

[1] A Florentine painter and sculptor who worked at Fontainebleau for Francis I, known in France as Francesque Pellegrin. His book, *La Fleur de la science de Pourtraicture: Patrons de Broderie, Façon arabicque et ytalique*, is dated 1530. A facsimile edition with an introduction by Gaston Migeon was published in Paris in 1908.

in the products of Muslim skill; but in knowledge of their technical excellence and their beauty master craftsmen such as Odericus of Rome, who in 1286 wrought Islamic patterns upon the inlaid marble pavement of the Presbytery of Westminster Abbey, and William Morris, who wove another into his velvet in 1884, together with a host of others before, since, and between them, have time and again refreshed Western art from a fund which has been to us rather an annuity than a legacy.

A. H. Christie.

ISLAMIC ART AND ITS INFLUENCE ON PAINTING IN EUROPE

There is no evidence of any Muhammadan paintings having been brought to Europe before the seventeenth century, and Rembrandt is believed to have been the first painter in the West who was sufficiently interested in Oriental art to make copies of some pictures that had reached Holland from the far East—portraits of members of the imperial family of Delhi.[1]

Any direct influence of the pictorial art of the Muslim world upon any individual artist in Europe is therefore excluded; still less is there evidence that any great movement in the art of painting in Europe has been stimulated by influences from the Muslim East; it is impossible, for example, to trace to Islam any new direction in pictorial art similar to that which manifested itself in Italian painting in the fifteenth and sixteenth centuries as the result of the revived interest in classical art. Such Muhammadan influences as are traceable, tend, therefore, to be superficial; but they make their appearance in Europe at quite an early period of the Arab domination in the waters of the Mediterranean. From Oriental fabrics were copied several

[1] F. Sarre, *Jahrbuch des Kgl. Preussischen Kunst-sammlungen*, 1904, p. 143.

representations of animals, such as appear in the eleventh-century manuscript of the commentary on the Apocalypse by Beatus in the Bibliothèque Nationale,[1] and in several other manuscripts, especially those of the school of Limoges during the early Middle Ages; but the effect of the direct contact of the Christian world with Muhammadan culture and of the importation of objects of Oriental art, was never so marked in painting as it was in sculpture, architecture, or metal-work. It exhibits itself chiefly in the adaptation of Oriental motifs for ornamental purposes and is for the most part confined to subordinate details. These decorative motifs, though brought to the notice of western artists by the importation of Muhammadan silks and other objects of Muhammadan manufacture, were not confined to such characteristic features as were devised by the followers of Islam themselves, but included also those which Muhammadans had taken over from their predecessors; and among such artistic heritages from the past are several conventional designs of great antiquity, such as the Chaldean sacred tree, which passed on, through Sāsānian art, into the Muslim period. This tree of life, in accordance with the primitive type, was often flanked by two beasts facing each other, but the Christian artists often omitted the central feature of the design, the sacred tree; among other primitive, pre-Muslim designs are the two animals, one the prey of the other, and animals with two heads and a single body. They occur more frequently in sculpture than in painting, and in the latter case were possibly often copied from similar carvings on capitals and bas-reliefs in churches.[2] Of the presence of Muslim artists working for Christian patrons on the continent of Europe during the early

[1] Lat. 8878 (J. Ebersolt, *Orient et Occident*, p. 99, Paris, 1928).

[2] A long list of these has been compiled, see André Michel, *Histoire de l'art*, t. i, 2me partie, pp. 883 sqq. (Paris, 1905); A. Marignan, *Un historien de l'art français*, Louis Courajod (Chap. IV, L'influence orientale sur les provinces du nord et du midi de l'Italie) (Paris, 1899).

Middle Ages, such as those who decorated the Palatine Chapel at Palermo for Roger II (1101–54), there appears to be no evidence.[1]

During the period of the Crusades more frequent intercourse with the Muslim East facilitated the importation of objects bearing specifically Muhammadan decorative motifs, and in the country of those centres of commercial communication with the East—Genoa, Pisa, and Venice—these motifs became introduced into paintings. Consequently, an interest in the Oriental world, stimulated largely by curiosity and the fascination of the unfamiliar, manifests itself in the early products of the Sienese school of painting, and becomes more prominent in Tuscan art. Turbaned figures and Oriental physiognomies make their appearance in such Italian pictures as early as the second half of the fourteenth century; such foreign personages generally take a subordinate place in the representation of a sacred scene, and it is in the accessories that Oriental influence make themselves especially felt, e.g. in the copying of Persian and other carpets, the clothing of even the more important persons in Oriental stuffs, and the introduction of exotic animals, such as leopards, apes, and parrots. In details of landscape, also, it is possible to recognize details of trees and foliage that appear to be deliberate imitations of Oriental designs.

A borrowing of a particularly Oriental character occurs in the frequent adaptation of Arabic letters for decorative purposes. This is one of the first examples of the direct influence of Muslim art on Christian workmen to attract the attention of European scholars, and since Adrien de Longpérier published his article, 'De l'emploi des caractères arabes dans l'ornementation, chez les peuples chrétiens de l'occident', in the *Revue archéologique*, in 1846, an increasing number of instances have been collected, the richest collection of which is to be found in the

[1] A. Pavlovsky, 'Décorations des plafonds de la Chapelle Palatine' (*Byzantinische Zeitschrift*, ii, 1893).

learned articles of Mr. A. H. Christie in the *Burlington Magazine* (vols. xl and xli, 'The development of ornament from Arabic scripts'). Such an ornamental use of Arabic characters appears in Italian painting as early as Giotto (e.g. on the right shoulder of the figure of Christ in the Resurrection of Lazarus, in the Arena Chapel, Padua). Fra Angelico and Fra Lippo Lippi (Fig. 73) were especially fond of this kind of decoration, and employed it even for the sleeves of the Virgin and the borders of her robe—obviously entirely in ignorance of the origin of such shapes. The source of their knowledge of this script must be sought in the many pieces of silk and other fabrics brought into Europe from the East, or in lamps and other brass vessels.

THOMAS ARNOLD.

BIBLIOGRAPHY

SIR THOMAS W. ARNOLD, *Painting in Islam. A study of the place of Pictorial Art in Muslim Culture*, Oxford, 1928.

FIG. 73. THE USE OF ARABIC LETTERING FOR DECORATIVE PURPOSES

The central scene from Fra Lippo Lippi's 'Coronation of the Virgin' (Uffizzi, Florence). Above, an enlargement of part of the scene, showing Arabic lettering on the scarf held by the angels

ARCHITECTURE

A GENERATION hence it may be possible to estimate with some confidence the legacy of the Islamic world to architecture; but in the present state of scholarship so much doubt exists as to several important aspects of Muhammadan architecture that only a violent partisan can feel sure of his ground. It is unfortunate that much recent research, which should have thrown light on uncertain points, has been presented to us in the form of polemical arguments. These are not mainly concerned with the nature of Muslim architecture in its maturer periods, still less with its effect on the evolution of architecture in our Western world, but rather with its origins and its earlier buildings. Nevertheless, they have a direct bearing on the question of its legacy to mankind, for we cannot fairly recognize a bequest from Islam unless there is some proof that Islam possessed the original title. In other words, so many things in Muhammadan architecture are said to have been stolen from non-Islamic peoples that some scholars actually hold that the Muslims were mere borrowers of the architectonic forms and had no architecture of their own worth the name. To reach a conclusion on this fundamental point, it is necessary in the first instance to attempt a brief outline of the origins and nature of Muhammadan architecture in general.

The Arabs, who within a half-century swept like a desert whirlwind from the Ḥijāz to the Pillars of Hercules in the West and to the confines of India in the East, conquered countries already civilized. Their dominions extended over an area wider than that of the Roman Empire at its greatest extent, and embraced many nations whose architecture differed from that of Rome and in some cases was far older.

Whatever position one may assume in the bitter controversy between those who believe in the mainly Roman origin of our Western medieval architecture, and those who attribute everything to Iran or Armenia, it is becoming clear that the latter school of thought demands our serious attention. A series of remarkable discoveries in Armenia, Mesopotamia, and Turkistan, though revealed to us in a bellicose way, has shaken our confidence in the ultra-Roman point of view. It may be that the Church has fostered for centuries a belief that our 'Romanesque' and Gothic buildings rose from the ashes of Imperial Rome, or that pedantic humanists of the Renaissance are to blame for our misconceptions. But whatever the cause, it is evident that now we must look eastwards with an impartial mind, at the outset getting rid of the habit of regarding 'the East' as a single entity. Hardly any one seriously doubts the fact of our debt to Rome; the time has come, however, to reconsider the extent of our obligation.

Of the territory subdued by the Arab conquerors, Syria, part of Armenia, and the habitable part of North Africa including Egypt were taken from the East Roman Empire; Spain was captured from the Visigoths, but had previously been a Roman province; and the lands from Mesopotamia to Turkistan and Afghanistan constituted the former Sāsānian kingdom of Chosroes II. Christianity had penetrated the whole of this vast area up to the eastern frontier of Armenia and Syria, and there was a sixth-century cathedral as far south as Ṣanʿā' in Yemen (southern Arabia).[1] The conquerors therefore found, ready to hand, skilled builders in every one of the subject provinces, and a great number of buildings which they, like the Coptic and Visigothic Christians before them, freely used as stone-quarries. Much has been made of this undeniable fact, but one must remember also that the Arabs found native craftsmen in the eastern provinces of their dominions who built in a style quite foreign to that of the Romans, and who, if we are to believe certain authorities, taught the Byzantine architects everything that makes Byzantine work differ from that of Rome.

[1] B. and E. M. Whishaw, *Arabic Spain* (London, 1912), p. 122.

There is no need to dispute the view commonly and justifiably held that the first Arab conquerors had no architectural skill or taste. In the nature of things it must have been so. Such a conquest was only possible to a race of soldiers inspired by religious enthusiasm, whose time was necessarily occupied mainly in fighting and praying. Moreover, they were not a town-dwelling people but nomads; and even when they forsook fighting to take up the task of government, they inevitably relied for technical skill in the building arts on craftsmen they found on the spot, or (and this is important) on craftsmen brought from one conquered country to another. Thus it is known that Armenian masons were employed not only in Egypt but in Spain, and perhaps at the ninth-century church of Germigny-des-Prés in France, which has several Muhammadan features.[1] But in spite of the Arabs' probable ignorance of architecture in the early years of conquest, the remarkable and incontrovertible fact about Muslim architecture is that in all countries and in all centuries it retained an unmistakable individuality of its own, although its origins were so diverse. There was something about it that differentiated it from the work of all the local schools of craftsmanship which were technically instrumental in bringing it into being.

The factor that transmuted and welded a host of varying modes of building into one style possessing individual characteristics was presumably the faith of Islam; for the buildings erected by the Arabs in their early years were chiefly mosques and palaces, and most of the important architectural works of subsequent centuries continued to be mosques or other religious buildings, such as madrasahs and convents, containing mosques. The mosque was the typical and principal Arab building, varying to some extent in form with different localities, but always retaining its main features. The annual pilgrimage to Mecca from all parts of the Islamic world doubtless contributed to the standardization of the mosque form, for in each town that the pilgrim passed

[1] J. Strzygowski, *Origin of Christian Church Art* (Oxford, 1923), p. 64.

through on his long journey he would make his prayers in the local mosque, and if he happened to be a building craftsman or an architect he would notice its design.

The primitive mosque at Madīnah, built by Muḥammad in 622, was the prototype of all others. It was a square enclosure surrounded by walls of brick and stone. Some part of it, probably the north portion where the Prophet led the prayers, was roofed. The roofs were probably made of palm-branches covered with mud and resting on palm-trunks. The congregation knelt facing north, the direction of the holy city of Jerusalem, and this direction (*qiblah*) was marked in some way. In 624 the direction for prayer was changed from Jerusalem to Mecca; that is (in the case of Madīnah) from north to south. In so elementary a building, there was no need to borrow architectural features from anywhere, for no architectural features were required.

The next mosque, built at Kūfah in Mesopotamia in 639, had its roof carried on marble columns brought from a former palace of the Persian kings at Ḥīrah, and was also square, but was enclosed by a trench instead of by a wall. A smaller mosque was founded by 'Amr at Fusṭāṭ (Cairo) in 642. It was square in plan, is said to have had no open court (*ṣaḥn*), and contained a new feature, a high pulpit (*minbar*). A few years later a *maqṣūrah* (screen or grille of wood) was introduced to protect the *imām* from the crowd. Minarets are said to have appeared about the end of the century, and the *miḥrāb* or prayer-niche (indicating the *qiblah*) a little later (Fig. 74). Thus, within eighty or ninety years from the building of the first mosque at Madīnah, all the essential features of the congregational mosque (*jāmiʿ*) had been evolved. Minor additions were *līwānāt* (plural of *līwān*, a corruption of *al-īwān*), which were colonnades or arcades surrounding the *ṣaḥn* to give shelter, and facilities for ablution. This short list includes all the chief ritual requirements of the mosque in all periods.

None of the buildings mentioned retains its original structure

FIG. 74. INTERIOR OF THE MOSQUE OF QĀIT BĀY *EXTRA MUROS*, CAIRO

The high pulpit (*minbar*) can be seen projecting in the centre, and to the right of it (left in the photograph) the miḥrāb

and even their plans have been lost in successive alterations. But the plan is all that matters, for the primitive mosque was barely a building and certainly not a work of architecture as we understand it. Nevertheless, M. van Berchem[1] has suggested the ascription of the origin of even this rudimentary mosque-plan to that of the early Christian church: the *ṣaḥn* being derived from the atrium, the principal *līwān* from the church proper, the *maqṣūrah* from the chancel-screen, the minaret from the church-tower,[2] and the *miḥrāb* from the apse. But such conjecture seems hardly necessary or appropriate: it is not until the Arabs begin to translate this religious enclosure and shelter into architecture that the question of origins arises.

The transition from bare necessity to attempts at dignity and splendour was very rapid—surprisingly so when one considers the austerity of the Islamic cult and the severity of the campaigning life led by so many of its votaries. Within twenty years of Muḥammad's death, his own mosque at Madīnah was rebuilt with walls and piers of dressed stone. And in the last years of the seventh century was built, near the rude mosque erected by the Caliph Omar at Jerusalem, after the Arab conquest of that city in 639, the magnificent 'Dome of the Rock', as it is commonly called, a building of impressive size and monumental character, gorgeously decorated (Fig. 75). At this point we plunge into the heart of all the acute controversy that still rages about the origin of Muslim architecture. The Dome of the Rock (*Qubbat al-Ṣakhrah* in Arabic) was an elaborate stone building, strictly speaking a *mashhad* ('place of witness') where pilgrims circumambulated the Rock, the spot whence Muḥammad was believed to have ascended to Heaven. Moreover, it remained unique; and for four centuries at least there was no important attempt at departure from the normal square congregational mosque with its open court. It has therefore been assumed, far too

[1] *Encyclopaedia of Islam*: article 'Architecture'.

[2] This theory is now discounted.

rashly, that the Dome of the Rock is simply a Roman or Byzantine type of structure, copied direct from pagan or Christian prototypes, executed by Christian craftsmen throughout, and therefore an alien work of architecture standing right outside the main stream of Arab art. There is a measure of truth, and more plausibility, in this view, but it must not be pressed too far.

In evolving this new type of building, an aisled rotunda, the Arabs had a definite purpose in mind. They wished to glorify and shelter the Sacred Rock of Jerusalem, already an ancient object of devotion to Muslims as well as Jews; and they desired to erect a building which should rival and surpass the famous Christian church of the Holy Sepulchre near by. The new *mashhad* was placed in the middle of a spacious rock plateau, known as the Ḥaram al-Sharīf, or 'Holy Sanctuary', on a great terrace or podium. (Aligned with it on the central axis of the plan already stood a mosque, that known as al-Aqṣā. A primitive building, its history is too obscure and complicated for discussion here.) In adopting the dome, or more precisely the 'annular rotunda', for the distinctive feature of their shrine, the Arabs showed sound judgement; and it is true that the dome had been used in this way, as the culminating and controlling element of a building designed to shelter a tomb or other venerated place, by both Romans and Byzantines before them. But these were not the only dome-builders on earth; and Strzygowski, the protagonist of Iranian inspiration, argues that the Eastern dome originated in Asia Minor or farther east, passed through Armenia to Byzantium, and thence to the Balkans and Russia under the patronage of the Greek Church.[1] Thus, though the Arabs here used a dome for the first time, they were adopting a feature which was not exclusively Christian or even exclusively Roman, and was probably copied from the famous 'Anastasis' dome, adjoining it and of almost identical size. Certainly there were domed churches in Syria and Armenia

[1] J. Strzygowski, op. cit., p. 27.

Fig. 75. INTERIOR OF THE DOME OF THE ROCK, JERUSALEM

long before the end of the seventh century; and churches of the type of the Dome of the Rock, that is, a rotunda within an octagon, already existed in Palestine. For the rest, the walls are of solid stone, the arches of the internal arcade and of the window-openings are semicircular, and the whole of the columns used in the two arcades are antiques, taken from older buildings, pagan or Christian. Hence neither the shafts nor the capitals of these columns are uniform in style. Across the springing of the arches are massive timber ties, probably introduced to resist the shocks of earthquakes prevalent in the locality, or perhaps because the builders were nervous of trusting the arch alone; similar precautions are to be found in Byzantine buildings. The dome itself is double and constructed entirely of timber, covered externally with lead and internally with modelled and painted plaster, but it is not the original structure. Much of the mosaic work is original, but most of the remaining decorations are of later date. Hence we find that, at the Dome of the Rock, the innovations are the domical plan, the use of semicircular arches, timber ties, and perhaps mosaic. The semicircular arch was decidedly not an Arab invention, the origin of timber ties is doubtful, and the earliest use of mosaic is pre-Islamic.

After the Dome of the Rock, the next important Muslim building in chronological order is the Great Mosque at Damascus, erected in the first years of the eighth century (Fig. 76). The principal *līwān* or sanctuary is a lofty apartment with doors or screens in the arches separating it from the *ṣaḥn*. Arcaded porticoes also surround the remaining three sides of the *ṣaḥn*. The new features in this mosque are numerous. The principal *līwān* has three aisles, crossed by a central transept, over the middle of which is a dome. At the end of the transept, that is, in the centre of the south wall of the principal *līwān*, is a prayer-niche (*miḥrāb*) indicating the *qiblah* or direction of Mecca. The arches surrounding the central court are carried partly on piers and partly on columns, and the arches are of the 'horseshoe' form which was destined to become characteristic of Western Muslim architecture, for some not very apparent reason. A horseshoe may be round or pointed at the top, but in either case its curve is carried down below the 'springing line'. At Damascus the round horseshoe arch is used. Above the main arcade, all round the *ṣaḥn*, is a range of semicircular-headed windows, two to each arch. Of the four Roman towers that once stood at the angles of the *temenos* within which the mosque was built, and which were used by the Arabs as minarets, only one (at the south-west angle) now remains, the other minarets being later in date. The interior of the building was richly decorated with marbles, mosaics, and apparently windows of coloured glass. The unusual plan of this mosque may have been influenced by the arrangement of Syrian churches converted into mosques, and the introduction of a transept and dome in the middle of the sanctuary may be evidence of a desire to enhance the importance of the *qiblah*, now represented for the third time[1] by a *miḥrāb*. The *miḥrāb* itself may have been an original idea: in a part of the world where diseases of the eyes are very common, it may even be possible, as an old *shaykh* once told me, that the *miḥrāb* was made in the form of a niche so that a blind man could recognize it as he groped his way round the walls, or it may have been borrowed from the Christian apse. The horseshoe arch has been found in pre-Islamic buildings, carved in the rock, but its occurrence at Damascus is one of the earliest cases where it has a true structural function. The purpose of the minaret is clear enough: it was provided[2] to give a position of vantage to the *mu'adhdhin* who summoned the faithful to prayer—a call invented perhaps intentionally as a contrast to the Christian custom of summoning worshippers with a clapper (before bells were introduced), or the Jewish use

[1] The first niche-*miḥrāb* was at Madīnah, the second at Fusṭāṭ (Cairo).

[2] The Arabic word for minaret (*ma'dhana*) signifies the place whence the call to prayer (*adhān*) is made; and the *mu'adhdhin* is the man who makes the call.

Fig. 76. THE GREAT MOSQUE, DAMASCUS

of a horn. The first instance of a tower being utilized for this purpose seems to have been at Damascus.

The earliest surviving minaret is that of the Great Mosque at Qayrawān near Tunis, and is recorded to have been built during the caliphate of Hishām (724–43). It is a huge and massive square tower, tapering slightly upwards, crowned with battlements, and surmounted by two stages, one built at a later date. Even if it is true that the four square towers at Damascus were the first minarets adapted to that end, it does not seem that a perfectly plain structure, such as that at Qayrawān, need be ascribed to Syria or any other special place of origin. It is an instance of ritual requirement met in the simplest and most straightforward way. Otherwise, the mosque at Qayrawān is of the congregational type, frequently altered, but retaining in the main the form in which it was rebuilt at the end of the ninth century. The mosque of Zaytūnah at Tunis, founded in 732, is another early and interesting example of the congregational type, with arcades formed of unpleasantly stilted arches supported on antique columns. Over the capitals of the arches are wooden blocks or abaci, connected by wooden tie-beams. This device mars the effect of many early Muslim buildings.

The Great Mosque at Córdoba in Spain, begun in 786, continues the succession (Fig. 77). Its area was more than doubled in the tenth century, but its original form may still be recalled by a careful study of the existing structure. It was a congregational mosque with a very deep sanctuary, containing eleven aisles separated by arcades, each with twenty columns. These columns, as in other cases already mentioned, were taken from older Roman buildings. The enormous size of the sanctuary made it desirable to have a proportionately lofty ceiling, much more lofty in fact than the height of the available columns with ordinary horseshoe arches above them. So a second range of arches was built at a higher level, creating a complicated and restless effect that is far from pleasing. Thus we find that the use of ready-made antique columns dictated the whole design of the arcade, both at Qayrawān and Córdoba, whereas the introduction of brick or stone piers, or of taller columns specially made for the building, would have enabled the architect to dispense with such regrettable subterfuges. The whole of the mosque at Córdoba was surrounded by a high buttressed wall, and there were arcades all round the *ṣaḥn*.

We must now retrace our steps to Mesopotamia, where a series of mosques built in the brick style traditional to that country connects the prototype at Madīnah with the famous mosque of Ibn Ṭūlūn at Cairo. Of these intermediate examples the most noteworthy are at Ukhaiḍir, Raqqah, Abū Dulaf, and Sāmarrā. The first two of these are now ascribed to the late eighth century, and the other two are of the mid-ninth century. They all carry on the tradition of Sāsānian architecture and all have the 'congregational' plan. The mosque at Ukhaiḍir, so admirably described in the late Gertrude Bell's monograph,[1] is of vital interest to us because one finds there in embryo the pointed arch which afterwards became the distinctive feature of Western Gothic architecture. The characteristic Sāsānian arch is semicircular, but occasionally one meets with isolated early examples of pointed arches. Horseshoe arches were probably used in Mesopotamia before this; there are several in Syrian churches (e.g. in the church of Qaṣr ibn-Wardān, *c.* 564), and actually a Hellenistic example at Chiusi in Italy. At Ukhaiḍir the arches are pointed ovoid and slightly stilted, as at Mashattā. But in the Baghdād Gate at Raqqah and at Abū Dulaf near Sāmarrā the arch had assumed the curve typical of later Muslim architecture, and by the end of the eighth century it was replacing all other arch-forms in Mesopotamia. The much earlier pointed arches found occasionally in India are cut out of solid rock, so are not really arches at all.

The Great Mosque at Sāmarrā is of enormous size and of con-

[1] G. L. Bell, *Palace and Mosque at Ukhaiḍir* (Oxford, 1914).

FIG. 77. INTERIOR OF THE GREAT MOSQUE OF CÓRDOBA

Photograph by Arxiu Mas

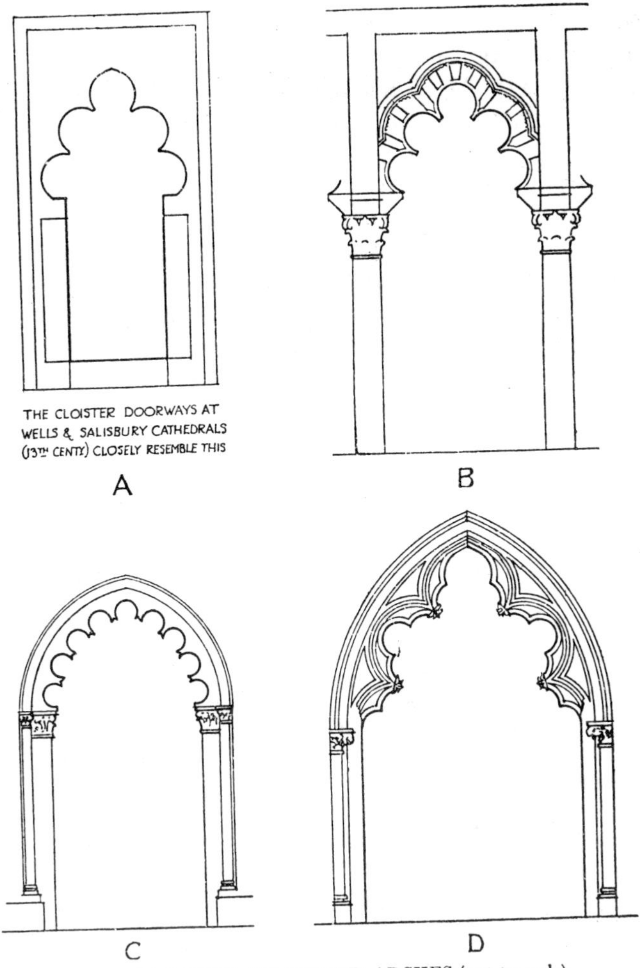
THE CLOISTER DOORWAYS AT
WELLS & SALISBURY CATHEDRALS
(13TH CENTY) CLOSELY RESEMBLE THIS
A
B
C
D

FIG. 78. PARALLEL OF CUSPED ARCHES (not to scale)

A. Sāmarrā, Great Mosque (846–52).
B. Córdoba, Sanctuary of Great Mosque (961–76).
C. Church of La Souterraine, France (*c.* 1200).
D. Cley Church, Norfolk (XIVth century).

siderable historical interest. It consists of a *ṣaḥn* with a deep sanctuary on the Mecca side and fairly deep porticoes round the remaining sides of the *ṣaḥn*. The great brick enclosing-wall has circular towers at each angle and semicircular towers intermediately. In the south wall of the sanctuary there is a row of small window-openings with cusped or multifoil heads. This remarkable feature, also found at Córdoba, may have originated in Buddhist India as Havell[1] suggests; otherwise it must be credited, with all its implications in Western art, to the Muslims (Fig. 78). Still more important is the substitution of brick piers to carry the arcades, in place of the antique columns used at Córdoba and elsewhere. These piers are octagonal in form on a square base, and have four circular or octagonal marble shafts to each pier. The shafts were jointed with metal dowels and had bell-shaped capitals. Here we have another feature that passed into Western architecture. The curious spiral minarets used at Sāmarrā, and later at the mosque of Ibn Ṭūlūn, led to no subsequent advance.

The mosque of Ibn Ṭūlūn at Cairo, commenced in 876, has been described at great length and by many writers,[2] but its importance in the history of Muhammadan architecture has been diminished to some extent since we have realized that some of its most distinctive features were anticipated in rather older buildings in Mesopotamia. It is a large congregational mosque, nearly square in plan, with a *ṣaḥn* surrounded on all sides by arcaded porticoes (Fig. 79), the sanctuary *līwān* being much deeper than the others. Outside the main walls is an open enclosing court (*ziyāda*), a feature that we have not met with before. The external walls are very massive and are crowned with ornamental battlements which, as will appear later, may be regarded as the prototype of Gothic pierced and crested parapets. (Battlements of various types were used in Assyria as early as the eighth

[1] E. B. Havell, *Indian Architecture* (2nd edition, London, 1927), pp. 85–6.
[2] See Chapter III of my *Muhammadan Architecture*, &c. (Oxford, 1924).

Fig. 79. MOSQUE OF IBN ṬŪLŪN, CAIRO

One of the Arcades

century B.C., in Egypt earlier still.) Below the battlements is a row of pointed window-openings filled with pierced plaster screens or *claire-voies*, alternating with pointed niches with multifoil or cusped heads. The arcades consist of massive brick piers with brick-engaged shafts at the angles, and above them are pointed arches which have a just perceptible 'horseshoe' curve at the springing. Thus the whole structure up to the level of the timber roof is of brick, covered with plain or ornamental stucco. It may be said without exaggeration that this mosque is, in all respects, Mesopotamian in type, and is derived from examples at Sāmarrā and Baghdād with which its founder, Ibn Ṭūlūn, had been familiar in youth. Besides the features already mentioned, other innovations include carved Kufic inscriptions in wood (a very skilful adaptation of lettering to ornamental purposes), and decoration in colour on practically all visible surfaces, mainly on white stucco, but also on the timber beams of the ceiling. There is a *miḥrāb* niche of bold design, since altered; a central fountain (*fawwārah*, not the original structure which had a wooden dome) in the *ṣaḥn*; and gorgeous lamps hung from the roof.

From the end of the ninth century to the end of the twelfth the number of surviving Muhammadan mosques is not large. Much military architecture was produced during that period, and it is admitted that the Crusaders gleaned ideas from the fortresses of Syria and Egypt, for masonry in Syria and Armenia had reached a high level centuries before this. The European use of machicolation,[1] for example, came from this source.

[1] Machicolation: an arrangement of bold brackets or corbels, closely spaced, carrying a projecting parapet. Between each pair of brackets is an opening (French *mâchicoulis*), closed with a trap-door, through which arrows, boiling oil or water, and other unpleasant things could be dropped on to the heads of besiegers attempting to mine the bottom of the walls below. Machicolation superseded wooden galleries, known as *hourdes* (hoardings) or *bretèches* (brattices) and used for the same purpose.

In an appendix to his work on the citadel of Cairo,[1] Mr. K. A. C. Creswell examined the origins of machicolation. He pointed out that six or seven of the ten alleged early examples in Syria were in fact small projecting stone latrines of a type that was common up to recent times; indeed there is one such, still in use, on the pier at Gorey in Jersey. Of the three remaining examples, which may have been used for the delivery of missiles from a height, the earliest dates from the middle of the sixth century A.D., that is, before the foundation of Islam. Since Mr. Creswell cited these instances, a Muslim example has been discovered at Qaṣr al-Ḥair near Ruṣāfa in Syria, dating from A.D. 729. There are two over the Bāb an-Naṣr (1087), a gateway at Cairo built by Armenian masons, and these were evidently *mâchicoulis* placed to cover the approach (Fig. 80). They antedate by a century the first instances known in Europe, viz. at Château Gaillard (1184), Châtillon (1186), Norwich (1187), and Winchester (1193). It is therefore clear that the Crusaders borrowed the idea from the Saracens, and not vice versa. Machicolation on rows of corbels eventually became very elaborate in French and English castles of the fourteenth century (Fig. 81).

Another feature of military architecture borrowed from Egypt and Syria was the 'right-angled' or 'crooked' entrance to a fortress through a gateway in the walls, by means of which an enemy who had attained the gateway was prevented from seeing or shooting through it into the inner courtyard. An entrance of this type does not seem to have been known to Roman or Byzantine military science, in which successive defensive gates were placed on the same axis, separated by a space known as the *propugnaculum*. These crooked entrances were first used, so far as is known, in the 'Round City' of Baghdād (eighth century), again at Saladin's citadel at Cairo (begun 1176), and culminated in a fine example at the citadel of Aleppo. They are seldom

[1] In *Bulletin de l'Institut français d'archéologie orientale*, vol. xxiii (Cairo, 1924).

Fig. 80. Bāb Al-Naṣr, Cairo (1087)

Fig. 81. Gateway of the Castle of Villeneuve-lès-Avignon XIVth century

MACHICOLATION

found in England, though there is a good example at Beaumaris; in France they were more popular, e.g. at Carcassonne. But both these countries favoured an oblique entrance for the more elaborately fortified castles, e.g. Pierrefonds and Conway.

India has no Muslim buildings of importance prior to the work at Old Delhi at the beginning of the thirteenth century. Nor is there anything in Asiatic Turkey, where the series of Seljūq buildings at Konia begins about the same time. In Spain and North Africa the chief remains, apart from military architecture, are the later work in the Great Mosque at Córdoba, where considerable extensions took place in the second half of the tenth century, and the fine minarets at Seville (the 'Giralda' tower, 1172–95) and at Rabāṭ (1178–84), both of which are decorated with cusped arcading resembling and anticipating later Gothic tracery (Fig. 82). This work is very interesting in character, and includes some remarkable dome-construction, but had no marked effect on architectural development outside Spain itself. In Sicily the Cappella Palatina was built in 1132, the church of the Martorana in 1136, La Ziza in 1154, and La Cuba in 1180. These are the accepted dates, and all of them fall outside the limit of Muslim domination in the island, which ended in 1060 for Palermo and in 1090 for Sicily as a whole. But even if they were built by the Normans they abound in pure Saracenic features which are also found on the mainland of Italy at Amalfi and Salerno. In Persia the chief buildings of this period are the 'Friday Mosque' at Ispahan and the Great Mosque (*c.* 1145–91) at Mosul, both large congregational mosques, but the former has been much altered. The Persian mosques, being constructed of brick, were decorated with stucco reliefs and with enamelled tiles, the latter a fashion afterwards adopted even in countries where stone was used, such as Syria and Egypt. The minarets were generally placed in pairs, were cylindrical in form, tapering slightly upwards, and were covered with glazed coloured tiles. M. Saladin has rather unkindly likened them to factory chimneys, and certainly they do not compare in gracefulness with the Cairene minarets. Persia also enthusiastically welcomed the curious 'stalactite' ornament described in the next paragraph.

The principal examples of the 'Syro-Egyptian' school are all to be found in Cairo, and are the large congregational mosques of al-Azhar (970) and al-Ḥākim (990–1012), the small congregational mosque of al-Aqmar (1125), and the small but important tomb-mosque of al-Juyūshī (1085). At al-Azhar and al-Aqmar the arcades are carried on antique columns, at al-Ḥākim on brick piers. At al-Ḥākim stone was used for the first time in Saracenic Cairo, though the Muqaṭṭam hills adjoining it furnish an excellent limestone. Evidently Cairo had leaned heavily on Mesopotamian tradition hitherto. The mosque of al-Juyūshī is the first example of a tomb-mosque, a type afterwards developed to great elaboration, with a dome over the founder's tomb and the *miḥrāb* on its south wall. The *ṣaḥn* is small, and between it and the dome is a vaulted transept. There is a square minaret in three stages, capped with a small high dome such as one sees on the Sicilian churches. The evolution of the dome is of the highest importance in the history of Muslim architecture, but, as it has no apparent bearing on Islam's legacy to Western building, it must be ignored in this brief survey. For the same reason, there is no object in discussing the origin of that unique feature the 'stalactite', which followed the Muslims everywhere and became a hall-mark of their architecture from India to Spain. Possibly of Mesopotamian parentage, its first authenticated occurrence is on the minaret of the mosque of al-Juyūshī; the next on the façade of the mosque of al-Aqmar, where it is used decoratively, and where there are also niches carved in the semblance of a scallop-shell; surely the prototype of the familiar Renaissance shell-niche? A band of ornamental Kufic lettering runs along the top of the façade. Another detail occurring in Cairene

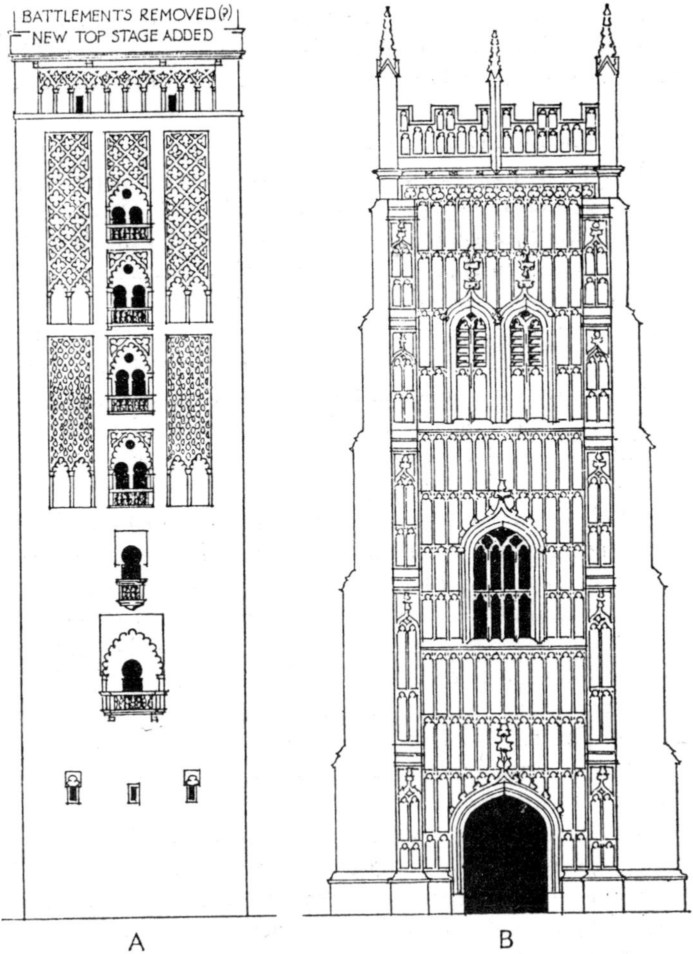

FIG. 82. PARALLEL OF TRACERIED TOWERS (not to scale)

A. Giralda Minaret, Seville (1172–95).
B. The Bell Tower, Evesham (1533).

mosques of this period is the 'saw-tooth' battlement, again probably derived from Mesopotamia. This *motif* may conceivably have inspired the architects of the ducal and other palaces at Venice.

From the thirteenth century onwards we have ample remains of Muslim architecture in all its provinces; India and Turkey have to be added to the list and Sicily struck off. Spain possesses the important palaces known as the Alhambra and the Alcázar, noteworthy for their profuse but graceful decoration; otherwise her later Moorish buildings are not of the first rank. Cairo furnishes the finest sequence of mosques and tombs up to 1517, when the city was captured by the Turks, and thereafter followed Ottoman fashions in the few mosques that were built. Anatolia provides a most interesting series of examples at Konia and Brusa from about 1200 up to 1453, when Constantinople became the capital of Turkey. From that date the Ottoman architects borrowed freely from the monuments of Byzantium, even when building so far afield as Cairo or Damascus. Persia, Turkistan, and India have an inexhaustible wealth of Muslim buildings of the later periods, and in India the tradition has persisted up to modern times. Strongly marked local characteristics differentiated the later work of the five main schools of Saracenic architecture: Syro-Egyptian, Hispano-Moresque, Persian, Ottoman, and Indian. These differences arose partly from the materials available, but were founded far more on local building traditions.

The 'Middle Ages' saw a great variety and development in mosque-planning. The congregational mosque continued to be erected in some countries, the domed tomb-mosque became very popular, and the *madrasah* (cruciform school-mosque), introduced in the twelfth century, has to be added to the list. The dome came to be a favourite feature of Muslim architecture. In Cairo its form was usually stilted, in Persia and Turkistan bulbous or ovoid domes were preferred, while in Constantinople

FIG. 83. PARALLEL OF BATTLEMENTS AND ARCHES (not to scale)

A. Mosque of Ibn Ṭūlūn, Cairo (868).
B. Persian arch, Mosque of al-Azhar, Cairo (970).
C. Mosque of Zayn al-Dīn Yūsuf, Cairo (1298).
D. Palazzo Ca' d'Oro, Venice (1431).
E. Cromer Church, Norfolk (XVth century).
F. Christ Church Hall, Oxford (XVIth century), 'Tudor' arch.

the mosques had low Byzantine domes. Externally, the stone domes of Egypt were decorated with lace-like patterning in the fifteenth century; in Persia they were covered with dazzling glazed tiles. Stalactite pendentives supported them, and indeed stalactites were used everywhere, often in excess, and sometimes hanging from the ceilings like the 'pendants' of our English fan-vaults. But whereas the Saracen dome had little influence on our Renaissance domes in the West, it seems possible that Muhammadan minarets of the graceful type found, especially, in Cairene buildings of the fourteenth and fifteenth centuries may have influenced the design of the later Renaissance *campanili* of Italy, and hence some of Wren's fine city steeples. Certainly Muhammadan architects had begun to realize the possibility of using dome and minaret in contrast, by this period; just as Wren afterwards used dome and towers so effectively in contrast at St. Paul's. The rather clumsy cylindrical minaret of Persia, and the pencil-shaped type beloved of the Ottoman Turks, never spread outside their natural homes.

As Saracenic architecture advanced, the round horseshoe and the pointed horseshoe arches continued to be favoured, the semicircular and the ordinary pointed or two-centred arch forms were frequently employed, and the so-called 'Persian' arch—of which the springing-curve turns into straight lines—was largely used in the country of its origin and elsewhere. It somewhat resembles our 'Tudor' arch (Fig. 83). Multifoil or cusped arches became general, and in the form of blind arcading and tracery were used as surface decoration. Battlements were elaborately foliated or cut into saw-teeth. Window-openings continued to be filled with pierced tracery or lattice-work, in stone or stucco, and were glazed with crudely coloured glass, perhaps before stained glass came into use in Western countries. Bands of decorative lettering, modelled in stucco or carved in wood or stone, alternated with geometrical surface ornament, for natural forms were prohibited by the theologians. Bold

FIG. 84. PARALLEL OF MINARETS AND CAMPANILI (not to scale)

A. Madrasah of Sanjar al Jauli, Cairo (1303–4).
B. Torre del Comune, Verona (1172, belfry 1372).
C. Duomo, Spoleto, C. Italy (1397).
D. Mausoleum of Barqūq, near Cairo (1400–10).
E. Duomo, Lecce, S. Italy (1661–82).
F. St. Mary-le-Bow, London (1671–83), by Wren.

carving in high relief is seldom found in the Muslim buildings of Egypt, though it may be seen in India, and effect is obtained by the free use of very delicate geometrical surface-patterns, incised rather than carved, in stone or stucco. Farther east, in Persia and Turkistan especially, where brick is the normal building-material, a plentiful use is made of glazed tiles. For their design geometrical and abstract forms were favoured up to late periods, when a more naturalistic treatment was adopted, introducing floral forms. The name 'arabesque', given to the conventional patterns in low relief used in England from Elizabethan days onwards, indicates that here we owe something to the Arabs of the Middle Ages.[1] Another form of ornament, common in Cairo but not so much used elsewhere, was the alternation of dark and light stone in horizontal courses. The origin of this practice may be ascribed to Rome or Byzantium, where 'lacing-courses' of brick were often introduced at intervals in stone walls, but the matter is open to doubt. Hence the striped façades of marble buildings in Pisa, Genoa, Siena, Florence, and other Italian cities may conceivably be derived from Cairo, with which they had close trading relations during the Middle Ages. Similar polychrome masonry may be seen at Le Puy in Auvergne, and, nearer home, at St. Peter's, Northampton.

Summing up the numerous points mentioned during this survey, it is clear that the accumulated architectural debt of the Western world to Islam is substantial. In the realm of military architecture alone we have seen that the Crusaders, who left many fine churches and fortresses in the Holy Land, themselves learned something of the art of fortification from their Saracen foes, who in their turn had profited by the skill of Armenian masons.

Excluding all count of our debt to the pre-Islamic stone buildings of Armenia and Syria and brick buildings of Iran (to

[1] On all these points see Chapter X, 'The Nature of Saracenic Ornament', in my *Muhammadan Architecture*, &c. (Oxford, 1924).

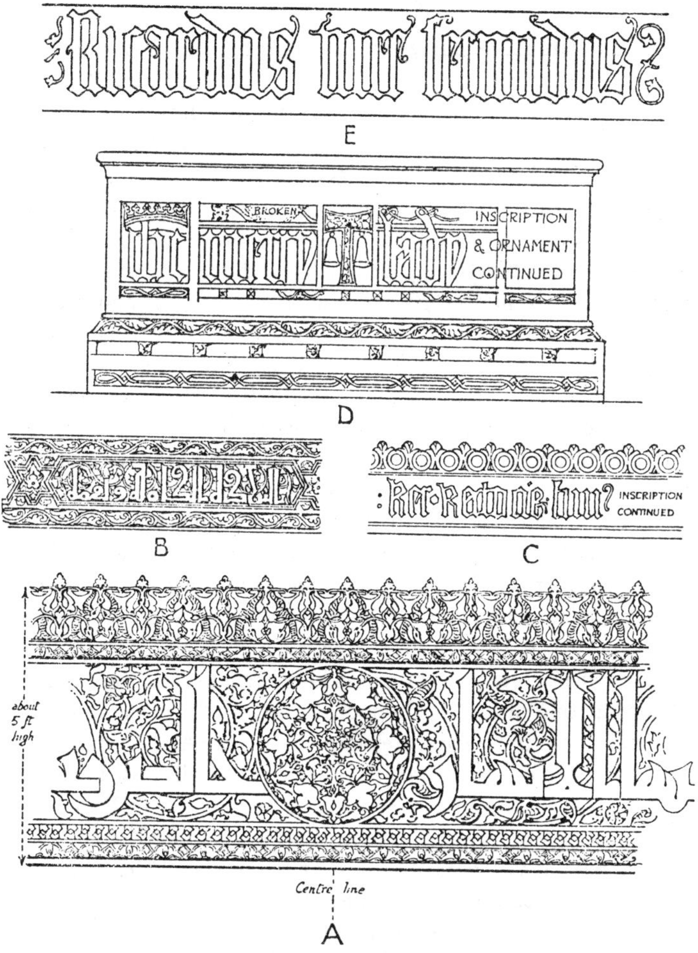

FIG. 85. PARALLEL OF KUFIC AND GOTHIC INSCRIPTIONS

A. Mosque of Sultan Ḥasan, Cairo (1356–63); in stucco.
B. Arat Museum, Cairo (XIIth century).
C. South Acre Church, Norfolk (*c.* 1550).
D. Fishlake, Yorkshire, tomb (1505).
E. Tomb of Richard II, Westminster (1399).

which scholars increasingly tend to attribute the beginnings of our medieval vaulting-system), we may reasonably ascribe the invention of the pointed arch to Muslim buildings in Syria and elsewhere. The ogee arch almost certainly, and the 'Tudor' arch possibly, have a similar origin. The use of cusps and of cusped or multifoil arches comes from the same source, as probably does the tracery-patterning of surfaces, and perhaps even the use of bar-tracery in windows. Plate-tracery may be derived from the pierced geometrical lattices in stone and stucco of the early mosques, or it may have originated still farther back in pre-Islamic Syrian or Mesopotamian buildings. The invention of stained glass is sometimes attributed to the East, but that attribution has not yet been proved. The use of engaged shafts at the angles of piers, so important in the history of Gothic vaulting, is a Saracen innovation of the eighth or ninth century. Ornamental and pierced battlements came from Mesopotamia to Cairo and were thence transmitted to Italy, afterwards becoming a feature of Gothic architecture. The carved inscriptions used decoratively in late Gothic work were anticipated in the ninth century at Ibn-Ṭūlūn's mosque at Cairo, but inscriptions in Kufic characters penetrated far into France during the Muslim occupation of her southern provinces,[1] and rare examples of ornament even in England are believed to show Arabic influence (Fig. 85). Striped façades may have come from Cairo, also possibly the design of Renaissance *campanili* and Renaissance shell-niches. The Arab *mashrabiyyah* or lattice of woodwork, used to conceal the women's apartments of a house or as a screen in the mosque, was copied in English metal grilles. The decoration of surfaces

[1] e.g. the carved wooden doors by the Christian master-carver Gaufredus in a chapel of the under-porch of the Cathedral of Le Puy, and another carved door in the church of La Voute Chilhac. Bands of ornament on the retable of Westminster Abbey and on certain early stained-glass windows are attributed by Prof. Lethaby to a similar origin. See A. H. Christie, 'The Development of Ornament from Arabic Script' in the *Burlington Magazine*, vols. xl–xli, 1922.

in low relief, by means of 'arabesques' or diaper patterns, and the use of geometrical patterns in decoration, is certainly a part of our debt to the Muslim peoples, who were also the source or channel of much of our knowledge of geometry.

All these are specific points, but the close contact of East and West during the Crusades and (more amicably) during the later Middle Ages must have contributed other influences on architecture which have escaped notice in this cursory sketch. In Spain the Moorish tradition in design persisted right into the late Renaissance period and helps to account for many of the complexities and peculiarities of Spanish Gothic architecture. Lastly, it may be observed that the development of Muslim building still proceeds in some of the remoter countries where it has flourished for more than a thousand years.

MARTIN S. BRIGGS.

BIBLIOGRAPHY

M. S. BRIGGS, *Muhammadan Architecture in Egypt and Palestine.* (Oxford, 1924.)

E. DIEZ, *Die Kunst der islamischen Völker.* (Berlin, 1915.)

J. FRANZ, *Die Baukunst des Islam.* (Darmstadt, 1887.)

A. GAYET, *L'art arabe.* (Paris, 1893.)

RICHMOND, E. T., *Moslem Architecture, 623–1516: some causes and consequences.* Royal Asiatic Society. (London, 1926.)

G. T. RIVOIRA, *Moslem Architecture: its origin and development.* (Oxford, 1918.)

H. SALADIN, *Manuel d'art musulman: tome I, Architecture.* (Paris, 1907.)

LITERATURE

THE literature of the Muslim Orient seems so remote from us that probably not one reader in a thousand has ever connected it in his mind with our own. The student of literary history, on the other hand, who knows how much in European literature has at different times been claimed, and how little has ever been proved, to be of oriental origin, may well be inclined to regard the whole subject with tolerant scepticism. There are certain facts, of course, which no one disputes. The oriental apologue and other works of its class enjoyed wide popularity in the Middle Ages. The first book printed in England, *The Dictes and Sayings of the Philosophers*, was a translation from a French version of a Latin recast of an Arabic work of this type. In the eighteenth century, again, the *Arabian Nights* ran through at least thirty editions in English and French, and has since been published more than three hundred times in all the languages of western Europe. Omar Khayyam is a name more familiar in England and America than in Persia. But are these merely isolated intrusions from the East, or do they illustrate a general tendency, and if so, how did such tendencies arise and what influence did they exert on the general course of literature? Unfortunately few of these questions may be answered with any finality, and little more can be attempted here than to suggest, on such evidence as is available, the lines along which an answer may be sought.

There is no more delicate problem than to assess the factors which determine the nature and degree of influence exerted by one literature upon another. The existence of a prolonged and close historical contact is clearly not necessary, though such contacts do invariably leave their mark on the literature of one or both of the peoples concerned. Nor does it seem to matter whether their historical relations are in the main friendly or hostile; the history of all the literatures of Europe serves to prove that literary fashions and movements do not stop at military frontiers. More essential than historical contact, and more difficult to prove by ordinary historical methods, is the fact of intercommunication. Whether it be personal or bilateral, or, as more frequently happens, scholastic and unilateral, it is only by literary analysis in the last resort that its existence can be affirmed or denied.

The most important factor is the most elusive of all. Before any kind of transference is possible there must be a condition of receptivity on one or both sides—a willingness to take what the other has to give, an implied recognition of its superiority in one or another field. It requires no close investigation to show that European receptivity of Arabic or Persian literary modes has been strictly limited both in time and in scope. There can be no comparison between the steady permeation of Western literature by Latin and, since the Renaissance, by Greek influences, and its fitful and half-concealed adaptation of elements of Eastern literature. There has scarcely been anything approaching a transference of any oriental literary art as a whole into European literature, but single elements of technique and occasionally certain established literary motives have been successfully transplanted. Why these should have been selected and the others left is a problem largely of national or popular psychology. It may be remarked, however, that oriental literature has exerted an influence less through its differences from that of Europe than through its similarities. The literary taste of Europe consistently rejected the strikingly unfamiliar features of Eastern literature, and was attracted instead to those elements of which the germ already existed, or had begun to develop in a tentative way, in European thought and letters. In such cases the oriental parallels served as a key to the door at which the West was knocking, or by their colour and brilliance of technique acquired such popular favour that they illuminated the lines along which the European movement should proceed. This is not to imply that they set a standard or served as models to be slavishly imitated; on the contrary, the branch of letters to which their impulse had been applied afterwards developed or expanded along its own peculiar lines, without reference to the East, and often in complete ignorance of its oriental forerunners.

Any attempt to draw an analogy between the influences exerted by oriental and classical literature respectively overlooks the difference between them, a difference not merely of degree, but of kind. The literature of Arabia and Persia is essentially 'romantic'. The student brought up to Greek ideals of literary excellence will find in it few of those qualities which constitute the perennial fascination of Greek literature. There is as full, or fuller, mastery of form, but it is rigid where Greek is various, and extravagant where Greek is severe. The classics achieve greatness by restraint and simplicity, the oriental weaves a laborious fabric of precious and obscure language, decorated with imagery often far-fetched and fantastic. The Greek appeals through beauty to the intellect, the Arab or Persian through richness of colour to the senses and the imagination. The assertion that Greek literature is creative, oriental literature fundamentally imitative and poor in intellectual qualities, though not without an element of truth, is an overbearing and extravagant generalization. Where the Muslim writer excels is in clothing the essential realism of his thought with the language of romance. But it would be false to conclude from this that there is an essential antithesis between the oriental spirit and the spirit of Europe. The antithesis exists, but it is between the oriental spirit and the classical spirit. Classicism in European literature has always been imposed from above; the literature of the people—especially in the north and west—shows closer kinship with the spirit of oriental literature. Their mutual feeling of remoteness is due to their isolation and ignorance; whenever a channel has been opened between them, the flow of oriental influence has generally brought such an access of strength to the popular currents in European literature as to enable them to challenge more or less successfully the classical supremacy.

The very fact of the popular appeal and transmission of oriental elements in the Middle Ages has still further obscured the process, rendering it more complicated in its effect and often difficult to prove by ordinary methods of historical criticism, the more so that most of the popular literature on both sides has perished. Even yet our literary histories show traces of the contemptuous aloofness which both Arabic writers and European scholars generally adopted towards the songs and tales of the people. There is every reason to believe that the modern study of folk-literature will throw fuller light on the diffusion throughout western Europe of both materials and technique derived immediately from the East. It is possible that this influence was at work already in the eighth century,[1] but it is principally with the development of the vernacular literatures that the question of oriental contacts arises.

The very first problem is perhaps the most difficult, and certainly the most disputed. A new type of poetry, with a new theme, a new social psychology, and a new technique suddenly comes into existence in southern France at the end of the eleventh century. There is little in the earlier literature of France which points in the direction of this development; on the other hand, the new poetry bears some strong resemblances to a certain type of contemporary poetry in Arabic Spain. What could be more natural than to suppose that the first Provençal poets were influenced by Arabic models? For several centuries this view met with almost unquestioned acceptance. It was never more confidently or sweepingly asserted than by Giam-

[1] See in Professor Leo Wiener's ingenious arguments for Gothic mediation of Arabic influences (*Contributions towards a History of Arabico-Gothic Culture*, vol. i. New York, 1917), more especially the chapter on Virgilius Maro the grammarian.

meria Barbieri in the full tide of the classical revival.[1] On the revival of medieval studies at the end of the eighteenth century, when public imagination was still obsessed with oriental romance, the general opinion, led by Sismondi and Fauriel, maintained the close association of Provençal with Arabic poetry. It was only in mid-nineteenth century that there appeared a revulsion, among both orientalists and students of Romance philology. The critics demanded documentary evidence of contacts between Provence and Andalusia, and failing to find them swung to the other extreme. If one may without malice attribute some share in the reaction to the overheated nationalism which animated all the western nations, it must be conceded that no self-respecting Romance scholar was likely to defend the theory of Arabic influences in the face of the contemptuous pronouncement of the famous Orientalist Dozy: 'Nous considérons cette question comme tout à fait oiseuse; nous voudrions ne plus la voir débattue, quoique nous soyons convaincu qu'elle le sera pendant longtemps encore. A chacun son cheval de bataille!'[2] On this ground the prevailing opinion appears to have taken its stand; Monsieur Anglade, for instance, is categorical: 'Ainsi fond et forme, les troubadours ont tout créé'.

Yet in spite of the assurance with which both positive and negative pronouncements have been made, both rest in fact upon little more than guesswork. Of systematic research into the problem from the orientalist side there has until recently been little or none, but the new evidence now coming to light goes far to remove all doubts that something at least of the poetic achievement of the south did in fact influence the earliest Provençal poets.[3]

[1] *Dell' Origine della Poesia Rimata* (published by Tiraboschi, Modena, 1790).

[2] *Recherches sur l'histoire . . . de l'Espagne*, 3rd ed. (1881). vol. ii. Appendix lxiv, note 2.

[3] It need hardly be said that in what follows there is no intention of denying

The novelty of Provençal poetry lies not in the theme itself, but in the conventional treatment of the theme. This palpitating love, expressed with such a wealth of fantastic imagery and literary refinement, is not the love expressed in the simple and passionate songs of the people. It is a sentimental doctrine, a romantic cult, a pathological condition which can be artificially stimulated, which finds its ideal not in the maiden but in the wife, from whose worship and service derives an ethical force by which the poet's life is enriched and ennobled. Whence came this art of love, this cult of the *dame*? Not from the manners of the time, as they are reflected in the literature of the people, whether Teutonic or Romance. 'Women', wrote Brunetière, 'in the bourgeois life of the Middle Ages seem to have bowed the head as low as in any age and in any place on earth beneath the law of force and brutality.' Nor was it by any means implicit in the new ideals of chivalry, which were beginning to inspire the upper classes. Such artificial sentimentality has nothing in common with its warrior creed. The feminine ideal of the new cult is flatly opposed to the Church's ideal of virginity. Had it arisen out of the natural relations between the professional poet and his patroness, its tone had been humbler. Greek and Latin literature, whether of the Golden or of the Silver Ages, offers little which could serve as its psychological basis. Yet it obviously depends upon an established literary tradition, and a possible source for that literary tradition may at least be looked for in the poetry of Arabic Spain.[1]

By the eleventh century Arabic poetry could look back on a long perspective of growth and development. But far as it might go there was never a time when love was not one of its mainsprings. In the old art-poetry of the desert, with its con-

the influence of other cultural sources, Latin, Celtic, &c., or of ruling out a certain measure of indigenous development.

[1] See for a discussion of this subject K. Burdach, 'Über den Ursprung der mittelälterlichen Minnesangs', in *S. B. preuss. Akad. Wiss.*, 1918.

ventional pictures expressed in polished language, elaborate similes, complex metres, and faultless rhymes (for Arabic was the first of the western languages to insist on perfect rhyme as an essential element in its poetry), every ode must open with a lament for the parting from some beloved, whose memory is evoked by revisiting a deserted camping-ground. As poetry migrated to the town, the love motive asserted itself more strongly, and a new delicacy replaced the frank hedonism of the desert. The ode gave place to the short lyric, in which the poet expressed his own personality and emotions. For a few decades Arabian poetry enjoyed a new spring, free, laughter-loving, true to life, before the lyric in its turn became stylized and conventional. Among the court poets, on the one hand, it gave rise to the sentimental lyric and delicate trifle, in which sensuous music combined with literary artifice to replace the warmth of genuine emotion. Among the people it was pressed into the service of a new art, the romance of the love-crazed swain whose life is consumed in pure devotion to an unattainable and idealized mistress. Among the mystics, again, the elements of idealism in these portrayals of an exalted and spiritual love were seized upon to serve as an allegory of the soul's unceasing devotion to the beloved. The bold and sensuous imagery of earthly love dominates the mystical poetry alike of Arab and Persian. Turgid, ecstatic, and expressed with traditional Arab fantasy by some Arab poets, subtilized and refined in others by metaphysical speculations, amongst the Persians it takes on a new sweetness and simplicity, graced with the rich imagery which springs naturally from the Persian imagination. Each of these types of love-lyric was destined to play a part in the history of European literature.

The most noteworthy feature of this new lyrical poetry was the emergence of a definite literary scheme of platonic love, combined with a social and ethical theory of love which was the distinctive contribution of Arabia. Already by the end of the eighth century some of the poets at the court at Baghdād were devoting their muse exclusively to this art of love. Less than a century later a boy barely in his teens, the son and successor of the founder of the most austere religious school in Islam, codified the scheme in a work of singular charm. In the *Book of Venus* Ibn Dāwud arranged, classified, and illustrated in verse all the aspects of love, its nature, laws, forms of expression and effects, in the spirit of the ideal put by Islamic tradition into the mouth of the Prophet: 'Whoso loves and conceals his love, remains chaste and dies, that one is a martyr.'

The unity of culture in the Muslim world ensured the cultivation of these poetic arts in Spain also. But here they developed farther on independent lines, through the assimilation and coalition of Spanish and Arabic elements in the population, and under the stimulus of the constant struggle with the Christian powers of the North. In no period of Arabic literature was there more widely diffused among all classes the spirit of poetry, the receptivity of mind and heart to impressions of beauty and the power of clothing these impressions in language both emotional and exquisite. Of these countless poets, named and nameless, the lyrics of the cavalier Sa'īd ibn Jūdī quoted by Dozy[1] may serve as examples. Here too the ideal of platonic love found universal acceptance. The name of Ibn Ḥazm is proverbial in Islam for religious puritanism and biting controversy, and honoured in the West as that of the founder of the science of comparative religion. Yet this man wrote and illustrated with his own verse a treatise on love which rivals and perhaps surpasses the *Book of Venus*.[2] He accepts the Platonic theory of love as the means whereby the severed portions of one sublime essence attain to earthly union, and in this spirit of purest

[1] *Histoire des Musulmans de l'Espagne*, ii. 227 ff. (English trans. by G. Stokes, *Spanish Islam*, pp. 332–5.)

[2] Ibn Ḥazm (*d.* 1064), *Ṭawq al-Ḥamāma* (*Le Collier de la Colombe*), edited with an introduction by Pétrof, Leiden, 1914.

romanticism unfolds an anatomy of love which is in many respects that of the troubadours of the next century, but to whose glowing altitudes they seldom attained.

Though so much of Spanish-Arabic poetry was natural and spontaneous, what has come down to us is mostly the carefully polished work of the court poets and poetesses, the aristocracy of their craft, with whom even princes and ministers did not disdain to compete, nay, who were themselves princes and ministers. In this courtly flower of Spanish-Arabic culture a new poetic technique was gradually built up. Alongside the epigram and the monoryhmed piece, with its verses of equal length and caesura, the Andalusian love-lyric began to show a preference for new stanza forms, with elaborate internal rhymes and complex metrical schemes. Though these metres are still syllabic it seems but a step to the poetry of the troubadours. That too was essentially art-poetry, the production of courtiers and court-poets, with artificial conventions and complex stanzas. There remains one difficulty. None of the early troubadours knew Arabic; who were the middlemen who transmitted the art from Andalusia to Provence?

It must be frankly conceded that a complete solution of this problem cannot yet be given, though much water has flowed under the bridge since Dozy's time. It is now proved beyond all question[1] that not only were the 'Moors' of Andalusia overwhelmingly Spanish in blood, but that all, from highest to lowest, understood and spoke Romance familiarly and habitually. These Spanish Muslims, while they absorbed Arabic culture, also contributed to it, and to their collaboration Spanish-Arabic culture owed many of its distinctive excellences. The Christians of Andalusia, who had become half-Arabicized (as is implied by their name of *Mozárabes*) and were often conversant with Arabic literature, in their turn communicated many seeds

[1] By Don Julian Ribera, *Disertaciones y Opusculos* (Madrid, 1928), i. 12–35, 109–12.

of Islamic culture to the northern kingdoms. Some such process of interaction underlies the history of Andalusian and of much Spanish poetry. The Spanish genius played a large part in the development of strophic measures, but in return the refinements of technique imposed by Arabic laws of forms and metre upon the strophe in its literary form (the *muwashshaḥ*) were reproduced in the popular bilingual ballad (the *zajal*), and thence found their way into purely romance poetry. The identity of the popular *villancico* with the *zajal* is scarcely open to question, and there is no reason to assume that such interaction was limited to technique or only to one kind of poetry, however few the proved Arabic elements in the *Romancero* generally may be. The *Crónica general* supplies an analogous example in Spanish prose literature of the combination of both Arabic and Spanish tradition.[1]

The medium of transmission was thus the popular *zajal* and its romance equivalent, the *villancico*. Fortunately one precious fragment of this popular literature has escaped destruction. This is a collection of some 150 pieces written in the vulgar mixed dialect in the early part of the twelfth century by the Andalusian poet Ibn Quzmān, who, though himself contemporary with the early troubadours, was by his own confession following an established tradition in Andalusia. The technique of his poetry is Arabic in its finish and rhymes, but already the prosodic revolution is complete—the metres are accentual, not syllabic. His stanzas are skilfully constructed with a view to the needs of choral singing, since most of his poems are (as Ribera has shown) dramatic episodes intended for performance by street minstrels. A comparison of these stanzas with the metrical systems of the first Provençal poets reveals some remarkable analogies. The poems of William of Poitiers are written in metres sometimes identical with those of Ibn Quzmān, some-

[1] See Fitzmaurice-Kelly, *A New History of Spanish Literature*, 1926, p. 24; R. Menéndez Pidal, *El Romancero*, p. 58.

times with slight variations which appear to be adaptations to monody of a scheme originally devised for choral singing. Moreover, the very licence and caprice of the Provençal poets shows that they were using metres which had no established traditions or *raison d'être* amongst them, whereas Andalusian choral poetry was kept by its musical and rhythmical necessities so true to type, that its influence can still be distinguished from that of Provençal poetry in the poems of Alfonso the Wise and later Spanish poets.[1]

A final point still remains to be dealt with. Ibn Quzmān's poems by no means reflect either the elevated sentiments of the court poetry of Andalusia or the honest romance of popular ballads. Although some of William of Poitiers's productions are not very far removed from the same gutter morality, there is a world of contrast between the tone of this Andalusian popular poetry and the conventional idealism of Provençal court-poetry. But Ibn Quzmān represents a startling degeneration in Spanish-Arabic society, and it is more than probable—judging from casual references in the Arabic writers to popular versions of famous poems—that in other popular productions (especially in the eleventh century, when the cultur · of Andalusia was at its most brilliant) the ideals of the court-poetry were more faithfully reflected.

From this brief review of the evidence it seems clear that, in view of the number and character of the coincidences between the court-poetry of Andalusia and the poetry of Provence, the theory of transmission cannot be simply waved aside. There are still many points which need to be cleared up, and there are other questions also, that of the musical accompaniment of Andalusian and Provençal poetry, for example,[2] which may throw

[1] Ribera, op. cit., i. 35–92.

[2] See Ribera, *Historia de la música árabe medieval*, 1927, and H. G. Farmer, *Historical Facts for the Arabian Musical Influence*, 1930. It may be suggested also, in the modest obscurity of a foot-note, that the technical terms

much light on the problem. But for the present the claim that Arabic poetry contributed in some measure to the rise of the new poetry of Europe appears to be justified, if we cannot yet go all the way with Professor Mackail in asserting that 'As Europe owes its religion to Judaea, so it owes its romance to Arabia'.[1]

The second area from which Arabic influences were transmitted to Europe was the Norman kingdom of Sicily, whose traditions were continued more especially by the Emperor Frederick II. That Arabic poetry was cultivated at the court of the Norman kings admits of no doubt But it was only under Frederick that the Sicilian school arose (unless all earlier works have perished), and at Frederick's court, as at that of Alfonso the Wise of Castille, though we hear much of translations of Arabic books and much about Muslim philosophy, and much too about Provençal and native troubadours, there is no definite mention of Arabic poets or poetry. On the other hand, Saracen ballerinas and singing-girls were certainly to be found in Frederick's suite. The cautious historian of medieval Sicily, while admitting that if we knew more of Sicilian-Arabic popular poetry we might possibly discover closer ties between it and the early Italian poetry in Sicily, goes no farther than to claim that

of Romance poetry might be re-studied from this point of view. Fauriel (iii. 326) has demonstrated the Arabic origin of *galaubia*, and Singer has referred to the *senhal*, the word *midons*, and *guardador* (= Arabic *raqīb*). F. W. Hasluck threw out a hint that *stanza* was suggested by *bayt* ('house', used in Arabic for a verse of poetry). The *tensio* resembles the Arabic *tanāzuʿ* in both function and name. Ribera (*Disertaciones, &c.* ii. 133–49) gives Arabo-Persian derivations for a number of other words, including *trobar*, which he derives from *ṭarab* = music, song. But even if *trobar* is to be connected with *trouver*, it is interesting to note that the Arabic *wajada* 'find' means also 'feel the pangs of love or sorrow'.

[1] *Lectures on Poetry* (1911), p. 97; cf. p. 125: 'To the kindred stocks of the Arabo-Syrian plateau—for of that single race and region Palestine is also a part—we owe largely or even mainly the vital forces which make the Middle Ages spiritually and imaginatively different from the world ruled over by Rome.'

the cultivation of poetry in the vulgar tongue was due to the example of the Arabic poets and the patronage they enjoyed from Muslim rulers.[1] Yet it is a significant fact that the metric of the early popular poetry of Italy, as represented by the canticles of Jacopone di Todi and the carnival songs, and with more elaboration in the *ballata*, is identical with that of the popular poetry of Andalusia.[2] Even Petrarch's violent nationalist outburst against the Arabs[3] proves at least, if it proves anything, that the more popular kind of Arabic poetry was still known in Italy in his day.

Whatever place may be assigned to Arabic poetry in stimulating the poetic genius of the Romance peoples, the debt of medieval Europe to Arabic prose literature is hardly open to question, though still far from explored in detail. The vogue of Arabic philosophical and scientific works brought with it an interest in other sides of Arabic literature, more especially in the apologues, fables, and tales, which constitute the bulk of Arabic belles-lettres. Already before this, however, oral transmission had broadcast elements of Arabic and other oriental story over a wide area. Until recently an oriental origin was claimed and accepted for the popular tales which flourished in Europe, in the various forms of *fabliaux*, *contes*, *exemples*, &c., during the thirteenth century, and which unquestionably present analogies with oriental and Indian tales. Although the exhaustive researches of Professor Bédier have now seriously weakened the arguments in support of this view,[4] there are still

[1] M. Amari, *Storia dei Musulmani di Sicilia*, 1868–72, iii. 738, 889. See also G. Cesareo, *Le Origini della Poesia lirica e la Poesia Siciliana sotto gli Suevi*, 1924, pp. 101, 107.

[2] See J. M. Millás, *Influencia de la poesía popular hispano-musulmana en la poesía italiana*, Revista de Archivos, &c., 1920, 1921. It is worth noting also that the Sicilian Richard of San Germano shows a characteristic feature of Arabic historical composition in the insertion of poems and verses into his chronicle.

[3] *Epist. Sen.* xii. 2.

[4] J. Bédier, *Les Fabliaux*, 5th ed., 1925.

large sections of popular literature which contain at least episodes from eastern story. Close analogies have been pointed out between Arabic romances and the story of Isolde Blanchemain, the German *Rolandslied*, and other northern tales. The author of one version of the Grail-saga even mentions an Arabic book as his source. The Arabic inspiration demonstrated for the Old French romance of *Floire et Blanchefleur* is the more significant because of its relationship with the lovely *Aucassin et Nicolette*, which itself bears unmistakable witness to its Spanish-Arabic provenance in the Arabic name of the hero (al-Qāsim) and in several details of the setting.[1] Nor does it in any way rob the French jongleur of the credit due to the creator of a masterpiece of beauty and delicacy to suggest that the *chante-fable*, unique in European literature, is a favourite form of popular Arabic romance.

Arabic travel-literature and cosmography have also left their traces in western literature, as was only to be expected when to travel implied for Europe mainly going on pilgrimage to the Holy Land. It was almost inevitable with oral transmission that the fabulous and marvellous elements should have spread farthest. They supplied embroideries for Marco Polo and 'Sir John Mandeville' amongst others, but their range was not limited to the Latin countries of the West. They penetrated even to Ireland and Scandinavia—possibly by way of the Caspian-Baltic trade-route—and reappear in such monastic tales as the *Legend of St. Brendan*. Merchants and jongleurs brought them back from the crusading states in Syria and the ports of the Levant. It was from oral sources, in all probability, that Boccaccio derived the oriental tales which he inserted in the *Decamerone*. Chaucer's *Squieres Tale* is an 'Arabian Nights'

[1] See for these generally S. Singer, 'Arabische und europaische Poesie im Mittelalter', in *Abh. Preuss. Akad. Wissenschaften*, 1918, and *Z. fur deut. Philologie*, lii (1927), 77–92; and for *Aucassin* the edition of F. W. Bourdillon (Manchester, 1919), xiv–xv.

story, which was probably brought to Europe by Italian merchants from the Black Sea, since the scene is laid at the court of the Mongol Khan on the Volga,

At Sarray in the land of Tartarye.

The oral dissemination of Arabic tales was supplemented in the fourteenth century by numerous translations of Arabic collections of stories made for the entertainment of the new reading classes. These oriental tales were preferred to the popular medieval stock, not only because of their variety and polished literary presentation, but above all because they displayed a richer imagination and a more edifying aim. Here the Christian and Islamic Middle Ages met on common ground, both in literary preferences and literary methods. The people told stories because they liked them, and in general their stories were intended to serve no moral purpose. But the story as a literary art takes its place in a moral framework. The general purpose of the writer is to define the art of government, or the duty of good living, or the profession of the virtues. Of such works there was an immense number in Arabic, drawn partly from the stores of old Indian fable, partly from other repertories in the East (including no doubt much of Greek origin), and partly from historical and legendary episodes in eastern history. There was no conception, of course, of literary proprietorship. Neither in Islam nor Christendom did either author or reader lay any weight on originality of material or power of psychological invention. The art of the moralizer (leaving aside for the present the question of literary style) lay in his faculty of selection and combination, in exhibiting familiar materials in a new setting. Thus the Arabic apologues came to play a great part in medieval and later European literature, passing from land to land, and inspiring as well as entering into much of the original composition of the time.

Of the many works of this type which were translated from

Arabic, chiefly by Jews, three may be selected as typical of the rest. The Arabic *Book of Sindbād* (*not* the Sailor), which was derived from a Sanskrit original, and is now, like the original itself, lost, was the medieval source of a number of versions, amongst others of a Syriac version (*Sindbān*), from which the medieval Greek *Syntipas* was derived, a Hebrew version (*Sindabār*), and several Persian versions, some of which, retranslated into Arabic and Turkish, were destined to reach Europe in the eighteenth century. The Hebrew *Sindabār* is the probable original on the one hand of the thirteenth-century Spanish *Libro de los Engannos*, on the other of the fourteenth-century Latin *Historia Septem Sapientium*, which was the source of several verse romances, amongst them the English *Seven Sages of Rome*.

The second work was a collection of sayings of the ancient philosophers, compiled in Egypt in the eleventh century by a certain Mubashshir ibn Fātik. This was translated into Spanish under the title of *Bocados de oro*, while the other western versions were based on a Latin translation (*Liber philosophorum moralium*), from which Guillaume de Tignonville made his version *Les ditz moraux des philosophes*, translated into English by Earl Rivers as *The Dictes and Sayings of the Philosophers*, and already noted as the first English book printed by Caxton.

The influence of these and similar works is most obvious in Spanish literature, especially in the earlier period. From them, for example, the Infante Don John Manuel (who was himself familiar with Arabic) drew the inspiration for *El Conde Lucanor*, in which even the prologue is modelled on the introductions with which all Arabic works are furnished.[1] There are indeed few early prose writings in Spanish which did not draw on materials translated from Arabic. But it has frequently been

[1] It cannot be proved, however, that Don John borrowed directly from Arabic sources (cf. G. Moldenhauer, *Die Legende von Barlaam und Josaphat*, 1929, 90–4).

remarked that the Arabic literary tradition was not directly disseminated from Spain; medieval Europe stood here, as in many other matters, on the shoulders of Italy and southern France, and only in much later days were such Arabic influences as had entered into Spanish literature transmitted to France and England.

The same comparative isolation of Spain is seen in the case of the third and still more famous collection, the animal fables of Sanskrit origin, which were translated into Arabic in the eighth century under the title of *Kalīla and Dimna*. This was retranslated into Spanish for Alfonso the Wise (1252–84), but the rest of Europe knew it only in a Latin translation, entitled *Directorium humanae vitae*, made in the same century by John of Capua, a converted Jew. This version was drawn upon for other Latin works, such as the *Gesta Romanorum*, and it was not until 1552 that it was first translated into the vernacular by Doni. The subsequent fortunes of this oriental tale show that even in the full flood of the classical revival oriental literature still had power to attract. Thomas North's *Moral Philosophy of Doni* (1570) was but the first of many English versions. The Latin and vernacular versions continued to be used for many decades by writers of *novelli* and even by dramatists (as, for example, by Massinger in the third act of *The Guardian*). Its subsequent revival, as the *Fables of Pilpay*, in the French translation (1644) of the late Persian version known as *The Lights of Canopus*, is of special interest, as the first direct contact of Persian literature with western Europe, and one of the sources of La Fontaine.

Yet another branch of Arabic belles-lettres may have contributed to medieval literature. This was the *maqāmāt*, the most elaborate of all Arabic compositions. Though literary convention demanded that *maqāmāt* should be written in rhymed prose and adorned with all manner of philological curiosities, the plan or plot of these works was of the simplest. They consist of a number of disconnected episodes, the hero of which is always a chevalier d'industrie, a vagabond with a large repertoire of more or less dishonest tricks for gaining a livelihood, but who is gifted with a fine literary wit with which he often expresses the loftiest moral sentiments. To this plan the Spanish picaresque novels offer certain analogies. It may be added that the *maqāmāt* found imitators among the Spanish Jews, and that *El Cavallero Cifar*, besides showing other oriental affinities, contains in at least one of the adventures of the Ribaldo—the first Spanish *pícaro*—an episode from the purely oriental cycle which is associated in the Arabic version with the character of *Juḥā*.[1] It is possible also that analogies may be found between episodes in the *maqāmāt* and early Italian tales of the realist or picaresque type, but the whole subject remains as yet unexplored.

This infiltration of Arabic literary themes into medieval Europe forms in reality one aspect of a general intellectual movement. Latin civilization was outgrowing the narrow ecclesiastical disciplines of the Dark Ages; men were becoming curious about matters which they had hitherto accepted on authority. Unable to find satisfaction in the narrowness, poverty, and lack of originality of such Latin literature as they possessed, they were forced to look elsewhere for what they desired. To the Islamic world they had hitherto conceded—and that grudgingly—only a military superiority; now they realized with shame that it was also their intellectual superior. With the flood-tide of Arabic science which followed this conviction there was borne a volume of prose literature, which entered more or less deeply into all the rising literatures of Europe, and prepared the way for the intellectual outburst of the Renaissance. Yet the most important Islamic contribution to the literature of the Middle Ages may have been rather the influence of Arabic culture and ideas on both poetry and prose, whether accompanied or not by material borrowings from Arabic sources. Though this subject strictly

[1] *Revue Hispanique*, x (1903), 91.

falls outside the scope of the present chapter, some mention must be made of the repeated suggestions of recent students, that elements of the Muslim cosmogony and legends of the ascent of Muḥammad (some of which may go back to older Persian legend) have entered into the *Divina Commedia* either direct or through earlier western legends, such as the *Legend of Tundal* and *St. Patrick's Purgatory*, as Arabic philosophical ideas and the imagery and eroticism of the Muslim mystics are certainly reflected not only in Dante's works, but also in the leading ideas of the other poets of the *dolce stil nuovo*.[1] The interest with which Arabic studies were pursued in Italy in Dante's time certainly renders the theory by no means improbable, though it cannot yet be held as proved, except on points of detail. But the thought is attractive, if only because the genius of Dante would tower all the higher could it be shown that he fused into one magnificent synthesis not only the great heritage of Christian and classical mysticism, but also the richest and most spiritual features of the religious experience of Islam.

Before leaving the Middle Ages we must return for a moment to Spain and take up again a point already touched on, the continued influence, namely, of Arabic oral tradition and Arabic culture in Andalusia, after the reconquest of the greater part of it by the Christians. This influence, though scarcely lending itself to dogmatic judgements, has none the less a perceptible bearing on Spanish, and, through Spanish, on European literature. Few would deny that something of the warmth and movement, the richer fantasy, which marks the literature of the south is due to the Arabic cultural environment of Andalusia during the early centuries and the impress which that culture left on the Andalusian. It is of course true that during the interval between the conquest of Seville and the fall of Granada the Andalusians were at one with their co-religionists of Castille in language, traditions, and literary style. But when, with the

[1] On this last point see H. J. Chaytor, *The Troubadours* (1912), 106.

weakening and downfall of the Moorish power, the chief cause of antagonism was removed, and friendly intercourse was restored between Moor and Christian, there was a remarkable literary revulsion. It seemed as if the Andalusians felt in the colder, sterner Castilian the lack of something that still touched a responsive chord in them, and turned back to the Moorish past to find it again. The influence of the Andalusian spirit is probably to be seen already in the polish and refinement which distinguish the *Amadis de Gaula* from other romances. It comes to full expression in the 'morisco' romance, reaching a climax in the *Historia del Abencerrage* (before 1550), and its continuation, the *Guerras Civiles* of Ginés Pérez de Hita. Whether or not these romances were based in part on Arabic originals is immaterial; the important fact is that they achieved a synthesis of Moorish and Spanish culture, which formed a turning-point in the history of modern European literature. It was the birthday of the modern novel. To this extent even Cervantes, whose *Don Quixote* is, in Prescott's phrase, totally Andalusian in wit, is indebted to Andalusian culture (though not, of course, through the medium of 'Cid Hamete Benengeli, Arabian historiographer'), and the same judgement may be applied to other names hardly less great in Spanish literature.

* * * * * *

The Renaissance, relegating the East to the background, erected a barrier and stemmed the tide of oriental influence. But the classical discipline could not last. The romantic spirit of Europe, the spirit which had expressed itself in Breton romances, in Teutonic folk-lore, in the English drama, stifled and repressed, sought an outlet. All its creations, pastoral romance, heroic romance, picaresque novel, failed one after the other. Perrault tapped a mighty source, but as yet the folk-tale was too weak to bear the weight of the assault. Then, in 1704, appeared Galland's translation of the *Arabian Nights*. Recent researches have shown that this translation was not an isolated event, but the culminating moment in a long process of artistic idealization, fed by the morisco romances, the beginnings of travel and colonization in the East, the descriptions of Indian and Persian life by Tavernier, Chardin, Bernier, and others, and the illusion of local colour created by the various eastern embassies which from time to time had dazzled Paris with their magnificence.[1] It was all doubtless very superficial, but during those years there was built up that 'romantic' image of the East, warm-coloured, exotic, and mysterious, which is still exploited in our own time. The success of the genuinely oriental *Arabian Nights* was immediate and complete. The imagination of the reading public was fired. Publishers competed for the privilege of ministering to the fashion. The *Arabian Nights* was followed by the *Persian Tales* ('Thousand and One Days'), the old *Book of Sindbād* came to life again as the *Turkish Tales*. When the supply of genuine material ran short, industrious writers set to work to supply the deficiency. Geullette filled the life of a generation with pseudo-translations, and the genius of Montesquieu created a new form of social criticism in the *Lettres persanes*.

In England the craze was hardly less. The *Arabian Nights*, the *Persian Tales*, the *Turkish Tales* were translated as soon as they appeared, and went through edition after edition. Numerous imitators learned from Geullette's example how to 'turn a Persian tale for half-a-crown'. It was a very strange Orient that was reflected in the 'Oriental' literature of the eighteenth century, an Orient which the romantic imagination of the time refashioned after its own ideas and peopled with grotesque figures clothed in the garb of caliphs, kadis, and jinns. So gross a perversion could not endure. The pseudo-oriental romance

[1] Pierre Martino: *L'Orient dans la Littérature française au XVII*^e^ *et au XVIII*^e^ *siècle*, 1906; see also M. P. Conant, *The Oriental Tale in England*, New York, 1908, and for the morisco romances M. A. Chaplyn, *Le Roman mauresque en France*, 1928.

wilted under the lash of Hamilton, Pope, and Goldsmith, but not before it had left its mark on literature. In England, fused with the kindred rhythms of the Old Testament, it produced *The Vision of Mirza* (the spark which first kindled the imagination of Robert Burns) and *Rasselas*. In France, reverting, by a strange coincidence, to the truly oriental form of apologue, it furnished Voltaire and the reformers with a setting for their political and social satires. And in both France and England it produced one remarkable book, which, by its fusion of 'Gothic romance' with oriental subjects and imagery, prefigured and influenced much of the imaginative work of the next half-century, Beckford's *Vathek*. More important, however, was its indirect influence, its share in predisposing public taste for the reversion to the non-classical and medieval which goes by the name of the Romantic movement.

But something more is needed to explain the success of the *Arabian Nights*. The cause is probably to be found in the crisis through which French and English literature was passing, owing to the expansion of the reading classes and the demand for a more popular type of literary production. Classicism, in England at least, had never been really popular, and the ponderous, slow-moving novels of the seventeenth century were not for the people. It was an age of experiment, when writers like Defoe, Steele, and Addison were feeling their way towards a new style. The *Arabian Nights*, essentially a production of the people, may have lacked all the finer elements of literary art, but it possessed in a superlative degree the one quality, hitherto overlooked by men of letters, but indispensable in a popular literature, the spirit of adventure. It is not over-rash to suggest that it supplied the clue for which the popular writers were searching, and that but for the *Nights* there would have been no *Robinson Crusoe*,[1] and perhaps no *Gulliver's Travels*.

[1] An original for *Robinson Crusoe* has sometimes been sought in the philosophic romance of Ibn Ṭufayl called *Ḥayy ibn Yaqẓān*, translated into Latin

The lengths to which the vogue for oriental tales was carried in the eighteenth century and the influence which they exerted are matters generally disregarded by our literary histories. The explanation of this neglect is doubtless to be sought in the poor literary quality of the direct imitations in both France and England, a fact which moved Brunetière to the criticism that contact with the Muslim Orient had enriched only a branch of letters which constituted a national disgrace. But there are other indications of the depth of the impress made by the oriental tale on the mind of the century. To Warton, writing his *History of English Poetry* in the seventeen-seventies, it seemed self-evident that the romantic movement in the Middle Ages was a purely Arabian product. Exaggerated out of all proportion though Warton's theory may be, its very existence and acceptance throws a strong light on the ideas with which his age was imbued. The same preoccupation can be seen in Southey's choice of subjects for his narrative poems *Thalaba* and *The Curse of Kehama*. To the modern critic these may well seem 'remotely and unpopularly conceived', but to a generation reared on *Maugraby the Magician* and other oriental fantasies they were no more remote and unpopular than are Ali Baba and Aladdin to the men and women of the twentieth century.

Above all the *Arabian Nights* remained. There was an element in them that never failed of appeal to the imagination. It was not only their rich colour and exotic setting—that element which has made the fortune of their imitators. For all their magic and mystery they stood on the solid ground of reality; though their characters might be standardized and undeveloped, their adventures were real adventures, told with an instinct for the dramatic. Beneath their fantasy and exotic appeal there was

by Pocock in 1671 under the title of *Philosophus Autodidactus*, of which Ockley issued an English version in 1708. The subject is now being more fully investigated by A. R. Pastór; see his work, *The Idea of Robinson Crusoe* (Part I, Watford, 1930).

a moral core, without which they could not have entered so deeply into the heart of Europe, nor have preserved for two centuries a place in the affections of both learned and simple. The real East became but the more vivid and its influence the more potent that it was freed from the cumbering extravagances that had hitherto obscured it.

It must not be forgotten that Europe was still profoundly ignorant of the true literature and thought of the East. A fresh page was turned when in 1774 William Jones issued, 'not as a philologist but a man of taste, not as an interpreter but a poet', his Latin *Commentaries on Asiatic Poetry*. For the first time it was open to the cultured, classically-educated circles of western Europe to understand and appreciate the qualities of Arabic and Persian poetry. But the weight of tradition lay heavy on the literature of France and England, and it was left for the leaders of the new German movement to grasp their possibilities. They were free agents, the creators, not the servants, of public taste. Moreover the poetry of Persia had already left its mark on German literature. More than a century before, the translations of Saʿdī's *Gulistān* and *Bustān* made by the traveller and scholar Olearius had 'refreshed and supplied a salutary stimulus to the German literature of that time',[1] and the continued influence of Persian literature is seen, for example, in the *Yūsuf and Zalīkhā* story in Grimmelshausen's tale *Joseph*. On the other hand, the literature of the eighteenth century could not but reflect the current French 'orientalism'. Lessing followed Voltaire in giving an oriental setting to his didactic work, and such early productions of the Romantic school as Oehlenschläger's *Ali und Gulhyndi* are typically eighteenth-century fantasies, while his later play *Aladdin* (1808), in spite of its mixture of *Arabian Nights*, fairies, elves, and Indian apologues, already shows glimpses of that better apprehension of the East which was eventually to relegate all such things to pantomime.

[1] *Allgemeine deutsche Biographie*, vol. 24, p. 275. Olearius died in 1671.

For this real understanding Germany was indebted to a remarkable line of poet-scholars, who continued the work begun by Sir William Jones. Through Herder's influence the passion for study, which was characteristic of the German romantic movement, extended also to oriental literature and thought. Schlegel and Hammer in the first generation, and Rückert in the second, revealed to the poets and writers of the West new and almost unsuspected treasures. The literature of the East, Indian, Persian, and Arabic, was thus able to enter into nineteenth-century German literature to a degree unparalleled in Europe since the literature of medieval Spain. The first and fairest flower in the western 'Gulistan' was Goethe's *West-östliche Divan*. His successors, who read and translated their oriental models for themselves, went farther. Like Rückert, they reproduced and imitated Persian ideas and images, if they did not, like Platen, go the length of using Persian metrical forms. Goethe, on the other hand, found in oriental poetry first of all a means of escape into the world of imagination from the brutal realities of the age. Mere imitation could not satisfy him; rather, by yoking the art and ideals of Persian poetry with those medieval and 'romantic' elements in the European tradition with which they were in closest harmony, he created a new idiom to express his own thought, and at the same time emphasized the cosmopolitanism which it was his aim to impress on German literature.[1]

For a time the Persian and Indian fashion held the field. Even Heine, though he did not spare his satire on it, could not keep the oriental note entirely out of his lyrics. But it failed, as it was bound to fail. It was a hothouse plant, and could not take root in European soil without hybridizing. There is much truth in the view that the more deeply impregnated the poet

[1] On the orientalist element in the German Romantic movement see A. J. F. Remy, Columbia Univ. Germanic Studies, vol. i. no. iv (New York, 1901).

with oriental thought, the less important was his work, considered as literature. The genius of Goethe instinctively rejected all the elements of Ḥāfiẓ which he found uncongenial, yet even among his works the *Divan* stands below the best. Only Bodenstedt, with his forged *Lieder des Mirza Schaffy*, was able to impress the imagination of the public. Nevertheless, if the oriental poetry of the German romantic movement cannot be given a high place as literature, nor be credited with achieving a fusion of the poetry of the East with modern European poetry, it made a valuable contribution to the ultimate heritage of Europe through its reproductions and translations, and opened a door never again closed.

The partial penetration of oriental currents into German literature might have raised, and did in fact raise,[1] expectations of an eastward movement on a much wider scale, but they were totally belied by the literature of England and France in the nineteenth century. For good or for evil, the mind of the West suddenly swung farther away from the East than ever. Distracted by its new philosophies, its new political ideas, its new inventions, its immense industrial development, it was in no mood to listen to the East, still less to seek patiently to understand its thought. Goethe's ideal of a *Weltliteratur*, broken on the wheel of nationalism, perished even in Germany. Yet the place occupied by the East, especially the Islamic East, in the literature of the nineteenth century and of our own times is not at all negligible. It seems a paradox that in an age when the East has become more closely linked to the West than ever in the past, and when it has exercised an unparalleled power of attraction over the imagination of the western peoples, the claims of oriental literature have been entirely ignored. The

[1] Cf. the passage from Schopenhauer quoted by Brunetière (*Études*, viii. 211): 'Le XIXe siècle ne devait guère moins un jour à la connaissance du vieux monde oriental que le XVIe siècle à la découverte ou à la révélation de l'antiquité gréco-romaine.'

explanation must be sought, at least in part, in the difference of quality between the Romantic movement in France and England and the movement led by Herder.

In France the Romantic movement, less exuberant and less allied with scholarship than in Germany, more under the influence of Scott and Byron than of Goethe and Schiller, showed few traces of the new orientalism. Political preoccupations, and that quality in French literature for which provincialism is perhaps too strong a word, kept the poets and writers of France concentrated on things nearer home. It was not that the East was overlooked; on the contrary—'In the age of Louis XIV', wrote Victor Hugo, in his preface to *Les Orientales*, 'all the world was hellenist, now it is orientalist'. And he confessed to strong poetic sympathies for the oriental world. 'He seemed to see in it from afar the gleam of a rich poetic art. It is a spring from which he has long desired to quench his thirst. There indeed all is vast, rich, productive, as in the Middle Ages, that other ocean of poetry.' But in spite of this declaration it would be difficult to trace any substantial oriental influence in his verse, certainly not of those Persian poets who cast their spell over Goethe and the Germans. His sympathies were rather with the Arabic poets. 'From the Arabs to the Persians the transition is violent; it is like coming to a nation of women after a nation of men. . . . Slavish people, fawning poetry. The Persians are the Italians of Asia.' For him the Orient, the Orient of *Zim-Zizimi* as of *Les Orientales*, was still in essentials the glittering and barbaric Orient of the eighteenth-century tradition, the Orient personified by Gautier in the character of Fortunio, or a decorative Byronic Orient, not the contemplative and melodious home of poets and scholars. He used it for the artistic effect of its glowing colours, as Delacroix painted Algerian subjects. The same may be said of almost all the French romantics. Some, like Gerard de Nerval and Gautier the Elder, more under the influence of the German School, felt a real attachment to the East, but their orientalism is too often patently at second-hand. The things of the East, in Brunetière's phrase, while becoming familiar, did not become 'interior'.

English literature in the nineteenth century stood substantially on the same footing as that of France. The effect of the new orientalism was more marked, as might have been expected, but the East continued to serve as little more than decorative background, enriched by the romantic insistence on 'local colour', a legacy of Scott and the German movement. It was Byron who made this other Orient popular, and its classic example is Moore's *Lalla Rookh*. The influence of the *Arabian Nights* is reduced to a few elements of the frame-story, and the poetical episodes are based on the works of Jones, d'Herbelot, and other orientalists. In order to saturate his imagination with eastern ideas and imagery, Moore secluded himself for two years, but despite his own satisfaction with the result,[1] his poem merely transports the accents of Scott from his native land to India. For the rest, the place of orientalism in the greater poets is negligible; *Sohrab and Rustum*, *Ferishtah's Fancies*, and the like, have little of the East in them but the name. In prose literature Shagpat stands alone in dependence upon Arabian models.

The solution of the paradox, then, is that, where the Muslim East was concerned, preoccupation with the romantic scene of their own imagining distracted the poets and writers of England and France from the reality behind the mask which served them so well. The East was treated as a mere colour-scheme, and its claim to have contributed to the spiritual heritage of mankind impatiently waved aside. Long ago Sir William Jones observed that no appreciation of Asiatic poetry was possible without a scholarly knowledge of the peoples and natural history of Asia.

[1] 'Although I have never been in the East myself, yet every one who *has* been there declares that nothing can be more perfect than my representations of it, its people, and life, in "Lalla Rookh".'

So long as this indispensable knowledge was confined to a few savants and civil servants, any productive influence of oriental literature and thought upon Europe was out of the question. Those who understood the East best, and who portrayed it, like Gobineau and Morier, with a certain ironic sympathy, doubtless owed something to oriental literature as well as to oriental life, but it is a debt not easily estimated.

Yet even the nineteenth century was not to be left without a witness to the essential kinship of East and West. Just as an Englishman created in *Vathek* the synthesis of the oriental and the Gothic tale, so now another Englishman was to demonstrate the power of an eastern poet to penetrate to the heart of western poetry. Fitzgerald's *Omar Khayyam* is at once truly Persian and truly English, not a translation, but a re-creation. If the mood expressed in the famous quatrains is not of the most heroic or exalted, none the less they caught the exact tone of the age, and voiced it as perfectly as eight centuries earlier they had voiced the polished hedonism of the cultured society of Ispahan.

On looking back over the field of European literature, the influence of the literatures of the Muslim East seems at first confined to a narrow and unproductive strip. Only when it is realized that the East has acted like a leaven on the spirit is it seen to possess a far wider importance. At three different periods, if our view is correct, it has reacted on western literature with results identical in nature, though not in degree. On each occasion its function has been to liberate the imagination from a narrow and oppressive discipline, to make the first breach in the wall of convention. It is in its power of calling into action creative impulses hitherto dormant or impotent that eastern literature has laid the West under its debt. The movement once started has gathered momentum from its own internal resources, and such oriental elements as have been absorbed are so blended with native elements that in the finished development they are often difficult to recognize. In so far as the East has supplied models for European literature it has played a subordinate part. In the Middle Ages, when there was a substantial identity of intellectual method between the civilization of Islam and Christendom, imitation on the part of the latter may well have been fruitful; after the Renaissance it could produce at best only harmless curiosities. For the same reason the result on medieval thought of contact with oriental literature was immeasurably greater than the result of later contacts.

Following on these three moments of casual contact, the German romantics turned again to the East, and for the first time made it their conscious aim to open a way for the real heritage of oriental poetry to enter into the poetry of Europe. The nineteenth century, with its new sense of power and superiority, seemed to clang the gate decisively in the face of their design. To-day, on the other hand, there are signs of a change. Oriental literature has begun to be studied again for its own sake, and a new understanding of the East is being gained. As this knowledge spreads and the East recovers its rightful place in the life of humanity, oriental literature may once again perform its historic function, and assist us to liberate ourselves from the narrow and oppressive conceptions which would limit all that is significant in literature, thought, and history, to our own small segment of the globe.

H. A. R. Gibb.

MYSTICISM

Not long ago, as I was turning over the first few pages of Miss Underhill's *Mysticism*, my eye fell on two quotations, one from a medieval German mystic, the other from an English author whose death had just been announced; and it struck me that I could recall exact Muslim parallels to both. Eckhart's famous saying, 'the word *Sum* can be spoken by no creature, but by God only; for it becomes the creature to testify of itself *Non Sum*', reminded me that three and a half centuries earlier, at Baghdād, Abū Naṣr al-Sarrāj, commenting on a definition of mystical unity (*tawḥīd*), had written 'None saith "I" except God, since real personality belongs to God alone'. The remark of Edward Carpenter, 'this perception seems to be one in which all the senses unite into one sense', caused me to look up some verses (580 foll.) in the *Tā'iyya* of the Egyptian poet and saint, Ibnu 'l- Fāriḍ (*ob.* A.D. 1235), where he describes his mystical consciousness as an experience in which all the senses are unified and exercised simultaneously:

> My eye conversed whilst my tongue gazed; my ear spoke and my hand listened;
> And whilst my ear was an eye to behold everything visible, my eye was an ear listening to song.

This is a 'coincidence' that obviously has evidential value. Concerning the problems of mystical psychology and speculation the West can still learn something from Islam. How much it actually learned of these matters during the Middle Ages, when Muslim philosophy and science radiating from their centre in Spain spread light through Christian Europe, we have yet to discover in detail, but the amount was certainly considerable. It would indeed be strange if no influence from this source reached men like Thomas Aquinas, Eckhart, and Dante; for mysticism was the common ground where medieval Christianity and Islam touched each other most nearly. The fact is founded on history, as we shall see. It explains why the ideas, methods, and systems produced by mystics—Roman Catholic and Muslim—of that period seem to bear the stamp of one and the same spiritual genius. But while the Catholic Church has kept her tradition unbroken, in Islam, after the thirteenth century, the main current runs in the channels of a new religious philosophy which, in the eyes of the orthodox, includes everything except religion.

The end of the second century of the Hijra (A. D. 719–816) is approaching when we meet, in Mesopotamia, with the name *Ṣūfī* by which the Muslim mystics soon afterwards became generally known; its derivation from *ṣūf*, the garment of coarse undyed wool worn by Christian ascetics, is one of many signs pointing the same way. Difficult questions of origin cannot be discussed here, but I may state the position as it appears to me. Let us take first the view that the basis of Ṣūfism is essentially *Islamic*. The claim of the Ṣūfīs to have inherited their doctrine from the Prophet deserves respect. In the *Qur'ān*, perhaps almost the only genuine record of his personality that has come down to us, ascetic and mystical elements are mingled with those of a different kind. The former, of course, are emphasized by the Ṣūfīs and given a deeper and more special significance than he himself attached to them, but this does not justify the assertion that Ṣūfism owes little to the *Qur'ān*. To Muslims, who have always venerated their Holy Scripture, learned it by heart in childhood, and studied it with intense concentration as the key to all human knowledge, such a notion would seem absurd. It is also historically untrue. Though Muḥammad left no system of dogmatic or mystical theology, the *Qur'ān* contains the raw materials of both. Being the outcome of feeling rather than reflection, the Prophet's statements about God are *formally* inconsistent, and while Muslim scholastics have embodied in their creed the aspect of transcendence, the Ṣūfīs, following his example, have combined the transcendent aspect with that of immanence, on which, though it is less prominent in the *Qur'ān*, they naturally lay greater stress. 'Allah is the Light of the heavens and the earth' (xxiv. 35); 'He is the first and the last and the outward and the inward' (lvii. 3); 'there is no god but He; everything is perishing except His Face' (xxviii. 88); 'I have breathed into him (man) of My spirit' (xv. 29); 'Verily, We have created man and We know what his soul suggests to him, for We are nigher unto him than the neck-artery' (l. 15); 'wheresoever ye turn, there is the Face of Allah' (ii. 109); 'he to whom Allah giveth not light hath no light at all' (xxiv. 40). Surely the seeds of mysticism are there. And, for the early Ṣūfīs, the *Qur'ān* is not only the Word of God: it is the primary means of drawing near to Him. By fervent prayer, by meditating profoundly on the text as a whole and in particular on the mysterious passages (xvii. 1; liii. 1–18) concerning the Night-journey and Ascension, they endeavoured to reproduce the Prophet's mystical experience in themselves.

Consider now the circumstances of time and place. The political revolution which transferred the seat of government from Damascus to Baghdād had brought Islam into immediate contact and conflict with the ideas of an older civilization; and if eventually these ideas were vanquished, yet history shows that in such encounters the victory is seldom complete. We are dealing with a widespread movement in lands where Hellenism had long been at home; where theological controversies were daily being carried on between Muslims on one side and Christians, Manichaeans, and Zoroastrians on the other; where members of the subject races, recently converted to Islam and anxious to adapt the new religion to their needs, might—sometimes in good faith—claim the authority of the Prophet for doctrines and practices which they valued. It is right to regard the Ṣūfīs as esoteric students of the *Qur'ān*, but not, I think, to see in Ṣūfism the pure result of Qur'ānic study. After A.D. 1000 it began to absorb and assimilate Hellenistic philosophy, and the evidence so far collected suggests that its origin and early development were influenced by Christian asceticism and Hellenistic mysticism. We may well believe that the *rāhib* (Christian monk or hermit), a figure familiar to Muḥammad himself, supplied his followers with a model for the life they led. The celebrated words put in his mouth, *lā rahbāniyyata fi 'l- Islām*, 'no monkery in Islam', are in fact a later protest against the Christian ideal and a proof of its influence. The Prophet is usually supposed to have condemned *rahbāniyya*, including celibacy, in the *Qur'ān*, but the exegesis of Sūra lvii. 27 that prevailed till the end of the third century A.H. makes him commend it as an institution divinely ordained: his censure falls only on those who had corrupted it.

Early Muslim asceticism, with its fearful visions of the wrath to come, its fasters and 'weepers', its austerities, devotions, and endless litanies, was a forcing-house for mysticism. Since 'there is no god but Allah', and to worship Him for the sake of being saved from Hell or rewarded with Paradise is to associate with Him a 'god', i.e. another object of hope or fear, the ascetic is impelled to trust in Him alone (*tawakkul*) and acquiesce entirely in His will (*riḍā*). But these words cannot be the last. Perfect detachment from 'gods' involves perfect attachment to God: in mystical language, union with God through *love*. This is the doctrine that inspires all religious and ethical Ṣūfism. The woman saint, Rābi'a of Baṣra (*ob.* A.D. 801), in whom our authorities find its first conspicuous exponent, is said to have been a slave, and her parentage is unknown. In the following verses, whether they be hers or not, the mystic's goal is depicted as ecstatic contemplation of the Beloved.

> Two ways I love Thee: selfishly,
> And next, as worthy is of Thee.
> 'Tis selfish love that I do naught
> Save think on Thee with every thought.

'Tis purest love when Thou dost raise
The veil to my adoring gaze.
Not mine the praise in that or this:
Thine is the praise in both, I wis.

The doctrine of a mystical union imparted by divine grace goes beyond anything in the *Qur'ān*, but is stated plainly in apocryphal traditions of the Prophet, e.g. 'God said, "My servant draws nigh unto Me by works of supererogation, and I love him; and when I love him, I am his ear, so that he hears by Me, and his eye, so that he sees by Me, and his tongue, so that he speaks by Me, and his hand, so that he takes by Me." ' Starting from a voluntary practice of devotion characterized by constant repetition (*dhikr*) of the name of Allah, the Ṣūfīs worked out a psychological method, a *via purgativa et illuminativa*, leading, or rather predisposing, the soul to attain to the gnosis (*maʿrifa*), which is defined as 'knowledge of the attributes of the divine Unity, peculiar to the saints who behold God with their hearts'. The first Muslim to give an experimental analysis of the inner life was Ḥārith al-Muḥāsibī of Baṣra (*ob.* A. D. 857); his treatise entitled *Riʿāya li-ḥuqūq Allāh*, or 'Method of religious observance', extant in a unique manuscript at Oxford, shows delicacy and originality, though he draws largely on Jewish and Christian sources for the purpose of edification. 'The Path' (*ṭarīqa*), as described by later writers, consists of acquired virtues (*maqāmāt*) and mystical states (*aḥwāl*). The first stage is repentance or conversion; then comes a series of others, e.g. renunciation, poverty, patience, trust in God, each being a preparation for the next. Details vary, but the general features are the same. The disciple learns to place 'the works of the heart' above 'the works of the members', the intention above the act, and even when scrupulously observing the religious law, to regard its ordinances as expressions or symbols of a deeper truth. These principles, notwithstanding their antinomian tendency, have permeated Muslim legalism and underlie the ethics expounded by the great theologian Ghazālī (*ob.* A. D. 1111) and illustrated by popular moralists like Sa'dī (*ob.* A. D. 1291). While the Ṣūfīs cannot be accused of loving themselves, it is true that they have sometimes loved God at the expense of their neighbours, especially those other than their own brethren. But in the end their conception of the divine Unity made it impossible for them to love God without loving His creatures too.

The foundations of a complete theory and practice of mystical religion were laid by the Ṣūfīs of the third century A. H. Dhu 'l- Nūn of Egypt introduced into Islam the idea of gnosis (*ma'rifa*)—a knowledge given in ecstasy, which differs altogether from intellectual and traditional knowledge (*'ilm*). Being asked how he knew God, he replied, 'I know Him through Himself'; and, like Dionysius, he declared that 'God is the opposite of anything you can imagine', and that 'the more one knows God, the more one is lost in Him'. Henceforth we note the increasing use of symbolism and technical terms proper to a doctrine reserved for the elect; it was felt that these high mysteries must not be divulged to profane ears. The Persian Abū Yazīd (Bāyazīd) of Bisṭām, possibly under the influence of Indian monism, developed the doctrine of *fanā* (the passing away of the self); and its positive counterpart, *baqā* (the unitive life in God), was added soon afterwards. Although his endeavour to reach the pure Unity by a process of negation pushed to extreme lengths culminated, as he himself confessed, in disillusionment, Bāyazīd became the legendary hero of the later Persian Ṣūfīs, who are never tired of quoting his ecstatic ejaculations (*shaṭḥiyyāt*), such as *Subḥānī*, 'Glory to me', and the story of his ascension to the Throne of God, which is said to have taken place in a dream. Among the sayings attributed to him are the following, 'Creatures are subject to "states", but the gnostic has no "state", because his vestiges are effaced and his essence is noughted by the essence of Another and his traces are lost in Another's traces'. 'Thirty years the transcendent God was my mirror, now I am my own mirror—i. e. that which I was I am no more, for "I" and "God" is a denial of the Unity of God. Since I am no more, the transcendent God is His own mirror. I say that I am my own mirror, for 'tis God that speaks with my tongue, and I have vanished.' 'I came forth from Bāyazīd-ness as a snake from its skin. Then I looked. I saw that lover, beloved, and love are one, for in the world of Unity all can be one.' While Bāyazīd is admired by those who prefer mystical 'intoxication' to 'sobriety', their opponents follow the teaching of Junayd of Baghdād, whose theory of 'union' was applied and exhibited to the Muslim world with uncompromising realism by his pupil, the famous Ḥallāj. It is not surprising that when Ḥallāj was arrested and imprisoned on grave charges of heresy, Junayd prudently disavowed him. The doctrine set forth in his *Kitābu 'l- Ṭawāsīn* would have shocked Muslims, even without the incisive formula, *Ana 'l- Ḥaqq*, 'I am God', in which its author summed it up, but is so original, profound, and historically important that an attempt must be made to sketch its leading ideas and call attention to some problems connected with it. This has only recently become possible through the recovery and exhaustive study of the scattered Ḥallājian texts by Professor Massignon of the University of Paris.

According to Ḥallāj, God, who in essence is love, created Man after His image to the end that His creature, loving Him alone, may suffer a spiritual transformation, find the divine image in himself, and thus attain to union with the divine will and nature. It is evident that the union of which Ḥallāj speaks and which he personally experienced is not pantheistic, though it has often been so described by Muslim as well as European writers. The term *ḥulūl*, which he used to denote it, was associated in the minds of his co-religionists with the Christian doctrine of incarnation. He does not appear to have attached this meaning to it in his own case, yet there are other parallels of an extraordinary kind which mark him out as the nearest of all Muslim mystics to the spirit of Christ. For him, the saint in union with God is superior to the prophet charged with an external mission, and the model of the saintly life is not Muḥammad, but Jesus, the type of glorified humanity, the deified man whose personality, transfigured and essentialized, stands forth as the witness and representative of God, revealing from within himself *al-Ḥaqq*, the Creator through whom he exists, the Creative Truth in whom he has all his being. Moreover, as Professor Massignon has observed, Ḥallāj conceives the mystical union as union with the Creative Word (*Kun*, Be!), which in the *Qur'ān* is appropriated to the birth of Jesus and the Resurrection, a union obtained 'by means of close and fervent adhesion of the understanding to the commandments of God'. And the result of this permanent acceptance of the divine *fiat* is the coming into the mystic's soul of the divine Spirit, which proceeds 'from the command of my Lord' (*Qur'ān*, xvii. 87) and thenceforth makes of each of the acts of that man 'acts truly divine'. Nor did Ḥallāj fail to prove how well he had learned the lesson that holiness is made perfect by suffering and self-sacrifice. His execution took place at Baghdād in A.D. 922. When he was brought to be crucified and saw the cross and the nails, he turned to the people and uttered a prayer, ending with the words:

> And these Thy servants who are gathered to slay me, in zeal for Thy religion and in desire to win Thy favour, forgive them, O Lord, and have mercy upon them; for verily if Thou hadst revealed to them that which Thou hast revealed to me, they would not have done what they have done; and if Thou hadst hidden from me that which Thou hast hidden from them, I should not have suffered this tribulation. Glory unto Thee in whatsoever Thou doest, and glory unto Thee in whatsoever Thou willest!

In Islam, where men are judged by their actions, mere heterodoxy cannot as a rule be effectively penalized, and however sharply the truth of mysticism may clash with the law of religion, nothing very serious is likely to occur so long as the mystic continues to worship with his fellow Muslims. It is agreed that Ḥallāj was scrupulous in the performance of his religious duties, and he never scorned, though he certainly did not flatter, 'the base degrees' by which one must ascend to the real religion that consists in the humble and ardent devotion of a pure heart. This represents the attitude of many Ṣūfīs towards the Islamic law, and it seems to be the best way in which they can serve two masters. But Ḥallāj was too much in earnest to compromise with his conscience. Against the public authority of the Muslim Church and State he sets up the personal authority immediately derived from God with whom the saint is one. And he was no theorist like Junayd: he was suspected of dealings with the Carmathians, he had preached his faith to believers and infidels alike, and, above all, sought to win converts by working 'evidentiary' miracles. On these grounds he was justly condemned. His crime was not that, as later Ṣūfīs put it, 'he divulged the mystery of the divine Lordship', but that in obedience to an inward call he proclaimed and actively asserted a truth which involves religious, political, and social anarchy. Other mystics have seen that truth. Ḥallāj lived it and died for it. Hence the intimacy and tenderness, so rare in Ṣūfism, of the verses in which he prays for union with his Beloved or tries to utter his feeling of perfect harmony with Him.

Betwixt me and Thee there lingers an 'it is I' that torments me.
Ah, of Thy grace, take away this 'I' from between us!

I am He whom I love, and He whom I love is I,
We are two spirits dwelling in one body.
If thou seest me, thou seest Him,
And if thou seest Him, thou seest us both.

I may remark by the way that the second of these four lines could not have been written by a pantheist. The monistic expression of the same idea is found in Jīlī's words, 'We are the spirit of One though we dwell in two bodies', and in the verse of Jalālu'ddīn Rūmī,

Happy the moment when we are seated in the palace, thou and I,
With two forms and with two figures but with one soul, thou and I.

That Ḥallāj declared himself to have become, at certain moments and in a certain sense, the God whose transcendence he nevertheless affirms in the strongest terms possible, will astonish no one who has remarked how often the paradoxes of logic are the truths of mysticism. Although his original doctrine did not long survive him, it furnished a basis for the development of speculations, e. g. concerning the nature of the Perfect Man, which play a large part in the writings of Ibnu 'l- ʿArabī and in Persian mystical poetry. But we do not find there any understanding of his character or of the tragic personal crisis which he has depicted in a widely echoed verse:

God cast him into the sea, with his arms tied behind his back,
And said to him, 'Take care, take care, lest thou be wetted by the water!'

The century following the death of Ḥallāj, though otherwise comparatively barren, produced the first systematic and general works on Ṣūfī doctrine, such as the *Kitābu 'l-Lumaʿ* by Abū Naṣr al-Sarrāj and the *Qūtu 'l- Qulūb* by Abū Ṭālib al-Makkī, which preserve much valuable material drawn from sources that have been lost. Ṣūfism was now beginning to drift from its anchorage in Islam towards pantheism and antinomianism, a tendency favoured by the growing influence of Greek philosophical ideas, especially that of 'emanation'. This is illustrated in striking fashion by the life and sayings of the Persian mystic, Abū Saʿīd (A. D. 967–1049). In some respects his teaching is admirable. 'The true saint', he said, 'goes in and out amongst the people and eats and sleeps with them and buys and sells in the market and marries and takes part in social intercourse and never forgets God for a single moment.' He saw all creatures 'through the eyes of the Creator', and set such store on charity and lovingkindness that he knew no better way of attaining to God than by bringing joy to the heart of a Muslim. What he says concerning the relation of the saint to the religious law may suggest a comparison with Ḥallāj; but the difference both in spirit and practice is immense. Whereas Ḥallāj would fain have kept the law and was faced with an insoluble conflict between loyalty to its ordinances and obedience to the higher authority which he felt within him, Abū Sa'īd regards the law as a state of bondage, necessary for those who are still on the Way, but superfluous after they have reached the goal. In his view, union with God is not an occasional or intermittent experience, but the permanent result of extinction of the individual self and assumption of the divine nature. It is related that he forbade his disciples to perform the pilgrimage to the Ka'ba, which he contemptuously described as 'a stone house'; and once, so it is said, on hearing the call of the muezzin he refused to interrupt the mystic dance of the dervishes, saying, 'This is our service of prayer'. Even if not literally true, these stories are typical. The famous *Epistle* of Qushayrī, written in A.D. 1045, contrasts the piety of the older school of Ṣūfīs, who had based their doctrine upon faithful observance of the *Sunna*, with the lawlessness and hypocrisy prevailing amongst the mystics of his own time. Thirty years later the author of the *Kashfu 'l- Maḥjūb* declares that his contemporaries give the name of 'law' to their lusts and call senseless fancies 'divine knowledge', the motions of the heart and affections of the animal soul 'divine love', heresy 'poverty', scepticism 'purity', and disbelief in positive religion 'self-abandonment'. While the saints, with their innumerable followers and worshippers, menaced the Islam of history and tradition, the orthodox party, divided against itself, either clinging fanatically to the letter of the *Qur'ān* or disputing over legal and ritual minutiae or analysing theological dogmas in the dry light of intellect, was fast losing touch with the inward spirit and life which makes religion a reality. Many earnest Muslims must have asked themselves how long such a state of things could last. Was there no means of preserving what was vital to the Faith without rending the community asunder? That question was decided by the intervention of one of the greatest men Islam has ever produced, Abū Ḥāmid Ghazālī (A. D. 1058–1111), known to medieval Europe as Abuhamet and Algazel.

The story of Ghazālī's conversion to Ṣūfism, as told by himself, is a classic of its kind. Here it will be enough to recall that in his younger days he had been a sceptic, but that a mystical experience cured him of this malady and caused him to devote all his powers to searching after absolute truth. His study of philosophy and scholastic theology convinced him that no light was to be found there; nor did the Ta'līmīs, with their doctrine of an infallible religious authority, come off any better when put to the test. Then he turned his attention to the mystic Way revealed in the writings of Ḥārith al-Muḥāsibī and the old masters of the third century A. H., and as he read, the truth dawned upon him. 'I saw plainly', he says, 'that what is most peculiar to them (the Ṣūfīs) cannot be learned from books, but can only be reached by immediate experience and ecstasy and inward transformation', in other words, by leading the mystical life. He saw, too, that his own salvation was at stake; but his worldly prospects were brilliant, and it cost him a hard struggle to give them up. His health broke under the strain, and at last he surrendered himself entirely, taking refuge with God 'as a man in sore affliction who has no resource left'. He was not yet forty when he quitted Baghdād with the resolve never to enter it again.

The truth, then, lay with the mystics; and it was Ghazālī's personal experience of this truth that inspired the great religious revival which his example no less than his works—notably the *Iḥyā*—brought about in circles hitherto unfriendly to mysticism. Henceforward the Ṣūfīs are definitely within the fold of Islam; for, according to Ghazālī and the majority of Muslims after him, the revelations bestowed on the saints supplement those of the prophets as the source and basis of all real knowledge. But at the same time he insists that sainthood is derived from prophecy and constantly appeals to the supreme authority of Muḥammad, whose law must be obeyed both in letter and spirit. And though his doctrine of the soul as a substance in which God causes His essence and qualities to be reflected—a mirror illumined by the 'divine spark'—might have led a bolder mystic into heretical speculations, he himself stood in no such danger. Perhaps what he thought in private went beyond what he taught in his books, though in the *Mishkātu 'l-Anwār* he says, for instance, that 'Allah is the Sun, and besides the Sun there is only the Sun's light'; but in Islam the use of pantheistic language does not necessarily mean that the writer is a pantheist. While Ghazālī sometimes pushes the doctrine of Unity to extreme lengths, he never forgets that God is the Creator whose absolute will brought the world into existence. Great as was his debt to Ṣūfism, he repaid it in full. Yet most Ṣūfīs think, and with justice, that he belongs not so much to themselves as to the Catholic Church of Islam, in which his heartfelt piety, moral enthusiasm, firm hold on tradition, and—however they may distrust it—his critical and objective philosophical method, established them securely. To a large extent he succeeded in making orthodoxy mystical; it was impossible in the nature of things that equal success should attend his efforts to make mysticism orthodox. He drew into the movement a strong and fairly tolerant body of conservative opinion, which acted as a brake in the stormy times ahead; but its driving force now came from another quarter, and the ideas that swung it irresistibly forward and were to dominate it in the future had little in common with his. The homage paid to the Prophet by many of the new school cannot hide the fact that their spiritual home is not Mecca but Athens and Alexandria. With Ghazālī an epoch in the history of Ṣūfism passes away. Hitherto the mystics had, in the main, represented the idea of an intimate personal relation between God and the soul as opposed to that of a formal worship based on authority and tradition, and this they combined with a theology constructed partly from the *Qur'ān* and partly with materials which had come down to them from Aristotle and the Neo-platonists. In proportion as the binding power of Islam grew feebler, the foreign elements gained ground until the collapse of the caliphate left them in full possession of the field. The result is a pantheistic philosophy which after seven hundred years still maintains its sway over large sections of the Muslim world and, as interpreted by Jalālu'ddīn Rūmī, Ḥāfiẓ and other Persian mystical poets, has charmed many who would find its original author, Ibnu 'l- 'Arabī (1165–1240), quite unreadable. Before returning to him, we may note another characteristic feature of the period. The twelfth century witnessed the beginnings of a vast organization of Muslim religious life, corresponding to the monastic orders in medieval Christendom. Formerly, though famous teachers had gathered round them groups of disciples, who sometimes lived together in a convent (*khānaqāh*), the schools thus formed were lacking in cohesion and sooner or later disappeared. These free associations of 'seekers' inspired by personal attachment to a shaykh were now supplanted by perpetual brotherhoods, each tracing its descent through a long line of saints from the Prophet to its own founder. The ritual varies in the different orders, which also diverge widely as regards their doctrine and their attitude towards the religious law. Celibacy is seldom demanded as a condition of membership; and through their lay members, belonging to all ranks of society but especially numerous amongst the poor, they have had a very great influence both for good and evil. Some European critics identify theoretical pantheism with practical immorality, but the mind of the East cannot be reduced to simple equations of this sort. Ṣūfī pantheism, as applied to life, generally includes a doctrine of divine personality and moral obligations. It must be admitted, however, that on account of the absence in Islam of a recognized doctrinal authority the mystics enjoy a freedom which many of them have abused.

Muḥyi'ddīn Ibnu 'l-ʿArabī, the greatest speculative genius among them, was born at Murcia in Spain and died in 1240 at Damascus. His system of universal philosophy is embedded in an enormous mass of writings, of which the most celebrated are the *Futūḥāt al-Makkiyya* (Meccan Revelations) and the *Fuṣūṣu 'l-Ḥikam* (Bezels of Wisdom). Much of it is abstruse and fantastic; yet no one who studies it can fail to be astonished by the intellectual and imaginative power of the author, though others, e.g. ʿAbdu 'l- Karīm Jīlī (*ob. circa* A.D. 1410), have explained it more lucidly and concisely than he himself has done. The following sketch comprises only a few points of outstanding importance.

Ibnu 'l-ʿArabī is a thoroughgoing monist, and the name given to his doctrine (*waḥdatu 'l- wujūd*, the unity of existence) justly describes it. He holds that all things pre-exist as ideas in the knowledge of God, whence they emanate and whither they ultimately return. There is no creation *ex nihilo*; the world is merely the outward aspect of that which in its inward aspect is God. While every phenomenon reveals some attribute of reality, Man is the microcosm in which all the divine attributes are united, and in Man alone does God become fully conscious of Himself. This doctrine, fusing together elements derived from Gnosticism, Neoplatonism, Christianity, and other sources, occupies the central place in Ibnu 'l-ʿArabī's system. It is essentially a Logos doctrine. Divinity is objectified and made manifest in the true idea of Humanity, of which Adam was the first incarnation. The Perfect Man (*al-Insān al-Kāmil*), as the image of God and the archetype of Nature, is at once the mediator of divine grace and the cosmic principle by which the world is animated and sustained. And, of course, the perfect man *par excellence* is Muḥammad. Long before Ibnu 'l-ʿArabī, the dogma of his pre-existence had established itself in Islam. His spiritual essence, the first thing that God created, was conceived as a celestial light (*nūr Muḥammadī*), which became incarnate in Adam and in the whole series of prophets after him from generation to generation until its final appearance in Muḥammad himself; according to the Shī ʿites, however, it passed from him to ʿAlī and the Imāms of his House, while the Ṣūfīs believe that it is immanent in the saints. Ibnu 'l-ʿArabī identifies Muḥammad, in his real nature, with the ἰδέα ἰδεῶν (*ḥaqīqatu 'l-ḥaqā'iq*), a phrase which is used by Origen to describe the Logos, and with the 'active intellect' of Aristotle. As such he is the agent in the creation of the world (*al-ḥaqq al-makhlūq bihi*), the vicegerent (*khalīfa*) of God on earth, and the pole (*quṭb*) on whom its existence depends and for whose sake it was created, the unique source and channel of all divine revelations; for he was a prophet when Adam was clay. This sounds like an echo of the doctrine of St. Paul and the author of the Fourth Gospel concerning Christ; and in some measure it may be so; at any rate Ibnu 'l-ʿArabī shows a peculiar sympathy with Christianity and applies the word *kalima* (λόγος) both to Jesus and Muḥammad, though not exclusively to them. A purely unitarian mysticism leads almost inevitably either to pantheism or saint-worship or, as in Islam, to a combination of the two. Apart from the bare divine nature, there remains as an object of personal devotion only the prophet or saint in and through whom God makes Himself known. The Islamic Logos doctrine seems to have arisen from the need of satisfying deep religious aspirations without impairing the divine unity. It substitutes for the Christian distinction of persons in God a distinction of aspects: the perfect man represents God *in relation to the world*. Hence the mystical worship of Muḥammad is frequently expressed in terms which the prophet of Mecca would have deemed rank blasphemy, e. g. 'were it not for the Light of our Lord Muḥammad, no mystery on earth would be revealed, no fountain would gush, no river flow'. The Ṣūfīs call him 'the Beloved of God', and he is the dispenser of every divine gift to those who love him and live in communion with his spirit.

For Ibnu 'l-ʿArabī, however, the popular adoration of the Prophet and the saints is but one of the many forms of belief in which God reveals Himself. The true mystic, he says, will find Him in all religions.

> My heart is capable of every form:
> A cloister for the monk, a fane for idols,
> A pasture for gazelles, the votary's Kaʿba,
> The tables of the Torah, the Koran.
> Love is the faith I hold: wherever turn
> His camels, still the one true Faith is mine.

The God of religion, as contrasted with the God of mysticism, is finite; hence it shows ignorance and injustice to praise one's own creed or blame that of another. Even infidels and idolaters are God's servants created in His image, and 'compassion towards His servants has the greater claim', though the law condemn them to die. From the fact that the soul is a mode of divine being, Ibnu 'l-ʿArabī infers that human actions are self-determined. But his system excludes free-will in the ordinary sense. God himself acts according to the necessity of His nature, which requires that the infinite variety of His attributes should produce an infinite variety of effects in the objects wherein they are displayed. This involves the appearance of light and darkness, good and evil, and all the opposites on which the possibility of knowledge depends. Since evil, as such, does not exist, hell is only a temporary state and every sinner will ultimately be saved.

There is much in Ibnu 'l-ʿArabī that reminds us of Spinoza, but it would be hazardous to suggest that the Spanish Jew was acquainted with the ideas of the Spanish Muslim, whose cabbalistic extravagances often disguise the fact that he is also a serious and original thinker. On the other hand, he certainly influenced some of the Christian medieval schoolmen, and, as Professor Asín Palacios has recently pointed out, many peculiar features in his descriptions of Hell, Paradise, and the Beatific Vision are reproduced by Dante with a closeness that can scarcely be fortuitous. 'The infernal regions, the astronomical heavens, the circles of the mystic rose, the choirs of angels around the focus of divine light, the three circles symbolizing the Trinity—all are described by Dante exactly as Ibnu 'l-ʿArabī described them'. Dante tells us how, as he mounted higher and higher in Paradise, his love was made stronger and his spiritual vision more intense by seeing Beatrice grow more and more beautiful. The same idea occurs in a poem of Ibnu 'l-ʿArabī written about a century earlier (*Tarjumānu 'l-Ashwāq*, No. LV):

Meeting with Him (the Beloved) creates in me what I have never imagined . . .
For I behold a form whose beauty, as often as we meet, grows in splendour and majesty,
So that there is no escape from a love that increases in proportion to every increase in His loveliness according to a predestined scale.

It may be added that Ibnu 'l-ʿArabī too had a Beatrice—Niẓām, the beautiful and accomplished daughter of Makīnu'ddīn—and that owing to the scandal caused by the mystical odes which he composed in her honour he wrote a commentary on them in order to convince his critics that they were wrong. Similarly 'in the *Convito* Dante declares his intention to interpret the esoteric meaning of fourteen love-songs which he had composed at an earlier date, and the subject of which had led to the erroneous belief that they dealt with sensual rather than intellectual love'. In short, the parallelism, both general and particular, reaches so far that only one conclusion is possible. Muslim religious legends, e. g. the *Miʿrāj* or Ascension of the

Prophet, together with popular and philosophical conceptions of the after-life—derived from Muslim traditionists and such writers as Fārābī, Avicenna, Ghazālī, and Ibnu'l-ʿArabī—must have passed into the common stock of literary culture that was accessible to the best minds in Europe in the thirteenth century. The Arab conquerors of Spain and Sicily repeated, though on a less imposing scale, the same process of impregnation to which they themselves had been subjected by the Hellenistic civilization of Persia and Syria. If in both cases direct evidence of transmission is frequently hard to obtain, the reason is that no written record can preserve the details of an intellectual communication carried on, over a long period of time, between two races living in daily intercourse with each other.

Let us turn to the East, where the golden age of Persian mysticism had already begun. It followed, 'as the night the day', an epoch of indescribable carnage and devastation, during which the Mongol barbarians swept across Asia, leaving only terror, misery, and chaos behind them. In nations, as in individuals, intense and prolonged suffering demands an anodyne. No wonder that Persia, too exhausted to help herself, turned for comfort to those who offered her on the one hand an ideal representation of things more prized because they seemed to have vanished from the earth—order, security, justice, beneficence, the social virtues bound up with established custom and tradition and forming the basis of any organized national life; and on the other hand, the mystic's vision of everlasting peace and joy to be attained by the pure in heart who contemplate within themselves the spiritual world that alone is real and enduring. To draw this picture was the task of the Ṣūfī poets, and the manner in which they accomplished it has made Persian mystical poetry famous even in countries where the language is read by few.

The intellectual groundwork of the picture comes from Ibnu 'l-ʿArabī. We shall see that under his influence Ṣūfism tends to become, not so much an affair of the heart and conscience, as a speculative philosophy out of touch with those intimate moral and religious feelings that inspired the earlier mystics. The typical saint is no longer one who has sought God with prayer and aspiration and found Him, after sore travail, in the transfiguration of dying to self through an inexplicable act of grace depending on nothing but the personal will of the Creator; he is rather the complete theosophist and hierophant from whom no mystery is hidden, the perfect man who identifies himself with God or the Logos.

> I was on that day when the Names were not,
> Nor any sign of existence endowed with name.
> By me Names and Named were brought to view
> On the day when there were not 'I' and 'we'.

Before considering the characteristics of this poetry, it may be well to state briefly the philosophical theory which underlies it.

The Essence of God is all that really exists; His attributes are distinguished from Him in thought, but in reality are not other than He. The aggregate of divine attributes, which we call the universe, is the ever-changing kaleidoscope wherein He displays Himself, and is real only in so far as He is reflected in it. Phenomena *per se* are not-being; they acquire a contingent existence from the efflux of Absolute Being by which they are irradiated. The position and function of man in the scheme of things has been explained above. In him the spiritual and physical worlds meet, and he stands at the centre of the universe of which he is the soul. But on his phenomenal side he is 'black with the darkness of not-being'; his bodily affections hold him in bondage, so that he thinks he is separate from God. That illusion, though supported by sense and reason, contradicts the first principle of the Ṣūfī philosophy, which teaches that all existence and all action is the manifestation of divine energy. What this means only the mystics who have experienced it can realize, and of course they cannot communicate it to others except symbolically. The erotic form of the poetry in which it is shadowed forth serves admirably to suggest to the imagination what the intellect is unable to apprehend. Moreover, the passion of love affords the most obvious analogy to the fits of ecstasy which Ṣūfīs have always associated with gnosis and sainthood. In the early period recitation of the *Qur'ān* was regularly employed to bring about the trance-state, and soon love-poems (in which at first there was no mystical intention) began to be used for the same purpose. Many odes of this kind were chanted, with or without the accompaniment of music, in order to stimulate enthusiasm and induce ecstasy; in some cases they were composed with that object. The aim of the writers is not only to convey transcendental truth, but also to create by their art a beautiful dream-world capable of suggesting the infinite and inexpressible, of attuning the soul to heavenly harmonies, and of preparing it for the highest mystical experience. The first of the following examples is taken from the Arabic *Dīwān* of Ibnu 'l-Fāriḍ (see p. 210 *supra*), while the second is part of a Persian ode by Jalālu'-ddīn Rūmī.

With my Beloved I alone have been
When secrets tenderer than evening airs
Passed, and the Vision blest
Was granted to my prayers,
That crowned me, else obscure, with endless fame,
The while amazed between
His beauty and His majesty
I stood in silent ecstasy,
Revealing that which o'er my spirit went and came.
Lo, in His face commingled
Is every charm and grace;
The whole of Beauty singled
Into a perfect face
Beholding Him would cry,
'There is no god but He, and He is the Most High!'

THE HOUSE OF LOVE

This house wherein is continually the sound of the viol,
Ask of the Master, what house is this?
If it is the Kaʿba, what means this idol-form?
And if it is the Magian temple, what means this light of God?
In this house is a treasure which the universe is too small to hold;
This 'house' and this 'Master' is all acting and pretence.
Lay no hand on the house, for this house is a talisman;
Speak not with the Master, for he is drunken overnight.
The dust and rubbish of this house is all musk and perfume,
The roof and door of this house is all verse and melody.
In fine, whoever has found his way into this house
Is the sultan of the world and the Solomon of the time.
O Master, bend down thy head once from this roof,
For in thy fair face is a token of fortune.
Like a mirror, the Soul has received thy image in its heart;
The tip of thy curl has sunk into its heart like a comb.
This is the Lord of Heaven, who resembles Venus and the moon;
This is the House of Love, which hath no bound or end.

While these lyrics, soaring beyond space and time, give free rein to an ecstasy that sees all things *sub specie unitatis*, another favourite form of Persian poetry, the love-romance, which had been brought to perfection by Niẓāmī (*ob.* A. D. 1203), is particularly well adapted to describe the pains and longings of the soul on its way towards God. Hence we find many mystical versions of old tales such as the passion of Majnūn for Laylā and of Zalīkhā (Potiphar's wife) for Joseph. A third and very large class of poems comprises those of which the object is mainly or entirely didactic. In their earliest form they are little more than versified homilies, illustrated by brief parables and anecdotes, like the *Ḥadīqatu 'l-Ḥaqīqa* ('The Garden of the Truth') composed by Sanā'ī of Ghazna; or allegorical descriptions of the ascending stages of the mystic's progress to unity. Both types rapidly attained their highest development: the former in the *Mathnawī* of Jalālu'ddīn Rūmī, and the latter in the *Manṭiqu 'l-Ṭayr* of Farīdu'ddīn 'Aṭṭār. 'Bird-speech', as the title of 'Aṭṭār's poem may be rendered, is the story of the birds which set out under the leadership of the hoopoe to seek the Sīmurgh, their mysterious king. After traversing the seven valleys of Search, Love, Knowledge, Detachment, Unity, Bewilderment, and Self-noughting, the survivors, thirty in number, are admitted to his presence and realize that 'they themselves are the Sīmurgh, while the Sīmurgh is nothing but those thirty birds (*sī murgh*).'

They besought the disclosure of this deep mystery and demanded the solution of 'we-ness' and 'thou-ness'.
Without speech came the answer from that Presence, saying, 'This sun-like Presence is a mirror,
Whosoever enters it sees himself therein; body and soul see therein the same body and soul'.

One may, perhaps, gather the poet's meaning from a passage, interesting for its own sake, in which Jīlī finds fault with the Christians for restricting the divine self-manifestation to the person of Jesus. 'God said, "I breathed my Spirit into Adam"; and here the name "Adam" signifies every human individual. The contemplation of those who behold God in man is the most perfect in the world. Something of this vision the Christians possess, and their doctrine about Jesus will lead them at last, when "the Thing shall be discovered as it really is", to the knowledge that mankind are like mirrors set face to face, each of which contains what is in all; and so they will behold God in themselves and declare Him to be absolutely One.'

The ecstatic state knows no law, and therefore 'the man of God is beyond infidelity and religion'. But, except by Ṣūfīs of the baser sort, this is not understood as sanctioning irreligious and immoral behaviour. The true saint keeps the law, not because he is obliged to do so, but through feeling himself one with God. The full circle of deification must comprehend both the inward and outward aspects of Deity—the One and the Many, the Truth and the Law. It is not enough to escape from all that is creaturely without entering into the eternal life of God the Creator as manifested in His works. To abide in God (*baqā*) after having passed away from selfhood (*fanā*) is the mark of the perfect man, who not only journeys *to* God, i. e. passes from plurality to unity, but *in* and *with* God, i. e. continuing in the unitive state, he returns with God to the phenomenal world from which he set out, and manifests unity in plurality. In this descent

> He makes the Law his outer garment
> And the mystic Path his inner garment,

for he brings down and displays the truth to mankind while fulfilling all the duties of the religious law. Theory apart, the great Muslim saints, many of whom were directors of souls, generally knew better than to cast their higher knowledge before those who had not yet mastered the lower. Like St. Paul, they distinguished 'between the milk which is necessary to one set of men and the strong meat which is allowed to others'. This doctrine of 'the double truth' enables them to harmonize the Qur'ānic conception of Allah with a pantheistic philosophy and build up a lofty ethical system of which the ultimate basis is the fact that evil is unreal.

The *Weltanschauung* of Persian Ṣūfism appears in popular form in the *Mathnawī-i Maʿnawī* or 'Spiritual Couplets' of Maulānā Jalālu'ddīn Rūmī, founder of the Maulawī (Mevlevī) order of dervishes, who died at Qōniya (Iconium) in A.D. 1273. The *Mathnawī* has been called 'the *Qur'ān* of Persia', and its author professes, indeed, to expound the inmost sense of the prophetic revelation; but any one looking through the work at random can see that its doctrines, interwoven with apologues, anecdotes, fables, legends, and traditions, range over the whole domain of medieval religious life and thought. Whereas in his odes he often writes from the standpoint of the mystic who sees nothing but God, the *Mathnawī* shows him as an eloquent and enthusiastic teacher explaining the way to God for the benefit of those who have entered upon it. The keynote is struck in the opening lines, where the reed-flute, 'the sacred musical instrument of the Mevlevī dervishes', represents the soul separated from God.

> Hark, how the Reed with shrill sad strain
> Of lovers' parting doth complain.
> 'From the reed-bed since I was torn,
> My song makes men and women mourn
> Love's pain and passion to impart,
> I want a sympathizing heart.
> He pines, the wretch who far must roam,
> For his old happiness and home.'

The poem has been well defined as 'an attempt to purify the religious sentiment by love'. According to Jalālu'ddīn, the faith that calls itself 'rational' and cannot be satisfied without intellectual proofs is just as worthless as that which is rooted in conformity, custom, and respectability.

> The blest initiates know and need not prove;
> From Satan logic, and from Adam love.

Rites and creeds count for little with God, who dwells neither in mosque nor church nor temple, but in the pure heart. The essential thing is a complete moral transformation, only to be wrought by ardent faith and humble prayer. Jalālu'ddīn is profoundly convinced of the goodness of God and the sinfulness of man; therefore, while denying the reality of evil in relation to its Creator, he affirms it in relation to the creatures. As regards God, it is good in so far as it makes manifest His perfection, just as the artist's power to depict the ugly as well as the beautiful affords evidence of his skill, not of his ugliness. But though the

Mathnawī illustrates copiously the view that all discord is

> harmony not understood,
> All partial evil universal good,

the Persian mystic preaches war to the death against the carnal self, which he describes as 'a Hell with seven gates' and as 'the mother of all idols'. The evil that men see in others is the reflection of their own.

> You are that evil-doer, and you strike those blows at yourself: 'tis yourself you are cursing at that moment.
> You do not see clearly the evil in yourself, else you would hate yourself with all your soul.

The poet devotes much space to a masterly description of the passions and vices, treating the topic with a realism which is sometimes embarrassing to his translators. Answering the necessitarian argument, he insists that our actions, though the effect of divine agency, are freely willed by us, so that we have no right to make God responsible for them. If sinners are conscious of acting under compulsion, why do they yield to it so readily and why do they afterwards feel ashamed and guilty? Yet this cannot be the final solution. Perfect freedom is impossible without perfect love and consists in union of the human will with the divine.

> The word 'compulsion' makes me impatient for Love's sake;
> 'Tis only he who loves not that is fettered by 'compulsion'.
> This is communion with God, not 'compulsion',
> The shining of the moon, not a cloud;
> Or if it be 'compulsion', it is not ordinary compulsion,
> It is not the compulsion of self-will inciting us to sin.

The moral purpose by which the *Mathnawī* is inspired asserts itself even in philosophical passages describing the emanation of the One Being through every grade of existence. This process is epitomized in the evolution of the soul which, as the form of universal reason, descends to the material world, passes through the mineral, vegetive, and animal kingdoms, attains to rationality in man, suffers probation, undergoes retribution, ascends to the sphere of the angels, and continuing its spiritual development till it is reunited with the infinite One, of which it is the mirror, realizes that all its experience of separation was 'such stuff as dreams are made on'.

First he appeared in the realm inanimate;
Thence came into the world of plants and lived
The plant-life many a year, nor called to mind
What he had been; then took the onward way
To animal existence, and once more
Remembers naught of that life vegetive,
Save when he feels himself moved with desire
Towards it in the season of sweet flowers,
As babes that seek the breast and know not why.
Again the wise Creator whom thou knowest
Uplifted him from animality
To Man's estate; and so from realm to realm
Advancing, he became intelligent,
Cunning and keen of wit, as he is now.
No memory of his past abides with him,
And from his present soul he shall be changed.

Though he is fallen asleep, God will not leave him
In this forgetfulness. Awakened, he
Will laugh to think what troublous dreams he had,
And wonder how his happy state of being
He could forget and not perceive that all
Those pains and sorrows were the effect of sleep
And guile and vain illusion. So this world
Seems lasting, though 'tis but the sleeper's dream;
Who, when the appointed Day shall dawn, escapes
From dark imaginings that haunted him,
And turns with laughter on his phantom griefs
When he beholds his everlasting home.

Be sure, the Day of Judgement will draw out
What good or ill soever thou hast done
In this life, and interpret all thy dream.
O tyrant who didst tear the innocent,
Thou from this heavy slumber shalt arise
A wolf, thy wicked passions one by one
Made howling wolves to rend thee limb from limb.

Space forbids further quotation from this great and many-sided poem which expresses the spirit of Persian mysticism with a power and insight that have never been equalled, though on account of its discursiveness, prolixity, and frequent obscurity few would care to read it through. The author has glimpses of the modern world and breathes a larger air than Ghazālī, whose religious attitude is that of an enlightened medieval theologian. It is the nature of mystics to soar, just as it is the business of legalists to imitate the old woman who clipped the wings and cut the talons of the king's falcon that fell into her hands. In Islam, however, such penalties are hard to enforce, and Ṣūfism followed its logical line of development within the Muslim community. This freedom was, on the whole, advantageous to both parties; it secured fair play in the inevitable conflict between them, it fostered mutual tolerance, and the diseases which some Roman Catholic writers attribute to it were at least no worse than the remedies formerly applied by ecclesiastical authority in Europe. As we have seen, the Ṣūfīs themselves, conscious of the dangers inherent in their doctrine, gradually organized a system of discipline under the direction of adepts who claimed and received unquestioning obedience. These were members of the hierarchy of visible and invisible saints, with the *Quṭb* (Axis) at their head, by whom according to Ṣūfī belief the spiritual government of the world is carried on. Their responsibility was the greater because practically every Ṣūfī has been trained by a shaikh and regards the self-instructed as alien to the brotherhood. But *quis custodiet ipsos custodes?* I do not speak of the saintly virtues; but what can the laws of conventional morality or anything else in the world matter to men who cultivate ecstasy by autohypnotic methods and feel themselves inspired to such an extent that their individuality is lost in God? Instead of judging them by ordinary standards, which is futile, let us rather reflect that sincere devotion to the Ideal—or as they would say, the Real—covers a multitude of sins, and acknowledge that in the course of their quest they reached, if not the goal, at any rate a purer religion and a higher morality than Islam could offer them.

R. A. Nicholson.

PHILOSOPHY AND THEOLOGY

Among the Muslim peoples it is commonly held that in the golden age of the caliphate there flourished world-wide systems of philosophy which were Arabian and Islamic, and that the Muslim academies were the forerunners and patterns of the European universities. This view, involving as it does the claim that Islam is the parent that begat and nourished European civilization, is not confined to mere propagandist literature, but is to be found, with or without qualification, in most of the serious contributions which modern Muslim scholars have made to the study of the development and history of Islamic institutions in the Middle Ages. In western literature, too, from time to time one reads of 'Arabian philosophy'. Some occidental writers profess to regard 'Arabian' philosophy as a hotchpotch of the opinions of the ancients into which heterogeneous matter of all kinds has been thrown and left to seethe. They maintain that there is no such thing as 'Arabian' philosophy: that the Arabic-speaking peoples merely took over the Greek philosophy which was current among the Syrian Christians and the cultured pagan community of Ḥarrān and added thereto a few ingredients borrowed from Persia and India.

Now it is true that the whole framework, scope, and material of Arabic philosophy is to be traced to the civilization of the empires which the Arabs conquered, and that Greek philosophy predominates in their system. Whatever has been said in more recent times there was no misapprehension of the truth among earlier Muslim scholars. Al-Jāḥiẓ (*d.* A.D. 869) of Baṣra, an able and versatile writer whose influence in Muslim Spain was destined to be of great importance, makes a generous recognition of the debt which his co-religionists owe to the intellectual achievements of the Greeks: 'Did we not possess the books of the ancients in which their wonderful wisdom is immortalized and in which the manifold lessons of history are so dealt with that the past lives before our eyes, did we not have access to the riches of their experience which would otherwise have been barred to us, our share in Wisdom would be immeasurably smaller and our means of attaining a true perspective most meagre.' Furthermore, the philosophers and scholastic theologians themselves for the most part made no attempt to conceal the origin of their theories. No literary pretence would have deceived the obscurantists who clung to the Quran and the Traditions of the Prophet, for a large number of condemnations on all intellectual pursuits which were unknown to the Arabs of Muḥammad's time are directed against those who introduce innovations of foreign origin. Philosophy was called 'wisdom mixed with unbelief'. Book-titles such as *An exposure of Greek infamies and a sip of religious Counsels* and *Ocular demonstration of the Refutation of Philosophy in the Quran*, tell their own story. A tale was circulated that a well-known philosopher on his death-bed recanted his doctrines, his last recorded utterance being 'Almighty God has spoken the truth and Avicenna is a liar'

Again, it is true to say that the positive contribution which the Arabs made to the sum of human knowledge by way of addition to the achievements of earlier thinkers is not of great importance: but even so, though one may convincingly prove that the Islamic civilization bequeathed little or no more than it had itself inherited, it seems somewhat unfair to deny to that civilization a right to the peculiar synthesis of philosophic thought which its doctors adopted as their own, and it would be a positive injustice to belittle the zeal and enthusiasm for learning for the sake of learning which animated large numbers of men throughout the vast Muhammadan empire. 'Arabic philosophy' does convey to orientalists a definite meaning.[1] They know that only one pure-blooded Arab—al-Kindī—distinguished himself by a

[1] And to others also: cf. Keicher's monograph *Raymundus Lullus und seine Stellung zur arabischen Philosophie*.

mastery of philosophical problems; but they also know that that strange and often irreconcilable combination of Aristotelian and neo-Platonic thought which even the greatest Muslim philosophers accepted as a reasonable explanation of the universe can best be called Arabian. Muhammadan it was not. Its foremost exponents were often nominal Muslims only, or self-confessed heretics who paid for their opinions with their lives or the loss of their liberty.

Had the Arabs been barbarians like the Mongols, who stamped out the fire of learning in the East so effectually that it never recovered, and possibly never will recover, from the loss of its libraries and its literary tradition, the Renascence in Europe might well have been delayed more than one century. Before the days of printing the life of a scholar must always have abounded in irritation and disappointment. Until, and even after, the foundation of the Muslim universities in East and West, many a student set out as a matter of course on a journey of a thousand miles or more in quest of a teacher. Vast journeys from Spain to Mecca or from Morocco to Baghdād were undertaken by young men who left their homes practically penniless to sit at the feet of a chosen master.

Here a word on the origin of the Muslim universities may not be out of place. The first was the famous Niẓāmī University of Baghdād which was founded by Niẓāmu-l-Mulk, the friend of Omar Khayyām and the Vizier of the Turk, Alp Arslān, in the year A. H. 457, the year before the Norman Conquest of England. Within a short time other universities sprang up at Nīshāpūr, Damascus, Jerusalem, Cairo, Alexandria, and other places: often, it will be noticed, in a city which had borne a reputation for learning centuries before the rise of Islam. In Europe Salerno[1] was already famous as a studium of medicine in the tenth century. If this school actually was a survival of the

[1] See Rashdall's *The Universities of Europe in the Middle Ages*, I, ch. 3, and *Cambridge Medieval History*, vi, p. 560.

old Greek school of medicine it would be due to the fact that southern Italy was a part of the Byzantine Empire until the eleventh century. Even after the Norman conquest it was the home of a large population which spoke Greek. Still, on the other hand, the Norman conquerors of Sicily patronized Arabian learning and adopted Islamic customs with such thoroughness that it is difficult to avoid the conclusion that Arabian medicine must have had a powerful influence on the school, sustaining if not creative.[1] In any case the large Saracen population must have been treated by Muslim physicians, and the earliest authors show that they were not ignorant of the writings of Arabian doctors.

Salerno was a medical school pure and simple: it was not a university. The oldest Christian universities of Bologna, Paris, Montpellier, and Oxford came into being in the twelfth century. The first 'Arabian' university in Europe owed its origin to Muslim learning, but not to Muslim initiative, and it came very late in the day. Alfonso the Wise (1252–81) secured the services of a certain Abu Bakr al-Riqūṭī, one of the most learned men of his generation, and built for him a school, where al-Riqūṭī gave instruction in all the sciences to Christians, Jews, and Muslims.

But the proudest of the Muslim universities was the Mustanṣiriyah which was founded in A.D. 1234 in Baghdād. 'We are told that in outward appearance, in stateliness of ornament and sumptuousness of furniture, in spaciousness and in the wealth of its pious foundations, the Mustanṣiriyah surpassed everything that had previously been seen in Islam. It contained four separate law-schools, one for each of the orthodox sects of the

[1] Guillaume le Bon (II) exhorted his subjects, the majority of whom were Saracens, to address their prayers to Allah; and his successors imitated Saracen money, court ceremonial, palace inscriptions, method of administration, and even, it is said, the harem. *Description de l'Afrique et de l'Espagne* par Edrisi, ed. Dozy and de Goeje, Int. p. 1.

Sunnīs, with a professor at the head of each, who had seventy-five students (*faqīh*) in his charge, to whom he gave instruction gratis. The four professors each received a monthly salary, and to each of the three hundred students one gold dīnār a month was assigned. The great kitchen of the college further provided daily rations of bread and meat to all the inmates. According to Ibn-al-Furāt there was a library . . . in the Mustanṣiriyah with rare books treating of the various sciences, so arranged that the students could easily consult them, and those who wished could copy these manuscripts, pens and paper being supplied by the establishment. Lamps for the students and a due provision of olive oil for lighting up the college are also mentioned, likewise storage places for cooling the drinking water; and in the great entrance hall . . . stood a clock . . . doubtless some form of clepsydra, announcing the appointed times of prayer, and marking the lapse of the hours by day and by night. Inside the college a bath house . . . was erected for the special use of the students, and a hospital . . . to which a physician was appointed, whose duty it was to visit the place every morning, prescribing for those who were sick; and there were great store-chambers in the Madrasah provided with all requisites of food, drink, and medicines.'[1] And all this in the early thirteenth century!

The origin of intellectual movements in the eleventh century is extremely obscure, and in the present state of our knowledge it would be safer to point to the vast importance of the role of Muslim savants in Spain in educating individuals rather than to the direct influence of their system of education on the Christian universities of Europe. The latter are of course junior to the Oriental universities, and the testimony of scholars in the Middle Ages abundantly justifies the thesis that Islamic learning provided them with much material for their studies. Many of

[1] *Baghdad during the Abbasid Caliphate*, G. le Strange, Oxford, 1900, p. 267 f.

these scholars are mentioned in *The Legacy of Israel* and in other chapters of this book. John of Salisbury[1] reminds his readers of the services of the Spaniards and those in touch with Africa and the Muhammadan East. Roger Bacon (*c.* 1215–92) can write 'philosophia ab . . . arabico deducta est. Et ideo nullus latinus sapientiam sacrae scripturae et philosophiae poterit ut oportet intelligere, nisi intelligat linguas a quibus sunt translatae'; and he tells us what Arabian authors especially justify this statement. But unfortunately the Christian travellers of earlier centuries do not tell us what they brought back with them from their journeys to countries under Muslim rule or Muslim influence. A comparison of the subjects studied among the Muslims in the tenth and eleventh centuries with the similar preoccupations of Christian students in the eleventh and twelfth centuries might be an indication that there is a closer connexion between Eastern and Western universities than has hitherto been supposed, but no decisive evidence is available. The very nature of systematic study, the relation of professor and pupil, the question of fees and endowments, the maintenance of discipline and the conferring of degrees or licences to teach, and the manifold activities of university life, must inevitably be more or less the same whether the centre of learning be in Baghdād or Oxford. Consequently, until some more definite proof of filiation is forthcoming, it would seem precarious to assert that the Christian university as an institution was moulded after the Islamic pattern. There are a good many points of resemblance, such as the grant by the Muslim professor of an *ijāza* or licence to teach or repeat the contents of a given document in the name and with the authority of the professor. Such a custom is evidently akin to the medieval *licentia docendi*, the earliest form of degree[2]; on the other hand the principle

[1] *Metalogicus*, iv. 6. I am indebted to Professor Clement C. J. Webb for this reference.

[2] However, the authorities who conferred the licence were not the same.

that nobody should set up as a teacher without having himself been taught for an adequate period by a duly authorized professor is too obvious to need a precedent so distant. Other superficial points of contact are the presence of large bodies of foreigners who were organized as *nationes*; also the early European practice of imparting instruction freely without exacting payment from pupils. This generous recognition of an obligation to hand on the torch of learning without requiring payment still lives on in the great university mosque of al-Azhar in Cairo, where students from all parts of the Muslim world are grouped in separate communal quarters, and are partially supported by pious benefactions and grants from the governing body.[1]

The way in which individual Latin scholars drew Arabian learning from Spain in the century before the official translators began their work has been sketched with great skill and probability in *The Legacy of Israel*.[2] In Europe Arabian ideas were propagated by wandering scholars, whose writings have not

[1] Rashdall writes: 'The Licence of the Rector to "read" a title or book, or rather the completion of such a course of lectures, made a man a Bachelor.' and 'A canonist could . . . lecture on a single title after four years of "hearing".' The technical sense of 'hearing' and 'reading' correspond to similar technicalities in Arabic, but these similarities and also the employment of pupil-teachers after five or six years of instruction are not necessarily of any significance and may well have arisen spontaneously in any university. Could an Arabic origin of that mysterious word *baccalareus* (which the *Oxford English Dictionary* can hardly be said to explain satisfactorily) be conjectured we should be on firmer ground. Originally a bachelor in a university appears to have been a student who was allowed to teach in a master's school, and though I have failed to find the exact expression in any Arabian writer *biḥaqq-al-riwāya*—'the right to teach on the authority of another'—would describe the baccalaureate and provide a tolerable assonance. However, the earliest use of the word is said (Hatzfeld et Darmesteter) to be in the *Chanson de Roland*. If the conjecture could be substantiated it would follow that the word of Arabic origin had been assimilated to 'bacheler'; the Arabic not providing a word for the person holding the degree but only for the office.

[2] See article by Charles and Dorothea Singer, p. 204 f.

survived; and though the channels through which the works of Avicenna, Algazel, and Averroes reached the Latins are well known, the more subtle penetration of ideas in the preceding centuries can only be conjectured: it cannot be proved.

Through the translations made by Dominic Gundisalvus, Archdeacon of Segovia, in the early years of the twelfth century, the Christian West became acquainted with Aristotle by way of Avicenna, al-Fārābī, and Algazel. Gundisalvus' own encyclopaedia of knowledge relies in the main on the information he has drawn from Arabian sources.[1]

The frequent statement that the West owed the recovery of Aristotle to the Arabs needs some qualification. It may be said that down to the time of Gundisalvus it was scarcely suspected that Aristotle was a philosopher. Bacon tells us that Boethius was the first to make the West acquainted with Aristotle. His translation of the *Categories* and the *De Interpretatione* together with his own logical treatises and commentaries formed practically the sum of Aristotelian knowledge in Europe down to about 1150. The West really knew no more of Plato than they knew of Aristotle by direct contact; but Platonism enjoyed the advantage of being firmly embedded in Christian thought. The earliest (but incomplete) version of the *Metaphysics* to reach Paris came in *c.* 1200 from Byzantium; a few years later another incomplete version translated from the Arabic arrived. The complete work was not in the hands of scholars till after 1260. The *Nicomachean Ethics* arrived first from Greek sources, then from Arabic, and lastly in its entirety, translated direct from the Greek, about 1250. The *Physics* and *De Anima* were received first from Greek.

Thus it may be said that the West owed the recovery of Aristotelian philosophy to the Arabs inasmuch as the interest of European scholars in the works of Aristotle was first kindled by acquaintance with Arabian thought. It can hardly be doubted

[1] See further *The Legacy of Israel*, pp. 254–6.

that Europeans took up the study of Aristotle because their zeal for philosophy had been quickened by contact with Arabian thought. Indeed, if the first effective influence was not Arabian, how are we to explain the fact that for generations Aristotle was confounded with the teaching ascribed to Averroes? Averroes himself knew no Greek, being content to rely on the translations of his predecessors. His system, which was extremely popular among the Jews, had penetrated Christian thought so deeply as to become a menace to the doctrines of the Church, and to St. Thomas especially belongs the merit of separating Aristotle from his commentator, and of criticizing the Arabian interpretation.

Our concern is not so much with the origin and development of Arabian philosophy and theology, as with their influence on the thought of the West. But a summary account of the system and its provenance is indispensable if we are to understand the place the Arabs occupy in the history of the transmission of philosophy. Here it may be remarked that it is difficult, if not impossible, to separate philosophy from theology in a survey of this kind. There is good authority for treating philosophy and theology as one subject, for Aristotle himself calls what we know as metaphysics both 'First Philosophy' and 'Theology'; and among the Greeks monotheism arose not in religious but in philosophical circles. This fact is of considerable importance in a discussion of the origin and development of the two studies in Islam. If philosophy in post-Christian times be primarily concerned with that which can be ascertained by human reason, while theology claims to teach the spiritual truths of things eternal which can only be ascertained through revelation, the Muhammadan world as a whole refused to recognize such a distinction of territory as valid. Both St. Thomas Aquinas and Duns Scotus recognize a distinction between philosophy and theology, and regard each as supreme in its own sphere; and like their Arabian predecessors they regard both reason and revelation as authoritative. But there is not always agreement as to what belongs to metaphysics and what to revealed religion. Roger Bacon, in his commendation of the study of philosophy, shows clearly his attitude to the question and indicates the oriental sources which determined the bent of his mind. 'Metaphysics among the philosophers', he says, 'occupies the place of one part of theology, being named by them together with moral philosophy *scientia divina*[1] and *theologia physica*, as appears from the first and eleventh books of Aristotle's *Metaphysics*, and from the ninth and tenth of the *Metaphysics* of Avicenna. Metaphysics surveys many matters concerning God and the angels and divine objects of this kind.'[2] And again, 'the end of speculative philosophy is the knowledge of the creator through the creatures'.[3] The Christian must always remember that 'in itself philosophy leads to the blindness of hell, and therefore it must in itself be darkness and mist'.[4]

Among the Arabian scholars there was no larger measure of agreement. Avicenna stressed being *qua* being as the proper subject of metaphysics, while Averroes, who claimed to depend more closely on Aristotle, asserted that God and the Intelligences were its proper province. Thus in the two Arabian philosophers best known to the Latins the domain of metaphysics and theology was quite different. Averroes claimed the right to submit everything save the revealed dogmas of the faith to the judgement of reason.

To return to the origin of philosophical studies among the Muslims. There is no reason for supposing that the Arabs who formed the victorious armies of the first caliphs differed markedly from the Arabs of to-day, save that the proportion of full-blooded Bedawin was probably considerably greater, a fact which is not

[1] Avicenna's treatise on metaphysics is called *'ilmu-l-ilāhiyyāt,* literally 'knowledge of matters pertaining to the divine'.

[2] *Opus Majus*, *Philog.*, ch. iii.

[3] Ibid., ch. viii.

[4] Ibid., ch. xix fin.

likely to raise exaggerated hopes among modern philosophers. Among such men interest in any form of learning was negligible. Not only stimulus to study but also material for study had to come from without. The stimulus came when the first generation or two had passed away, and the conquering caste had to justify their right to exist as a separate religious community. While the newcomers ruled by force of arms, preserved all or at any rate most of the distinctive customs of the desert, and spoke a different dialect, there was no need of any intellectual justification; the more especially when, in Syria, for example, their Christian neighbours regarded them as a new sect of Arian tendencies, while the Arabs themselves looked with an indulgent eye on the worship of the Trinitarians. But before many years had passed distinctions between the Semites of the Desert and the Semites of the Sown became blurred. The caliphs' armies had enrolled thousands of Arabs who had served the 'Romans' as auxiliaries. In Syria, Mesopotamia, and Egypt the Arabs were often welcomed because they put an end to imperial exactions and relieved the schismatic churches from the unwelcome pressure of the central government, displaying a better knowledge of local feeling and sentiment than foreigners. Islam at first was all but inarticulate. Its simple creed of One God did not involve any necessary contradiction of Christian belief. It was only when the contradictory and controversial aspects of the two religions were emphasized that Islam found its voice and sought for formulas in which to give it utterance.

In the course of time large numbers of Jews and Christians became Muslims in order to escape the poll-tax which was exacted from all non-Muslim monotheists, or people who possessed inspired scriptures.[1] These people carried with them the culture of the Byzantine and Persian empires. Such widespread secessions alarmed the authorities of the Church, and they proceeded by

[1] I have described the influence of the Jews in *The Legacy of Israel*, pp. 129 ff.

argument to attack the foundations of Islam. What was the nature of Allah? What was meant by the assertion that he was Almighty, Omniscient? What was the relation of His knowledge to Himself. If He had predestined all things by an immutable decree wherein lay man's free will and responsibility? Such were some of the problems which the Christian churches had been debating for centuries. They handed them on with ironical satisfaction to the Muhammadan community, where they caused as much bitterness and strife as in their original home. There were times and areas where these questionings could be silenced by the voice of authority, but among the more earnest and intelligent classes they called for some sort of answer. Such answers as were given were at first halting and tentative. The language and the ideas were new and strange to a people whose governing classes had not known even of the existence of philosophy. St. John of Damascus when he argues can dismiss his Muslim opponents with kindly condescension. The Muslims, however, were not long content to leave their adversaries in undisputed possession of the weapons of Greek dialectic, and they gradually familiarized themselves with the system of thought which was contained in the writings of the Greeks and Syrians. Little has come down to us from this early period save the tradition that various philosophical works were translated into Arabic, and some sayings of earlier speculative theologians which show that philosophical doubts had already begun to work in their minds.

It was under the patronage of the Abbasid Caliph al-Ma'mūn (198–218, i.e. A.D. 813–33) that philosophy really came into its own. From the fact that this caliph held that the Qurān was created in time in opposition to the orthodox tenet that it was eternal before all worlds, and was confessedly an upholder of the doctrines of the Muʿtazila[1] or Liberal theologians on the subject of the divine nature, it may be inferred that the Muslims had long been familiar with Greek thought and Christian theology.

[1] See p. 262.

Ma'mūn founded a school of savants at Baghdād in which the study and translation of Greek works was pursued with the utmost vigour. In the task of translation the Nestorian physician Ḥunayn ibn Isḥāq al-ʿIbādī (809–73) and his family played an important part. Ḥunayn did not work only at Baghdād: he travelled through Syria and Palestine on his way to Alexandria to learn all that the ancient world knew of medicine and to gain a better working knowledge of Greek. Apart from the medical and mathematical treatises he translated into Arabic, Ḥunayn is to be credited with the *Categories*, *Physics*, and *Magna Moralia* of Aristotle; the *Republic*, *Laws*, and *Timaeus* of Plato, though these books are not always translated in full. His son Isḥāq (died *c.* 910) was perhaps responsible for Arabic versions of the *Metaphysics*, *de anima*, *de generatione et corruptione*, and the *Hermeneutics*, together with commentaries of Alexander of Aphrodisias and others, so that when the work of Ḥunayn's nephew Ḥubaysh was added there was not a great deal of contemporary knowledge which remained unrepresented in the Arabic language. In the poetry, drama, and history of the classical age the Arabs felt no interest.

Thus far there has been found very little independent thought and no justification of the term 'Arabian philosophy'. The school of translators which these men founded was continued by Jacobites whose claim to independent value stands no higher than their predecessors' with the exception of the treatise which a certain Qusṭā ibn Lūqā wrote on the difference between the soul and the spirit. This work exercised considerable influence when it was translated into Latin.

In this era falls the work of the first and last philosopher the Arabs produced. Abū Yūsuf Yaʿqūb ibn Isḥāq al-Kindī was an Arab whose family came from the south of the peninsula; he was born about 850 in Kūfa and educated at Baṣra and Baghdād. Not much of his work has survived in its original language, but a good deal is still extant in Latin translations made by Gerard of Cremona and others. With his achievements in mathematics, astrology, alchemy, and optics we are not concerned here. Quite the most important thing he did was to lend his name and authority to the translation of a book which influenced the whole subsequent course of philosophy and theology in East and West until St. Thomas Aquinas, not without aid from Arabian sources, drove it from the field. The work in question bears the following superscription in Arabic: 'The first Chapter of the Book of Aristotle the Philosopher which in Greek is called *Theologia* (*Uthūlūjiyya*) which is a discussion about Divine Government (*rubūbiyya*). The Commentary of Porphyrius the Tyrian which ʿAbdu-l-Masīḥ ibn ʿAbd Allah Nāʿima of Emessa translated into Arabic and which Abū Yūsuf Yaʿqūb ibn Isḥāq al-Kindī (May God have mercy on him!) corrected after collation with the original for Aḥmad ibn al-Muʿtaṣim billāh.'[1] From this it is clear that though the book is ascribed to Aristotle the superscription openly proclaims that it is a commentary attributed to Porphyry. Possibly the *Theology* was ascribed to Aristotle at a later period when the mystical tendencies of neo-Platonism were firmly entrenched in Islam and when the authority of Aristotle as *al-failasūf*—the philosopher *par excellence*—was paramount. The book is not a commentary in any sense of the word, but a neo-Platonic treatise based on books iv–vi of the *Enneads* of Plotinus.

Inasmuch as the theories of the soul which occur in this book recur, with various individual modifications, throughout the course of Arabian philosophy, it may be worth while to summarize them briefly. The soul (*nafs*) is a pure intellectual substance (*jauhar ʿaqlī*) incorporeal and immortal, which descended from the world of intelligence to the world of sense and corporeality. The intellectual substance dwells eternally in the world of intelligence, from which it cannot depart, but it falls short of the pure and passionless intellect in that it con-

[1] Ed. by Fr. Dieterici, Leipzig, 1883.

ceives a desire to give birth to the forms which are present to itself, and desire begets pain until it accomplishes its desire in the world of perception. Out of this desire the soul is formed. Therefore the soul is intellect: sometimes it is in a body and sometimes it is external to it. The intellect works in this world through the soul. The soul of all animals has 'taken a wrong path'. There is, too, a plant-soul which is endowed with life, and springs from the same source as the others. The human soul has three parts, plant, animal, and rational. The soul leaves the body at its dissolution, and the pure soul which has kept itself unspotted from the world will return at once without any delay to the intellectual substances. On the other hand, souls which have defiled themselves in this world and have become subject to the lusts of the body will only attain to their original state after grievous exertion. In answer to the question as to what the soul remembers when it has returned to the world of intelligence it is answered that it only thinks and does what is befitting in that world. The proof that it will not remember its former pre-occupations, its desires, or its philosophy is that even in this world it takes no interest in temporal matters when its gaze is fixed on the heavenly world. All knowledge in the heavenly world is timeless, and therefore souls are timeless. Therefore, too, souls know timelessly the things thought in this world.

The manifold operations of the soul at different times form no argument against the soul's faculty being one simple entity. Its working is manifested at different times because corporeal substances cannot receive its workings at one and the same time. The intellect is all things and its essence comprehends all things, so that when it sees its own essence it sees all things.

God is the cause of the intelligence, which is the cause of soul, which is in turn the cause of nature, while nature is the cause of all individual things. Though one thing may cause another, God is the cause of all, for he is the creator of cause. The two worlds of sense and intelligence are related to one another as a rough to a carved stone. Beauty in nature proceeds from the beauty which is in the soul.

The results of secondary causes are not to be attributed to a will residing in the stars. The body, which is merely the instrument of the soul, perishes and disintegrates when the soul has no further use for it and leaves it. Because of the soul man is what he is. The soul remains ever in one state subject neither to corruption nor dissolution.

Such are a few of the ideas which were fathered on Aristotle, and it is strange to reflect that the subsequent Arabian philosophers did not think of questioning the authenticity of a document which contained many statements that they instinctively ignored. To this corruption of the sources of authoritative Aristotelianism may be traced the general confusion and lack of unity of conception which the West inherited from the East, and from which St. Thomas delivered Christendom. However, the mysticism inherent in the Neo-Platonic doctrines met the need of many who found refuge therein from the doubts and difficulties which the system as a whole created when it was circulated as a part of Aristotelianism. On the other hand, the confusion which a piecing-together of incoherent philosophies engendered in the minds of earnest Muslim seekers after truth must have contributed not a little to the hatred and intolerance of all philosophy which so many of their writers express.

By philosophers (*falāsifa*—an arabized plural of *failasūf*) the Arabs meant those whose primary interest was philosophical rather than theological. Al-Shahrastānī (*d.* 1153) says that they all followed the Aristotelian path, save in a few details which they borrowed from Plato and the earlier philosophers. This statement must, of course, be read in accordance with the Islamic belief that the Neo-Platonic theories attributed to Aristotle were really his. Al-Shahrastānī begins his list of Arabian philosophers with al-Kindī and Ḥunayn ibn Isḥāq, and ends it with Abū ʿAlī ibn Sīnā (Avicenna) who, he says, is held by the majority to have had the keenest insight and judgement. Doubtless to these he would have added, had he lived longer, the Spanish philosopher Ibn Rushd (Averroes *d.* 1198), Aristotle's most learned commentator. The physics of these men were founded on Aristotle's doctrine of the four causes: they recognized the existence of forms and natures by which beings can be differentiated, and they sought to discover the principle of being in these forms and natures.

Al-Kindī's own theory of the universe was akin to *The Theology of Aristotle.* The divine intelligence is the cause of the world's existence: its activity is mediated through the heavenly spheres to the terrestrial world. The world-soul is intermediate between God and the world of bodies. This world-soul created the heavenly spheres. The human soul is an emanation from the world-soul. There is thus a duality in man: inasmuch as the soul is tied to the body it is influenced by the heavenly spheres, but in so far as it is true to its spiritual origin it is free and independent. Both freedom and immortality are only attainable in the world of intelligence, so that if man would attain thereto he must set himself to develop his intellectual powers by acquiring a right knowledge of God and the universe.

In the opinion of an exceptionally well-informed biographer, Ibn Khallikān, the greatest of the earlier Islamic philosophers was al-Fārābī (*d.* A. H. 339=950) who was ultimately of Turkish origin. He was a prolific commentator on Aristotle and those works of Plato with which his co-religionists were acquainted. His treatises on *The Soul* and *The Faculties of the Soul* and on *The Intelligence* were well known to the Latins. Al-Kindī and al-Fārābī handed on to their successors the problem of the *intellectus agens.* Aristotle had brought his theory of the human mind under the sway of his theory of the antithesis of power and act, potentiality and actuality; and to him human reason (*intellectus* as it was called in the Middle Ages) was only a capacity for knowledge: sometimes it knows or thinks, sometimes it does not. There must then be an actual being which can rouse the potential human intellect to actuality, and this must itself be intellect ὁ ποιῶν, *al-faʿʿāl*. But what was this active or creative intellect, what its relation to the human soul, to the intelligences which moved the spheres, and to God? Al-Fārābī divided the intellect into four, namely intellect in power, in act, the acquired intellect, and the agent intellect. By the third he seems to have meant the state of the intellect in act at the moment of its understanding the intelligibles. By the agent intellect he meant a pure form which does not reside in matter. It is that which makes the potential intellect actual and the potential intelligible actually intelligible.

Before we leave this subject it may be said that Averroes (see p. 275) held that the active intellect and also the potential intellect were one in all men. Such a belief was destructive of personal immortality and of individual personality. It was combated by St. Thomas Aquinas, who taught that the possible or potential intellect and also the active intellect was a part of the soul of each individual, so that the number of active intellects and possible intellects is identical with the sum of the human race. Avicenna had followed al-Fārābī in asserting the unity of the active though not of the potential intellect in all men, but this the great Dominican rightly saw was inconsistent with the individual's control over his own actions.

In al-Fārābī we meet those arguments for the existence of God which are derived from the *Timaeus* and the *Metaphysics* and recur with tedious iteration in all the Islamic scholastics—the necessary and the potential, the impossibility of an infinite chain of causes and the postulate of a first cause necessarily existent in and for itself. Al-Fārābī was an enthusiastic exponent of the theory that the world had no beginning, a doctrine which was an offence to Islam and Christianity. His definition of time as the movement which holds things together deserves mention.

A name far better known in the West than al-Fārābī was Avicenna (Abū ʿAlī al Ḥusayn ibn ʿAbd Allāh ibn Sīnā, 980–1037) whose family sprang from Bukhārā. His posthumous fame rested more on his medical than his philosophical writings. He had the gift of popular writing and could make a subject his own and explain it briefly and succinctly to the world, so that he was justly regarded as representative of the best Arabian philosophic thought before the rise of Averroes in the West. The Latins knew Avicenna before they became acquainted with the work of Averroes. Raymond, Archbishop of Toledo, between the years 1130 and 1150, ordered translations to be made by his Archdeacon Dominic Gundisalvus and Juan Avendeath of Seville. Avicenna's general position is similar to that of his predecessor, but his doctrines are much more clearly articulated. Pure intelligences emanated from the necessary being, simple substances, not subject to change. These beautiful things turned always towards the necessary being whom they sought to imitate, rapt in the intellectual delight of contemplating the divine throughout eternity. Avicenna's interpretation of his predecessors exercised a powerful influence in the West when his works had been translated into Latin.[1]

One of the many words and ideas which Avicenna handed on to the West was *intentio*,[2] the Arabic *maʿqūlāt*, i.e. what is understood by the intellect, intelligibles. There were two kinds of 'intentions', the primary conception of a thing such as a tree, and the secondary intention or logical concept of a thing in relation to abstract universal conceptions. Avicenna's contention that the subject of logic was second intentions by which one proceeded from the known to the unknown was taken over by Albertus Magnus, and became part of the scholastic tradition.

Avicenna made for himself and posterity a problem which taxed his ingenuity to the utmost. He laid down the principle

[1] Cf. *Legacy of Israel*, p. 211.

[2] See the article on this word in *New English Dictionary*.

that from the one and indivisible only one being can originate.[1] Therefore it is not permissible to assert that form and matter spring directly from God, for that would involve the assumption that there are two different modes in the divine essence. Matter, indeed, is not to be thought of as coming from God, because it is the very principle of multiplicity and diversity.

Again, argued Avicenna, we may not suggest that a necessary being which has no final cause is influenced by a purpose in the sense that he acts for the sake of something other than himself. For if he did he would be dominated in his actions by regard for a being inferior to himself. It would then be necessary to distinguish within the divine nature: (*a*) the good of the thing which made it desirable; (*b*) the divine knowledge of that good; and (*c*) the divine intention of acquiring or producing that good. Therefore something intermediary between God the necessary being and the world of multiplicity must be postulated. The problem, therefore, was how to account for the fact of a complex universe and a simple creator.

Avicenna began by combining the notions of the necessary and the possible with the notions of consciousness and knowledge. The first caused, the pure intelligence, derives its being from the first being. It is therefore necessary. But in itself it is merely contingent, since there was no necessity for the first cause to cause it. Thus arose a duality in the universe by which the first cause was unaffected, and from this duality there came triplicity. Thence came the series of emanations which ended in the sphere of the moon, where the intelligence of the moon engendered a last pure intelligence which produced human souls and the four elements. Here Avicenna got into serious difficulty. He had lost the principle which he had held through the spheres, the principle that 'from one only one can proceed'.

[1] No doubt Plotinus, who was conscious of the difficulty in showing how plurality can emanate from unity, is the source of this and many other doctrines of Avicenna.

The elements might be one materially by reason of a common substratum, but what of their forms? He attributed the existence of 'four elements' to a knowledge within the pure intelligences that they were four in God's thought. To endeavour to safeguard his principle and still to leave room for multiplicity Avicenna advanced the theory that matter was 'prepared' or 'disposed' to accept a particular form. This disposition was produced by the motions of the spheres in such a way that the form had simply to occupy or appropriate the matter which had been prepared to receive its proper form.

The scale of creation, according to many Muslim philosophers, was constructed thus:

First Principle, i.e. God.

The First Intelligence, knowing its essence and its origin.

The Second Intelligence knowing itself as (*a*) necessary (*b*) possible.	(*a*) the soul and (*b*) body of the ninth sphere.
The Third Intelligence knowing itself as (*a*) necessary (*b*) possible.	(*a*) the soul and (*b*) body of the sphere of Saturn.
and so on till	
The Sphere of the Moon	the soul and body of the sphere of the Moon.
The Active Intelligence:	human souls and the four elements.

Although it is anticipating the march of learning, it is convenient to insert here Roger Bacon's account of the state of philosophical knowledge in his day (1292): 'The greater part of Aristotle's philosophy failed to have any effect [in the West] either because manuscripts were hidden away and extremely rare, or because the subject matter was difficult or distasteful, or because of the wars in the East, until after the time of Mahomet when Avicenna and Averroes and the rest brought back Aristotle's philosophy into the light of comprehensive exposition. Although some logical and other works had been translated from the Greek by Boethius, yet only from the time of Michael the Scot, who translated certain parts of Aristotle's books on Nature and Metaphysics with his own expositions, has the philosophy of Aristotle been highly prized by the Latins. Of the thousand books which contain his great and comprehensive wisdom only a mere modicum has even been translated into Latin up to the present, and less still is in general use among students. Avicenna in particular, Aristotle's imitator and expositor, who completed philosophy as far as he could, composed a work on philosophy in three volumes, as he says in the prologue of his book *The Sufficiency*. One was a popular work like the dicta of the Peripatetic philosophers who are of the school of Aristotle; the second according to the pure truth of philosophy which "fears not the thrusts of opponents' spears" as he says himself; the third, which he completed at the end of his life, in which he explained the earlier volumes and gathered together the more obscure facts of nature and art. But two of these volumes have not been translated. The Latins possess certain parts of the first which is called the book of Assipha (variant Assepha) that is the *Book of Sufficiency*.[1] After him came Averroes, a man of solid wisdom who corrected many statements of his predecessors and contributed a good deal of new material himself, although he too must be corrected in some particulars and needs amplifying in many others. However, as Solomon writes in Ecclesiastes, "Of making many books there is no end".'[2] There are grounds for regarding Bacon as an embittered scold, and he certainly failed sometimes to keep abreast of the knowledge of

[1] This is a mistranslation. The correct title, *Liber Sanationis*, was, I think first given in 1887 in *Analecta Orientalia*, ed. D. S. Margoliouth.

[2] *Philosophiae*, xiii.

his own day; but nevertheless there is value in his statements if we apply them to his immediate past.

Inasmuch as Muhammadan Spain was a faithful mirror of all the warring sects of Oriental Islam and was drawn into the many controversies, philosophical and dogmatic, which agitated the ancient centres of Hellenism, it is essential that some account should be given of those thinkers whose teaching exercised strong influence on early Spanish philosophy and scholasticism. Some of Bacon's words still hold good. The time has not yet come when a history of Muslim philosophy can be written. Even were all the relevant material which is contained in manuscripts stored in the various libraries of Europe and the Muhammadan world published and placed in the hands of scholars, we should have to wait till monographs and detailed studies had prepared the ground for a general survey of its vast content. At the present time there are many gaps in our knowledge which are being filled up slowly; but almost every accession to our knowledge of medieval Arabian philosophy also throws fresh light on the development of medieval thought in the West. The Muslim East was closely bound to the West by the ties of religion which political disunion could not sever. When once Western Islam was opened to the flow of Eastern speculation a close connexion in thought and the subjects of study became apparent. There was a unity—a common interest—which bound together the scattered scholars of the vast Islamic empire in an intellectual brotherhood of understanding which Europe has lost to-day. Muslim *Fachgenossen* enjoyed the inestimable advantage of thinking, writing, and speaking a common language: consequently we are bound to look for the antecedents of the Muslim thinkers of Spain—who did not become active till the third century of the Hijrah—in the Orient.

In Spain the Church had lost contact with philosophy, so that instead of the Christians being the tutors of the invading Muslims they had to become their pupils. Mozarabic literature is notoriously poor and decadent, and it would be vain to look for the seeds of medieval scholastic in its territory. Spain remained the most orthodox Muslim country for some three centuries, and there is no trace of any important theological or rational movement till the writings of al-Jāḥiẓ, a Muʿtazilite of a prodigious industry who wrote on almost every subject known to the ancient world, were brought in by Spanish Arabs who had attended his lectures in the Orient. Immediately, the Muʿtazilite doctrines met with a response from the more intelligent classes and orthodox teaching was called in question.

The relation of the divine omnipotence to human will had been hotly debated as early as the first century of the Hijrah. This problem, which our own Pelagius raised and discussed with such vigour that the views he propounded soon rose to the rank of a new heresy, was entirely after the hearts of the Greek theologians, who seized with avidity upon a fresh subject of debate. Predestination and Free Will became the burning question. From thence it passed like an infectious disease to the Muslim Church. Those who held the view that God could not predestinate men's actions because He was a moral being who was bound to do that which was righteous came to be known as Muʿtazila, i.e. Secessionists, and the name was subsequently applied to those who departed from a strictly orthodox attitude towards the Quran and apostolic tradition. We are not concerned to follow the fortunes of the liberal theologians in the East, except in so far as their attitude influenced the subsequent course of Muslim thought which poured into western and southern Europe. The great service which the Muʿtazila rendered the civilized world was not so much their insistence upon certain doctrines such as the eternal principle of the divine righteousness[1]; but their demand that theology should be subject to in-

[1] In this they were not innovators, but upholders of the ancient Semitic conception of a *Ṣedeq* or righteousness which is far older than monotheism.

vestigation by the mind. They would not be silenced by such phrases as 'God Most High has said'. Instead they demanded to be told the meaning of 'God' and 'said'. The danger of such an attitude became obvious in those extremists who carried the questionings of the Muʿtazila too far and fell into agnosticism or open atheism. Fitzgerald's famous quatrains well illustrate the pessimism into which many of these men fell. But doubt and pessimism are states of mind which man instinctively regards as unwholesome, and the strength of the Muʿtazilite movement lay with those who laboured to establish the theology of Islam on a firm philosophical foundation. They insisted that the foundation should be logical, and that nothing that was repugnant to philosophy as they knew it should be taught as *de fide*. If we see in the voluminous literature of the Muʿtazilite controversy about the divine attributes merely a dispute about names, we shall as gravely underestimate the issue at stake as Gibbon did when he accused the Christian churches of convulsing the world for the sake of a diphthong.

The Quran can hardly be said to have furnished its devotees with the material for a doctrine of God. It referred to Him as The Knower, The Mighty, the Lifegiver, and the Death-bringer, and so on: it spoke of Allah sitting upon his throne and ascribed to Him the figure of a man. The Muʿtazila regarded such expressions as figurative—mere anthropomorphic concessions to man's limitations. The exaltation of seven attributes: Power, Will, Knowledge, Hearing, Seeing, Speech, and Life, into separate qualities within the Divine nature they condemned as polytheism. Some went so far as to deny that anything whatever could be predicated of God: others rejected only some of these qualities. Duns Scotus, who owed a great deal to the Spanish Arabian School, held that the First Being was living, active, intelligent, and possessed of will.

The name Muʿtazila originally meant one who held that a mortal sinner had 'seceded' from the community of the faithful.

A discussion as to what was meant by God possessing the attribute of speech became fundamental, and eventually led to the suppression of the Muʿtazila by the power of the secular arm. The Muʿtazila argued that if speech was a divine attribute it was necessarily eternal and pre-existent before all worlds, uncreate; otherwise when God spoke in time he suffered change in that He had become what He was not before, and 'becoming' may not be predicated of God. Therefore, if speech was a divine attribute, and the Quran was the record of that speech, the Quran as the word of God must, *ex hypothesi*, be uncreate. But that was absurd, because it was demonstrably a thing of the created world, revealed and written in time and place, as its sometimes domestic and purely local verses plainly indicated. God's attributes were identical with His being, and though his relations with His creatures engendered certain operative attributes, e.g. creation and preservation, they pertained only to time.

The Caliph al-Ma'mūn, himself a Muʿtazilite, made belief in the Quran as a thing of time a test of conformity. Unfortunately the Muʿtazila showed themselves intolerant in the day of their power, and their persecution of the orthodox party who held firmly to the doctrine of the pre-existence of the Quran and a fairly literal exegesis of it, together with an acceptance of the vast number of traditions which circulated in the name of Muḥammad, recoiled on their own head.

However, in the fourth century of the Hijrah it had become abundantly plain that some concession must be made to the claims of the Muʿtazila. Men's minds had become unsettled, and there was urgent need of the restatement of the dogmas of the faith in the light of current philosophy. This task was taken in hand by two men who were the founders of orthodox *kalām*, or scholastic philosophy, namely Abu' l-Ḥasan al-Ashʿarī[1]

[1] Al-Ashʿarī's exposition of his system is now being published in Germany for the first time. Till this is in the hand of scholars it is not possible always

of Baghdād (*c.* 932) and Abu'l-Manṣūr al-Māturīdī (*d.* 944) of Samarqand. *Kalām* is a speculative science, especially, though not exclusively, dealing with theological matters. The *Mutakallimūn*, i.e. 'speakers', the *Loquentes* mentioned by St. Thomas, define *kalām* as 'the science of the foundations of the faith and the intellectual proofs in support of the theological verities'. Originally the word *mutakallimūn* was not applied to any particular school, and could be used of orthodox and unorthodox alike, though in the course of time it came to be applied more exclusively to the defenders of the orthodox Islamic position.

Muʿtazilite doctrines made very little headway in Spain for a good many years, because the heresy was associated in the popular mind with the dangerous Fāṭimid secret society which threatened the whole fabric of Muslim institutions. Consequently philosophers were driven to work in secret. Of the three influential Arabian thinkers whom Spain produced, Ibn Masarra, Ibnu-l-ʿArabī, and Ibn Rushd (Averroes), to whom it fell to hand on the amalgam of philosophy and theology which had come down to them from Neo-Platonic, Pseudo-Empedoclean and Aristotelian writings, the first two were essentially mystics. They imitated the austerities which their Oriental co-religionists had taken over from Christian monks, and combined with the practices of devout recluses a pantheistic speculative philosophy.

The first of these, Muḥammad ibn ʿAbd Allāh ibn Masarra, was born in the year 269 of the Hijrah, i.e. A. D. 883. His father ʿAbd Allāh, a native of Córdoba, had become an enthusiastic student of Muʿtazilite doctrines, which prudence bade him conceal. He died while his son was still a youth, but not before he had instilled into him a love of speculative theology and the ascetic life. Accordingly Ibn Masarra, before he had reached thirty years of age, went into the mountainous district of the

to say how far al-Ashʿarī's own opinions warrant the doctrines of his school.

Sierra de Córdoba and there, surrounded by his disciples, gave himself up to the study and the teaching of an esoteric theology. Secrecy, which fear of the secular power inspired, gave his teaching a depth which would have been denied to a faith more widely disseminated, and secured for Ibn Masarra and his school a lasting influence on the thought of the subsequent centuries. In course of time it became known that Ibn Masarra's retreat was the centre from which doctrine dangerous to the fundamental theses of Islam was being promulgated; and, fearful of the consequences of a charge of atheism, Ibn Masarra deemed it prudent to leave the country under the pretext of undertaking the pilgrimage to Mecca. Not till the accession of the tolerant and scholarly ʿAbd al-Raḥmān III did Ibn Masarra return from Arabia to Spain; and when he was once more established as a teacher the esoteric character of his instruction became more marked. To the outside world he was the pious and austere ascetic who followed the path of penitential exercises and devotions; to his ordinary hearers he was a mystic whose utterances were free from all suggestions of unorthodoxy; but to the inner circle of his initiates he was a master of esoteric truth, whose words bore an inner and mysterious meaning which only the chosen few could understand. Ibn Masarra was the first to introduce into the West an intentionally ambiguous and obscure use of common words, and his example has been followed by most subsequent esoteric writers. So successful was his method that when he died in 931 he was respected as a man of saintly character and pious austerities rather than remembered as a teacher of dubious theology.

No written work of Ibn Masarra is extant; but a learned Spanish Orientalist has collected the material for a reconstruction of the essential features of his system.[1] From these it would seem that Ibn Masarra was an enthusiastic advocate of the philosophy which was fathered on Empedocles. Among the

[1] Professor M. Asín, *Abenmasarra y su escuela*, Madrid, 1914.

Muslims Empedocles was regarded as the first of the seven great philosophers of Greece. By the fiction that he was an auditor of the saints and sages, David, Solomon, and Luqmān, he was clothed with extra-canonical authority, and thus given some sort of standing as one in the line of authoritative tradition, though born out of due time.

The principal difference between the Masarrian and the Oriental version of Neo-Platonism lay in the postulate of a Prime Matter or Element (*ʿunṣur* or *al-hayyūlā al-awwal*) as the first object of God's creation. This element was spiritual and was symbolized by the throne of God.

The ideas which Ibn Masarra seems to have been the first to propagate in the West exercised enormous influence in the succeeding centuries. The famous Jews Avicebron (Ibn Gabīrōl *c.* 1020–1050 or 1070) of Malaga, Judah ha-Levī of Toledo, Moses ibn Ezra of Granada, Joseph ibn Saddīq of Córdoba, Samuel ibn Tibbon, Shem Tōb ibn Joseph ibn Falaqīrā, all adopt the salient doctrines of the pseudo-Empedocles, though it would be hazardous to assert that they necessarily drew them from Ibn Masarra.

Although Jewish philosophical thought in the Middle Ages has already been discussed in this series[1] it is only right that the Jewish debt to the Arabs should receive recognition here. One has only to remember that there was never a Hebrew translation of Aristotle, and that the Jews were content with the versions they were given in al-Fārābī, Avicenna, and Averroes, to realize how profoundly Jewry was influenced by Arabian culture. Hebrew scholars may have looked askance at the Arabic translation of Aristotle (which inspires respect for the Arabist who can translate it rather than for the original translator) and have decided to make use of the accepted paraphrases and commentaries of the authors mentioned above.

The Muʿtazila especially exercised a profound influence on Jewish thinkers: indeed it is sometimes impossible to tell from

[1] *The Legacy of Israel*, pp. 189 f. *et passim*.

the context of a *kalām* book whether the author is a Jew or a Muhammadan. As would be expected, the orthodox Ash'arite view of God, which explicitly denies the operation of natural laws and the relation of cause and effect, had no more influence on Jewry than on Christendom.

From Sa'adia ben Joseph al-Fayyūmī (892–942) down to Joseph Albo (1380–1444) Jewish philosophy concerned itself with the problems and the arguments it inherited from the Arabs. There is no need to catalogue the list of men who were generally abreast with, and sometimes in advance of, the philosophical position of their time.[1] By far the most important was Moses Maimonides (1135–1204) whose searching criticism of the Arabian *Mutakallimūn* was freely used by St. Thomas Aquinas. Maimonides followed the example of al-Fārābī and Avicenna in going back to Aristotle for the material for his proof of the existence, unity, and incorporeality of God.

Among a section of Christian scholastics Avicebron gained an astonishing reputation after his *Fons Vitae* was translated from Arabic into Latin by Avendeath and Dominic Gundisalvus, in the first half of the twelfth century. Almost without exception the Franciscan school came under the spell of the *Fons Vitae*; while the Dominicans, inspired by St. Thomas Aquinas, subjected its doctrines to a sharp and destructive criticism. Gundisalvus himself wrote three works, *De Unitate*, in which he explained that everything save God is composed of matter and form, *De Processione Mundi* and *De Anima*, which propagated the pantheistic theories of the Spanish-Arabian school. So devoid of all polemic was the *Fons Vitae* that many Christian writers thought the author was an Arab, while Guillaume d'Auvergne thought he was the only Christian thoroughly conversant with Arabian philosophy who was sound in the doctrine of the *Verbum Dei*. However, as Guillaume does not share Avicebron's view that spiritual beings are composed of matter,

[1] See further *The Legacy of Israel*, pp. 192–202 and especially 437 ff.

it is reasonable to assume that his praise of him as the noblest of all philosophers was based upon a partial acquaintance with his works.

Alexander of Hales also adopts Avicebron's view of prime matter and speaks of angels as possessed of matter and form. To the Spanish Jew he owes the idea that every active and passive relation indicates form and matter respectively.

Avicebron gave the title *Source of Life* to his work because it claimed to point to an esoteric knowledge of the principle behind all phenomena, a knowledge which was hidden from the ignorant and foolish and revealed to the philosopher who meditated on the divine mysteries. The universe was thus to be explained not by a study of the nature of things, but by a knowledge of the principle which had given them being. Illuminative wisdom was known to Bacon, who speaks of philosophy as 'coming into being through the influence of a divine illumination'.

The revival of peripatetic studies reinforced the opposition of many Christian scholastics to the Spanish-Arabian doctrines, and those who had espoused them were forced to endeavour to clothe them with the authority of the Fathers. St. Thomas therefore takes pains to show that St. Augustine did not explicitly ascribe matter to spiritual beings. With possibly one or two exceptions he expounds Avicebron's theories simply in order to refute them. His *de substantiis separatis* contains a conspicuous example. He asserts that it is impossible to prove that spiritual beings are of matter, and he advances arguments for rejecting the doctrine of emanations in place of the immediate creative activity of God.

Another writer whose work had great influence in the West was Algazel (Abū Ḥāmid ibn Muḥammad al-Ṭūsī al-Ghazālī, 1058–1109). Surnamed *Ḥujjatu-l-Islām*, 'Islam's convincing Proof', his varied life was lived amid the significant intellectual and religious movements of his day. In turn he had been philosopher, scholastic, traditionist, sceptic, and mystic. A man of unquestionable sincerity and firm moral purpose—one of the comparatively few men of his race who consistently exerted himself to awake in his co-religionists a zeal for morality—he has retained in Islam a position somewhat comparable with that of St. Thomas Aquinas in Christianity. In reading his theological treatises one remembers only with an effort that the author is a Muhammadan, unless a reference to the Trinity or the Incarnation is called for.

In early manhood he took up the study of theology and canon law as a career. Before he was twenty he began to question the dogmas which were held to be authoritative and to inquire into theological problems for himself. He was elected assistant to the professor at Nīshāpūr, and from there he passed on to the Niẓāmī Academy at Baghdād, where as a specialist in law his fortune was secure. Here, after some years of conflict between faith and reason he succumbed to a severe nervous breakdown, and left the capital in search of quiet and peace. Regaining the power of ordered thought, he set himself to study afresh the four 'ways' which claimed to lead to the truth: (1) scholastic theology; (2) the Taʿlīmites, who believed that there was an infallible teacher; (3) the 'Aristotelian' philosophers, and (4) the Ṣūfīs or mystics who held that God could be mystically apprehended in ecstasy. He went carefully through all these systems, and finally emerged a mystic. Al-Ghazālī's spiritual pilgrimage is a fascinating story which deserves to be better known in its details. Its importance for our purpose is that Algazel set himself to study afresh the several systems of philosophy and theology and embodied his results in works which were translated into Latin. His books on logic, physics, and metaphysics became known through the translators of Toledo in the twelfth century, though so far as concerns metaphysics Algazel's influence did not equal that of Avicebron, which, being in the main stream of Spanish thought, was firmly established among the Latins until Averroes and St. Thomas drove it into a backwater.

Two Spaniards, Raymund Lull and Raymund Martin, must be mentioned. The controversy which has gathered round the origin of Raymund Lull's philosophy well illustrates the point which was made at the beginning of this chapter. Spanish Orientalists claim to have found very many examples of Arabian inspiration in Lull's work; while certain modern French scholastics have asserted that the genesis of his system is to be found in Augustinianism and the classical tradition of the Church. Where controversy runs high it is begging the question to speak of a 'common-sense view'; but probably many will agree that the facts justify the general conclusion of this chapter: a classical tradition, lost or obscured in Christian Europe, returned under the aegis of Islam and caused enthusiastic study of Arabian writings, of Aristotle, and of the Fathers of the Church. There can be no necessity to write of a '*reproche* d'arabisme' when Christian scholars sought the aid of those who had, on the whole, faithfully transmitted the lore of the ancients. Christians who lived during the Arabian Renascence felt no false shame in learning from the Arabians; nor, to do them justice, did the Arabians display more than a legitimate pride in their intellectual pre-eminence. Ibn Ṭumlūs of Alcira—he died in 1223 and was thus almost a contemporary of Lull—writes in no vainglorious spirit: 'In the sciences of Geometry, Arithmetic, Astronomy, and Music the scholars of Islam have surpassed their ancient predecessors. Still, although it can be said with great probability that men nowadays have access to fuller knowledge than the ancients, it is only fair to remember that it is likely that a good many of the works of the ancients have perished.' Modern scholarship endorses[1] the claim which Ibn Ṭumlūs puts forward with the scrupulous fairness of a scholar who would rather magnify than decry the achievements of his

1 See chapters x, xi, and xii.

predecessors. His claim that Muslim thinkers have achieved as much in the realm of metaphysics as in the positive sciences is not on such sure ground. We have seen what had happened to Aristotelianism in its Arabian dress.

The absence of any considerable body of philosophical opinions which can be labelled Arabian unduly complicates the question of immediate source, but any one who considers that Lull was the founder of a School of Oriental Studies; that he wrote and spoke Arabic; that the great aim of his life was to commend the Christian faith to the Saracens on intellectual grounds; and that he is said to have met a martyr's death preaching to the Arabs of Tunis, will probably feel that to exclude direct Arabian influence from his life is to narrow unduly the range of his overflowing sympathies. He lived in an age (1235–1315) when the West was going back to the real source of its philosophy, and the extent to which he relied on the Muslim philosophers can only be determined by close study of none too decisive data. Certainly in the theological, or rather devotional, section of his writings he borrowed a great deal from the Arabs. His treatise on the *Hundred Names of God* speaks for itself; while in *Blanquerna* he writes with manifest approval of the *marabout* or dervish system of exciting devotional and ecstatic states by the rhythmical recitation of certain words. It seems more natural to suppose that the parallels between the language and habits and the mode of existence adopted by Lull and those current in the Muhammadan world are due to his observation of, and interest in, the religious life of his Muslim contemporaries, rather than to attribute such coincidences to the influence of remote Christian eremites of the early centuries.

The first School of Oriental Studies in Europe was founded at Toledo in 1250 by the Order of Preachers. Here Arabic and Biblical and Rabbinical Hebrew were studied with a view to making men competent to undertake missionary work among Jews and Muslims. The greatest scholar this School produced was Raymund Martin, a contemporary of St. Thomas, whose knowledge of Arabian authors has probably not been equalled in Europe until modern times. Not only was he familiar with the Quran and the collections of apostolic tradition in Islam, but he also quotes the principal theologians and philosophers of Islam from al-Fārābī down to Averroes, with critical observations on the points of difference between them. The *Summa contra Gentiles* and the *Pugio Fidei adversus Mauros et Judaeos* had a common origin in that they were both composed by command of the General of the Order of Preachers.

It was Raymund Martin who perceived the value of Algazel's *Tahāfut al-falāsifa*, or Incoherence of the Philosophers, and incorporated a great deal of it, which is a polemic against the philosophers and scholastics of Islam, into his *Pugio Fidei*. Henceforward Algazel's arguments in favour of the *creatio ex nihilo* and his proofs that God's knowledge comprises particulars, and of the dogma of the resurrection of the dead were employed by Christians in many scholastic treatises. Raymund translates the title of Algazel's attack on the philosophers *Ruina seu Praecipitium Philosophorum*. Algazel's mental and religious attitude appealed to Christian scholars from the moment that his writings could be read, and they still repay careful study. Martin's *Pugio* is remarkable for the ease with which it moves in the world of Oriental letters. The Hebrew of the Old Testament, the Talmud, and the Hebrew version of Maimonides Martin cites in Hebrew, after the manner of a modern scholar writing for a learned circle of readers. Algazel, Rasi (al-Rāzī), and Averroes he cites in Latin, always giving the title of the book from which his quotation is drawn.

Among Algazel's works was a treatise on the place of reason as applied to revelation and the theological dogmas. This work presents many parallels in its arguments and conclusions with the *Summa* of St. Thomas, a fact which can hardly have more than one explanation. The *Summa contra Gentiles* and the

Pugio Fidei had a common origin in so far as they were both written at the request of Raymund de Pinnaforte, General of the Dominican Order; the similarity of some chapters in the *Summa* and in the *Pugio* is suggestive. Some of the more important questions on which St. Thomas and Algazel agree are the value of human reason in explaining or demonstrating the truth about divine things; the ideas of contingency and necessity as demonstrating the existence of God; the unity of God implied in His perfection; the possibility of the beatific vision; the divine knowledge and the divine simplicity; God's speech a *verbum mentis*; the names of God; miracles a testimony to the truth of the prophets' utterances; the dogma of the resurrection from the dead.

As we have seen, St. Thomas refers sometimes to the views of different schools of Muslim theologians: thus in *Contra Gentiles*, iii. 97, he writes: 'First, there is the error of those who maintained that all things are the result of God's simple will without any reason. This is the error of the Muslim theologians *Loquentium* in the law of the Saracens *ut Rabbi Moyses dicit*, according to whom the sole reason why fire heats rather than chills is because God so wills. Secondly, we refute the error of those who assert that the ordering of causes proceeds from divine providence by way of necessity.'

From St. Thomas's citation of Moses (Maimonides, *Guide to the Perplexed*) it is clear that the source of his information about the Ashʿarites and the Muʿtazila in this case was not immediately Arabian. But for the reasons given above Maimonides is unlikely to have been his only source of knowledge. Intellectually Algazel was a man of lesser stature than the Angelic Doctor, but nevertheless they had much in common. Their intention, their sympathies, and their interests were essentially the same. Both endeavoured to state the case for the opposition before they pronounced judgement; both laboured to produce *Summas* which would provide a reasonable statement of their faith, and both found a happiness in the mystical apprehension of the divine which they confessed made their earlier strivings seem as nothing.

Passing over Ibn Bājja (Avempace) and Ibn Ṭufail we must end with a mention of Averroes *che il gran comento feo.* Abū'l-Walīd ibn Rushd (A. H. 520–95, i.e. 1126–98) belongs to Europe and European thought rather than to the East. In Italy his influence lived on into the sixteenth century, and gave rise to the famous disputes of Achillini and Pomponazzi. Averroism continued to be a living factor in European thought until the birth of modern experimental science. Latin has preserved more than one of Ibn Rushd's works which Arabic has lost. In the West at one time Averroism could claim the attention of the first scholars of the age: in Islam Averroes never gained an authoritative position.

Ibn Rushd came of a family of Córdoban lawyers; his grandfather, his father, and he himself were all qāḍīs of Córdoba. He devoted himself to the writing of philosophical works and commentaries during the leisure won from his legal duties. He was for a time in high favour at the Moroccan court, but the systematic opposition of the theologians brought about his downfall. He was accused of heresy and even of apostasy to Judaism and banished from Córdoba, though he was restored to favour before his death and recalled to Marrakesh, where he died in 1198. His tomb may still be seen there.

For centuries Averroes has stood as the representative of the thesis that philosophy is true and revealed religion is false. Siger of Brabant as much as any one is responsible for this, in that when he put forward a thesis which contradicted Christian dogma he claimed the authority of Aristotle and referred obscurities in the interpretation of the philosopher to the commentary of Averroes. To Siger faith and reason were mutually contradictory. In default of accurate study of what Averroes actually wrote and taught it was inevitable that the

Church should condemn with Siger the source from which he claimed to draw his doctrines. Averroes was naturally regarded as the author of Averroism. Similarly, until quite recently, Nestorius has had to bear the reproach of Nestorianism. The Angelic Doctor's treatise *de unitate intellectus contra averroistas*, in which he fulminated against the thesis that belief in the unity of the intellect is necessary *per rationem* while it must be firmly rejected *per fidem*, was in itself sufficient to stamp Ibn Rushd as a false doctor. The famous letter of Stephen, Bishop of Paris, which prefaces the 219 propositions of the Averroists that were condemned, set the seal on Averroes as the father of free thought and unbelief.[1] Of course, Averroes' teaching that the soul was one in all men, and that its parts were only kept apart by the bodies in which they dwelt, was anathema to Christians and Muslims alike. A clear discussion of the question which Martin declares to be 'phreneticorum deliramentis simillimum' will be found in his *Pugio*.[2]

Now, when the authentic writings of Averroes can be examined and he is allowed to speak for himself, it becomes plain that he is not altogether responsible for the intellectual position of the so-called Averroists in Christian countries. On the contrary Averroes and St. Thomas stand side by side as defenders of the same ideal, the harmony of faith and reason. And further the Angelic Doctor has made use of many of the arguments which the Muslim Doctor had previously employed. Any one who will be at the pains to consult Ibn Rushd's *Kitābu-l-Falsafa* and especially his *Faṣlu-l-maqāli fī muwāfaqati-l-ḥikmati wal-sharīʿa*[3]

[1] Still, a distinction must be drawn between Averroes as a philosopher and as the commentator of Aristotle. The same University of Paris which condemned the 'Averroistic' doctrines required its alumni a century later by a solemn oath to teach only those things which were consistent with Aristotle as expounded by Averroes (quod textum Aristotelis et sui commentatoris . . . firmiter et tanquam authenticum observabit). Rashdall, *Universities*, i. 368.

[2] Paris, 1651, p. 182.

[3] Translations of this work have been published in French by L. Gauthier.

(the latter title means 'A true and critical discussion of the question of the agreement between Philosophy and Revealed Religion'), and the relevant portions of his reasoned reply to Algazel's attack upon the Philosophers, namely the *Tahāfutu-l-Tahāfut*, will be prepared at the outset to find that Averroes is the determined adversary of that particular kind of rationalism which was known in the West as Averroism, and his expectation will be realized.

There is a similarity in the attitude of Averroes and St. Thomas which suggests something more than intellectual affinity. The determination to give reason its proper place, to make use of the philosophy of the ancients and at the same time to submit their conclusions to the criticism which the reflection of subsequent centuries demands, to demonstrate the reasonableness of the middle course between a sceptical mysticism and a rationalism which is divorced altogether from belief in the possibility of a revealed religion—these were the motives and aims of both Christian and Muslim doctors. The opposition which both of them met with sprang from a similar source, the party which was hostile to the application of peripatetic principles to theology.

The Angelic Doctor's famous chapters on the domain of faith and reason, with their emphasis on the impotence of reason to penetrate the divine mysteries which have been made known by revelation, have their counterpart in the Córdoban's *Apologia pro vita sua*. To them conflict between philosophy and revealed truth as it was enshrined in the Bible and the Quran respectively was unthinkable. Where there is an apparent discrepancy between revealed and philosophical truth it must be the reader's interpretation which is at fault. The plain and literal meaning

Accord de la Religion et de la Philosophie. Traité d'Ibn Rochd (Averroes), Alger, 1905; and in Spanish with Thomistic parallels and a most valuable historical and critical analysis by M. Asín, *Homenaje à D. Francisco Codera* Madrid, 1904, pp. 271 f.

of the text was not always the right one, especially where anthropomorphisms were used of the deity.

St. Thomas was always able to ride triumphantly over texts which seemed to conflict with his conclusions, because he was able to appeal to authoritative allegorical interpretation. The Bible was the guarantee that a statement or a doctrine was true, but the Church alone could say how the text of the Bible was to be interpreted. Obviously Averroes could not go so far as this, but he went as far as he could. He laid down a number of rules to govern cases where allegorical interpretation is necessary and the plain meaning of the text must be abandoned or left to the ignorant and uninstructed who have not sufficient intelligence to understand the philosophical difficulty inherent in the literal meaning, and whose faith would be destroyed if they were told that a Quranic text was not literally true. In reply to objectors he denies that the doctrine of Ijmāʿ (Islam's nearest approach to *quod ubique, quod semper, quod ab omnibus*) was ever valid. If it is argued that there are certain texts which all Muslims take *au pied de la lettre* while they are unanimous in interpreting others allegorically, and therefore it cannot be right to apply the one method to the other text and vice versa, Averroes replies that were catholic consent definitely established it would not be lawful to do so; but when this consent is only presumed it is permissible. He maintains that, except within extremely narrow limits, it has never been possible to assert that all doctors in any one age were unanimous on any one question.

Christian Averroists had not the same freedom as their master in peripatetic studies, and so they had to give an altogether unwarranted extension to his doctrines. Averroes had said that the science of Quranic interpretation was not for the ignorant multitude, and that they had better be allowed to retain their crude ideas while the philosopher interpreted the sacred text in the light of reason. Admittedly there would then be a discrepancy between the words of the Quran and the belief of the educated, but such a discrepancy could not authorize the bold theory that faith demanded belief in a proposition which reason denied to be true. Bald and uncritical Latin translations of Averroes shared the responsibility for making the Arabian the author of a theory of double truth. The translators did not always understand the technical significance of words which dealt with metaphorical and allegorical expressions. 'Metaphor' and 'symbol' or 'similitude'[1] were understood to mean falsehoods and fables. Averroes was perfectly orthodox in asserting the legitimacy of allegorical interpretation, whatever his co-religionists may have thought of the texts he chose for the exercise. He was merely applying a principle which had been in existence in Christianity and Islam from the very first.[2]

Coincidences between the theology of St. Thomas and Averroes are extremely numerous. None is more important than the dogma that God's knowledge embraces particulars, and the arguments advanced in its support. The famous proposition of the Angelic Doctor that the Divine Knowledge is the cause of things is none other than Ibn Rushd's *al-ʿilmu-l-qadīmu huwa ʿillatun wa-sababun lil-maujūd.*[3] The Muslim peripatetics denied that the knowledge of God comprised particulars on the ground that if it did a change in the known would involve change in the knower. Algazel replied that if God could not see and hear all that was going on in the sub-lunar world He, the author of sight and hearing, would be inferior to His creatures.

The resemblances between Averroes and St. Thomas are so numerous that they must be traceable to something firmer than mere coincidence. A common desire to reconcile philosophy and theology is not of great significance, but when the plan is worked

[1] *Majāz* and *mithāl.*

[2] Cf. Matt vii. 6; *Sūrah* iii. 5; Averroes *Faṣl.* p. 8; *Sum. Theol.* 1a q1[a] *et passim.*

[3] See *Damīmatu-l-mas'alati 'llatī dhakarahā Abu-l-Walīd fī faṣli-l-maqāl*, ed. Asín, op. cit. This letter was translated by Raymund Martin and incorporated in his *Pugio* i, ch. xxv.

out on parallel lines it is only natural to conclude that Averroes has bequeathed something more than a commentary on Aristotle to Christian scholarship. In both writers we find after the philosophical proofs of dogma quotations from the Quran or Bible; both begin by setting out doubtful or apparently contradictory testimonies. We find the same proof of God's existence from movement, and the providential guidance of the world; the same argument for God's unity from the unity of the world. In advancing the proposition that in order to acquire knowledge of God one must use the method of *via remotionis*, both temper it with the *via analogiae*.

These parallels could be multiplied freely, and a great many of them would be found to be common to Islamic writers in East and West. But enough has been said to demonstrate the course of the procession of philosophical and theological speculation in its journey from the Orient. From the year 1217 onwards, the commentaries of Averroes were made available to the western schools by Michael Scot in Toledo. Many of Averroes' ideas were incorporated in Maimonides' great work which St. Thomas sometimes quotes. In his *Quaestiones Disputatae* St. Thomas refers to Averroes' statements on the controversy about the nature of God's knowledge.

It is fitting that this chapter should end with St. Thomas Aquinas, for he puts the elusive idea 'influence' in its proper setting. We have traced the presence of Arabian influence in his writings, but it would not be true to say that he was dependent upon Arabian writers. He cannot be made the servant of any school or any century.[1] His habit of turning back from

[1] 'He did not simply piece his authorities together; he thought out for himself each point as it came up, and produced, despite the impediments to the free play of speculative thought which constant deference to various authorities demanded, a masterpiece of sober criticism and of keen insight into the general significance and affinities of the positions adopted or rejected.' Clement C. J. Webb, *A History of Philosophy*, London, 1915, p. 120.

the ideas current in the present to the doctrines of the Fathers in the Church's past is a valuable reminder that from the Arabians the West was recovering its lost patrimony. To say this is not to depreciate or undervalue the achievements of the Arabians. They kept alive the light of learning, and however small their contribution towards the advancement of purely philosophical thought may have been, their service to theology was of the greatest value.[1] We may be sure that those who accuse the Muslim scholars of lack of originality and of intellectual decadence have never read Averroes or looked into Algazel, but have adopted second-hand judgements. The presence of doctrines of Islamic origin in the very citadel of Western Christianity, the *Summa* of Aquinas, is a sufficient refutation of the charge of lack of originality and sterility.

To do justice to the many ramifications of Muslim influence a history of medieval culture would have to be written, and far-reaching controversies would be stirred. The streams of national culture flow into the vast ocean of human thought; once they reach the sea it is difficult, if not impossible, to separate the fresh from the salt. Each must rely on his own taste.

During the four centuries or more of Muslim predominance there was a spirit of religious and philosophical inquiry in all centres of learning. The colour and charm characteristic of the Oriental mind linger still in the writings of this age when every merchant was a poet and as likely as not any poet a merchant. Travel and reading, fighting and love, music and song, all these were of Allah's bounty. Life might be short, especially if lived too near a throne or court, but it was sweet. In such an age what matter if there were religious uncertainties? The doubting could and did take refuge in a mystic pantheism which found

[1] The Muslim atomistic philosophers' theory of continuous creation and atomic time is of peculiar interest at the present day. See Maimonides *Guide for the Perplexed*, tr. by M. Friedländer, London, 1925, pp. 120 ff. ,and D. B. Macdonald in *Isis* (ix.2) 1927 ;pp. 326 f.

God within and without him. Apocalyptists and Essenes could enjoy prophetic ecstasies or practise austerities which found their way to Europe and inspired or reinforced the zeal of the Albigenses or the Cathari. The Messianist had his *mahdī*, and the orthodox his hope of 'solid joys and lasting pleasures' in the garden of fair women. Dour students like Ibn Ḥazm of Córdoba could sit down and compose Europe's first comprehensive *Religionsgeschichte* and the first systematic higher critical study of the Old and New Testaments. Phantasy could mix with fact and imagination gild the common metal of life until men like Ibnu-l-ʿArabī produced their astonishing prototypes of the *Divina Commedia.*

The barrier of language decreed that our forefathers could only savour a fragment of this rich and varied life, and so, when the Muslim empire in Europe came to an end, all the knowledge that had not already been assimilated was banished with the defeated Moors. But even so East and West were intellectually much more closely aligned in the thirteenth century than they have ever been since. Save for the central dogmas of the Trinity and the Incarnation the scholastics, as we have seen, could as often as not find as many allies in the opposing camp as in the ranks of their own army. When all the rich material in Europe's libraries has been brought to light it may yet be seen that the abiding influence of the Arabs on medieval civilization is much greater than has hitherto been recognized.

ALFRED GUILLAUME.

BIBLIOGRAPHY

This article should be read in conjunction with that by C. and D. Singer on 'The Jewish Factor in Medieval Thought' in *The Legacy of Israel*, the sister volume to this.

S. MUNK, *Mélanges de Philosophie juive et arabe*, Paris, 1857, reprinted 1927.

M. HORTEN, *Die philosophischen Systeme der spekulativen Theologen im Islam*, Bonn, 1912.

BARON CARRA DE VAUX, *Gazali*, Paris, 1902.

M. ASÍN Y PALACIOS, *Algazel*, Zaragoza, 1901.

El Averroismo teológico de Santo Tomas de Aquino extracto del *Homenaje à . . . Codera*), Zaragoza, 1904.

Abenmasarra y su escuela, Madrid, 1914. (These works are indispensable.)

In *Beiträge zur Geschichte der Philosophie des Mittelalters*:

M. WITTMANN, *Die Stellung des hl. Thomas von Aquin zur Avencebrol*, Münster, 1900.

Zur Stellung Avencebrol's im Entwicklungsgang der arabischen Philosophie, 1905.

A. SCHNEIDER, *Die abendländische Spekulation des Zwölften Jahrhunderts in ihren Verhältnis zur aristotelischen und jüdisch-arabischen Philosophie*, 1915.

E. GILSON, '*Pourquoi saint Thomas a critiqué saint Augustin*' in *Archives d'histoire doctrinale et littéraire du moyen âge*, Paris, 1926, pp. 5 f.

C. R. S. HARRIS, *Duns Scotus*, Oxford, 1927.

DE L. O'LEARY, *Arabic Thought and its Place in History*, London, 1922.

S. VAN DEN BERGH, *Die Epitome der Metaphysik des Averroes*, Leiden, 1924.

CLEMENT C. J. WEBB, *Studies in the History of Natural Theology*, Oxford, 1915.

LAW AND SOCIETY

THE social structure of ancient Arabia was founded upon blood kinship. A group of men descending, or claiming descent, from a common ancestor, associated together for the sake of mutual defence; they were united by common worship and by common habits, but first and foremost by a blood tie, whether genuine or fictitious, which produced an effective brotherhood: the Arab tribe, in fact, was a great family.

As in all primitive societies, the original social unit in Arabia was not the individual, but the group. The individual counted for little by himself, but only through the family or aggregate to which he belonged. The family summed up the life of all its members under its social and legal aspects; it claimed their rights, it avenged their injuries, it answered for their crimes, and inherited their property after death, pursuant to a custom (*sunnah*) which derived all its authority, which was considerable, from immemorial practice.

Islam preserved this organism in all its essential features; one element only it changed; for the blood tie, which was the political and social foundation of the Arab tribe, it substituted the community of faith.

In the primitive Semitic tribe, worship was already the centre of tribal life. God and the worshipping tribe were one. The god was a friend to the friends of the tribe, an enemy to its enemies; he impersonated and embodied the continuity of tribe and kin. To change one's god was to the primitive Semite what a change of nationality would be to us.

Thus Muḥammad only recalled Arab society to its primitive beginnings and built up a social structure on the base which appealed to its deepest instincts, a fact which has not escaped the keen eye of Ibn Khaldūn. The traditional frame of tribe and family was pulled down. There was no longer any question of *gentes*, of clientship, of tribal confederations. He who adopted Islam had to forget all connexions, even his own kith and kin, unless they were his companions in the faith. Like Abraham, he must say to his own people, so long as they adhere to the old faith: 'Between you and me there is nothing in common.' Such was the aspect of the new social order inaugurated by Muḥammad.

Out of the anonymity of collective life, we see personal life emerging. Henceforward man is reckoned as an individual, and the individual in his turn derives what claims and duties he may have, not from his connexion with the community, but from his faith. The body of these believers make up the 'Islamic community'.

Those who profess belief in the Only God (Allāh), in the mission of Muḥammad, and adhere to the few precepts he taught, belong by right to the 'people' or 'community' (*ummah*) of Muḥammad, which now supersedes the ancient *ummah*, or tribe founded upon kinship. This community is different from any other: it is the chosen, the holy people, to whom is entrusted the furtherance of good and the repression of evil; it is the only seat of justice and faith upon earth, the sole witness for God among the nations, just as the Prophet had been God's witness among the Arabs.

All these ideas are already set forth in the oldest historical document of Islam, the charter promulgated at Medina in the year One of the Hijrah.

The people of Muḥammad were a large family, pitted against every other group not worshipping the same God, 'one hand against all others'. 'Brethren in the faith, partners in the sharing of booty, allies against the common foe', as Abū Bakr said, addressing the people of Medina. Hence the ethically religious character of the whole system, in which mutual help is considered as a legal duty, according to the precept that every Muslim should be the helper and protector of every other

Muslim in case of need. 'The Muslim', says a ḥadīth, 'are a single hand, like a compact wall whose bricks support each other.' These ideas are to be found in every part of the law, both public and private. A corollary of brotherhood is equality. Equal before God, the Muslims are equal among themselves. Among the believers superiority is marked only by priority in the faith or by a stricter observance of its precepts. 'O Quraysh, God has suppressed among you the pride of nobility and the arrogance of the times of ignorance. All men are descended from Adam, and Adam was built up from clay.' Equality before the law is a fundamental basis of the whole system, political as well as civil. 'Let them all be equal before thee', say the celebrated instructions of the Caliph 'Umar to Abū Mūsā al-Ash'arī, 'in respect of thy justice and tribunal, lest the powerful put their hope in thy partiality, and the weak despair of thy justice.' Whether authentic or not, these rules are to be found in every legal manual, and are the basis of procedure and of civil law.

At the head of this community of equals, brethren in the faith as in Israel of old, is God himself. The rule of Allāh over his people is immediate and direct. The gods of the ancient Arab tribes had been the patrons and protectors of their worshippers. Allāh, patron and defender of his chosen people, now takes the place of the ancient gods, and rules the Muslim community. When the chief of a tribe that had adopted Islam said to the Prophet, 'Thou art our prince', the Prophet answered quickly: 'The prince is God, not I'.

Islam is the direct government of Allāh, the rule of God, whose eyes are upon his people. The principle of unity and order which in other societies is called *civitas*, *polis*, State, in Islam is personified by Allāh: Allāh is the name of the supreme power, acting in the common interest. Thus the public treasury is 'the treasury of Allāh', the army is the 'army of Allāh', even the public functionaries are 'the employees of Allāh'.

No less direct is the relation between Allāh and the individual believers; for between Allāh and the believer there is no mediator; Islam has no church, no priests, no sacraments. What is the good of mediators between man and his Maker, who has known him before his birth and is 'nearer to him than his jugular vein'? After the Prophet who has transmitted to mankind the final word of Allāh, Allāh can have no other interpreter and no other agent of his will. Man is alone in the presence of God, in life and in death; he may always address him directly, without introduction and without ceremony, as he would address an Arab Sayyid. From birth to death man is alone under the eye of God, Whom nothing escapes, to Whom is present every action, every word, even the most hidden thought; alone he will answer for his deeds, and alone will he face the judgement of God, before Whom neither intercessions nor mediators will be of any avail,[1] in that *dies irae* when every creature will be summoned to receive the requital of his deeds. The most rigid protestantism is almost a sacerdotal religion, compared with this personal monotheism, unbending, and intolerant of any interference between man and his Creator.

Alone and defenceless in the presence of the All-seeing Judge, what can man do in order to shelter himself from the power of God, but surrender himself to His mercy, 'from Him to Him', according to the Muslim formula? This surrender of man to God, a surrender full of humility and hope, is true faith, and that is why Islam (i.e. the abandonment of oneself to God) is the only true religion, because it is the only disposition of a religious soul in the presence of God. Man realizes who God is and man's lowly estate in His eyes. This total surrender, which is often a characteristic of Semitism, is the ensign of Islam, its badge among the nations, and it was perhaps an obscure consciousness of the affinity of this teaching with the religious instinct of his own people that led Muḥammad to proclaim himself

[1] Many Muslims, however, believe in the effective intercession of Muḥammad.

the Restorer of the genuine and undefiled faith of Abraham, and the last of the Prophets.

Foundations of the Islamic Community

The Divine Law (*sharīʿah*). The nature of this brotherhood grouped round the symbol of faith, and governed by God, determines the conception of law. Law, according to the ancients and ourselves, is the legal norm approved by the people, directly or through the organs that represent them, and derives its authority from the reason and will of man, and his moral nature. The Muslim conception is quite different. If it be true that the chief and ruler of the Islamic community is God himself, law is naught save the will of God. It is the rule according to which Allāh, the legislator to the people whom He has chosen, will try it.

Submission to this law is at the same time a social duty and a precept of faith; whosoever violates it, not only infringes the legal order, but commits a sin, because there is no right in which God has not a share. Juridical order and religion, law and morals, are the two aspects of that same will, from which the Muslim community derives its existence and its direction; every legal question is in itself a case of conscience, and jurisprudence points to theology as its ultimate base.

What is the nature and proper function of this law? The Quranic revelation styles itself a law of liberty, an act of mercy vouchsafed by God to mankind, in order to soften the rigidity of the preceding revelations. Islam is a reversion to natural law, to the primitive faith of the patriarchs (Noah or Abraham) which had been corrupted and adulterated by Jews and Christians. The new law suppresses the austerities and the numerous inderdictions imposed upon the Jews by the Mosaic law, abolishes the macerations of Christianity, and declares its willingness to comply with the weakness and frailty of man, and the practical necessities of life. 'Ease the way, do not make it rougher': such were the instructions usually imparted by the Prophet to his *missi dominici*. 'Allāh lays upon each man only what he can fulfil.' Islam has a tendency towards mysticism, but not towards asceticism. It formally disapproves of the exaggeration of austerity, which weakens the body and suppresses the natural instincts of man. It exhorts the believer to enjoy the 'good things' granted by God, provided he observes due measure and obeys the precepts, not numerous in themselves nor very strict, of the Quranic revelation.

Islamic law favours every practical activity, and holds in great esteem agriculture, commerce, and every kind of work; it censures all those who burden others with their maintenance, requires every man to keep himself by the produce of his own labour, and does not despise any sort of work whereby man may make himself independent of others. 'L'Islam est une religion d'hommes', says Renan. Considering its spirit, therefore, we see that the tendency of Islamic law is to allow human action the widest limits, and we may agree with the Muslim jurists, when they teach that the fundamental rule of law is liberty.

But this liberty (*ibāḥah*) cannot be unlimited. Man is by his very nature greedy and ungrateful, covetous of other men's goods, niggardly of his own, disposed to sloth, ungrateful for the blessings that God has bestowed upon him. Human society would not have been possible, and the individual himself would not have been able to subsist, had God allowed free scope to the appetites of every individual as well as to the injustice and violence of all. God has therefore set a bound to human activity, and this bound (*ḥadd*) is precisely what we call law (*ḥukm*), which restrains human action within certain limits, forbidding some acts and enjoining others, and thus restraining the primitive liberty of man, so as to make it as beneficial as possible either to the individual or to society.

Naturally, law cannot deal with every detail, but only with a restricted number of cases having legal significance. The Roman jurists had said: *Legis virtus haec est, imperare, vetare, permittere, punire.*

Islamic law, true to its religious character, adds to these two fresh provinces of legal interference, namely 'things admissible' and 'things reprehensible'. Leaving aside for the moment the penal section, we thus obtain five categories representing the whole body of positive law. Whatever their form, these rules tend to the same end and have the same purpose, that is the public weal (*maṣlaḥa*). Accordingly, law, divine in its origin, human in its subject-matter, has no other end but the welfare of man, even if this end be not at first sight apparent: for God can do nothing which does not express the wisdom and mercy of which He is the supreme source.

Man, being both soul and body, has a twofold life, moral and physical. Among the rules or limits laid down by God for the discipline of mankind, some have reference to the life of the soul, some to the life of the body. Religion and law are two distinct orders, but complementary to each other, being strictly connected through their common end, which is the welfare of man. The principles of faith ('beliefs') regulate the spiritual life and determine what man should believe in order to attain eternal life. Positive law (*s̲h̲arīʿah*, the straight way) is the discipline of human activity as directed to earthly purposes, and is the necessary complement, the body of that organism of which faith is the soul. The proper sphere of faith is the heart, that is to say the inner life of man. Positive law cannot take this into account. Faith is a personal affair, of which God is the sole judge, because He alone knows the heart of man. The proper sphere of positive law is the actions of man as far as their external manifestations are concerned. Some of these refer to the observance of the fundamental precepts of Islam, i.e. the profession of the Divine Unity, prayer, fasting, the payment of tithes or poor-tax, and pilgrimage. Here there is no question of faith ('the actions of the heart'), for the heart escapes the competence of the lawyers;

but rather of the actions of the body, namely, those external acts of piety or worship made binding upon the believer by the precepts of Muslim law. These precepts (as well as those duties of public law which will be mentioned presently) are called 'God's rights', their subject-matter being the duties of man towards his Creator, which do not depend on personal choice.

But man is not only a soul, he is also a body, and as such has to provide for his earthly existence. Hence the supremely important fact of social life. It is said in the *Durr-al-mukhtār*: 'Man is by nature a political animal, because he cannot live by himself as other animals do, but requires the help and society of fellow-creatures.' But the aptitudes of individuals are different, their needs numerous, the faculties of each, as well as their forces, very limited. Man is obliged to seek the help of his fellows, and hence the complicated and manifold interests, relations, and exchanges, which are the origin and mainspring of society, and of which money is the instrument. From the preceding quotation we may perceive how deep and far-reaching is the influence of Hellenic ideas. Amongst others, we may trace this influence in the functions of money, as they are developed in Dimashqī, in a way parallel to that of *Digest*, Book XX.

The relations arising from social life are the origin and proper matter of positive law. The necessity of reproduction gives rise to sexual union, as well as to the constitution of the family. Hence the legal connexion arising from matrimony. The division of labour and the various needs of the individual give rise to that net of relations and exchanges to which jurists refer under the general name of legal transactions, corresponding to our civil and commercial law, which are not separated into different branches in the Muslim legal system, any more than they were in Roman law. The death of the individual gives rise to succession, which is governed by the rules concerning devolution and division of inheritance. Finally, the protection of the social order gives rise to a penal system, of which more will be said later.

Law is a social fact: one section refers to society, and another to the individual. Whatever does not concern private interests is termed God's right, because God is substituted in the Muslim concept for the old idea of *civitas*. Among God's rights are the rules relating to freedom, to patronage, to matrimony, to kinship, to the prohibition of usury, to penal law. These rules cannot be disregarded, for they appertain to the general welfare, or, as we should say, to public order, and are independent of the individual will. The other class of relations refer to the private concerns of individuals, and are called the rights of man.

Starting from liberty as the fundamental basis of law, Islamic jurists have reached a twofold conclusion:

1. Liberty finds its limit in its very nature, because liberty unlimited would mean self-destruction—and that limit or boundary is the legal norm, or Law.

2. No limit is arbitrary, because it is determined by its utility or the greatest good of the individual or of society. Utility, which is the foundation of law, traces also its boundary and extent.

A cursory review of the various legal institutions may be of some help towards realizing the practical bearing of these principles. As God's vicar upon earth, man is endowed with a personality making him susceptible both of rights and duties: chief amongst these is the right of man as an individual to personal safety and freedom. Freedom is the inborn right of every man, slavery being only an exception to the rule: 'Adam and Eve were free', a proposition from which jurists have drawn various inferences: (*a*) the foundling whose status is unknown is presumed to be free; (*b*) the freeman claimed as a slave is not bound *prima facie* to prove his freedom, until the reverse has been legally shown against him; (*c*) in case of doubt, the presumption is for liberty.

Liberty means the power of self-disposal. The freeman has no master but God, the supreme Lord of all human existence, to whom alone subservience is due. Hence liberty cannot be disposed of at pleasure, and even a spontaneous admission of slavery is not recognized by law as valid. In the same spirit law forbids and religion deprecates suicide.

The same principles and the same methods apply to the doctrine of proprietary rights. Potentially any man is entitled to any thing because all the world's goods have been created for the use of man. By instituting property God has set a limit to this right; thus enabling every man to know the lot assigned to him by God in the general stock of wealth, and securing social order. But it would be erroneous to suppose that property as a right is unlimited—it finds a limit in its very nature and the end to which it may be subservient. Earthly goods are bestowed upon man in order that he may provide for his existence, that is to say, in order to employ them usefully, not to squander them without a purpose or according to his whim. Following the precepts of the Qur'ān and tradition, Muslim law ignores the *jus utendi et abutendi* of Roman law, brands as a form of squandering any consumption of wealth not required by real use, considers every useless consumption a sin. In its eyes prodigality is a form of mental disease, which ought to be legally restrained. It insists on moderation, following the middle way in the use of riches, as most consonant with the nature of law and with the purpose for which God has bestowed His goods upon mankind.

The doctrine of contractual capacity presents similar features. Every man is able to enter into an obligation and impose obligations towards himself upon others, inasmuch as, by his very existence, he is endowed with legal capacity. But this abstract faculty also has a limit, which is determined by the interest or utility of the subject; it is expressed by the various restrictions imposed on the contracts of infants, and of persons afflicted with mental disease, or prodigality, or sickness, or bankrupt. These limitations of capacity are generally called bonds or fetters, and are grounded on the intention of law to protect the estate of the incapable against the consequences of his own incompetence. Likewise, every man is entitled to make use of his right without caring whether, in so doing, he may inconvenience others, the object of every right being essentially to procure the advantage of its holder. But this faculty of procuring one's own advantage has a limit, expressed by a twofold rule: (*a*) no one is entitled to exercise his right with the sole object of injuring others without any profit to himself; (*b*) neither is one entitled to exercise his right, when this use entails an injury to others out of proportion to his own benefit. This rule applies to every part of the system. Hence the limits set to paternal authority over daughters, to the rights of the master over his slave, of the husband over his wife, and the rules concerning neighbourly relations. The logical process followed in all these cases is always the same: once the principle is laid down, the lawgiver is careful to set a limit, without which law, instead of helping, might become the enemy of mankind.

This system of rules comprising every part of a Muslim's life, from the humblest details up to the principles of his moral and social existence, is termed 'the straight way' '*s̲h̲arīʿah*' and must be followed by every believer.

Hence the importance assumed by the science of law (*al-fiqh*), which is linked up with theology, as an essentially religious science, conferring great merit on those who cultivate it, as may be inferred from the Ḥanafī definition: 'the science of Law is the knowledge of the rights and duties whereby man is enabled to observe right conduct in the world, and prepare himself for the future life'. Truly one may apply here with more truth what Roman lawyers said of their own pursuit: 'Rerum humanarum atque divinarum scientia'.

The leader of the Community

The sovereign is an integral part of law: he is as necessary as law itself. Law is a social fact, based, as we have seen, on human society and the social nature of man. Unfortunately man, although social by nature, is not a good animal. 'Men are the enemies of each other' (Qur'ān, xx. 121). Were they left to their instincts of violence and greed, they would utterly lay waste the earth. Law is a permanent struggle against the wicked instincts of man. Law would be an empty word had it not a defender and sustainer.

The same reasons which make it necessary for the welfare of men that their activity should have a limit, which is law, make it imperative that they should have a ruler to lead, and when necessary to compel them to obedience. God has therefore perfected the edifice of law by establishing a ruler (*imām*, or *khalīfah*), and prescribing obedience to his behests. Supreme power can be conferred by God alone, because no man, as such, is entitled to rule over his fellow beings. Every form of authority among men, the relation of father and children, of guardian and pupil, of master and slave, of ruler and subject, has no other foundation than the will of God, to whom alone power belongs, and Who confers it in different measure on some men for the benefit of others: 'God establishes princes and God deprives them of power'.

The establishment of the chief and obedience to his directions are both a religious duty and a necessity of existence for the Muslim community, as they would be for any other, because, if there were not a firmly established power, there would be no human society, no religion, only a rabble, lawless or misguided, wherein all that makes life worth living would be lost, including the supreme interest of faith, whose foundation rests upon order and security for each and all. 'The Prince is the main pillar of the pavilion of the State.' Hence the establishment of such a chief is a religious duty; every Muslim possessing the necessary requisites must concern himself with it. To shirk such a duty is to desert the community of believers. 'He who dies without an *imām* dies the death of a pagan.'

On the same grounds the headship can only be held by one head at a time: (*a*) because the unity of the divine law requires the unity of the sovereign who has to enforce it; (*b*) because social order cannot be secured if the sovereign authority be shared between more than one —'were there more than one God, the universe would go to ruin', says the Qur'ān (xxi. 22).

This one chief must be endowed with the moral and physical qualities necessary to fulfil his office, viz.: freedom—the caliph cannot be a slave, because he who cannot freely dispose of himself cannot have the authority necessary to be a chief; masculine sex, because, as the ḥadīth expresses it, 'a people whose chief is a woman cannot prosper'; legal capacity, i.e. puberty and moral sanity; physical integrity, i.e. immunity from physical imperfections which might hinder him in the fulfilment of his duty; knowledge of divine law—although it is controverted how far this must extend—wisdom and courage in order to maintain in peace and war the interests entrusted to his care; a moral life, in conformity with the precepts of the divine law and of Muslim ethics; last, but not least, *Descent*, viz. the fact of belonging to the Quraysh. The Quraysh are the tribe to which the Prophet belonged. Their pre-eminence amongst Arab families seems to have been acknowledged from ancient times and to have gradually grown into a maxim. This does not mean that supreme power should be vested in a special branch of that tribe: the original purport of this strange restriction is essentially that the caliph should belong by blood to the Arab race. It is therefore contrary to principle that the caliphate should belong to an alien, and this is one of the reasons of the illegitimacy of the modern caliphate.

Given these requisites, it is evident that the choice of a chief for the Islamic community cannot be left to chance or violence, but must be founded on the ripe reflection of those best qualified to appreciate whether the candidate is a fit subject for choice. The elective body cannot therefore be the whole of the Muslim people, but only those who by their culture, their social rank, their experience of worldly affairs, and their morality, are suited to be judges. The electorate will be entrusted to the 'men of the pen and the sword', in other words, to the civil and military notables; to them is given power 'both to bind and to loose', that is to say, to stipulate in the name of the whole community the bond on which rests the power of the prince and the obedience due from his subjects. Election is in law the act by which the people, or the notables on their behalf, confer the supreme power on the object of their choice; it is an offer of contract (*ʿiqād*) which, if accepted by the person chosen, becomes a binding contract (*ʿaqd*).

In the first century of the Hijrah, another way of instituting the caliphate was introduced by custom—viz. the appointment of a successor or heir by the reigning caliph. Such an appointment is equivalent to an offer of contract, which, if accepted, becomes a contract.

The form in which the contract is perfected is called *bayʿah*, a word which was formerly used to express the consummation of a bargain, and is symbolized by the traditional handshake which, since the time of Abū Bakr, has been the token of acceptance on the part of the person elected.

Let us now consider the effects of the *bayʿah* or homage: (*a*) with regard to the caliph himself; and (*b*) with regard to the people under his rule.

(*a*) By accepting the investiture, the caliph binds himself to exercise his power within the limits laid down by the divine law. This is the first and most essential of his duties, the end of man being not the interests of this world, a thing in itself vain and futile, ending in corruption and death, but faith which leads man to eternal life.

(*b*) The caliph undertakes to provide for the temporal interests of Islam, such as the protection of the frontiers, the conduct of war against the unbelievers, internal security, management of public property, and the administration of justice.

In the performance of this twofold duty the chief of the Muslim community effectively acts as the vicar or *locum tenens* of the Prophet (*khalīfah*). The successors of the Prophet were not the heirs of his spiritual mission. They were in fact, and claimed to be, nothing more than substitutes or vicars, who carried on his work by furthering the religious and temporal interests of the community. Abū Bakr declined the title of Vicar of God (*khalīfat Allāh*), and was content to be called 'the Vicar of God's Apostle'. Later on, under 'Umar, the title of *Amīr al-mu'minīn*, 'Commander of the Faithful', came into use and defined still better the representative of supreme power who was not a sovereign (*malik*) but a prince, in the original sense of the word, namely *primus inter pares*.

The name *imām*, signifying properly *antistes*, director of prayer, remains through all time to designate one of the highest prerogatives of the sovereign, viz. his religious office, the source of all others, which are, according to the canon law of Islam, justice, holy war, and censorship of customs. When writers mention the imām without further explanation they mean thereby the ruler of the state, the supreme source of power, in whose name all public functions are performed. None of these functions confers on the caliph a sacerdotal or holy character, as has been assumed by certain authorities.

The truth is that the caliph in his capacity as religious chief is not a pontiff: he has no priestly character whatsoever, because Islam has no hierarchy nor apostolic succession. Neither is he a master (*rabb*) in his political capacity. The caliphate is not an office instituted by the divine law in order to provide for the general welfare; it is a public trust having as its object the service, the protection, and the enforcement of the holy law. The caliph is often compared to a shepherd, and embodies in his person the unity of the flock that is gathered round him. As the shepherd watches over his flock, and the guardian assists his pupil, so the prince is established to further the interests of Muslims who are unable, as a body, to take care of them. He is the trustee (*wakīl*) of the community of believers—his actions derive their legitimacy and their limitation from the principle that a prince must seek the welfare of the community, 'for to this end are Princes set over the people'. The trustee is bound to give his master a truthful account of what he has done. The caliph is bound likewise to reckon with God. 'I advise thee', writes Abū Yūsuf to the Caliph Hārūn al-Ras͟hīd, 'to watch over the flock entrusted to thy care . . . since the shepherd must answer for the flock committed to him, and the master may call thee to account for it.'

Jamā'ah, imām—Congregation, leader—these two simple terms sum up the whole political system of Islam, as well as its conception of the state.

The representative and executive power of the state is centred in the caliph, whose function is to apply it, when the law is explicit and formal. In this case he has no authority to alter it in the least, and must apply it such as it is; for instance, when the law does not allow the judge to grant a reprieve. In the cases for which no positive rule is laid down his freedom is practically unlimited: for he is not an ordinary agent but a trustee, and the execution of the law is left to his discretion. Besides this judicial discretion, he possesses discretionary powers in many other matters of public concern, such as the conduct of war, the division of booty, and the assessment of the land-tax, the employment of the public revenue, the appointment of public officials.

As regards the people, the acceptance of the *bayʿah* signifies an engagement to follow and obey their chief: 'whosoever rebels against the imām rebels against God'; 'obey, though your chief be a black slave'. The duty of assistance or help (*nuṣrah*) is connected with the duty of obedience, and binds the person who has done homage to respond to any call made by the prince for help against an enemy challenging his authority or threatening the safety of Muslims.

The only limit to these duties is the sheer impossibility of giving help, be it physical or moral. When a command exceeds men's powers or is clearly contrary to the divine law, for in-instance if the prince commands any one to commit murder or adultery, to drink wine, or to omit a ritual prayer, the prince's authority is in abeyance. 'No obedience in sin', says the tradition. The mutual engagement between caliph and people is inviolable, so long as the caliph is fit to fulfil his duty of protecting the Muslim community. When he is no longer able to give the people what they have a right to expect, his authority lapses, and the contract is legally cancelled. This change may happen through physical incapacity, or through loss of liberty, such as captivity among infidels.

The caliphate thus outlined embodies the political programme of the orthodox school of jurists, the 'prophetic Caliphate', as it is termed—the only legitimate form of sovereignty. To them it seemed to coincide with the golden age of Islam under the first four successors of the Prophet, the 'well-directed', as they are called. After that time jurists point to a progressive decline, growing more rapid in proportion as Islam departs from its origins. The true caliphate is succeeded by the kingship, viz. power pure and simple, 'the rule of the sword', which has nothing to do with religious law. A tradition referred to the Prophet, in different versions, says: After me there will be amīrs (commanders) and after these kings and after these tyrants.' These traditions give an outline ~~of the~~ history of the caliphate from the orthodox point of view, and are on the whole confirmed by history.

In point of fact, the caliphate as it is fondly imagined by jurists never had a real existence. But in its beginnings, under the first two caliphs, it nearly attained that programme; and had circumstances been favourable, it might have developed the germs of good government. But hardly had the first Muslim generation died away when the practical needs of a great polity, and the unruly temper of the Arabs, combined to transform the caliphate first into a personal rule under the Umayyads; then, under the Abbasids, into a monarchy on the Persian pattern, whose apparent orthodoxy but ill concealed the despotism, the violence, and the administrative mismanagement which were pushing the empire to its ruin.

In the third century of the Hijrah the sultanate superseded the caliphate, which was reduced henceforth to a purely decorative function. The military chieftains who rose on the ruins of the empire imposed their rule as *de facto* authorities, and the Caliph of Baghdad had to be satisfied with investing them with a show of legitimacy.

The jurists had to accept the inevitable, and they tried to make the best of the actual situation, hard as it was. The schools began to teach that government, even if it were not in accordance with the requirements of the divine law, and even if it were based on violence pure and simple, was still deserving of homage as a protection against anarchy and a check to private violence, thus providing that social peace which is the essential aim of the *Sharīʿah*. Jurists realize that the old programme is too lofty for practical use. It is admitted by many teachers that the imām may not be the blameless man required by the *Sharīʿah*, that descent from the Quraysh is not indispensable for the caliph, and even that there may be more than one imām. The believer must obey him who holds power, either rightfully or *de facto*. The actual holder may be a tyrant, or lead a scandalous life.

What has a believer to do in such a case? 'Be patient, give to Caesar what is due unto Caesar and wait until justice be done.'

Al-Ghazālī, towards the end of the fifth century, puts the problem with his customary frankness—'the concessions made by us', says Ghazālī, 'are not spontaneous, but necessity makes lawful what is forbidden. We know it is not allowed to feed on a dead animal: still, it would be worse to die of hunger. Of those that contend that the caliphate is dead for ever and irreplaceable, we should like to ask: which is to be preferred, anarchy and the stoppage of social life for lack of a properly constituted authority, or acknowledgement of the existing power, whatever it be? Of these two alternatives, the jurist cannot but choose the latter.'

In 656 A.H. (A.D. 1258) the Mongols stormed Baghdād, put the caliph to death, and destroyed the whole Abbasid family. The caliphate, which had been long dead as a political power, was thus effectively brought to an end. After that epoch, history mentions only sultans, save in Egypt where an Abbasid, either authentic or fictitious, perpetuated the title of caliph. This empty puppet was kept only for the convenience of the Mamlūk rulers. When the Turks took Cairo in 1517, they found the last remnant of this line. It has been maintained that there was a formal transfer of power from this last Abbasid to the Turkish ruler; but this transfer, had it really happened, would have been legally null and void: for the caliphate is not a proprietary right transferable at will, but a trusteeship held on behalf of the Muslim community. The caliphate, therefore, has really been extinct since 1543 if not 1258. The real state of things is given by the Qāḍī Ibn Jamā'ah of Damascus (about 700 A.H.): 'The sovereign has a right to govern until another and stronger one shall oust him from power and rule in his State. The latter will rule by the same title and will have to be acknowledged on the same grounds; for a government, however objectionable, is better than none at all; and between two evils we must choose the lesser.' Jurists in Morocco have summed up the rule in the brief maxim: 'To him who holds power obedience is due.'

Penal Law

There is not much to say respecting the penal system. Based as it is, like the Hebrew law, on the principle of an eye for an eye and a tooth for a tooth, and the primitive conception of retaliation, it reproduces too literally, and without the least mitigation, the old legal ideas we find in the biblical text. Those conceptions have a historical and traditional value. The later generation of jurists, even in Arabia, dare not oppose the literal interpretation of the Qur'ān to the progress of ideas, and they try by interpretation and commentary to shirk the strict application of the text.

The Legacy of Islam

Is it allowable to speak, even in a very wide sense, of a legacy of Islam? According to a current opinion, it is useless to try and find a common meeting-ground for Eastern and Western Law. Enclosed within the rigid frame of dogma, the system of Islam cannot be reduced to our formulas; being, as it is, a religious law it is at variance with our ideas, quite incapable of development. A confusion is usually made in this respect between two distinct fields. Like Christianity and any other religion Islam has special dogmas pertaining to it, which of course cannot be exposed to discussion by its votaries. But it would be as unjust to tax it with rigidity as it would be to bring a similar charge against Christianity. Every great religious system has something more than mere dogma. It has been said by St. Thomas Aquinas with great truth: 'The common weal, which is the ultimate scope of law, has many different origins, according to persons, to circumstances, and epochs'. The thinkers of Islam have perceived this quite clearly. The political doctrine of Aristotle, combined with the principle of Revelation, has produced in Arab science a system which offers some analogies to the political ideas of medieval Christianity which are both natural and striking. On these we should like to dwell briefly.

Society, as we have seen, is a necessary fact; it is not a confused rabble, but an aggregation held together by a common end and by ties of mutual help; hence the social and moral conception of the state: 'The object of Government is to lead men to prosperity in this world and to salvation in the next'. This purpose is effected by law: the structure of law is determined by the very structure of society, and from this in fact derives its legitimacy.

Its beginnings are traced by Muslims much in the same way as in Christian theory. A moment existed at the dawn of history when mankind was one single flock. Ignorant of evil they lived in a state of peaceful anarchy, according to the precepts of natural law. The end of the golden age came with the crime of Cain. The passions of men gained the upper hand and brought about social disorder, the loss of the true faith, and the introduction of particular laws. The object of law is the prevention of evil, hence two main principles: equality and good faith.

1. Equality: 'The white man is not above the black nor the black above the yellow; all men are equal before their Maker', said the Prophet. Equal before God, members of a great family in which there is neither noble nor villein, but only believers, Muslims are equal before the civil law; and this equality was proclaimed at a time when it was practically unknown throughout Christian society.

2. This law, equal for all, rests essentially on *good faith*. Muslims must keep their pledges. No one may profit from what belongs to another Muslim, except with the owner's consent. 'Be honest towards those who have confidence in your honesty'; 'do not betray those who have betrayed you'—these traditions and a great many others referred to the Prophet are also among the general rules of Muslim law. This conception of good faith

is essentially an ethical one, and is elevated to an abstract and universal notion. It strikes us as being more akin to our mind than the feudal and Germanic conception of good faith springing from personal fealty. The system thus allows a wide scope to the human will, and attaches importance to the spirit rather than to the letter. Human will, whatever its expression, is sufficient to create a legal bond. It is but seldom that the validity or nullity of an act does depend in Muslim law on the point of form. Contrast this with the unending formal minutiae of Germanic procedure. The rule 'consensus solus obligat' is fundamental in the eyes of the doctors of law.

Having as its scope social utility, Muslim law is essentially progressive, in much the same way as our own. Being a product of language and logic it is a science. It is not unchangeable and depending on mere tradition. The great schools of law agree on this point. 'The legal rule', say the Ḥanafites, 'is not unchangeable, it is not the same as the rules of grammar and logic. It expresses what generally happens and changes with the circumstances which have produced it.'

Law is also liable to change with regard to its application. Mālikites and Ḥanafites agree on this point also. 'Utility is the rule of the lawyer.' The Arabs have perceived very clearly the reason of this flexibility. It is again usage. Societies are living organisms and undergo ceaseless change during their life. 'In the time of Adam the condition of men was weak and miserable. The sister was permitted to the brother and God extended his indulgence to many other matters. When society became wealthier and more numerous, precepts were multiplied.' This continuity of life may be seen in the course of Islamic history.

'We can see that the Companions of the Prophet took different decisions on the ground of their utility, without being authorized by any precept. For instance they decided that the Qur'ān should be committed to writing, although they were not empowered to do so by any precedent. They set up offices for the different branches of government, struck money, built prisons. It is for the same reason of utility that law submits the deposition of legal witnesses to strict conditions which are not found in tradition . . . so that, of necessity it has given certain contracts, e.g. loans, a wide interpretation . . .'

Such are the foundations of the great authority given by Muslim jurists to custom. It is a kind of unwritten rule which has the power of making law and even of modifying it. 'What the Muslims approve, is approved of God.' When it is uniform, enduring, and is not *contra bonos mores*, or against the general rules of law, usage has the same force as law itself; and becomes part and parcel of it.

'Necessity', say the Ḥanafites, 'has opened the way to the re-admission of many things which would not be admissible according to strict rule.' For instance, mortgage is admitted, in order to relieve the condition of debtors. Interest on loans, theoretically forbidden because, as in most primitive economies, it promptly degenerates into usury, finds a devious way back into the accepted practices. We might add *emphyteusis*, the hire of a labourer against part of the product, the contract made with a broker or with a town crier: all of which conventions, according to the letter of Muslim law, ought to be null and void on account of the uncertainty of their object and the element of risk which they entail, are nevertheless admitted by the two orthodox schools of law.

Not only does the law admit custom, but it follows it in its changes.

'It is a general rule that every law based on use or custom changes with the custom itself . . . It might be said on one side: we must follow what is established, for we cannot make law, having neither the knowledge nor the authority required: we must solve questions which are submitted to us according to what is to be found in the books. But on the other hand, to apply laws which are founded on ancient usage, once that usage is changed, is to set oneself against general opinion, and to prove one's ignorance of religion. The truth is that whenever a law is based upon the custom of a particular time, that law must change when the conditions which called it into being have changed.'

The mainspring of this development is the prince or ruler. He is a trustee: he cannot substitute his own authority for traditional law, but he may prefer one of the accepted systems of law before another. He may make a certain custom so prevalent that it ultimately becomes a law. Finally, in case of need, he may take the measures called for by the circumstances, as a good trustee must do on behalf of his beneficiary. Does this mean that the religious idea has had no share in the development of Muslim law? It would be a misapprehension of that powerful unity of thought which is the main strength of Islam. The science of law is only a part of theology. Even more perhaps than in Christianity, theocracy has superseded the classical notion of city-state. But we must not go astray in this interpretation. Looking more closely into the matter, we shall see that the meaning of the Muslim jurists is identical with our own. The distinction between the *rights of Allāh* and the rights of man has no more meaning than the distinction between public law and private law.

The religious idea has had no doubt a very great influence, but it is not what one would suppose. That influence consists in the moral bent it has given to law, that is to say in the connexion, amounting often to a blending, between legal rules and moral precepts. Partnership, loan, the character of witnesses, the relations between master and servant, plaintiff and defendant, every convention and bargain forming the subject-matter of legal relationships takes a moral turn and is considered under an aspect superior to mere private interest. Deposit, for instance, is a form of assistance and of mutual help, because thereby one helps the proprietor to preserve his property; and this is recommended because God says: 'Help each other in good works', and the Prophet says: 'God helps man so long as man helps his brother'. The man who receives knowingly a payment which is not due to him incurs a twofold sort of obligation: he is guilty before God, and guilty towards the victim of his fraud. The debtor who has the means to pay his debt and postpones payment is guilty of a serious sin, and endangers his salvation. The Prophet uttered some charming words with regard to neighbourly relations: 'Be kind to your neighbour. Draw the veil over him. Avoid injury. Look upon him with an eye of kindness. If you see him doing evil, forgive him. If you see him doing good to you, proclaim your thankfulness'.

The consequence of this spirit is that the exercise of a right is actually regarded as the fulfilment of a duty: for if right is good, it is not possible 'to omit it without sin'. He who claims his property from an unrightful possessor fulfils also a moral obligation: for if he kept silence, he would allow the unjust possessor to continue in his sin. 'Help thy brother even if he is unjust', says the Prophet. 'Assistance in this case consists in preventing his being unjust.' But if everybody's right is not only his private interest, but is also his moral obligation, this right has certain limits which moral law and social interest determine. Conciliation and compromise are everywhere asserted to be most laudable. Reprisals are forbidden. Vexatious proceedings against a debtor are contrary to law, as well as abusive exercise of right. 'No one may make use of his right so as to cause another an evident damage.' The Muslim jurists have in these matters a more delicate feeling than we should suppose. It is forbidden, for instance, to give a power of attorney to the enemy of the party against whom it is proposed to proceed; to hire a beast of burden to a man known for his rough treatment of animals; to sell a young slave girl to a libertine who might persuade her to impiety or debauch her. Everywhere the limit of law and its measures is traced by morality.

Hence it has been rightly said: 'Man has no right in which God has not a share; God's share is His command to give every one his due and not to encroach on what belongs to another'. We have thus reached a point of pure right which is common ground for all civilized communities.

Such is, in its essential features, the Muslim system of law. It may rightfully claim a high rank in the appreciation of experts. It stands out as immeasurably superior to the barbarous practices and crude formalism of early feudal law, with which its *floruit* was contemporaneous.

What was lacking in Muslim law is what has been wanting in every other respect, viz. a more synthetic spirit. A tendency to anarchy, and a fundamental incapacity for organization and discipline, the causes of the political incapacity of the Arabs, have been intellectually a source of weakness within their legal system. Another cause of weakness is that the Arabs have immoderately exaggerated the fundamental basis of their system. The idea that justice consists in reciprocity has been pushed to its extremest consequences by them, as well as by our canon lawyers. The philosophy of Aristotle contributed to this result at least as much as religious dogma: the prohibition of interest under every form, the dislike of every kind of risk, the exclusion of any uncertainty in contracts, all the peculiarities, in a word, of Muslim law, spring from that origin, and depend from the same general idea, which is that in all these cases the rule of equality is infringed, and with it justice; and the lawyer has only in view the readjustment of the balance, that is to say the suppression of every device which may trouble the strict application of the rule—*ut aequalitas servetur*, as our own doctors of canon law used to say.

The constant endeavour to attain this objective has led to an excess of regulation, an attention to minutiae that would have stifled every form of business, if precepts had not been eluded by means of a more or less plausible system of fictions, or had not remained for the most part purely theoretical.

Among our positive acquisitions from Arab law, there are legal institutions such as limited partnership (*qirāḍ*), and certain technicalities of commercial law. But even omitting these, there is no doubt that the high ethical standard of certain parts of Arab law acted favourably on the development of our modern concepts; and herein lies its enduring merit.

D. DE SANTILLANA.

SCIENCE AND MEDICINE

THE treasure-houses of Islamic science are just beginning to be opened. In Constantinople alone there are more than eighty mosque libraries containing tens of thousands of manuscripts. In Cairo, Damascus, Mosul, and Baghdād, as well as in Persia and India, there are other collections. Few have been listed, much less described or edited. Even the catalogue of the Escorial Library in Spain, which contains a large part of the wisdom of western Islam, is not yet complete. During the last few years the mass of material recovered has gone far to subvert our former conceptions and has thrown a flood of new light on the early history of scientific thought in the Islamic world. Thus at present even an outline of the medical and scientific achievement of Islam can, at best, be but tentative.

§ 1. *Early Period to* A.D. *750*

When, in the seventh century, the Arabs first entered into the heritage of an ancient civilization, they brought with them apart from their religious and social ideals, no spiritual contribution save their music and their language. The rich and flexible tongue of Arabia was destined to become the scientific idiom of the Near East, just as Latin grew into a medium of scientific understanding in the West.

The Arabian pre-Islamic and early Islamic poetry shows that the Bedouins possessed a certain knowledge of the animals, plants, and stones of their vast peninsula. Their poets had a predilection for describing the qualities of their riding-camels and horses, and from their accounts in later centuries was derived a definite class of literature. In medicine, hygiene, and meteorology their knowledge was most rudimentary. The Qurān expresses no clear conception of the nature of disease and gives hygienic directions only for social purposes. More elaborate material is afforded by Quranic traditions and commentaries formed during the first centuries of the Islamic faith. The contents of these, however, are of but little scientific value, being mere lists of diseases and remedies mingled with magic practices, descriptions of talismans against the evil eye and protective prayers.

By the time the Arabs had penetrated into the Byzantine and Persian Empires, Greek science had for centuries ceased to be a living force. It had passed into the hands of scholars who copied or commented on the works of Aristotle, Hippocrates, Galen, Ptolemy, Archimedes, and the rest. The Greek medical tradition had found its most effective expositors in Aëtios of Amida (*fl. c.* 550) and Paul of Aegina (*fl. c.* 625) who dwelt in Alexandria, in Alexander of Tralles (525–605) domiciled in Rome, and Theophilos Protospatharios of Constantinople, (*fl. c.* 640).

During the centuries preceding the Arab invasion, the capital of Egypt saw some feeble revival of its ancient academy. Here a new basis for medical learning was created by abstraction of the main works of Galen. The Alexandrian Johannes Philoponus stands out as a bold advocate of the views of Aristotle. The writings bearing the name of Hippocrates had been condensed by Alexandrian scholars at an earlier period. Egypt, however, provided on the one hand a population fanatically Christian, and on the other abounded in occultism and mysticism. The soil was not favourable for any scientific development.

For such reasons Egypt failed to act as an effective intermediary between Greek and Arabic medicine and science. For that we must look to the Syriac-speaking world. The Neo-Arāmaic or Syriac idiom had, from the third century onwards, gradually replaced Greek in the learned circles of western Asia. The bearers of this Syro-Hellenistic civilization were mainly the Nestorians. This Christian sect was founded in A.D. 428 by Nestorius, patriarch of Constantinople. Its adherents were condemned as heretical by the Council of Ephesus in 431 and thereon migrated to Edessa. Expelled thence in 489 by the Byzantine Emperor Zeno, they emigrated to Persia, then under Sāsānian rule, where they were well received. Pushing yet farther eastward, with missionary zeal, they penetrated the heart of Asia and reached even as far as western China.

The Nestorian scientific centre, which included a medical school, was transferred from Edessa to Nisibis in Mesopotamia, and again in the first half of the sixth century to Jundēshāpūr in south-west Persia. There, besides a large hospital, an academy had been founded in the fourth century by the Sāsānian monarch. The great king Chosroes Nūshīrwān (531–79) made the city the most important intellectual centre of the time. Here Greek scholars who had left Athens when Justinian closed the philosophical schools in 529 came to meet Syrian, Persian, and Indian sages. Thus arose a scientific syncretism which later became important for the development of Islamic thought. Chosroes sent his own physician to India in search of medical books. These were then turned from Sanskrit into Pahlavi (Middle Persian), and many other scientific works were translated from Greek into Persian or Syriac. A disciple of the medical school of Jundēshāpūr and a contemporary of the Prophet was the first scientifically trained medical man in Arabia, and is cited by the Quranic traditionists.

The first important scientific figure in the Syriac-speaking world was Sergius of Rêsh-'Ainâ (*d.* 536) who was not a Nestorian but a Monophysite (Jacobite) Christian priest and chief physician in his Mesopotamian birth-place. It was he who began the task of translating the Greek medical literature into Syriac. Versions of many important works of Galen are ascribed to him. Though crude, they were sufficient to maintain Greek medical tradition in western Asia for more than two centuries. During this period scholars began to write medical treatises of their own, based on Greek medicine. The best known of these were the *Pandects* of Ahron, a Christian priest and physician in Alexandria shortly before the rise of Islam. The work was perhaps originally composed in Greek, but soon translated into Syriac and later into Arabic. The writing of Ahron has not survived, but it seems to have contained the first description of small-pox, a disease unknown to ancient Greek medicine.

References to works on the natural sciences, from the centuries immediately preceding the rise of Islam, are rarer than those of a medical character. At some early period the *Parva naturalia* of Aristotle and certain pseudo-Aristotelian books *On the cosmos* and *On the soul*, appeared in Syriac, as did also the *Physiologus*, a Christian theological treatise on animals and their legendary powers and qualities. In the same language appeared versions of Greek treatises on cattle-breeding, agriculture, and veterinary medicine, as well as alchemical tracts. Some early Syriac fragments on metallurgic technical procedure still survive. It is probable that during the Sāsānian rule the main centres of alchemical and astrological study were the great towns in the eastern and northern provinces of Persia, where Chinese and Indian influences were being welded to form a new civilization.

When the Arabs overran north Africa and western Asia they left the Byzantine and Persian administrative and scientific institutions almost untouched. The academy of Jundēshāpūr continued as the scientific centre of the new Islamic empire. From here, during the Umayyad period (661–749), learned men, especially physicians, came to Damascus, the capital. They were mostly Christians or Jews bearing Arabic names. It was a Persian Jew, Māsarjawaih, who translated Ahron's *Pandects* into Arabic, and was responsible for what was probably the earliest scientific book in that language. History however is almost silent concerning scientific aims at the court of the Umayyad Caliphs.

§ 2. *Age of Translations from about 750 to about 900.*

The rise of the Abbasids about 750 inaugurated the epoch of greatest power, splendour, and prosperity of Islamic rule. At the very dawn stands the figure of a Muslim whose shadow lies athwart the science of the Middle Ages in the Orient as in the Occident. Jābir ibn Ḥayyān called aṣ-Ṣūfī (that is 'the Mystic'), the *Geber* of medieval Latin literature, was the son of an Arabic druggist in Kufa who died a martyr of the Shī'ite propaganda. Jābir practised as a physician, but no record of his medical writings has come down to us, though the author of this essay has recently been able to recover a work ascribed to him on poisons. Jābir is famous as the father of Arabic alchemy. As we write there arrives evidence, however, that the works ascribed to him are of the tenth century, where we shall accordingly consider them (p. 325).

Jābir is said to have been closely attached to the family of the Barmecides, the powerful viziers of Hārūn ar-Rashīd. He was implicated in their downfall in A.D. 803 and died in exile at Kufa, his father's birthplace, where it is said that his laboratory was found in ruins two hundred years later.

In the time of the second Abbasid Caliph al-Manṣūr (754–75) the task of translation of Greek wisdom was taken up again, notably at Jundēshāpūr. From there the ruler, when sick, sent for Jūrjīs (George) of the Christian family of the Bukht-Yishû' ('Jesus hath delivered'), chief physician at the renowned hospital. Another member of the same family was later consulted by the Caliphs al-Hādī (*d.* 786) and Hārūn ar-Rashīd (*d.* 809). The Bukht-Yishû' family produced no less than seven generations of distinguished physicians, the last of whom lived into the second half of the eleventh century A.D. It was doubtless the skill of the first Bukht-Yishû' that made the caliphs desire to propagate Greek medical knowledge among the physicians of their empire.

The ninth century was the period of greatest activity in the work of translation. The old Syriac versions of Sergius were revised and new ones added. The translators, mostly Nestorian Christians, had a command of the Greek, Syriac, and Arabic languages and often also of Persian. Most of them wrote first in Syriac. The venerable Yūḥannā ibn Māsawayh (d. 857), however, who was for half a century physician to Hārūn ar-Rashīd's successors, produced a number of medical works in Arabic. In general the Syriac versions were prepared for Christian disciples and friends, while those in Arabic were intended for Muslim patrons who were themselves sometimes men of learning.

During the reign of the Caliph Al-Ma'mūn (813–33) the new learning reached its first climax. The monarch created in Baghdād a regular school for translation. It was equipped with a library. One of the translators there was Ḥunayn ibn Isḥāq (809–77), a particularly gifted philosopher and physician of wide erudition, the dominating figure of this century of translators. We know from his own recently published *Missive* that he translated practically the whole immense corpus of Galenic writings. This amounted to a hundred Syriac, and thirty-nine Arabic versions of Galen's medical and philosophical books. His disciples, of whom his son Isḥāq and his nephew Ḥubaysh were the most prominent, produced some thirteen Syriac and sixty Arabic translations. Thus was transmitted to the Islamic world the whole legacy of the most voluminous of the Greek scientific writers.

Ḥunayn's predilection for the scholastic turn in Galen's theories is everywhere apparent. It was Ḥunayn who gave Galen his supreme position in the Middle Ages in the Orient, and indirectly also in the Occident. Concerning the works of Hippocrates we are less well informed. Ḥunayn himself translated his *Aphorisms*, and this version remained classical for the later

Arabs who frequently commented on it. Most of the other Hippocratic works were translated by Ḥunayn's disciples. These versions were often revised by the master, who himself rendered into Syriac and Arabic nearly all the commentaries that Galen had himself written upon Hippocrates. Ḥunayn translated moreover the great *Synopsis* of Oribasius (325–403), the *Seven Books* of Paul of Aegina—both voluminous works—and the important and exceedingly influential *Materia Medica* of Dioscurides (*fl. c.* 60) which had been badly rendered by a former translator. This work was yet again translated into Arabic in Spain during the second half of the tenth century (see p. 330). Magnificent illustrated Arabic manuscripts of these Arabic translations of Dioscurides are contained in various libraries. Among the Arabic translations ascribed to Ḥunayn are works of other Greek physicians and veterinary writers, together with several Aristotelian physical works and the Greek Old Testament (*the Septuagint*). Many of Ḥunayn's translations are still extant in manuscript, particularly in the libraries of Constantinople. They exhibit a free and sure mastery of the language, an easy adaptation to the Greek original, and a striking exactness of expression without verbosity. The superiority of Ḥunayn's workmanship was so generally recognized that many of the minor translators ascribed their productions to the great master.

Ḥunayn's own compositions are nearly as numerous as his translations. They include many summaries of, and commentaries on, Galen's works, and skilful extracts and recapitulations in the form of text-books for students. Among the Arabs and Persians the most renowned of his books were the *Questions on Medicine*, a manual in the form of query and answer, and *Ten Treatises on the Eye*, which is the earliest systematic text-book of ophthalmology known. Several important works of Galen, though lost in their Greek original, have been preserved for us in the Arabic translations made by Ḥunayn or his pupils.

Ḥunayn ibn Isḥāq had several contemporaries who are considered 'great' translators, besides some ninety pupils who undertook similar work of less importance. In the former class were his nephew Ḥubaysh, his son Isḥāq (*d.* 910), the great physician and mathematician, Thābit ibn Qurra (825–901) of Ḥarrān in Mesopotamia, and Qustā ibn Lūqā (Constantine, son of Luke, *fl. c.* 900). All these except Thābit were Christians, like the majority of the physicians of the ninth century. Thābit himself was a heathen 'Ṣābian' or star-worshipper. Ḥunayn and Ḥubaysh translated medical writings almost exclusively, their colleagues devoted themselves rather to astronomical, physical, mathematical, and philosophical Greek works. All of them produced also works of their own composition, the titles of which run into many hundreds. In the first half of the ninth century scientific works in the Syriac language predominated, but as the century wore on Arabic works became more numerous. Accompanying this process was the disappearance of the old school of Jundēshāpūr, all its famous physicians and scientists having been gradually transferred to Baghdād and Sāmarrā, the brilliant residences of the caliphs.

About 856, al-Mutawakkil re-founded at Baghdād the library and translation school, the direction of which was entrusted to Ḥunayn. The caliphs and their grandees furnished the necessary means to allow the Christian scholars to travel in search of Greek manuscripts and to bring them to Baghdād for translation. Thus Ḥunayn himself relates concerning a work of Galen now lost, and rare even at that date, 'I sought it earnestly and travelled in search thereof in Mesopotamia, Syria, Palestine, and Egypt, until I reached Alexandria. Yet I was not able to find aught save about half of it at Damascus.' He says that he always tried to work from at least three manuscripts of a Greek book so as to collate them and restore their text properly—a very modern conception of the duty of an editor.

As for medical learning in Baghdād, an interesting passage in Ḥunayn's recently published *Missive on the Galenic Translations* shows us the Greek traditions fully alive there in 856. Thus he gives a picture of how the *Twenty Books* of Galen were being studied. 'The reading of the students of the Medical School at Alexandria was confined to these books, keeping to the order which I have followed in my list. They were accustomed to meet daily to read and interpret one of the standard works, as in our days our Christian friends meet daily at the educational institutions known as *scholē* (*uskūl*) to discuss a standard work from among the books of the Ancients. The remainder of Galen's books they used to read each for himself, after an introductory study of the afore-mentioned books, just as our friends to-day do with the explanations of the books of the Ancients.' At this period, as well as later, full liberty to teach was granted in the schools and mosques of Baghdād.

Besides the translations of Greek works and their extracts, the translators made manuals of which one form, that of the 'pandects', is typical of the period of Arabic learning. These are recapitulations of the whole of medicine, discussing the affections of the body, systematically beginning at the head and working down to the feet. Most of these pandects are lost. One however was republished at Cairo only a few months ago. It was ascribed to Thābit ibn Qurra (p. 318), more celebrated as a translator and astronomer than as a physician. It is divided into thirty-one sections. The subjects treated are hygiene, 'hidden' and general diseases, e.g. those of the skin; then comes a section occupying the bulk of the work—on diseases of parts from the head, down through the breast, stomach, and intestines to the extremities; then follows a discussion on infectious diseases, among which are small-pox and measles; and here also poisons find a place; next is an account of climate, then of fractures and dislocations, then of food-stuffs and diet, and lastly of matters of sex. The exposition of each disease, its causes, symptoms, and treatment, is given in clear and succinct language. Many Greek and Syriac authors are quoted.

Another kind of medical literature, much in favour with the Arab scholars, was the cram book in the form of questions and answers. Such books have survived in hundreds of manuscripts and have done much to give to Arabic medicine its scholastic aspect.

As regards the process of translation of the Greek works on the sciences other than medicine, our sources of information are somewhat meagre. Most of the Aristotelian scientific corpus was rendered into Syriac and Arabic by unknown translators. The *Physics*, the *Meteorology*, the *De Anima*, *De Sensu*, *De Coelo*, *De Generatione et Corruptione*, the *Historia Animalium*, together with works on botany, mineralogy, and mechanics spuriously ascribed to the great philosopher, all became accessible in these languages. Some treatises of neo-Platonic origin such as the *Secret of Creation* and the famous *De Causis*, ascribed to Apollonius of Tyana (called Bālīnūs by the Arabs), and other apocryphal works of Hellenistic scientists appeared in Arabic dress. Many Greek alchemical works, all or most under false ascriptions, were also translated. During the ninth century A.D., however, no progress in chemistry is recorded, and two of the great scientists, Ḥunayn and al-Kindī (*d. c.* 873), were violent opponents of alchemical practices which they considered fraudulent.

We turn now from the translations to the original works of the period. In physics al-Kindī is the most frequently named scholar. No less than 265 works are ascribed to this first Muhammadan 'Philosopher of the Arabs'. Of these at least fifteen are on meteorology, several are on specific weight, on tides, optics and notably on the reflection of light, and eight are on music. Unhappily the bulk of al-Kindī's scientific output is lost. His *Optics*, preserved in a Latin translation, influenced Roger Bacon and other western men of science.

The technical arts were rapidly developing in Mesopotamia and Egypt, where irrigation works and canals for water-supply and communications were created. Theoretical mechanics roused much interest, and many books on elevation of water, water-wheels, on balances and on water-clocks were written. The earliest treatise on mechanics extant appeared about 860 as the *Book of Artifices* by the mathematicians Muḥammad, Aḥmad, and Ḥasan, sons of Mūsā ibn Shākir, who were themselves patrons of translators. This book contains one hundred technical constructions of which some twenty are of practical value, among them being accounts of vessels for warm and cold water, and water wells with a fixed level. Most are descriptions of scientific toys such as drinking-vessels with musical automata and the like, based on the mechanical principles of Hero of Alexandria.

In natural history a special type of literature arose during the eighth century. It took the form of accounts of animals, plants, and stones composed with a literary aim, but containing useful information. One of the most prominent authors of such works was the famous Arabic philologist al-Aṣmaʿī of Baṣra (A.D. 740–828). He composed books *On the Horse*, *On the Camel*, *On Wild Animals*, *On Plants and Trees*, *On the Vine and the Palm-Tree*, *On the Making of Man*, and several other writers produced comparable works. A book that has caused much controversy is the *Nabataean Agriculture* of Ibn Waḥshiyya (*c.* A.D. 800). It contains some useful information on animals, plants, and their cultivation, mingled with legends and forged translations from Babylonian and other Semitic sources. The Syriac version of the work on husbandry (*Geoponica*) by the Byzantine scholar Cassianus Bassus (*c.* 550) was translated into Arabic by different scholars.

After the Arabic edition of Aristotle's apocryphal *Mineralogy* many Islamic writers composed books on stones, particularly precious stones, which form a special *genre*, the 'lapidary', afterwards both translated and imitated in the West. Nearly all those we have mentioned, from 'Jābir' to al-Kindī, were authors of such pamphlets. Al-Kindī moreover wrote several small works on iron and steel for weapons. The increasingly close connexion between the caliphs' empire and eastern and southern lands, e.g., Turkistan, India, and the east African coasts, increased the afflux of rare and precious stones and the knowledge of them. Thus some modern names of stones still bear traces of Arabic or Persian contacts, for example the *bezoar* (Persian: *pād-zahr*, i.e. protecting against poison). So too many plants, drugs, and species unknown to the Greeks came through the Persians, e.g. camphor (an Arabic word of Persian origin) and galanga-root (Persian *khūlinjān* from Chinese *kawliang-chang*) from the Sunda Islands, musk from Tibet, sugar-cane from India, amber from the coasts of the Indian Ocean. Pharmacological and toxicological treatises were composed by many of the Arabic-writing physicians from Jābir ibn Ḥayyān onwards. Paper was introduced from China into the Islamic world in the eighth century and in A.D. 794 the first Islamic paper-manufacture was established in Baghdād.

§ 3. *The Golden Age from about 900 to about 1100.*

At the end of the period of translation, the physicians and scientists of the Islamic world stood on a firm foundation of Greek science, increased by a large share of Persian and Indian thought and experience. Their work had been learned but not very original. From this time on they begin to rely upon their own resources and to develop from within.

The sciences, particularly medicine, now pass rapidly from the hands of Christians and Ṣābians into the possession of Muslim scholars, mostly Persians. In medicine, in place of *pandects* compiled from antique sources, we find imposing encyclopaedic works in which the knowledge of former generations is carefully classified and set against that of the moderns.

The first and surely the greatest of the writers of this new school is al Rāzī, the author known to the Latin West as Rhazes (*c.* 865–925), a Persian Muslim born at Rayy near modern Ṭehrān. Rhazes was undoubtedly the greatest physician of the Islamic world and one of the great physicians of all time. He studied in Baghdād under a disciple of Ḥunayn ibn Isḥāq, who was acquainted with Greek, Persian, and Indian medicine. In his youth Rhazes practised as an alchemist, but in his later years, when his reputation attracted pupils and patients from all parts of western Asia, he devoted himself exclusively to medicine. His erudition was all-embracing, and his scientific output remarkable, amounting to more than 200 works, half of which are medical.

The writings of Rhazes on medicine included many short missives of an ephemeral character. Their very titles bring a human element into what must be, for most readers, a somewhat arid theme. *On the fact that even skilful physicians cannot heal all diseases*; *Why frightened patients easily forsake even the skilled physician; Why people prefer quacks and charlatans to skilled physicians; Why ignorant physicians, laymen, and women have more success than learned medical men*, are among his lighter topics. Other of his missives treat of separate diseases, for example of stone in the bladder and in the kidneys, both very common conditions in the near East. We have also by him treatises on anatomy. The most celebrated of all the works of Rhazes is that *On Small-pox and Measles*. It was early translated into Latin and later into various languages, including English, being printed some forty times between 1498 and 1866. It gives the first clear account of these two diseases that has come down to us. An extract will convey to the reader something of the observing spirit of the original.

'The outbreak of small-pox is preceded by continuous fever, aching in the back, itching in the nose and shivering during sleep. The main symptoms of its presence are: back-ache with fever, stinging pain in the whole body, congestion of the face, sometimes shrinkage, violent redness of the cheeks and eyes, a sense of pressure in the body, creeping of the flesh, pain in the throat and breast accompanied by difficulty of respiration and coughing, dryness of the mouth, thick salivation, hoarseness of the voice, headache and pressure in the head, excitement, anxiety, nausea and unrest. Excitement, nausea and unrest are more pronounced in measles than in small-pox, whilst the aching in the back is more severe in small-pox than in measles.'

Rhazes gives sound and detailed advice as to the treatment of the pustules after the full development of small-pox. These pustules are of course the cause of the unsightly scars left by the disease, which is still common in the East.

The greatest medical work of Rhazes, and perhaps the most extensive ever written by a medical man, is his *al-Ḥāwī*, i.e. 'Comprehensive Book', which includes indeed Greek, Syriac, and early Arabic medical knowledge in their entirety. Throughout his life Rhazes must have collected extracts from all the books on medicine which he had read, together with his whole medical experience. These he combined in his last years into this enormous manual. The Arabic biographies agree in saying that he could not finish his work and that after his death his disciples gave it its actual form. Of the more than twenty volumes of which the *Ḥāwī* consisted about ten only are in existence, scattered in eight or more public libraries. Half a century after Rhazes only two complete copies were known, but I have myself found a note in the book of an oculist of the Bukht-Yishūʿ family of about A. D. 1070 to the effect that he had hado ccasion to consult five copies of the *Ḥāwī's* ophthalmic section. For each disease Rhazes first cites all the Greek, Syrian, Arabic, Persian, and Indian authors, and at the end gives his own opinion and experiences, and he preserves many striking examples of his clinical insight.

The *Ḥāwī* was translated into Latin under the auspices of Charles I of Anjou by the Sicilian Jewish physician Faraj ibn Sālim (Farragut) of Girgenti, who finished his enormous task in

1279. He rendered the name *al-Ḥāwī* by *continens*, and as the *Liber Continens* (see *Legacy of Israel*, p. 221) this greatest work of Rhazes was propagated in numerous manuscripts during the following centuries. It was repeatedly printed from 1486 onwards. By 1542 there had appeared five editions of this vast and costly work, besides many more of various parts of it. Its influence on European medicine was thus very considerable.

Besides medicine, Rhazes left writings on theology, philosophy, mathematics, astronomy, and the 'natural sciences'. The last deal with matter, space, time, motion, nutrition, growth, putrefaction, meteorology, optics, and alchemy. The importance of Rhazes' alchemical work has been brought to light during the last few years only. His great *Book of the Art (of Alchemy)* was recently discovered in the library of an Indian prince. Although dependent partly on the same sources as 'Jābir', Rhazes excels him in his exact classification of substances, and in his clear description of chemical processes and apparatus, which is always devoid of mystical elements. While 'Jābir' and the other Arabian alchemists divide mineral substances into 'Bodies' (gold, silver, &c.), 'Souls' (sulphur, arsenic, &c.), and 'Spirits' (mercury and sal-ammoniac), Rhazes classifies alchemical substances as vegetable, animal, or mineral, a conception which comes from him into modern speech. The class of minerals he divides into spirits, bodies, stones, vitriols, boraxes, and salts. He distinguished volatile 'bodies' and non-volatile 'spirits', placing among the latter sulphur, mercury, arsenic, and salmiac.

A prominent contemporary of Rhazes was the writer known to the West as Isaac Judaeus (855–955). This Egyptian Jew became physician to the Fāṭimid rulers of Qairawān in Tunisia. His works were among the first to be translated into Latin, the task being accomplished by Constantine the African about 1080. They exercised much influence on Western medieval medicine, and were still being read in the seventeenth century. Robert

Burton (1577–1640) quotes them freely in his *Anatomy of Melancholy*. The books of Isaac *On Fevers*, *On the Elements*, *On simple Drugs and Aliments*, and above all, his treatise *On Urine* dominated medicine for many centuries. Very remarkable is his little tract, extant in a Hebrew translation only, *Guide for Physicians*. It shows a high ethical conception of the medical profession. Some of the aphorisms in this work are worthy of record: 'Should adversity befall a physician open not thy mouth to condemn, for each hath his hour.' 'Let thine own skill exalt thee and seek not honour in another's shame.' 'Neglect not to visit and treat the poor, for there is no nobler work than this.' 'Comfort the sufferer by the promise of healing, even when thou art not confident, for thus thou mayest assist his natural powers.' A practical piece of advice excellent when dealing with Oriental patients is: 'Ask thy reward while the sickness is waxing or at its height, for being cured he will surely forget what thou didst for him!'

Isaac's most distinguished disciple was Ibn al-Jazzār (*d.* 1009), a Muslim, whose chief work *Provision for the Traveller* was early translated into Latin as the *Viaticum*, Greek (*Ephodia*) and Hebrew. It was very popular with medieval physicians, because it gave a good record of internal diseases, but it was ascribed by its translator Constantine to himself and not to the real author (see p. 346).

The alchemical writings to which the name of 'Jābir' is attached have long been a puzzle to scholars. If this 'Jābir' be the eighth-century mystic of that name, it is difficult to understand how he could have obtained any knowledge of the still inaccessible Greek alchemical literature. As already indicated, however (p. 315), evidence is now available that the works bearing the name of 'Jābir' were produced early in the tenth century. It appears that they were the work of a secret society similar to the so-called 'Brethren of Purity'. In the medical work of 'Jābir' only Greek authors are quoted, but the diction is independent of theirs and shows a distinct scholastic trend. Syrian and Indian names of drugs are rarely used, but Persian terms abound. Thus we may consider this remarkable book to be a mixture of Greek scientific research and Persian practical knowledge of medicines and poisons. Anyhow it is doubtless the last link in a long chain of scientific development during pre-Islamic and Islamic times.

'Jābir' is world-famed as the father of Arabic alchemy. This word, *al-kīmiyā*, is usually said to be derived from the Egyptian *kam-it* or *kem-it*, 'the black', or, as some have thought, from the Greek *chyma*, 'molten metal'. The fundamental premises of this 'science' as established by Egyptian and Greek scholars were (*a*) that all metals are in reality the same, and that consequently a transmutation of one into another is possible; (*b*) that gold is the 'purest' of all metals, and silver next to it, and (*c*) that there is a substance capable of continuously transforming base into pure metals. These conceptions had the merit of provoking experiment, but were unfortunately accompanied by an inordinate tendency to theorize. Moreover, at Alexandria, the centre of Greek learning, and indeed throughout the Islamic realm, certain mystical tendencies derived from the Gnostics and the neo-Platonists had a very detrimental effect upon the experimental spirit. Alchemy, which in the hands of 'Jābir' was a matter for experimental research, tended to become the subject of ineffable speculation and superstitious practice, passing into fraudulent deception.

About a hundred alchemical works ascribed to 'Jābir' are extant. Many are little but confused jumbles of puerile superstition. But there are others which prove that the author recognized more clearly, and stated more definitely, the importance of experiment than any other early chemist. Thus he was enabled to make noteworthy advances in both the theory and practice of the subject. His influence can be traced throughout the whole historic course of European alchemy and chemistry.

On the practical side, 'Jābir' described improved methods for evaporation, filtration, sublimation, melting, distillation, and crystallization. He described the preparation of many chemical substances, e.g. cinnabar (sulphide of mercury), arsenious oxide, and others. He knew how to obtain nearly pure vitriols, alums, alkalis, sal-ammoniac, and saltpetre, how to produce so-called 'liver' and 'milk' of sulphur by heating sulphur with alkali, and so on. He prepared fairly pure mercury oxide and sublimate, as well as acetates of lead and other metals, sometimes crystallized. He understood the preparation of crude sulphuric and nitric acids as well as a mixture of them, *aqua regia*, and the solubility of gold and silver in this acid.

Several technical terms have passed from 'Jābir's' Arabic writings through Latin into the European languages. Among these are *realgar* (red sulphide of arsenic), *tutia* (zinc oxide), *alkali*, *antimony* (Ar: *ithmid*), *alembic* for the upper, and *aludel* for the lower part of a distillation vessel. A new chemical substance unknown to the Greeks which appears in 'Jābir's' works is *sal-ammoniac*. The *ammoniacon* of the Greeks was rock-salt, and it seems that the transference of the old name to a new salt was effected by the Syrians. A full appreciation of 'Jābir's' merits in chemistry will only be possible when the bulk of his chemical writings have been published, particularly his great *Book of the Seventy*. This composition of seventy discourses was till recently known only in an inferior and incomplete Latin version. The author of this article has had the good fortune to find the almost complete Arabic original.

The chemical writings to which 'Jābir's' name is attached were soon translated into Latin. The first such version, the *Book of the Composition of Alchemy*, was made by the Englishman Robert of Chester, in A.D. 1144. The translation of the *Book of the Seventy* into Latin was one of the achievements of the famous Gerard of Cremona (*d.* 1187, see p. 347). A work entitled the

FIG. 86. The 'bath'

FIG. 87. Symbolic figures of mixtures

TWO ILLUSTRATIONS FROM A MODERN ARABIC ALCHEMICAL MS.

Sun of Perfection is ascribed to 'Jābir' by the English translator Richard Russell (1678) who describes him as 'Geber, the Most Famous Arabian Prince and Philosopher'. Much evidence linking 'Geber' of the Latin writers with the Arabic alchemists has recently appeared from the pen of Dr. E. J. Holmyard.

In the Eastern caliphate there arose a generation of prominent physicians of whom we will first mention the Persian Muslim known to the Latins as Haly Abbas (*d.* 994). He composed an excellent and compact encyclopaedia, *The Whole Medical Art*, known also to the Latins as *Liber regius* (*al-Kitāb al-Malikī*). It deals with both the theory and practice of medicine. It begins with a most interesting chapter containing an explicit critique of previous Greek and Arabic medical treatises. This book was twice translated into Latin at an early date, but it was superseded by the *Canon* of the great Avicenna.

Abū 'Alī al-Ḥusayn ibn Sīnā, known universally to the West as Avicenna (980–1037), was one of the greatest scholars of the Islamic world, though less remarkable as a physician than as a philosopher and physicist. Nevertheless his influence on European medicine has been overwhelming. Ibn Sīnā concentrated the legacy of Greek medical knowledge with the addition of the Arabs' contribution in his gigantic *Canon of Medicine* (al-Qānūn fī'ṭ-Ṭibb), which is the culmination and masterpiece of Arabic systematization. This medical encyclopaedia deals with general medicine, simple drugs, diseases affecting all parts of the body from the head to the feet, special pathology and pharmacopoeia.

The system of classification adopted in the *Canon* is most complex, and is in part responsible for the mania for subdivision which affected Western scholasticism. The book was translated into Latin by Gerard of Cremona in the twelfth century (p. 348) and his version exists in innumerable manuscripts. The demand for it may be gleaned from the fact that in the last thirty years of the fifteenth century it was issued sixteen times—fifteen editions being in Latin and one in Hebrew, and that it was reissued more than twenty times during the sixteenth century. These figures do not include editions of parts of the work. Commentaries on it in Latin, Hebrew, and the vernaculars, both in manuscript and in print, are without number, and the book continued to be printed and read into the second half of the seventeenth century. Probably no medical work ever written has been so much studied, and it is still in current use in the Orient.

Some fifteen other medical works of Avicenna are known, together with about a hundred writings by him on theology, metaphysics, astronomy, and philology. Nearly all are written in Arabic except some poems which are in Persian, a language which acquired new importance during the tenth century. With Avicenna 'the Prince and Chief of Physicians' Islamic medicine reached its zenith in the East. To this day pious veneration surrounds the tomb of the great physician and philosopher at Hamadān in western Persia.

While the eastern Islamic world was gradually acquiring supremacy in medicine, western Islam developed also as a centre of this science. In Spain during the glorious reigns of the caliphs ʿAbd al-Raḥmān III and al-Ḥakam II of Córdoba, Ḥasday ben Shaprūṭ (*d.c.* 990), a Jew, was at once minister, court-physician, and patron of science. In his younger years he translated into Arabic, with the help of the monk Nicholas, the splendid manuscript of the *Materia Medica* of Dioscurides which had been sent as a diplomatic present from the Byzantine emperor Constantine VII. Later Ibn Juljul, court-physician and medical historian, corrected this version and wrote a commentary on it.

The Muslim known to the Latins as Abulcasis (*d.c.* A.D. 1013) was likewise court-physician in Córdoba. His name is associated with a great *Medical Vade mecum* (*at-Taṣrīf*) in thirty sections, the last of which deals with surgery, an art which had till then been neglected by Islamic authors. The surgical treatise of

FIG. 88. AVICENNA GIVING A LECTURE ON ANATOMY

From a XVIth-century manuscript of Mansur's *Anatomy* (composed in Persia about A.D. 1400) in the collection of Dr. Max Meyerhof

Abulcasis is based largely on the sixth book of Paul of Aegina, but with numerous additions. His work contained illustrations of instruments which influenced other Arabic authors and especially helped to lay the foundations of surgery in Europe It was early translated into Latin, Provençal, and Hebrew. The celebrated French surgeon Guy de Chauliac (1300–68) appended the Latin version to one of his works.

In Egypt, Syria, and Mesopotamia there was much medical activity in the eleventh century A. D. 'Alī ibn Riḍwān of Cairo (*d.c.* 1067) known to the Latins as Haly Rodoam, produced a fine medical topography of Egypt and was an ardent follower of Galen and the Greek authors. He declared that one could become a good physician solely by the study of the ancient works, which opinion gave rise to a long and violent polemic with his contemporary Ibn Buṭlān of Baghdād (*d.c.* 1063). Ibn Riḍwān's commentary on Galen's *Ars parva*, as well as Ibn Buṭlān's *Synoptic Tables of Medicine*, a scholastic masterpiece, were translated into Latin.

Before leaving this period of Islamic medicine we have to consider some productions which are peculiar to it.

First come the treatises on simple drugs which form parts of the great encyclopaedias, but which were also composed as separate monographs by a series of other authors. Such treatises are still highly esteemed in the Orient. Abū Manṣūr Muwaffaq of Herāt in Persia wrote about 975 in Persian, *The Foundations of the True Properties of Remedies* describing 585 drugs. It contains besides Greek and Syriac, Arabic, Persian, and Indian knowledge. It is, moreover, the first monument of modern Persian prose. There were many treatises of the same type in Arabic. Among them we may mention those of Māsawayh al-Māridīnī of Baghdād and Cairo (*d.* 1015) and Ibn Wāfid in Spain (*d.c.* 1074). Both are well known in their Latin translations and were printed together some fifty or more times. In Latin they appeared as *De Medicinis universalibus et particulari-*

bus by 'Mesue' the younger, and *De Medicamentis simplicibus* by 'Abenguefit'.

Ophthalmology was another branch of medicine which reached its height about A.D. 1000. The Christian oculist ʿAlī ibn ʿĪsā of Baghdād known to the Latins as Jesu Haly, and the Muslim 'Ammār of Mosul, known as 'Canamusali', left two excellent treatises, increasing the Greek canon of ophthalmology with numerous additions, operations, and personal observations. Both were translated into Latin. They were the best text-books on eye-diseases until the first half of the eighteenth century when the Renaissance of ophthalmology set in in France.

In science we have mentioned the achievements of Rhazes and 'Jābir' in *Alchemy*. The two greatest spirits of the age, Avicenna and al-Bīrūnī, were firmly opposed to the subject. On the other hand we owe to Avicenna a treatise on the formation of mountains, stones, and minerals. It is important for the history of geology as discussing the influence of earthquake, wind, water, temperature, sedimentation, desiccation, and other causes of solidification.

Abu Rayḥān Muḥammad al-Bīrūnī (973–1048) called 'the Master' (*al-Ustādh*), a Persian physician, astronomer, mathematician, physicist, geographer, and historian, is perhaps the most prominent figure in the phalanx of those universally learned Muslim scholars who characterize the Golden Age of Islamic science. His *Chronology of Ancient Nations* and his Indian studies are known in good English translations. Most of his mathematical works and many other writings are waiting for publication. In physics his greatest achievement is the nearly exact determination of the specific weight of eighteen precious stones and metals. A voluminous unedited lapidary by al-Bīrūnī is extant in a unique manuscript in the Escorial Library. It contains a description of a great number of stones and metals from the natural, commercial, and medical point of view. He composed, moreover, a pharmacology (*ṣaydala*). Important information could certainly be obtained from his unedited works on the origin of Indian and Chinese stones and drugs which appear early in Arabic scientific works.

Al-Mas'ūdī (*d.* in Cairo *c.* 957) is in a restricted sense the 'Pliny of the Arabs'. In his *Meadows of Gold* he described an earthquake, the waters of the Dead Sea, and the first windmills, which are perhaps an invention of the Islamic peoples, and he also gives what has been described as the rudiments of a theory of evolution.

The 'Brethren of Purity' (*Ikhwān aṣ-Ṣafā*), a secret philosophical society founded in Mesopotamia in the tenth century, wrote an encyclopaedia composed of fifty-two treatises, seventeen of which deal with natural science, mainly on Greek lines. We find here discussions on the formation of minerals, on earthquakes, tides, meteorological phenomena, and the elements, all brought into relation with the celestial spheres and bodies. The work of the Brethren, although burnt as heretical by the orthodox clergy in Baghdād, spread as far as Spain where it influenced philosophic and scientific thought. Water-clocks were frequently constructed in the Islamic countries. One example was presented to Charlemagne by an embassy sent by Hārūn ar-Rashīd.

The famous philosopher al-Fārābī, a Turkish Muslim (*d.c.* A.D. 951), must be mentioned here for his treatise *On Music*, the most important oriental work on the theory of music. He also wrote an important book on the classification of sciences. Two similar works of classification were composed some time after. One was the *Keys of Sciences*, written in 976 by Muḥammad al-Khawārizmī. The other was the famous work *Fihrist al-'Ulūm*, i.e. *Index of Sciences* (988), by Ibn an-Nadīm. The latter is of primary importance for our knowledge of early Islamic (and Greek) scientists and philosophers.

Optics was developed to its highest degree by Abū 'Alī al-

Ḥasan ibn al-Haytham (Alhazen) of Baṣra (965). He moved to Cairo where he entered the service of the Fāṭimid caliph al-Ḥākim (996–1020) and tried to discover a method of regulating the annual Nile inundation. Failing in this task he had to hide from the caliph's wrath and simulate madness until al-Ḥākim's death. He nevertheless found time not only to copy ancient treatises on mathematics and physics, but also himself to compose many works on these subjects and on medicine, his original profession. His main work is *On Optics*: the original Arabic is lost, but the book survives in Latin. Alhazen opposes the theory of Euclid and Ptolemy that the eye sends out visual rays to the object of vision. He discusses the propagation of light and colours, optic illusions and reflection, with experiments for testing the angles of incidence and reflection. His name is still associated with the so-called 'Alhazen's problem': 'In a spherical concave or convex, a cylindrical or conical mirror to find the point from which an object of given position will be reflected to an eye of given position.' It leads to an equation of the fourth degree which Alhazen solved by the use of a hyperbola.

Alhazen examines also the refraction of light-rays through transparent mediums (air, water). In detailing his experiments with spherical segments (glass vessels filled with water), he comes very near to the theoretical discovery of magnifying lenses, which was made practically in Italy three centuries later, whilst more than six centuries were to pass before the law of sines was established by Snell and Descartes. Roger Bacon (thirteenth century) and all medieval Western writers on optics—notably the Pole Witelo or Vitellio—base their optical works largely on Alhazen's *Opticae Thesaurus*. His work also influenced Leonardo da Vinci and Johann Kepler. The latter modestly entitled his fundamental work on dioptrics *Ad Vitellionem Paralipomena* (Frankfort 1604).

Commentaries on Alhazen's *Optics* were written by Oriental authors, but most of his successors did not adopt his theory of vision; nor did the oculists of later periods of Islamic science. Al-Bīrūnī however and Avicenna share independently and fully Alhazen's opinion that 'it is not a ray that leaves the eye and meets the object that gives rise to vision. Rather the form of the perceived object passes into the eye and is transmuted by its transparent body (i.e. the lens)'.

Alhazen left several minor writings on physical optics, among them one *On Light*. He regards light as a kind of fire that is reflected at the spheric limit of the atmosphere. In *On Twilight Phenomena*, which is extant only in Latin, he calculates that this atmosphere is about ten English miles in height. Other of his treatises deal with the rainbow, the halo, and with spherical and parabolic mirrors. These and some other books on shadows and eclipses are of a highly mathematical character. On the basis of his calculations he constructed such mirrors of metal. Most of these works were products of the last ten years of Alhazen's life, as was his fundamental study *On the Burning glass*, in which he created a dioptric far superior to that of the Greeks. The work exhibits a profound and accurate conception of the nature of focussing, magnifying, and inversion of the image, and of formation of rings and colours by experiments. Alhazen wrote moreover a commentary on the optical works of Euclid and Ptolemy, on the *Physics* of Aristotle, and on the Aristotelian *Problemata*. He observed the semi-lunar shape of the image of the sun during eclipses on a wall opposite a fine hole made in the window-shutters—the first record of the *camera obscura*.

We may glance at the scientific institutions during this golden age of Islamic science. *Hospitals* were early founded, probably on the models of the old and celebrated academy-hospital of Jundēshāpūr. From the Persian name for this is derived the title used for a hospital throughout the Islamic world (*bīmāristān*). We have authentic information concerning at least thirty-four such institutions. They were distributed through the

Islamic world, from Persia to Morocco, from northern Syria to Egypt. In Cairo the first hospital was founded by the governor Ibn Ṭūlūn about A.D. 872 and still existed in the fifteenth century, and several others were later established there.

In Baghdād the first hospital was created at the order of Hārūn ar-Rashīd at the beginning of the ninth century, and five others were installed during the tenth. Travelling hospitals were known in the eleventh century. The Islamic chronicles give very exact information concerning the administration of these institutions. We know not only their budgets but even the amount of the salaries of physicians, oculists, and employees. The chief physicians and surgeons gave lectures to students and graduates, examined them, and gave diplomas (*ijāza*). Medical men, druggists, and barbers became subject to inspection. The orthopaedists were, for example, examined as to whether they were acquainted with the anatomy and surgery of Paul of Aegina. Arrangements were made for practical instruction. The hospitals were divided into two sections, for men and women, and each had its own wards and a dispensary. Some hospitals possessed a library. Many physicians were trained by an apprenticeship in the practice of a master, often their father or uncle. Others journeyed to foreign towns in order to follow the lessons of some celebrated practitioner. A report from Spain says that a physician at Cadiz installed in the parks of the governor a botanical garden in which he cultivated rare medicinal plants brought back from his travels.

Sciences other than medicine were mostly taught in mosques. In the early centuries of Islam these were liberally placed at the disposal of scholars. There are also records of academic libraries founded by caliphs, princes, and other prominent men. The Arabic chronicles furnish abundant information concerning these institutions.

Every important mosque had and still has its library not only of theological, but also of philosophical and scientific works

We have already mentioned the 'House of Wisdom', created in Baghdād by the Caliph al-Ma'mūn about A.D. 830. His nephew al-Mutawakkil followed his example, as did many grandees of his court. The caliph's friend and secretary 'Alī ibn Yaḥyā (*d.* 888) had a beautiful library in his country seat. In Cairo the Fāṭimid caliph al-Ḥākim founded in A.D. 995 a 'House of Science' the budget of which is known exactly. As orthodox theology became supreme it was suspended because of the danger of heresy.

The pilgrimage to Mecca and Medina, the duty of every Muslim, favoured the spread of science, since it compelled students from India and Spain, from Asia Minor and Africa, to pass through many lands where they could visit mosques and academies and have intercourse with prominent scholars. Moreover many came from Tunis to Persia, and from the Caspian Sea to Cairo and Córdoba, to follow the courses of famous teachers. The actual process of teaching was much as it is to-day. The professor sat with his back to a column, and round him gathered a ring of disciples. In the al-Azhar mosque of ancient fame in Cairo the tourist may usually see twenty or thirty such groups within the great hypostyle hall, giving what is in all probability a true picture of academic lessons as they were held in the days of ancient Greece and Córdoba.

§ 4. *Age of Decline from about* 1100

Whilst the orthodoxy of early Islam tolerated the sciences, we may say that, from the time of the famous religious teacher al-Ghazālī (*d.* 1111) onwards, this tolerance gave place to persecution of these studies 'because they lead to loss of belief in the origin of the world and in the creator'. Whether or no this attitude was alone sufficient to prevent the rise of great independent thinkers, it was certainly a very important factor in their suppression. The twelfth century marks a standstill. The works of Rhazes, Avicenna, and 'Jābir' are reproduced, summarized, commented on, but outstanding and independent works are becoming rare.

Among the physicians an increasing number of Jews is to be observed, particularly at the courts of Baghdād and Cairo, and in Spain, perhaps because Jews were relatively free from the restraints of orthodox Islam. The prototype of the eminent Jewish court physician, practitioner, philosopher, and religious teacher, is Maimonides (1135–1204). Born in Spain, he spent most of his active life in Cairo under the great Saladin and his sons. His best medical work is his *Aphorisms* in which he even ventured to criticize the opinions of Galen himself. As a court official he wrote hygienic treatises for the sultan which are very typical specimens of medical literature during the later centuries of Islam. The influence of orthodoxy on the otherwise rather liberal court of Cairo is evident from the excuse given by Maimonides at the end of one of his tracts, in which he has a lengthy scientific apology for his advice to the sultan that he should indulge in the forbidden wine and music as a cure for his melancholy.

Maimonides' younger contemporary, the Muslim ʿAbd al-Laṭīf, travelled from Baghdād to Cairo to see renowned scholars and the land of Egypt, of which he then gave his famous description. After describing the famines and earthquakes in Egypt from A.D. 1200 to 1202 he gives an interesting account of his osteological studies in an ancient cemetery in the north-west of Cairo. He checked and corrected Galen's description of the bone of the lower jaw and of the sacrum.

Pharmacological treatises abounded at this period. They were either on simple drugs, the most famous of which was that by Ibn al-Bayṭār (*d.* 1248), or on compound remedies. The latter treatises were called *Aqrābādhīn* (mutilation of Greek *graphidion*, i.e. small treatise). The word masquerades very frequently in Latin manuscripts and early printed books as

Grabadin. A *Collection of Simple Drugs* was composed by Ibn al-Bayṭār, who collected plants and drugs on the Mediterranean littoral, from Spain to Syria, described more than 1,400 medicinal drugs, and compared them with the records of more than 150 ancient or Arabian authors. It is a work of extraordinary erudition and observation, and is the greatest of the Arabic books on botany.

Later Arabic books on compound remedies are still in favour with the native druggists throughout the Islamic world. Among the most popular at the present day is the *Management of the Drug Store* by the Jew Kohēn al-ʿAṭṭār 14(th century) and the *Memorial* by Dāwūd al-Anṭākī (*d.* 1599), both composed in Cairo. Many of the old and complicated recipes of these books passed into the European dispensaries. Several names of remedies came thus to the West from the East. Among these we may note *rob* for a conserve of inspissated fruit-juice with honey, *julep* (Persian *gulāb* rose-water) for a medicinal aromatic drink, and *sirup* (Arabic *sharāb*).

With the beginning of the fourteenth century magic and superstitious practices began to creep into the medical works of the Muslim writers, whose medical knowledge was often derived from religious writings. There is thus a further deterioration of the general standard of the material.

In Spain, the philosophical bias predominated among medical men. The prototypes of this combination are the two Muslims, Ibn Zuhr (Avenzoar) and Ibn Rushd (Averroes). The former (*d.* in Seville 1162) was an aristocratic physician at the court of one of the Almohade rulers. He displayed disdain for surgery and surgeons and was more a consulting physician than a general practitioner. His chief work is the *Facilitation of Treatment* known by its Arabic name *al-Taysīr*, translated into Latin as *Theisir* in 1280 by Paravicius, with the help of a Jew, in Venice, where it was later repeatedly printed. This book gives proof of remarkable independence of thought, being largely based on personal experience. It is this, perhaps, which caused it to enjoy less success with the Arabs than in Europe.

Averroes (*d.* in Morocco in 1198), disciple and friend of Avenzoar, was among the very greatest of Aristotelian philosophers. He also wrote some sixteen medical works, one of which is well known in its Latin translation. This is the *General Rules of Medicine* (Kulliyyāt fī'ṭ-Ṭibb) translated in 1255 by the Paduan Jew Bonacosa under the title of *Colliget*. It was several times printed, in conjunction with Avenzoar's *Theisir*. Everywhere in his book Averroes reveals himself as an Aristotelian thinker, particularly in the second part where he deals with physiology and psychology. Often he pits the opinions of Rhazes and Avenzoar against those of Hippocrates and Galen.

The great plague of the fourteenth century, the 'Black Death', furnished an occasion for Muslim physicians in Spain to free themselves from theological prejudice which regarded plague as a divine punishment and to consider the epidemic as a contagion. The celebrated Arab statesman, historian, and physician Ibn al-Khaṭīb of Granada (1313-74) described it in a famous treatise *On Plague*. In it we find, for example, the remarkable passage:

'The existence of contagion is established by experience, study, and the evidence of the senses, by trustworthy reports on transmission by garments, vessels, ear-rings; by the spread of it by persons from one house, by infection of a healthy sea-port by an arrival from an infected land . . . by the immunity of isolated individuals and . . . nomadic Beduin tribes of Africa. . . . It must be a principle that a proof taken from the Traditions has to undergo modification when in manifest contradiction with the evidence of the perception of the senses.'

This was a very bold statement in the days of darkest orthodoxy.

The Moorish physician Ibn Khātima (*d.* 1369) wrote a book on the plague which ravaged Almeria in Spain in 1348-9. This treatise is far superior to all the numerous plague tracts edited in Europe between the fourteenth and the sixteenth centuries. He says:

'The result of my long experience is that if a person comes into contact with a patient, he is immediately attacked by the disease with the same symptoms. If the first patient expectorated blood, the second will do so. . . . If the first developed buboes, they will appear on the other in the same places. If the first had an ulcer, the second will get the same; and the second patient likewise transmits the disease.'

To appreciate the teaching of these writers it must be remembered that the doctrine of the contagious character of disease is not emphasized by the Greek physicians and is almost passed over by most medieval medical writers.

In the sciences other than medicine the output of books during the period of decline was very great, but the deterioration no less marked. Thus there are known books of some forty Arabic and Persian alchemists after the eleventh century. Yet their works add very little to the subject. It is noteworthy that Ibn Khaldūn (*d.* 1406) the talented Arabian philosopher of history, the greatest intellect of his century, was a violent opponent of alchemy.

Mineralogy stood in close relation to alchemy. Nearly fifty Arabic lapidaries have been named. The best known of them is the *Flowers of Knowledge of Stones*, by Shihāb al-Dīn al-Tīfāshī (*d.* in Cairo A. D. 1154). It gives in twenty-five chapters extensive information on the subject of the same number of precious stones, their origin, geography, examination, purity, price, application for medicinal and magical purposes, and so on. Except for Pliny and the spurious Aristotelian lapidary he quotes only Arabic authors.

The only important Muslim work on *Zoology* is the *Life of Animals* by Muḥammad ad-Damīrī (*d.* 1405 in Cairo). The author was a religious teacher, and therefore his book is not the result of personal experience but a compilation from all the available literary sources. Although a purely scholastic book it achieved a great reputation in the Orient. In some parts it contains useful information on folklore, popular medicine and racial psychology, but always overgrown with a bewildering mass of incoherent narratives.

The many cosmographical encyclopaedias of the Arabs and Persians all contain sections on animals, plants, and stones. The best known is that of Zakariyyā al-Qazwīnī (*d.* 1283) still imperfectly edited. Many manuscripts of this work are beautifully illustrated.

There exists a considerable number of books and sections of encyclopaedias dealing with the subject of physics, most of them from a philosophical point of view.

Metrological studies were much in favour with the Muslims of the later centuries, particularly those on balances. Al-Khāzinī, originally a Greek slave who lived about 1200 in Merv (Persia), left a voluminous book *The Balance of Wisdom*, of which parts only have been edited. He takes up and continues Thābit b. Qurra's investigations of the so-called 'Roman' balance, or steelyard, which is itself of Greek origin. His work comprises, moreover, valuable remarks on specific gravity and the specific weight of alloys. Khāzinī also dealt with the problem of the greater density of water when nearer to the centre of the earth, shortly before Roger Bacon propounded and proved the same hypothesis.

Very fine manuscripts, full of good illustrations, exist on hydrostatic automatons and on clocks, particularly such as were moved by water, mercury, weights, or burning candles. Al-Jazarī finished, in 1206, in Mesopotamia, a great book on mechanics and clocks, the best extant in the Islamic world. At the same time (in 1203) the Persian Riḍwān described the water-clock constructed by his father Muḥammad ibn 'Alī near one of the gates of Damascus, an artifice much admired throughout the Islamic world, the memory of which survived until the sixteenth century. The authors refer to Archimedes, Apollonius, and

Ktesibius, but are remarkable in their exact description of all the mechanical details.

Prominent in optics was the Persian Kamāl ad-Dīn (*d.* about 1320). He repeated and improved on Alhazen's experiments with the *camera obscura* (p. 335). He also observed the path of the rays in the interior of a glass sphere in order to examine the refraction of sunlight in raindrops. This led him to an explanation of the genesis of the primary and secondary rainbows.

A curious example of the lively interest shown by laymen in scientific questions is seen in the optical book of Shihāb al-Dīn al-Qarāfī, a theologian and judge in Cairo (*d. c.* 1285). He discusses—in a more speculative than scientific manner—fifty optical problems, three of which are of special interest because they concern questions put to Muslim scholars by 'the Emperor the king of the Franks in Sicily'. This was no other than Frederick II of Hohenstaufen who between 1220 and 1230 set philosophical and geometrical problems for Muslim scholars in Spain and Egypt. The three questions on optics are: 'Why do oars and lances, partly covered with water, appear to be bent? Why does Canopus appear bigger when near the horizon, whereas the absence of moisture in the southern deserts precludes moisture as an explanation? What is the cause of the illusion of floating specks before the eyes of those suffering from incipient cataract and other eye trouble?'

Finally we must cast a glance at two bio-bibliographical works of high importance for the history of Islamic medicine and science. First the *History of Philosophers* by Ibn al-Qifṭī (*d.* in Damascus 1248), containing 414 biographies of Greek, Syrian, and Islamic physicians, astronomers, and philosophers. It is a mine of information for the knowledge of Greek literature possessed by the Arabs and it tells us much about Greek antiquity which has not survived in classical sources. No less important is the *Valuable Information on the Classes of Physicians* by Ibn Abī Uṣaybiʿa, a very learned physician and oculist who lived chiefly in Cairo (*d.* 1270). He deals with the life and work of more than 600 medical men, taking his information partly from works now lost, partly from his intimate knowledge of many thousands of medical books. All the modern histories of Arabian medicine are based on this work, which also contains valuable classical traditions.

The dependence of the Copts in Egypt, and the Armenians, on Arabic medical science is evident from such of their works as are available in modern dress. Lack of space prevents the author from giving an analysis of them.

§ 5. *The Legacy*

We turn now from the storehouse of Arabic science to its passage to the West. The legacy of the Islamic world in medicine and natural science is the legacy of Greece, increased by many additions, mostly practical. Rhazes, the Persian, was a talented clinical observer, but not a Harvey. ʿAbd al-Laṭīf, the Arab, was a diligent seeker in anatomy, but in no way to be compared to Vesalius. The Muslims possessed excellent translations of the works of the Hippocratic Corpus and of Galen. All, even the long theoretical explanations of the latter, were well understood and well rendered by such intelligent and polyglot scholars as Ḥunayn. But the additions of the Islamic physicians refer almost solely to clinical and therapeutic experience. The theory and the thought of the Greeks were left untouched and treasured up after careful systematization and classification. It must be remembered that Muslims were strictly prohibited from dissecting either human bodies or living animals. Thus experiment was practically impossible in medicine, so that none of Galen's anatomical and physiological errors could be corrected. On the other hand, they received some impetus from the experience of Persian, Indian, and Central Asian scholars concerning particular lines of treatment, operations, and the knowledge of drugs and minerals. This knowledge helped them to make progress in chemistry, although we are, as a matter of fact, not yet sufficiently informed to be able to state what is the share of Greece and what that of the Orient in the development of alchemy.

In other sciences some of the best Greek works were unknown to the Muslims, as, for example, the *botany* of Theophrastus. Their own share in this branch is a considerable one, but again, of purely practical importance. The Muslim scholars, although acute observers, were thinkers only in a restricted sense. It is the same in zoology, mineralogy, and mechanics. The glory of Muslim science is in the field of optics. Here the mathematical ability of an Alhazen and a Kamāl al-Dīn outshone that of Euclid and Ptolemy. Real and lasting advances stand to their credit in this department of science.

When Islamic medicine and science came to a standstill, about 1100, they began to be transmitted to Europe in Latin translations. The state of monkish medicine at that period is vigorously described by Charles Singer in his *Short History of Medicine*: 'Anatomy and Physiology perished. Prognosis was reduced to an absurd rule of thumb. Botany became a drug-list. Superstitious practices crept in, and Medicine deteriorated into a collection of formulae, punctuated by incantations. The scientific stream, which is its life-blood, was dried up at its source.'

Only in one corner of Europe, at Salerno near Naples, a medical school preserved some traces of Greek medicine, and it was here that the Tunisian adventurer and renegade, Constantine the African, passed several years before he became a monk at the famous convent Monte Cassino in Campania. There he took up the work of translation about 1070 to continue it until his death (1087). Constantine's Latin versions are corrupt, confused, full of misunderstood Arabic terms, in parts incomprehensible, the true prototype of the Barbaro-Latin literature of the Middle Ages. But they had the merit of planting the first sparse seed of Greek learning in the sterile soil of medieval Europe.

Constantine was a shameless plagiarist claiming for himself many works which he had translated from Arabic into Latin. We may, however, remember that the rights of authorship were but lightly regarded in those times. He translated into Latin Hippocrates' *Aphorisms* from Ḥunayn's Arabic version, with Galen's commentary from Ḥubaysh's version; Hippocrates' *Prognostica* and *Diaeta Acutorum*; together with many works of Galen. The fate of one book issued as Constantine's *De Oculis* is characteristic of the times. It was later turned again into Latin by a certain Demetrius, perhaps in Sicily. In reality it is nothing but Ḥunayn's book *The Ten Treatises on the Eye*. Constantine was, however, the first to render Greek scientific works accessible. He also placed the works of Haly Abbas and Isaac Judaeus in the hands of his successors. The alchemical *Liber Experimentorum* of Rhazes was translated into Latin by Constantine, who had disciples among the monks of Monte Cassino. One of these was Johannes Afflacius 'the Saracen', who helped him in the translation of Arabic works into Latin.

During Constantine's lifetime the struggle between Christendom and Islam was active both in Spain and in Sicily. In 1085, Toledo, the greatest centre of Muslim learning in the West, fell before the Spanish Christians. Latin students began to come to the new capital to admire the remains of Moorish civilization and to study the *Artes Arabum*. The intermediaries for the learning and later on the translation work were native Jews and former Muslim subjects (*Mozarabs*). Charles and Dorothea Singer, in another volume of this series, have painted a lively picture of this collaboration, which gives a clear idea of a curious scientific syncretism. The first prominent European man of science who came to Toledo was Adelard of Bath, an English mathematician and philosopher. On the other hand a Spanish

Jew converted to Christianity, Petrus Alphonsi, went to England where he became physician to Henry I and spread the science of the Muslims there for the first time. Both scholars translated Arabic astronomical and mathematical works into Latin during the first half of the twelfth century. Many others followed their example.

The scientific life which expanded in Toledo during the twelfth century is reminiscent in many ways of the translation period of Baghdād three centuries before. Just as the Caliph al-Ma'mūn installed the 'House of Wisdom', so Archbishop Raymond founded, under the direction of the Archdeacon Dominico Gundisalvi, a school of translation which flourished in Toledo until the thirteenth century. The part of the polyglot Christian and Ṣābian translators of Baghdād was played in Toledo by the Jews who spoke Arabic, Hebrew, Spanish, and sometimes Latin. The converted Jew Avendeath (Ibn Dāwūd, i.e. son of David) translated a great many mathematical, astronomical, and astrological works of the Arabs into Latin, as the Ṣābian Thābit ibn Qurra had turned those of the Greeks into Arabic. Gerard of Cremona did for the Latins what Ḥunayn ibn Isḥāq did for the Arabs in translating the works of philosophers, mathematicians, physicists, and physicians.

Gerard, born in Cremona in Italy in 1114, came to Toledo to find Ptolemy's *Almagest*. He translated it into Latin in 1175. He soon became the most prominent and prolific of all the translators from Arabic, being helped in his task by a native Christian and a Jew. In the two decades before his death in 1187 he produced nearly eighty translations, some of them of the utmost importance. By opening wide the doors of the treasure-house of Greek and Arabic learning, at the same time he gave many followers the impulse to imitate his example. He is the real father of 'Arabism' in Europe.

In medicine we owe to Gerard versions of the works of Hippocrates, of Galen, of nearly all Ḥunayn's translations, of works of al-Kindī, of Avicenna's vast *Canon*, and of the important and influential *Surgery* of Abulcasis. In physics he rendered from the Arabic many of the works of Aristotle, including the apocryphal *Lapidary* ascribed to the great philosopher, as well as writings by al-Kindī, al-Fārābī, Isaac Judaeus, and Thābit.

Mark, Canon of Toledo, perhaps a younger contemporary of Gerard, also did good service. He translated the treatise on *Airs, Waters, and Places* of Hippocrates and many works of Galen, all from Ḥubaysh and Ḥunayn's Arabic versions. Ḥunayn's famous *Quaestiones medicae* were translated by Rufino, a scholar of Alessandria in Italy who lived at Murcia in Spain. Abraham, a Jew of Tortosa, helped Simon of Genoa (*Januensis*) to translate Abulcasis' *Liber Servitoris* and Serapion the Younger's *De Simplicibus*.

Other portions of Abulcasis' output were translated by a certain Berengar of Valencia, and by Arnald of Villanova (*d. c.* 1313). The latter is the last renowned medical translator of Spain. We owe to him the versions of works of Avicenna, al-Kindi, Avenzoar, and others.

Sicily, which had been under Muslim control for 130 years, fell definitely into the hands of the Normans in 1091, and became a fertile centre for the spread of Arabic science. Among the population Greek, Arabic, and Latin were in constant use as vernacular dialects, but some scholars, particularly Jews, also knew the literary form of these languages. The kings, from Roger I to Frederick II, Manfred, and Charles I of Anjou, drew learned men to Palermo regardless of language or religion. Here, as in Toledo, a troop of learned translators began to make Latin versions from Greek and Arabic. These translations mainly deal with astronomy and mathematics.

In medicine no important translations wer eaccomplished in Sicily during the twelfth century. In the following century, in the reign of Charles of Anjou, however (1266–85), we meet the great Jewish translator 'Farragut' of Girgenti and his translation of Rhazes' *Continens* (p. 324). He finished his task, which would have occupied half a normal lifetime, in 1279.

Another Jew, Moses of Palermo, was trained as a Latin translator at the order of King Charles. Of his works we know only the version of a pseudo-Hippocratic work on the diseases of horses. Michael Scot (*d.* 1235), favourite of Frederick II, translated into Latin from Arabic and Hebrew versions the entire biological and zoological works of Aristotle, particularly the abstract of *De Animalibus* with Avicenna's commentary which he dedicated to the emperor in 1232.

It is well known that Frederick II exhibited great interest in zoology, that he used his wealth and his friendly relations with Muslim rulers to keep a menagerie of elephants, dromedaries, lions, leopards, falcons, owls, &c., which he then took with him on his travels. The emperor himself wrote a work on hunting, *De Arte Venandi*, largely based on a work of Michael Scot, and on the same scholar's translation of Aristotle's zoology. (With regard to Frederick's interest in optical questions see p. 343.)

The influence of the Crusades on the transmission of the Islamic sciences to Europe was surprisingly little. The only important work we can trace to that movement was by a certain Stephen of Pisa, who was trained in Salerno and in Sicily. He came to Antioch and translated there in A. D. 1127 the *Liber regalis* of Haly Abbas. In it he severely criticizes the former translation of the same work made by Constantine the African.

We may suppose that the foundation of hospitals throughout Europe during the thirteenth century, hospitals which were no longer under clerical supervision alone, was partly due to the influence of the Crusades. They may well have been imitations of such splendidly installed *Bīmāristāns* as that of the contemporary Seljūq ruler Nūr al-Dīn in Damascus, and that of the Mamlūk sultan al-Manṣūr Qalāwūn in Cairo. The latter institution was much admired by European travellers of later centuries, and after a period of decay has seen a renaissance in our time. In Italy Pope Innocent III founded in Rome at the beginning of the thirteenth century the Hospital San Spirito from which a network of kindred institutions soon spread over western Europe. The asylum and hospital 'Les Quinze-Vingt' was founded in Paris by Louis IX after his return from his unhappy crusade in 1254-60. Originally intended for three hundred poor blind men, it had added to it later a hospital for eye-diseases which is now one of the most important in the French capital.

The Muslims who came in touch with Frank physicians during the Crusades expressed much scorn for their professional skill. This appears for instance from anecdotes related by the Syrian prince Usāma based on the reports of his Arabic Christian physician Thābit. This man about A. D. 1140 observed two cases which ended fatally owing to the barbarous surgery of a Frank.

Some of the Latin translators worked in northern Italy. Here, for instance, Burgundio of Pisa had made translations of ten Galenic works direct from the Greek (*c.* A. D. 1180). Accursius of Pistoia translated Galen's *De Viribus Alimentorum* from Ḥubaysh's Arabic version about 1200; the Jewish convert Bonacosa translated Averroes' *Colliget* into Latin in Padua in 1255, and Paravicius rendered Avenzoar's *Taysīr* in Venice, with the help of the Jew Jacob, in 1280.

Of other translators the period and origin are unknown, as for example, of David Hermenus who translated Canamusali's ophthalmology. Many works too are extant in Latin translations by anonymous authors, among them being treatises by Maimonides, Avicenna, Geber, Rhazes, and Alhazen. We note particularly that most of the alchemical writings are anonymously rendered.

The process of translation went on well into the sixteenth century. Thus Andrea Alpago of Belluno in Italy (*d.* 1520) must be mentioned as a prominent translator of Avicenna's *Canon*, *Aphorismi*, *De Anima*, and minor works of Averroes and Johannes Serapion, and Ibn al Qifṭī's biographical lexicon. There are many translations of even later date which were widely used in the universities, especially in those of northern Italy and France.

In this way hundreds of translations from the Graeco Arabic literature descended on the barren scientific soil of Europe. The effect was that of a fertilizing rain. In Salerno, under the influence of Constantine's versions, arose a generation of prominent medical teachers. Anatomy showed signs of revival. Better text-books of surgery were produced. Gynaecology and obstetrics, hitherto the monopoly of midwives, became the subject of scientific study. Ophthalmology passed from the hands of wandering cataract-couchers to those of learned physicians.

Universities were established in numbers from the twelfth century onwards and became the centres of the new learning. Such were Bologna, Padua, Montpellier, and Paris. As in Byzantine Alexandria and in the Baghdād of the caliphs, teaching consisted entirely of readings of ancient authors, at last accessible in Latin. Experimental science did not yet exist, and botany, zoology, physics, and alchemy followed the lines of the Graeco-Arabic tradition entirely. It was not until the end of the sixteenth century that human bodies were publicly dissected at Bologna, and at first only to obtain evidence for legal processes (Singer). They served in no way to correct the anatomical and physiological errors of Galen as transmitted by Avicenna. Tradition remained stronger than autopsy.

On the practical side, however, in surgery, hygiene, and perhaps above all in the provision of hospitals, some progress was made. Guy de Chauliac (*d.* 1368), the surgeon of Montpellier, took up the scorned operations for rupture and cataract. Lanfranchi of Milan, who established himself in France, introduced advanced methods in ligature of blood-vessels and suture of wounds. For some time in northern Italy the non-suppurative treatment of wounds with wine-compresses was practised.

Natural science had its home in the University of Paris. The Aristotelian science as introduced from Toledo with Averroes' commentaries was the foundation of learning. Roger Bacon and his scientific opponent Albert of Bollstaedt (Albertus Magnus), among others, here expounded the works of the great Muslim scientists. We have already seen how Roger Bacon's Optics was based on Alhazen's *Thesaurus Opticae*. Albert repeated the alchemical teachings of 'Jābir' (*Geber*) and other Arabic writers in his *De Mineralibus*. He is original only in his zoological and botanical studies, and even in these he relies greatly on translations from Arabic. The influence of *Geber* is very pronounced in the encyclopaedia *Speculum Naturale* by Vincent de Beauvais. The alchemical tracts ascribed to Arnald of Villanova and to Raymund Lull are full of quotations from *Geber*. Arabic alchemy, associated as it was with astrology, predominated throughout the thirteenth and fourteenth centuries.

After the sixteenth century medicine and science, particularly in northern Italy, begin to refer more and more to translations from the Greek rather than the Arabic. 'Hellenism' was opposed to 'Arabism', though there was no fundamental difference between them. As long as the books of the Ancients formed the almost exclusive basis of scientific research, Scholasticism maintained its supremacy. After the invention of the art of printing, in the second half of the fifteenth century, all the Graeco-Arabic works on medicine and science were eagerly and repeatedly printed. It was in the period 1530 to 1550 that Arabism received its death-blow. Simultaneously with the revolution of astronomy by Copernicus (*d.* 1543), Paracelsus (*d.* 1541) reformed alchemy and medicine, and incessantly urged his students to abandon Galen and Avicenna and to return to the observation of nature: *Experimenta et ratio auctorum loco mihi suffragantur!* In the same year, 1543, in which Copernicus published his *De Revolutionibus Orbium caelestium*, Andreas Vesalius edited his fundamental new anatomy. This year marks the end of the Middle Ages in medicine and science, and with it the effective end of the direct influence of Arabian science.

Still Arabism lingered on. In Vienna in 1520, and in Frankfurt on the Oder in 1588, the medical curriculum was still largely based on Avicenna's *Canon* and on the ninth book *Ad Almansorem* of Rhazes. Even in the seventeenth century in France and Germany some scholars kept to Arabic erudition, whilst the struggle between Hellenists and Arabists went on in northern Italy until both were crushed by the advent of the modern scientific method. Arabic pharmacology survived until the beginning of the nineteenth century. Parts of the Latin version of Ibn al-Bayṭār's *Simplicia* were printed as late as 1758 at Cremona; Serapion and Mesuë the younger were studied and summarized for the use of European pharmacopoeias until about 1830. The Armenian compilation of medicine from Greek, Arabic, and Persian sources composed by Mechithar in A.D. 1184 was reprinted in Venice in 1832. In an old German treatise on zoology of 1838 I have found all the legends relating to the poisonous nature of the gecko—a harmless oriental house-lizard—which are to be read in ad-Damīrī's *Life of Animals*.

In certain branches of medicine the Graeco-Arabic tradition survived long, even in practice. Vesalius himself left several errors of Galen and Avicenna concerning the anatomy of the eye unchanged, and they were not corrected before *c.* A.D. 1600. The real nature of cataract as a solid opacation of the lens, not as a congealed liquid, was discovered by Pierre Brisseau, a French practitioner, in 1604. And the old couching operation for cataract, with a needle, as described by Antyllos of Alexandria and as handed down by Rhazes and 'Alī ibn 'Īsā, was still practised by Percivall Pott in England about 1780, and in Germany even as late as 1820.

In the Islamic Orient the old scientific and medical tradition is still fully alive in popular medicine and among village barbers. The author saw in Cairo, on the very day on which he wrote these lines, a man operated on for cataract by a wandering Sudanese charlatan in accordance with the directions of Antyllos and Avicenna. The native druggists from Morocco to India habitually compose their remedies in accordance with the *Aqrābādhīns* (p. 338) of the Arabic physicians.

Looking back we may say that Islamic medicine and science reflected the light of the Hellenic sun, when its day had fled, and that they shone like a moon, illuminating the darkest night of the European Middle Ages; that some bright stars lent their own light, and that moon and stars alike faded at the dawn of a new day—the Renaissance. Since they had their share in the direction and introduction of that great movement, it may reasonably be claimed that they are with us yet.

MAX MEYERHOF.

SOME BOOKS OF REFERENCE

This article should be read in conjunction with that by C. and D. Singer on 'The Jewish Factor in Medieval Thought' in *The Legacy of Israel*.

1. ARABIC MEDICINE AND SCIENCE.

F. Wüstenfeld, *Geschichte der arabischen Aerzte und Naturforscher*, Göttingen, 1840, is still an indispensable standard work on the subject, as are L. Leclerc, *Histoire de la médecine arabe*, 2 vols., Paris, 1876, and C. Brockelmann, *Geschichte der arabischen Literatur*, 2 vols., Weimar, 1898–1902. Works covering a wide area in a more readable fashion are Baron Carra de Vaux, *Les penseurs de l'Islam*, 5 vols., Paris, 1921–6; Joseph Hell, *The Arab Civilization*, Cambridge, 1926; M. Meyerhof, *Le monde islamique*, Paris, 1926; De Lacy O'Leary, *Arabic Thought and its Place in History*, London, 1926. In special departments the following are of value: E. G. Browne, *Arabian Medicine*, Cambridge, 1921; E. J. Holmyard, *Book of Knowledge concerning cultivation of gold by Abulqāsim Muḥammad ibn Aḥmad*, Paris, 1923; and *Avicennae De congelatione et conglutinatione lapidum*, Paris, 1927; O. von Lippmann, *Entstehung und Ausbreitung der Alchemie*, Berlin, 1919; H. Suter, *Die Mathematiker und Astronomen der Araber*,

Leipzig, 1900; J. Berendes, *Die Pharmacie bei den alten Culturvölkern*, 2 vols., Halle, 1891; J. Stephenson, *Zoological Section of the Nuzhatu-l-Qulūb of ... al Qazwīnī*, London, 1928; H. Duhem, *Le Système du Monde*, 5 vols., Paris, 1913–17; J. Hirschberg, *Geschichte der Augenheilkunde bei den Arabern*, Leipzig, 1905; Abū Manṣur Muwaffak, *Liber fundamentorum pharmacologiae*, ed. R. Seligmann, Vindobonae, 1830–3; G. Bergsträsser, *Ḥunain ibn Isḥāq über die syrischen und arabischen Galenübersetzungen*, Leipzig, 1925. O. C. Gruner, *A Treatise on the Canon of Medicine of Avicenna*, London, 1930.

2. TRANSMISSION TO THE WEST.

The indispensable reference book is M. Steinschneider, *Die Europäischen Uebersetzungen aus dem Arabischen bis Mitte des 17 Jahrhunderts*, 2 parts, Vienna, 1904–5. There is also much valuable information in E. Wiedemann, *Beiträge zur Geschichte der Naturwissenschaften*, 69 fasc., Erlangen, 1904–29; G. Sarton, *Introduction to the History of Science*, Baltimore, 1927; and Lynn Thorndike, *History of Magic and Experimental Science*, 2 vols., 2nd edition, Cambridge, Mass., 1927. Works covering a wide area in a more readable fashion are Charles Singer, *From Magic to Science*, London, 1928; and *Studies in the History and Method of Science*, vol. ii, Oxford, 1921; C. H. Haskins, *Studies in the History of Medieval Science*, 2nd edition, Cambridge, Mass., 1927. In special departments the following are of value: Charles Singer, *Short History of Medicine*, Oxford; Max Neuburger, *History of Medicine*, 2 vols, Translation, Oxford, 1910–25; D. Campbell, *Arabian Medicine*, 2 vols, London, 1926; F. H. Garrison, *An Introduction to the History of Medicine*, 4th edition, Philadelphia, 1929; E. J. Holmyard, *Chemistry to the Time of Dalton*, Oxford, 1925; E. Darmstaedter, *Die Alchemie des Geber*, Berlin, 1922; Dorothea Waley Singer, *Catalogue of Latin and Vernacular Alchemical Manuscripts in Great Britain and Ireland*, 3 vols., Brussels, 1928–9; H. Schelenz, *Geschichte der Pharmazie*, Berlin, 1904; Julius Ruska, *Arabische Alchemisten*, 2 vols., Heidelberg, 1924; J. Ruska, *Tabula Smaragdina*, Heidelberg, 1926; G. Sobhy, *The Book of al-Dhakhīra*, Cairo, 1928; Hirschberg, *Die arabischen Augenärzte*, 2 vols., Berlin, 1904–5; Max Meyerhof, *The Ten Treatises on the Eye, by Ḥunain b. Isḥāq*, Cairo, 1928; E. Wiedemann, Al-Kīmiyā, in *Encyclopaedia of Islam*, vol. ii, 1927 (Leyden and London); L. Leclerc, *Traité des simples par Ibn al Beïthar*, 3 vols., Paris, 1877; Jayakar, *Al-Damīrī's Ḥayāt al-Ḥayawān, a zoological Lexicon*, 2 vols., London and Bombay, 1906–8; M. Berthelot, *La chimie au Moyen-Âge*, vol. iv, Paris, 1895; J. Ruska and P. Kraus, *Der Zusammenbruch der Ǣschābir-Legende*, Berlin, 1930.

The author is very much indebted to Dr. Charles Singer for his revision of this section, for his corrections, and for some suggestions.

MUSIC

WHEN we consider the wide gulf which separates the Eastern and Western arts of music, it is difficult to realize that there could be any Arabian or Islamic legacy to music in Europe at all. We Europeans conceive music vertically whilst the Arabs apprehend it horizontally. That is, broadly, the cognizable difference between the harmonic and melodic principles which underlie the art of music in the West and East respectively. Further, the Arabian notions of a tonic, of rhythm, and of ornamenting the melody, are quite alien to ours. Before the tenth century, however, the separation between the two arts was not so great. Indeed, there was actually very little difference between them, since they could both be reduced to a common denominator. At one period they both had the same Pythagorean scale, and both had inherited certain Greek and Syrian elements. Above all, harmony, such as we understand the term to-day, was unknown. The outstanding difference between them was that the Arabs possessed a system of mensural music as well as a definite conception of the 'gloss' or ornament to the melody, both of which were eventually to influence the West.

The source of Arabian music was the Semitic theory and practice of an earlier date, both of which had influenced, if they had not been the actual foundations of, Greek theory and practice. At a period just prior to Islam, the Arab kingdoms of al-Ḥīra and Ghassān were doubtless influenced by Persian and Byzantine customs respectively, and both probably possessed the Pythagorean scale, which had originally come from the Semites.

In the early days of Islam we find that al-Ḥijāz, then the political centre, had adopted mensural music which was called *īqāʿ* or 'rhythm'. About the same time the Arabs adopted a new theory of music at the hands of a musician named Ibn Misjaḥ (*d. c.* 705–14). This theory contained both Persian and Byzantine elements, but, as the late Dr. J. P. N. Land remarked, 'The Persian and Byzantine importations did not supersede the national music, but were engrafted upon an Arabic root with a character of its own'. This system, the scale of which appears to have been Pythagorean, obtained until the fall of Baghdād (1258).

Meanwhile, several changes took place, and in the scale these were so disturbing that Isḥāq al-Mauṣilī (*d.* 850) found it necessary to recast the theory in its former Pythagorean mould. This held good until the time of al-Iṣfahānī (*d.* 967), when the above ideas again asserted themselves. These latter were the Zalzalian and Khurāsānian scales. What helped to keep the older system as the basis was the acquisition of ancient Greek theory by means of translations of Aristotle, Aristoxenus, Euclid (or pseudo-Euclid), Nicomachus, Ptolemy, and others. Yet, in spite of borrowings, we know from al-Kindī (*d. c.* 874), al-Iṣfahānī, and the Ikhwān al-Ṣafā' (10th century), that the Arabian, Persian, and Byzantine systems of music were different. By the eleventh century Persian and Khurāsānian ideas had been adopted, noticeably in the modes. Later, a theorist named Ṣafī al-Dīn 'Abd al-Mu'min (*d.* 1294) introduced or systematized a new theory (the Systematist Theory), while before the close of the Middle Ages another scale found acceptance, the Quarter-Tone System, which obtains to-day among the Arabs of the East. That Arabian music was influenced by Persian and Byzantine practice is openly admitted by the Arabs. In turn, the Persians and Byzantines also borrowed from the Arabian art.

The Practice of Music

What music meant to the Arabs is illuminatingly revealed in the *Thousand and One Nights*. The best insight, however, into the Arab's intense appreciation of the art is to be gained from such works as Ibn 'Abd Rabbihi's *Unique Necklace*, al-Iṣfahānī's

Great Book of Songs, both written in the tenth century, and al-Nuwairī's *The Extreme Need*, composed in the thirteenth century, all of which, unfortunately, are still only available in Arabic. Here we see that music accompanied the Arab from the cradle to the grave, from the lullaby to the elegy. Every moment of his life seems to have had its particular music—joy and sorrow, work and play, battle-throng and religious exercise. Almost every Arab of substance in those days had his singing-girl, who appears to have been as much in evidence in the household as the pianoforte is with us to-day.

It is not, however, the music of 'the people' that we are primarily concerned with here. As Ibn Khaldūn (*d.* 1406) says, no art really begins until there are artists. We see a professional class of musician in pre-Islamic days, and with the rise of the caliphate, in spite of the ban of Islam which did not regard 'listening to music' with favour, this class was held in the highest esteem. Indeed, the cultivation of music by the Arabs in all its branches reduces to insignificance the recognition of the art in the history of any other country.

Vocal music has always been more keenly appreciated by the Arabs than purely instrumental music. Their ardent taste for poetry determined this to some extent, although the pressure of legal opinion which frowned on instrumental music (*per se*), also contributed to the preference. Among the verse forms of vocal music there were, besides the ode or *qaṣīda*, many shorter forms such as the *qiṭ'a* or fragment, the *ghazal* or love song, and the more popular *mawāl*. In the West, later forms, such as the *zajal* and *muwashshaḥ*, were introduced. The melody, which was set to certain modes or scales, might be in mensural form, i.e. set to rhythm (*īqā'*), or it might not. Every performer sang or played in unison or octave. Harmony was unknown in the form in which we understand the term. In its place the Arabs had the 'gloss' or ornamentation of the melody, which sometimes included the striking of a note of the melody simultaneously with its fourth, fifth, or octave, a procedure known as the *tarkīb* or compound. The instrumental accompaniment, which followed the melodic scheme, was invariably furnished by the lute (*al-'ūd*, from which our word is derived), pandore (*ṭanbūr*), psaltery (*qānūn*), or flute (*qaṣaba*, *nāy*), whilst the drum (*ṭabl*), tambourine (*duff*), or wand (*qaḍīb*) strengthened the rhythm. There were also instrumental pieces, but far oftener they were used as preludes or interludes to vocal items. Perhaps the most important musical form was the *nauba*, a sort of vocal and instrumental suite of several movements, which was especially developed in the West. So far, the music dealt with is what might be termed chamber-music, for although we sometimes read of very large orchestras, the general rule was for quite small numbers.

Open-air music, appropriate to a procession or military display, was usually confined to such instruments as the reed-pipe (*zamr*, *surnāy*), horn or clarion (*būq*), trumpet (*nafīr*), drum (*ṭabl*), kettledrum (*naqqāra*, *qaṣ'a*), and cymbal (*kāsa*). The military band played an important part in Muslim martial display, and it was recognized as a special part of military tactics. Senior officers had bands allotted to them, the size of which depended on their rank, as did also the number of movements or fanfares in the military *nauba*.

In spite of the legal condemnation of music and musical instruments, especially the latter, the spiritual effects of music were clearly recognized. The *ṣūfī* looked upon it as a means of revelation attained through ecstasy, whilst the dervish and marabout fraternities regulated their rituals by it. Al-Ghazālī quotes: 'Ecstasy means the state that comes from listening to music'. Elsewhere in his treatise on *Music and Ecstasy* he gives seven reasons for holding that singing is more potent in producing ecstasy than the Quran itself. As we read in the *Thousand and One Nights*: 'To some people music is meat, and to others medicine'. This conceit grew out of the doctrine of the 'influence of music', which, with the belief in the principles of the *ethos*, the harmony of the spheres, and the theory of numbers, attracted unusual attention. This doctrine of musical therapeutics had a fairly wide acceptance.

Among the people at large on festive occasions all sorts of musical instruments were to be found, while with the women the tambourine was a special favourite. The itinerant minstrel also had his place. He was generally equipped with a tabor (*ṭabl*) and pipe (*shāhīn*), one hand beating the former and the other fingering the latter, whilst he shook his head which was crowned by a cap furnished with small bells.

That the Arabs contributed to the practical art in the East there is ample evidence in the technical nomenclature from Samarqand to the Atlantic.

Musical Instruments

The names of musical instruments in Arabic are legion, and it would be impossible here to deal with even a tithe of them. The Arabs carried the manufacture of musical instruments to a fine art. Treatises were written on their manufacture, and some towns, like Seville, were famous for their production. In the lute family alone there were all sorts of species and sizes. Besides their pre-Islamic lute (*mizhar*) with a skin belly, they had their classical lute (*'ūd qadīm*), which approximated to the modern mandoline, as well as a larger instrument called the perfect lute (*'ūd kāmil*). Their *shāhrūd* was an archlute, and we have pictorial designs of some enormous instruments. In the pandore group they possessed instruments as large as the *ṭanbūr turkī* and as small as the *ṭanbūr bighilma*. Then there was the guitar, known as the *murabba'*. It was a flat-chested rectangular instrument. Later it came to be known as the *qītāra*. More important to us were their bowed instruments, known at first under the generic term *rabāb*. These, too, were found in all shapes and sizes, and among them those known as the *kamānja*

'Ūd

Zamr

Fig. 89. HISPANO-MOORISH MUSICIANS OF THE Xth–XIth CENTURY
From an ivory box in the Victoria and Albert Museum, London

Chang (Jank) Rabāb

Fig. 90. PERSIAN MUSICIANS OF THE XIIth CENTURY
From a silver casket in the Procuratorio di S. Marco, Venice

and *ghishak*. Among the instruments with open strings were the harp (*jank*, *ṣanj*), psaltery (*qānūn*, *nuzha*), and dulcimer (*sinṭīr*).

The wood-wind family included flutes in many sizes, from the *nāy bamm* and others, which were about three feet in length, to the smaller *shabbāba* and *juwāq*, about a foot long and even less. The *ṣaffāra* was a *flûte à bec*. Among the reed-blown types were the *zamr*, *surnāy*, *zulāmī*, and *ghaiṭa*, as well as the reed-blown *būq* which was made of metal.

The term *duff* stood for any tambourine, but specifically it was the square instrument. The round instrument had a dozen different names according to its size or construction, such as *ṭār*, *dā'ira*, &c. The drums, also, were to be found in many varieties under such names as *ṭabl*, *naqqāra*, *qaṣ'a*, &c. The cymbal was the *kāsa*, a name also given to the bowl-shaped castanet, the flat form of which was called *ṣinj*.

Both the pneumatic organ (*urghanūn*) and the *hydraulis* were known to the Arabs, and probably also the *organistrum* (*dūlāb*), well known in medieval European art and resembling the modern hurdy-gurdy, and the *eschaquiel* (*al-shaqira*).

That the Arabs were both inventors and improvers of musical instruments we have various statements to prove. Al-Fārābī (*d.* 950) is said to have 'invented' (? improved) the *rabāb* and *qānūn*; al-Zunām (early 9th century) designed a wood-wind instrument called the *nāy zunāmī* or *zulāmī*; Zalzal (*d.* 791) introduced the *'ūd al-shabbūṭ*; al-Ḥakam II (*d.* 976) improved the reed-blown *būq*; Ziryāb (early 9th century) added to the range of the lute; both al-Bayyāsī and Abū'l-Majd (11th century) were organ constructors, whilst Ṣafī al-Dīn 'Abd al-Mu'min (*d.* 1294) invented a square psaltery called the *nuzha*, as well as an instrument known as the *mughnī*.

Although some sort of musical notation existed from the early years of the ninth century, most of the performers learned their music by ear. Some of the composers believed that their works were inspired by the genii. The dress and general appearance of the Arab minstrel is worthy of notice. Long hair, painted face and hands, and bright colours, appear to have been affected by this class, a relic perhaps, of the effeminate *mukhannathūn* of early Islamic days. Many of the singers were *evirati*, some as a punishment, others probably because of the popularity of the boy's voice. The singer was patronized at the caliph's court not only on account of his art, but also because of his political use. The musician's vocation took him into many households, where the wine-cup often revealed a secret of political import. Further, there was many an opinion that could be more effectively propagated by means of a song than otherwise, as the *jongleurs* of the heretical troubadours of Provence, who imitated the Arabs, found eventually to their cost.

Writers on Music

An enormous amount of Arabic literature was written about music—histories, collections of songs, books on musical instruments, the legal aspect of music, aesthetics, and the lives of musicians. The greatest of all these writers were al-Mas'ūdī (*d. c.* 957) and al-Iṣfahānī (*d.* 967). In the former's *Meadows of Gold* we get interesting data on the early practice of Arabian music, whilst in his other books the author dealt with the music of foreign lands. More valuable still is the monumental work of al-Iṣfahānī—the *Great Book of Songs* in twenty-one volumes, which Ibn Khaldūn has called 'the *dīwān* of the Arabs'. This author also wrote four other books on music. A mine of information regarding writers on the theory and science of music, as well as on the general literature of music, is *The Index* of Muḥammad ibn Isḥāq al-Warrāq (*d. c.* 995–6).

In the West we have much the same. *The Unique Necklace* of Ibn 'Abd Rabbihi (*d.* 940) contains the lives of the celebrated musicians, as well as a spirited defence of music against the puritans. Yaḥyā al-Khudujj al-Mursī (12th century) wrote a *Book of Songs* in imitation of al-Iṣfahānī in the East. Ibn al-

'Arabī (*d.* 1151) and others contributed works on the 'permissibility' of music, at the same time furnishing much information about musical instruments.

After the fall of Baghdād (1258) the 'fine writers' on music almost ceased to exist. Their place was taken by a host of legists who argued for or against the 'permissibility' of music. The few who did write on music in the older manner included it as part of a larger work, as we see in the *Prolegomena* of Ibn Khaldūn (*d.* 1406), and the *Mustaṭraf* of al-Ibshīhī (*d.* 1446).

Theorists

The first writer on the theory of music of whom we have definite information is Yūnus al-Kātib (*d. c.* 765). He was followed by al-Khalīl (*d.* 791), the systematizer of Arabian prosody and the first Arabic lexicographer. His *Book of Notes* and *Book of Rhythms* are catalogued in *The Index* (late 10th century). Probably it was al-Khalīl's theories that Ibn Firnās (*d.* 888) introduced into Spain. The latter was 'the first who taught the science of music in al-Andalus'. Isḥāq al-Mauṣilī (*d.* 850) recast the 'Old Arabian System', and his theories were put forward in a *Book of Notes and Rhythms*.

Between the eighth and tenth centuries many of the treatises of the Greeks on the theory of music and the science of sound were translated into Arabic. A work attributed to Pythagoras was known in Arabic, as well as Plato's *Timaeus*, the latter having been translated by Yūḥannā ibn al-Baṭrīq (*d.* 815), and again by Ḥunain ibn Isḥāq (*d.* 873). Among Aristotelian writings the Arabs possessed the *Problemata* and *De anima*, both translated by Ḥunain ibn Isḥāq. Among the commentaries on *De anima* by Greek writers known in Arabic were those of Themistius and Simplicius, the former having been rendered by the same Ḥunain who was also responsible for Galen's *De voce*. It was from these works that the Arabs derived their more scientific ideas on the theory of sound.

Aristoxenus was known in two works in Arabic—*The Principles [of Harmony]* and a book *On Rhythm*, the former title bearing out the opinion that the *Elements of Harmony* that we now possess in Greek was originally made up of two works—the *Principles* (ἀρχαί) and the *Elements* (στοιχεῖα). In Arabic Euclid had two books on music attached to his name—*The Introduction to Harmony* and *The Section of the Canon*. Nicomachus was read in a *Grand Book on Music* and in several compendia, which seems to show that Nicomachus did write that 'larger work' which he refers to in his *Manual of Harmony*, the latter being made up of his compendia, as we know it in Greek. His *Introduction to Arithmetic*, which incidentally deals with music, was translated by Thābit ibn Qurra (*d.* 901). Ptolemy was known by a *Book on Music*, which was probably his *Treatise on Harmony* that we know to-day. Other works from the Greek that have come down to us in Arabic are the treatises on hydraulic organs attributed to Archimedes and Apollonius Pergaeus, and those by a certain writer known in Arabic as Mūrṭus or Mūrisṭus, who wrote on the pneumatic organ, the *hydraulis*, and the chimes.

The earliest extant works on the theory of music in Arabic showing the influence of the Greek writers are those of al-Kindī (*d. c.* 874). Seven treatises on the theory of music were composed by him, and three, if not four, have been preserved, viz.: *The Essentials of Knowledge in Music*; *On the Melodies*; *The Necessary Book in the Composition of Melodies*, and another. Al-Sarakhsī (*d.* 899) and Manṣūr ibn Ṭalḥa ibn Ṭāhir were his disciples. Contemporary theorists were Thābit ibn Qurra (*d.* 901), Muḥammad ibn Zakariyyā al-Rāzī (*d.* 923), and Qusṭā ibn Lūqā (*d.* 932). These were followed by the greatest of all the Arabic theorists—al-Fārābī. Among his books on music were the *Grand Book on Music*, *Styles in Music*, and *On the Classification of Rhythm*. Besides these, he dealt with music in two of his celebrated compendia of the sciences—*The*

Classification of the Sciences and *The Origin of the Sciences.* Al-Fārābī tells us that he wrote his *Grand Book on Music* because he found *lacunae* as well as obscurities in what the Greeks had written on music, at least as he found them in Arabic translation. After him came al-Būzjānī (*d.* 998), the greatest of Arabic writers on mathematics, who composed a *Compendium on the Science of Rhythm.* At the same time there lived the encyclopaedists known as the Ikhwān al-Ṣafā' (10th century) whose treatise on music was widely read, and Muḥammad ibn Aḥmad al-Khwārizmī (10th century), the author of the *Keys of the Sciences,* one of which unlocked the theory of music.

Of particular fame was Ibn Sīnā or Avicenna (*d.* 1037) who, after al-Fārābī, contributed the most important works on the theory of music in Arabic. These are to be found in the *Shifā'* and the *Najāt.* He also wrote an *Introduction to the Art of Music,* whilst a few definitions are to be found in his *Divisions of the Sciences.* Ibn Zaila (*d.* 1048), his disciple, wrote a *Book of Sufficiency in Music,* whilst a contemporary, Ibn al-Haitham (*d.* 1039), a brilliant mathematician and physicist, compiled two studies of the works attributed to Euclid—a *Commentary on the Introduction to Harmony,* and a *Commentary to the Section of the Canon.* He wrote in Egypt where another gifted author, Abū'l-Ṣalt Umayya (*d.* 1134), composed a *Treatise on Music.* Other theorists who crowd into the twelfth century are Ibn al-Naqqāsh (*d.* 1178), al-Bāhilī and his son Abū'l-Majd (*d.* 1180), and Ibn Man'a (*b.* 1156). The thirteenth century brought theorists of even greater renown. 'Alam al-Dīn Qaiṣar (*d.* 1251) was looked upon as the most eminent mathematician in Egypt and Syria, and was especially famed in the theory of music. Further east similar celebrity was accorded Naṣīr al-Dīn (*d.* 1274), whose fragment on music has been preserved.

In Muslim Spain, after Ibn Firnās (*d.* 888), we read of Maslama al-Majrīṭī (*d.* 1007) and al-Kirmānī (*d.* 1066), who popularized the treatises of the Ikhwān al-Ṣafā', whilst other theorists were Abū'l-Faḍl Ḥasdāy (11th century), a Jew, and Muḥammad ibn al-Ḥaddād (*d.* 1165). Greater merit as a writer on the theory of music was reserved for Ibn Bājja or Avempace (*d.* 1138). His treatise on music enjoyed the same reputation in the West as that of al-Fārābī in the East. Ibn Rus̲h̲d or Averroes (*d.* 1198) wrote the famous *Commentary on Aristotle's De anima*, dealing perspicuously with the theory of sound. In the thirteenth century there followed the famous Ibn Sab'īn (*d.* 1269) and his contemporary al-Raqūṭī, who after the fall of Murcia to the Christians was engaged by them to teach the *quadrivium*.

In the thirteenth century the new Systematist School was founded by Ṣafī al-Dīn 'Abd al-Mu'min (*d.* 1294). His theories were expounded in the famous *S̲h̲arafiyya* and in a *Book of Musical Modes*. Ḥājjī K̲h̲alīfa says that he was amongst those 'taking the front rank' in the writers on the theory of music. Most of the names that follow here belong to his school. S̲h̲ams al-Dīn Muḥammad ibn al-Marḥūm (*c.* 1329) wrote a treatise in verse entitled *The Jewels of Arrangement in the Knowledge of the Melodies*, and Muḥammad ibn 'Īsā ibn Karā (*d.* 1358) composed *The End of the Enquiry into the Knowledge of the Melodies and the Rhythms*.

More imposing was a treatise known as the *Maulānā Mubārak-s̲h̲āh Commentary on the Musical Modes*, dedicated to S̲h̲āh S̲h̲ujā' (1359–84), which was one of the numerous commentaries written on the theories of Ṣafī al-Dīn 'Abd al-Mu'min. Another treatise dedicated to the same patron is the encyclopaedia known as the *Discourses on the Sciences*. It contains a section on music. The work was probably written by al-Jurjānī (*d.* 1377).

'Amr ibn K̲h̲iḍr al-Kurdī (*c.* 1397) was the author of *The Treasure of the Enquiry into the Modes and the Rhythms*. Ibn al-Fanārī (*d.* 1430) deals with music in his encyclopaedia of the sciences. S̲h̲ams al-Dīn al-'Ajamī (15th century) wrote a useful *Epistle on the Science of the Melodies*. Al-Lād̲h̲iqī (*d.* 1445) composed an estimable work known as *The Fatḥiyya*. Ḥājjī Khalīfa appears to rank this writer with Ṣafī al-Dīn ʿAbd al-Muʾmin and ʿAbd al-Qādir ibn Ghaibī. Lastly, and probably the most important treatise since the works of the founder of the Systematist School, is the anonymous *Muḥammad ibn Murād Treatise*[1] (*c.* 1421–51), now in the British Museum.

Value of the Arabian Theorists

Most of the Arabic theorists, being skilled in the *quadrivium*, were good mathematicians and physicists. The speculative theory of music and the physical bases of sound, which the Greek treatises had opened up to them, led many of these theorists to make experiments on their own account. That is one of the most interesting phases of their work. More than once we find them saying that they had put such and such a theory to practical test and experiment and found it wanting or otherwise. The criticisms of Ṣafī al-Dīn on the definitions of al-Fārābī and Ibn Sīnā reveal the temper of these inquirers, who will not meekly bow the knee to the statements of their predecessors, however great their names, if they are not correct.

We have seen that both al-Fārābī and Ibn Sīnā are claimed to have added to what the Greeks taught. Just as the Arabic astronomers corrected Ptolemy and others, so the Arabic musical-theorists improved on their Greek teachers. The Introduction to al-Fārābī's *Grand Book on Music* is certainly equal, if not superior, to anything that has come down to us from Greek sources. In the theory of the physical bases of sound the Arabs certainly made some advance, especially in the question of the spherical propagation of sound. Indeed, it is highly probable that when the works of the Arabic theorists have been edited with an adequate *apparatus criticus*,

[1] I have given it this name because it is dedicated to the Sultan Muḥammad ibn Murād.

many a debatable word or passage in the Greek writers will be illuminated.

The careful descriptions of musical instruments made by the Arabic theorists, which included measurements, enable us to know the precise scales used. We have instruments of the lute, pandore, harp, and wood-wind families described by al-Kindī (*d. c.* 874), al-Fārābī (*d. c.* 950), al-Khwārizmī (10th century), and the Ikhwān al-Ṣafā' (10th century), that is centuries before we have any such attempt made in Europe. That they were not content with Greek tuning is evident from their experiments with the neutral third of Zalzal ($\frac{27}{22}$) and the Persian third ($\frac{81}{68}$).

The Systematist School, fathered by Ṣafī al-Dīn (*d.* 1294), produced what Sir Hubert Parry considers to be 'the most perfect scale ever devised', whilst Helmholtz says that 'their use of the Major 7th of the scale as a leading note to the tonic marks a new conception, which admitted of being used for the further development of the tonal degrees of the scale, even within the domain of purely homophonic music'.

The Legacy of Arabian Music

The legacy left to the world of music by the Arabs was a substantial gift. Look where we will in the East, we find the influence of the Arabian practical art. That Persian, Turkish, and other theorists also benefited there is ample written evidence. In Persia the *Gladness of the Soul* of 'Abd al-Mu'min (12th century), the *Assembling of the Sciences* of Fakhr al-Dīn al-Rāzī (*d.* 1209), the *Precious Sciences* of al-Āmulī (14th century), and the *Assembling of the Melodies* and other works of 'Abd al-Qādir ibn Ghaibī (*d.* 1435) reveal the Arabian legacy. In Turkey, we find that the treatises of al-Fārābī, Ṣafī al-Dīn, and 'Abd al-Qādir were translated into Turkish. The son of the latter, 'Abd al-'Azīz, and a grandson, both of whom were in the service of the 'Uthmānlī sultans, wrote treatises which show their dependence on their Arabic masters, as do the works of Khiḍr ibn 'Abdallāh and Aḥmad Ug͟hlu S͟hukrullāh (15th century). Even in India we find that the Arabic treatises were drawn upon.

As for western Europe, the benefits which accrued from contact with Arabian culture were greater still. Europe received its legacy from the Arabs in two ways—(1) by means of the *political contact*, which brought the legacy of the practical art by hand and by word of mouth, and (2) by means of the *literary and intellectual contact*, which brought the bequest of the theoretical art through translations from the Arabic and *viva voce* through scholars who had studied at the Muslim schools in Spain and elsewhere.

In spite of the very considerable Arabic literature on the theory of music which existed in the Middle Ages, very little has come down to us in Latin or Hebrew translations. Of the Greeks, Aristotle's *De anima*, translated by Johannes Hispalensis (*d.* 1157), and Galen's *De voce*, of which we have a thirteenth-century MS., are known to have been rendered from the Arabic into Latin. Of the Arabs, the two encyclopaedias by al-Fārābī (*d.* 950) were translated into Latin by Johannes Hispalensis and Gerard of Cremona (*d.* 1187) as *De scientiis* and *De ortu scientiarum*. Avicenna (*d.* 1037) was also known in Latin by his *Compendium of Aristotle's De anima* which was done by Johannes Hispalensis. It was translated again by Andreas Alpagus (*d.* 1520), who also turned his encyclopaedia into Latin as *De divisione scientiarum*. Of special value was the *Great Commentary on Aristotle's De anima* by Averroes (*d.* 1198) which was latinized by Michael Scot (*d.* 1232).

There was also much that appeared in Hebrew translation from the Arabic which became accessible to western Europe. Euclid's *Section of the Canon* had evidently been translated into Hebrew from the Arabic, since we have a *Commentary on the Canon* by Isaiah ben Isaac. Moses ibn Tibbon (*d.* 1283) was responsible for a translation of the *Problemata*. There is also a work on music in the Vatican attributed to Abraham ibn Ḥiyya (*d.* 1136) which is said to be a translation from the Arabic. Probably the *Treatise on Music* by Abū'l-Ṣalt Umayya (*d.* 1134) was also known in Hebrew. The Introduction to al-Fārābī's *Grand Book on Music* is recommended by Ibn 'Aqnin (*fl.* 1160–1226). Shem-Ṭob Isaac of Tortosa (*d. c.* 1267) translated the *Middle Commentary on Aristotle's De anima* by Averroes. Kalonymus ben Kalonymus (*d. c.* 1328) made a version of al-Fārābī's *Classification of the Sciences.*

A first glimpse of the transmission of the Arabian legacy in music by means of literary contact is to be seen in Constantine the African (*d.* 1087), one of the early translators of Arabic works into Latin, who introduces the Arabian theories on the influences of the planets and the curative effects of music in his *De humana natura* and *De morborum cognitione.* It had been a maxim of Avicenna '*inter omnia exercitia sanitatis cantare melius est*'.

Gundisalvus (*fl.* 1130–50) has a section on music in his *De divisione philosophiae*, much of which is a verbal reproduction from al-Fārābi's *De scientiis* and *De ortu scientiarum*, which he may have had a hand in translating. Borrowings from the same source may be found in the treatise *De musica*, which bears the name of [pseudo-] Aristotle, and in the *Speculum doctrinale* of Vincent de Beauvais (d. 1264), where al-Fārābī is quoted with Boëthius, Isidore of Seville, and Guido of Arezzo. From a definition in the *Ars musica* of Johannes Ægidius (*c.* 1270), a Spanish theorist who was acquainted with the works of Constantine the African, it would appear that al-Fārābī was again the source. The same may be said of Robert Kilwardby (*d.* 1279), Raimundo Lull (*d.* 1315), Simon Tunstede (*fl.* 1300–69), and Adam de Fulda (*c.* 1490).

Roger Bacon (*d.* 1280) quotes al-Fārābī, in company with Ptolemy and Euclid, in the section on music in the *Opus tertium*, especially mentioning the book *De scientiis.* He also draws on Ibn Sīnā on the question of the therapeutic value of music. The latter is also borrowed by Walter Odington (*c.* 1280) in his *De speculatione musices*, and by Engelbert (*d.* 1331) in his *De musica.* Jerome of Moravia (13th century) devotes a chapter to al-Fārābī in his *De musica*, whilst in another chapter he quotes him side by side with Boëthius, Isidore, Hugo of St. Victor, Guido of Arezzo, and Johannes Garlandia. Al-Fārābī still continued to attract the attention of scholars until the seventeenth century, as we know from George Valla's *De expetendis et fugiendis rebus* (1497–1501), George Reish's *Margarita philosophica* (1508), and Camerarius, who re-issued *De scientiis* (1638).

The benefits that resulted from the literary contact, as outlined above, were not considerable. Of far greater importance was the transmission of Arabian theory *viva voce*. Ibn al-Ḥijārī (*d.* 1194) says that during the Umayyad rule in Spain (8th–11th centuries) 'students from all parts of the world flocked . . . to learn the sciences of which Córdoba was the most noble repository'. Music, which was part of the *quadrivium*, was studied, and European students could have benefited from the Arabic fount direct, without the intermediary of Latin translations. Arabic was probably spoken by the Mozarabs (the Christians living under Muslim rule in Spain), and these people played an important part in the diffusion of the Arabian sciences. We know that Roger Bacon, when lecturing to Spanish students at Oxford, and using faulty Latin translations from the Arabic, was ridiculed by them because they knew his authorities *ab origine*. It is no wonder that the *doctor mirabilis*, like his predecessor Adelard of Bath (early 12th century), recommended his readers and listeners to abandon the European schools for those of the Arabs. Whilst European theorists only knew of Greek theory from Martianus Capella, Boëthius, Cassiodorus, and Isidore, the Arabs possessed the works of Aristotle, Aristoxenus, Euclid, Nicomachus, Ptolemy, and others. It would appear, therefore, that whether the best of the treatises on music in Arabic were known in Latin or not, the mere fact that the Arabs studied them must have yielded beneficial results.

That the Arabs influenced Europe in the question of solfeggio and an alphabetic notation cannot be said with any degree of certainty. In instrumental tablature the borrowing is far clearer, and it is openly acknowledged in the earliest Latin work on the subject that we possess, the *Ars de pulsatione lambuti*. As for a diastematic notation, the earliest use of it in the Islamic East only dates from about 1200.

Probably the most important legacy left to Europe by the Arabs was mensural music. Prior to Franco of Cologne (*c.* 1190?) the *cantus mensurabilis*, or measured song, was unknown. Under the name of *īqā'* (pl. *īqā'āt*) or rhythm, it had been a constituent part of Arabian music since the seventh century, and we have it described in a work by al-Kindī (*d. c.* 874). Not only mensural values in the notes, but even the rhythmic modes that we see in Franco and his school, appear to have been derived originally from the Arabs. In the Latin treatise *De mensuris et discantu* (*c.* 1273–80) we have particular kinds of notes bearing such names as *elmuahym* and *elmuarifa*, which are of Arabic origin, whilst in Johannes de Muris (14th century) we have a reference to a device known as the *alentrade*, also of Arabian origin. The medieval *hocket*, which Robert de Handlo (*c.* 1326) says is 'a combination of notes and pauses', is the Arabic *īqā'āt*, just as the Latin *alhash* in Avicenna's *Canon* is the Arabic *al-'ishq*.

The Practical Art

The diffusion of the Arabian practical art was due to the minstrel class who were the real disseminators of music in the Middle Ages. Perhaps the gaudy raiment of the Occidental musicians, their long hair and painted faces were due to Oriental influences. The Morris dancers, i.e. Moorish dancers, with their hobby-horse and bells, are certainly reminiscent of the Arab minstrels, and as late as Thoinot Arbeau (1589) these Morris dancers still dyed their faces in imitation of the Moors. The Basque name for the hobby-horse—*zamalzaïn*, is simply the Arabic *zāmil al-zain* ('gala limping horse'). The Spanish word *mascara*, like the English *masker* ('play actor'), is the Arabic *maskhara* ('buffoon'). There are dozens of words connected with music in the Iberian peninsula, such as *zambra*, *zarabanda*, *huda*, *mourisca*, which are apparently of Arabic origin.

The superior culture enjoyed by the Arabs was bound to be reflected in western Europe. We know that the Spaniards were imitating Arabian models in rhyme and metre in the ninth century, and in the tenth century even the Jews were influenced. Obviously, the music that accompanied the verse was also borrowed since the two were inseparable. We see both the Arab and the Jew among the *juglares* of Christian Spain, and in the twelfth century, when the Counts of Barcelona became the rulers of Provence, the troubadour (a word which may have been derived from the Arabic *ṭarrāb* 'minstrel') and his *jongleur* re-acted the parts of the Arab *amīr* and his *mughannī*.

The legacy to western Europe in musical instruments and in instrumental music was of the greatest importance. That the Arabs were responsible for the names and even the actual types of a number of musical instruments in western Europe is generally acknowledged. The origin of the words *lute*, *rebec*, *guitar*, and *naker*, from the Arabic *al-'ūd*, *rabāb*, *qītāra*, and *naqqāra*, is well established.

Much of the alien nomenclature adopted by Europe does not always represent fresh types of instruments being adopted. It may have been due to political pressure. There were many distinctly novel Arabian types introduced, and these were of considerable moment to European music. Firstly, there arrived a whole family of stringed instruments of the lute, pandore, and guitar groups. Secondly, there came bowed instruments of various types. Of the early diffusion of these we have the evidence of the St. Médard Evangel (8th century), and the Lothair and Labeo Notker Psalters (9th–10th centuries).

With these instruments came several material benefits. European minstrels, prior to the Arabian contact, only had the cithara and harp among stringed instruments, and they only had their ears to guide them when tuning. The Arabs brought to Europe their lutes, pandores, and guitars, with the places of the notes fixed on the finger-board by means of *frets* (cf. Arab. *farīḍa*, *farḍ*) which were determined by measurement. This alone was a noteworthy advance. Indeed, it was perhaps the fretting of the Arabian lute that registered the employment of the major mode for Europe.

Of course the greatest of the benefits which accrued from the Arab contact was undoubtedly the acquisition of mensural music, which must have been passed on by the minstrels long before the theorists took cognizance of it. Secondly, the 'gloss' or adornment of the melody, the counterpart of *arabesque* in the other arts, was placed under contribution. It was the type of 'gloss' known as the *tarkīb* or 'compound', which was the striking of a note simultaneously with its fourth, fifth, or octave, that probably gave Europe its first prompting towards harmony. It is also worthy of notice that the word *conductus*, a medieval form of composition, is identical with the Arabic *majrā*. It was the Arabian lute perfected by the Spanish masters that led to the *musica ficta*.

With the fall of Baghdād to the Mongols (1258), the capitulation of Granada to the Christians (1492), and the surrender of Egypt to the Turks (1517), the political and cultural superiority of Arabic-speaking peoples ceased. Art and politics may appear to be poles asunder, but the truth is that they are closely bound together. Irrespective of this, Europe had taken the lead in the world's culture long before the last-mentioned date.

From time to time attempts have been made to introduce Arabian and Muslim melodies and 'oriental' effects of orchestra-

1 2 — *Būq* 3 — *Naqqāra* 4 — *Ṭabl* 5 — *Kāsa*

Fig. 91. EGYPTIAN MILITARY BAND OF THE FOURTEENTH CENTURY

From a MS. of Al-Jazarī in the Museum of Fine Arts, Boston

tion into Western music. In the nineteenth century experiments in this direction were made by Rubinstein, Félicien David, and Saint-Saëns; while later composers have also attacked the problem. A study of their endeavours might be of considerable interest, but it would be too long and too technical to undertake in this essay.

H. G. FARMER.

ASTRONOMY AND MATHEMATICS

We must not expect to find among the Arabs the same powerful genius, the same gift of scientific imagination, the same 'enthusiasm', the same originality of thought that we have among the Greeks. The Arabs are before all else the pupils of the Greeks; their science is a continuation of Greek science which it preserves, cultivates, and on a number of important points develops and perfects. One of the greatest of them, al-Bīrūnī, said in considering all the conditions necessary for scientific research—early education, knowledge of languages, long life, the possession of means sufficient to enable one to make journeys and acquire books and instruments: 'all these conditions are rarely found in a single individual, especially in our day. That is why we ought to confine ourselves to what the ancients have dealt with and endeavour to perfect what can be perfected. The middle way is in all things the most praiseworthy; and he who attempts too much ruins himself and his estate'.

Al-Bīrūnī is here, however, obviously too modest; for with this limited ambition the Arabs have really achieved great things in science; they taught the use of ciphers, although they did not invent them, and thus became the founders of the arithmetic of everyday life; they made algebra an exact science and developed it considerably and laid the foundations of analytical geometry; they were indisputably the founders of plane and spherical trigonometry which, properly speaking, did not exist among the Greeks. In astronomy they made a number of valuable observations. They preserved for us in their translations a number of Greek works, the originals of which have been lost: three books of the *Conics* of Apollonius, the *Spherics* of Menelaus, the *Mechanics* of Hero of Alexandria, the *Pneumatics* of Philo of Byzantium, a short book on the balance attributed to Euclid and another to Archimedes on the clepsydra—for which services we cannot be too grateful to them. Another reason for our interest in Arab science is the influence it has had in the West. The Arabs kept alive the higher intellectual life and the study of science in a period when the Christian West was fighting desperately with barbarism. The zenith of their activity may be placed in the ninth and tenth centuries, but it was continued down to the fifteenth. From the twelfth century every one in the West who had any taste for science, some desire for light, turned to the East or to the Moorish West. At this period the works of the Arabs began to be translated as those of the Greeks had previously been by them. The Arabs thus formed a bond of union, a connecting link between ancient culture and modern civilization. When at the Renaissance the spirit of man was once again filled with the zeal for knowledge and stimulated by the spark of genius, if it was able to set promptly to work, to produce and to invent, it was because the Arabs had preserved and perfected various branches of knowledge, kept the spirit of research alive and eager and maintained it pliant and ready for future discoveries.

Before going into details, one fact must be impressed upon the reader; in the history of the sciences, the words 'Arab' and 'Muslim' must be taken in a very wide sense. The majority of the learned men who have flourished in the world of Islām and under the protection of Muslim sovereigns were not Arabs by birth, and several were not even Muslims. The centre of intellectual life, which in the later Hellenistic period was at Alexandria in Egypt, was transferred in the most flourishing period of Arab learning to a district which now seems very remote and backward in civilization, to eastern Persia (Khorāsān) and beyond to the valley of the Oxus, to Khwārizm, Turkistan and Bactria. Al-Khwārizmī for example was a native of Khiva, al-Farghāni of Transoxania, Abu'l-Wafā' and al-Battānī were of Persian origin, as was al-Bīrūnī; al-Kindī was of pure Arab stock. Fārābī was a Turk by origin and Avicenna (Ibn Sīnā) hailed from near Bal<u>kh</u>. Al-<u>Gh</u>azālī and Naṣīr al-Dīn came from Ṭūs in the east of Persia. Omar Khayyām, who wrote his *Algebra* in Arabic, enjoys in our day a great fame as a Persian poet. Several of these scholars wrote in both languages. Avicenna made a Persian version of the one of his books which is perhaps the most important for physics: 'The Philosophy dedicated to 'Alā'; and Naṣīr al-Dīn al-Ṭūsī wrote in the same language a very fine treatise on ethics and a little manual of astronomy. As to Averroes (Ibn Ru<u>sh</u>d), Arzachel (al-Zarḳālī), and Alpetragius (al-Biṭrūjī), they were Arabs of Spain.

As to religion, Ḥunain b. Isḥāḳ, his son Isḥāḳ, Ḳusṭā b. Lūḳā and others who did great work as translators were Christians. <u>Th</u>ābit b. Ḳurra, the great geometer, and al-Battānī, the illustrious astronomer (Albategnius) belonged to the Ṣābians, a pagan sect which worshipped the stars and was devoted to scientific studies and long survived under Islām. Others like Mā<u>sh</u>ā'allāh were Jews: and it may be mentioned that at the period of the Renaissance the Jews contributed very much by their translations and their teaching to the spread of Arab learning in the Latin West.

These scholars, so very different in origin, have however several features in common. Their object was to simplify and make lucid. Without having sufficient genius to make generalizations or any great synthesis, they are very good arrangers. They arrange logically. They classifiy and enumerate, and this simple gift of orderliness and lucidity is almost sufficient to explain the progress which they made. Their manner is didactic; they appear to address themselves not, like the Greeks, to some particular amateur or to some Maecenas interested in learning for itself alone, but rather to all intelligent students. Their books remind one of good secondary or university text-books. The Arabs were traders, travellers, and lawyers; they had the positive mind; their science therefore had a practical object; arithmetic had to serve the needs of commerce, and the division of estates;

astronomy the requirements of travellers and those who cross the deserts, or of religion which has to know the hours of prayer, the azimuth of Mecca and the moment of the first appearance of the moon of Ramaḍān.

The Arab is always practical and never becomes lost in reverie. The Arabic language moreover is dry, precise, and recalls somewhat the style of Voltaire in French. It is more suitable for an exact and precise science than for eloquence and poetic flights. It has the further advantage of lending itself readily to the formation of technical terms. The Arab scholars did not write in verse like the Hindus who composed their algebras in *ślokas*; they did not propound historical problems like the Greeks; they had no taste for enormous numbers and vast periods of time. We do not find among them any *kalpa*, *yoga*, or 'days of Brahma' as among the Hindus, nor names for very high numerals. They are more positive than the Greeks themselves who were interested in very large numbers, as we see from the *Arenarius* and the cattle-problem of Archimedes and the 'great year' of Aristarchus of Samos.

II

We have no books of the time of the Umayyads; the documented history of Arab learning only begins with the 'Abbāsids.[1] Under the second caliph of that dynasty, al-Manṣūr, the centre of the Muslim Empire was transferred from the Byzantine to the Persian part of the Empire: al-Manṣūr founded Baghdād in 145 (762). He had at his court a number of learned men, engineers, and astronomers. The plans of the town were drawn

[1] Much has been written, more particularly in recent years, about science among the Arabs; it is a subject which would require a long bibliography; a bibliography will be found in Volume II of my *Les Penseurs de l'Islam*, Paris, Geuthner, 1921. Special mention must, however, be made here of the excellent work done by Prof. E. Wiedemann of Erlangen who has gathered round him a body of pupils and collaborators. Cf. also H. Suter, *Die Mathematiker und Astronomen der Araber und ihre Werke*, Leipzig, 1900.

up under the direction of the celebrated minister Khālid b. Barmak, by the astronomer Naubakht, a Persian, and by Māshā'allāh, a Jew. In 154 (770) an astronomer, Ya'qūb al-Fazārī, presented at the court of al-Manṣūr a learned Hindu named Manka who introduced the *Sindhind* (*Siddhānta*), a treatise on astronomy according to Hindu methods. This work was translated by al-Fazārī the younger, but the translation is now lost. Al-Fazārī was the first Muslim to construct an astrolabe. He wrote on the use of the armillary sphere and prepared tables according to the years of the Arabs. The translations from the Greek begin in the same period: Abū Yaḥyā b. Baṭrīḳ translated—in addition to medical works—the *Quadripartitum* of Ptolemy. Māshā'allāh (*d.* 815) is a scholar of importance; he wrote on astrology, on the astrolabe, and on meteorology; his book on prices, *de mercibus*, is the oldest scientific work that we possess in Arabic. Johannes de Luna Hispalensis translated several of his works into Latin in the Middle Ages. 'Omar b. al-Farrukhān (*d.* in 200 = 815), a friend of the vizier Yaḥyā the Barmecide, was one of the engineers and architects of Baghdād; he translated some works from the Persian and annotated the *Quadripartitum* of Ptolemy.

This movement, begun under al-Manṣūr, developed still more under his grandson al-Ma'mūn. A prince with a fine intellect, a scholar, philosopher, and theologian, al-Ma'mūn caused the works of the ancients to be sought out and established an office for translating them. Euclid as well as the Almagest was now translated into Arabic by al-Ḥajjāj b. Yūsuf whose activity begins in the reign of Hārūn al-Rashīd. His translation comprises the first six books of Euclid. Al-Ma'mūn had a degree of the meridian measured in the plain of Sinjār by a method different from that of the Greeks: A number of observers setting out from the same point walked, some to the north, the others to the south, until they had seen the pole star rise and sink one degree. They then measured the distance traversed and took the mean of the results. They did not, however, actually keep to this mean but adopted the larger of the two values, 56⅔ miles corresponding for the great circle to 47.325 kilometres, a result rather too large. At the same time observations were taken at Baghdād and at Jundēshāpūr. An observatory was established at Baghdād near the Shammāsīya gate; its erection is attributed to Sind b. ʻAlī, a Jewish convert to Islām. From these observations the tables called 'Tested Tables' or 'Tables of al-Ma'mūn' were prepared according to the method of the *Sindhind*. Al-Farghānī (Alfraganus) is one of the astronomers of this time who were known to the medieval west. He belonged to Farghāna in Transoxania. His *Compendium* of astronomy, a work much esteemed, was translated into Latin by Gerard of Cremona and by Johannes Hispalensis. Regiomontanus at the Renaissance studied it and the great Melanchthon published an edition based on the work of Regiomontanus at Nuremberg in 1537.

Arithmetic and algebra also flourished alongside of astronomy. This was the period of the celebrated al-Khwārizmī, (i.e. the native of Khwarizm) [*d.* between 220 (835) and 230 (844)] whose name, corrupted by the Latin writers of the West, gave us, it is believed, the term algorism (sometimes written algorithm). Besides an important treatise on astronomy, he also wrote a book on the Indian (*Hindī*) method of calculation and another on algebra. The first was translated into Latin by Adelard of Bath, the two others by Gerard of Cremona; the treatise on astronomy and that on arithmetic are known only from these Latin translations.

The *Algebra* of al-Khwārizmī[1] is lucid and well arranged. After dealing with equations of the second degree, the author discusses algebraic multiplication and division; he then treats of problems relating to the measurement of surfaces and deals with others relating to the division of estates or to various legal

[1] Edited with English introduction and translation by F. Rosen, London, 1831.

questions; these latter, which are generally equations of the first degree, although very complicated to look at, are all propounded in the form of numerical examples. The method of approaching the equation of the second degree is important. The author, following Diophantus, distinguishes six cases, one of which, however, is given only for the sake of completeness, for it is identical with the simplest case of the first degree, $bx=c$. The six cases are: squares equal to roots, $ax^2 = bx$; squares equal to numbers, $ax^2 = c$; roots equal to numbers $bx = c$; squares and roots equal to numbers $ax^2+bx = c$; squares and numbers equal to roots $ax^2+c = bx$; roots and numbers equal to squares, $bx+c = ax^2$. We see from this list that the science of this time had not yet completely grasped the manipulation of signs since the different positions of the terms on the opposite sides of the equations seem to it to require separate solutions. The Arabs give the name *muḳābala* (opposition, comparison) to this opposition of the two sides of an equation. This word is usually associated by them with the word *jabr* which means 'restitution'. Jabr (*al-jabr*, algebra) is adding something to a given quantity or multiplying it so that it becomes exactly equal to another. This term seems to have originally meant the two simplest operations of algebra, $a+x=b$ and $ax=b$; its application was later extended and it came to mean the whole subject. It is also found contrasted to *ḥaṭṭ*, 'descent', which means to diminish a number by subtraction or division so that it becomes equal to a given quantity:

$$a-x = b; \frac{a}{x} = b.$$

Al-Khwārizmī, having thus enumerated the six possible cases, gives the rules for their solution and in letters of the alphabet, for at this period algebraic notations were not yet invented. He then proves the rules. The demonstration is geometrical; the Arabs indeed were primarily geometers; they did not then conceive an algebra existing by itself and not based on geometry. This demonstration, repeated several times with the variations demanded by the differences of the cases, is rather a pretty one: here is an abbreviated example.

To solve the equation: a square and 10 roots are equal to 39 dirhams. Let us imagine a square the side of which is unknown; this is the one of which we desire to know the root: Let *AB* be

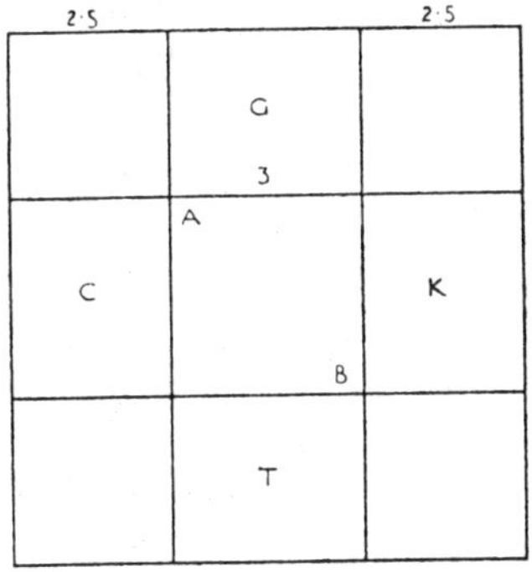

this square: If we multiply its side by a number, the product is this number of roots which we add to the square. Here we have to add ten roots: Let us therefore take a quarter of 10 or 2·5 and make on each side of the square the 4 parallelograms *CGKT*; the value of the square and these rectangles will be 39. But the small squares which are in the angles are each $2{\cdot}5 \times 2{\cdot}5$ or 6·25, that is 25 in all. The whole large square therefore amounts to $39+25$ or 64. Its side is therefore 8 and if we deduct twice the side of the small squares at the angles, i.e. twice 2·5 or 5, there remains 3, which is the root of the square sought.

The question has been asked what difference there was in this case between the Hindu and Arab methods. According to M. Rodet, the Hindus were more analytical than the Arabs, less pure geometers; they had in addition the idea of the double sign; they transfer more easily a term from one side of an equation to the other; method with them is thus beginning to generalize. It must, however, be recognized that as regards exposition, their language, pompous and encumbered by its verse form, has not the clearness, exactness, and scientific simplicity of that of the Arabs.

There is a case in al-<u>Kh</u>wārizmī where the idea of the double sign seems just to emerge. It is the fifth: $ax^2+c=bx$; 'in this case', he says, 'addition and subtraction may be equally well employed'. The theory of equations of the second degree remained down to the sixteenth century exactly as we find it in the Arab algebraist. In the eighteenth century Leonardo Fibonacci of Pisa, an algebraist of considerable importance, says that he owed a great deal to the Arabs. He travelled in Egypt, Syria, Greece, and Sicily, and learned the Arab method there, recognized it to be 'superior to the method of Pythagoras' and composed a *Liber Abaci* in fifteen chapters, the last of which deals with algebraic calculation. Leonardo of Pisa enumerates the six cases of the quadratic equation just as al-<u>Kh</u>wārizmī gives them. The idea of negative and imaginary roots is not clearly defined till Cardan in his *Ars Magna* (1545).

Al-<u>Kh</u>wārizmī's other work, *De Numero indico*,[1] raises the often-discussed question of the origin of the numerals. What the Arab scholar calls Indian (*Hindī*) calculation is counting with the numerals which we call Arabic in contrast to counting with the letters of the alphabet which was then usual in the East. It is evident from this qualification of *Hindī* that the Arabs did not claim to have invented the numerals; but we must not be too quick to conclude from this that they are really of Indian origin; for, as I have observed, the word *Hindī* is easily confused in the Arabic script with *hindasī* which means what relates to geometry or the art of the engineer; in various cases in which the word *Hindī* is used, the meaning of *hindasī* fits better; thus

[1] Latin text edited by Prince Boncompagni in the series *Trattati d'Aritmetica*, Rome, 1857, No. 1.

there is in astronomy a graduated circle which is called *Hindī* which ought perhaps to be translated 'mathematical circle'. The numerals thus called might therefore be simply 'the mathematical characters'. On the other hand the Persians call the numerals 'figures of *end*', which means in their language: 'characters of the little or of small quantities'. As to the forms of the numerals, Woepcke wished to derive them from the initials of the names of the numerals in Sanskrit. But, apart from the fact that the connexion of the forms is not at all obvious, it may be objected that, in the arithmetical systems in which letters are used, it is not as a rule the initials of the numerals that are used, but the letters of the alphabet in their order; this was the case among the Greeks and among the Arabs themselves. The learned Arab al-Bīrūnī in the tenth century says that the numerals came from 'the most beautiful form of the Indian figures'. He does not, however, say exactly what this form is nor in what part of India it was in use. It appears on the contrary that the numerals have a simpler and handier form among the Arabs than anywhere else; this must be their original form. The first five numerals are formed from 1, 2, 3, 4, 5 strokes ligatured; the next four seem to be formed by very simple conventions. The zero is a little circle or dot. It is very likely that the Arabs obtained these signs, like so much of their science, from the tradition of the neo-Platonic schools.

We know that in the numeral system the zero is of capital importance, for it is the zero that enables us to keep the figures in the series of powers of ten, units, tens, hundreds, &c. in the case where one of these powers is not represented. If we did not have a zero, we should have to use a table with columns, columns of units, tens, hundreds, &c., to keep each figure in its place. This table is what is known as the abacus. We find that the zero was known to the Arabs at least 250 years before it was known in the West. The abacus is first found in Rome with Boethius in the fifth century, but its use did not spread then. It reappears with Gerbert in the tenth century. Gerbert had travelled in Spain and studied the sciences of the Moors. He spread the use of the abacus but was not acquainted with the zero. It was not till the twelfth century that Christian arithmeticians began to write treatises on counting with the numerals, without columns, completed by the zero. This method was called algorithm. Now among the Arabs the numerals appear from the first with the zero. The author of the 'Keys of the Sciences', *Mafātīḥ al-'Ulūm*, writing in the tenth century in a period when the use of the numerals had not yet become general, says that if a power of ten is not represented, a little circle is used 'to keep the rows'. This little circle is called *ṣifr*, 'empty'. Some reckoners put a little bar called *tarḳīn*, from the Nabataean *rīḳān* which also means 'empty', 'nil'.

It may be noted that the Latin word *cifra* has a double meaning: it is sometimes zero, sometimes the ciphers themselves. In the sense of zero, it is evidently the Arabic *ṣifr* empty; in the meaning of numeral it is clearly the *sifr* (with *s*) which means something written, a book or character. These words algebra, cipher, algorithm survive as witnesses of the part played by the Arabs in the foundation and diffusion of the science of calculation.

III

Under al-Ma'mūn's successors, especially Mu'taḍid, who was quite an important caliph, there flourished a number of scholars who threw a vivid light on Arab learning and most of whom were known to medieval scholars. Geometrical studies progressed and conic sections began to attract attention. Three brothers, known as Banū Mūsā, distinguished themselves in this period; they were sons of a certain Shākir who, says a biographer, had been a brigand in his youth and harassed the roads of Khorāsān; he became an intimate of al-Ma'mūn and one of the most esteemed scholars of his time. We owe a number of works to these three brothers, one of which, on the measurement of plane and spherical surfaces, was translated into Latin by Gerard of Cremona under the title *Liber Trium Fratrum*. They wrote a treatise on mechanics which is preserved in the Vatican. This work does not deal mainly with the principles of mechanics nor with simple machines like that of Hero, which was translated into Arabic about the same time by Ḳusṭā b. Lūḳā; it resembles the *Pneumatics* of Hero and Philo; in it are described automata and various apparatus constructed with great ingenuity. Another Arabic treatise of the same kind but later in date is that of Badīʿul-Zamān al-Jazarī, a copy of which with very fine miniatures is preserved in Constantinople. The Arabs were very skilful in the construction of clepsydras, water-clocks with automata; it will be remembered that Hārūn al-Rashīd sent one as a present to Charlemagne.

Abū Maʿshar of Balkh in Khorāsān, who died at the age of a hundred in 272 (886), was an astronomer and astrologer of great renown. Four of his works, including the book *De Conjunctionibus et annorum revolutionibus*, were translated into Latin by Johannes Hispalensis and Adelard of Bath.

Thābit b. Ḳurra of Ḥarrān in Mesopotamia is often regarded as the greatest Arab geometer. It was he who did science the service of translating into Arabic seven of the eight books of the conic sections of Apollonius and thus preserving three which are now lost in the original text. The Banū Mūsā were associated with him in this work: they presented him to the future caliph Muʿtaḍid and gave him a pension of 500 dinars a month. Thābit knew Greek and Syriac and made translations from these languages into Arabic. He improved the translation of Euclid's *Elements* by Isḥāḳ b. Ḥunain and that of the *Almagest* by the same. He wrote a number of short treatises or memoirs on astronomy and geometry, elucidating numerous passages in ancient works, inventing new propositions, annotating and facilitating study. Almost all the scientific subjects that could be studied in his day seem to be touched upon in his works. There are references to memoirs by him on the postulates and axioms of Euclid, on the transversal figure (translated into Latin by Gerard of Cremona), on method in geometry, on mechanics, on irrationals, conceived in the manner of Euclid and Plato, and an introduction to Euclid, a work much esteemed. His work on the shadows of the gnomon, i.e. on the sundial, is the earliest that we know on this subject. His treatise on the balance, *Liber Carastonis sive de Statera*, was translated into Latin by Gerard of Cremona. Arabic literature contains several treatises on the balance, one of which, that of al-Khāzinī, is of particular interest. The idea of equilibrium and of gravity is highly developed in it; specific gravities are also discussed.

Thābit made astronomical observations in Baghdād, notably to determine the altitude of the sun and the length of the solar year. He recorded his observations in a book. Belonging to the pagan sect of the Ṣābians and at heart deeply attached to paganism, this scholar is one of the most eminent representatives in the Middle Ages of the traditions of classical culture.

In the next generation there stands out one of the most illustrious scholars of the East, perhaps the one whom the Latin scholars of the Middle Ages and Renaissance most admired and eulogized, al-Battānī (Albategnius). He made his astronomical observations from 264 to 306 (877–918). He wrote a large treatise and compiled astronomical tables,[1] which show in many respects an advance on the work of al-Khwārizmī and diverge still farther from Indian methods. Calculations or observations like those relating to the first appearance of the new moon, to the inclina-

[1] Edited in Arabic and Latin by Nallino, 1903.

Al-Khwārizmī's astronomical treatise has been edited in Latin by H. Suter from Adelard of Bath's version (Copenhagen, 1914). At this period the Arab astronomers reckoned longitudes from the meridian of 'Arin'. This name is a corruption: it is really Ujjain, a town in Central India which had then an observatory; at a much later date in the eighteeenth century Jay Singh re-established the observatory there.

tion of the ecliptic, to the length of the tropic and sidereal year, to lunar anomalies, to eclipses, to parallaxes, are more complicated and more accurate in al-Battānī than in al-Khwārizmī. But his greatest claim to fame is undoubtedly that if he did not discover he at least popularized the first notions of trigonometrical ratios as we use them to-day. Ptolemy used chords, for the calculation of which he had only one main theorem, a very clumsy one. Al-Battānī substituted the sine for the chord. He used tangent and cotangent and he was acquainted with two or three fundamental relations in trigonometry. The sine is called in Arabic *jaib*, which means 'a bay or curve' (in Latin *sinus*), and this is evidently the origin of the word sine. The cotangent to the Arab astronomer is the 'horizontal shadow' of the gnomon, and the tangent is the 'vertical shadow'. They did not yet reckon directly according to the arcs of the circle; but the gnomon itself is divided into 12 parts. Ḥabash, contemporary of al-Battānī, divides it into 60 parts. Hence we get tables of cotangents in parts of the gnomon, based on the equation $\cot\alpha = \frac{\cos\alpha}{\sin\alpha}12$. The altitude of the sun is determined, starting from the cotangent, by the formula

$$\sin(90-\alpha) = \frac{\cot\alpha \,.\, 60}{\sqrt{(12^2+\cot^2\alpha)}}$$

The formulae

$$\sin\alpha = \frac{\tan\alpha}{\sqrt{(1+\tan^2\alpha)}}, \quad \cos\alpha = \frac{1}{\sqrt{(1+\tan^2\alpha)}}$$

are explained in al-Battānī. This brings us very far beyond the point reached by the Greeks and really opens the era of modern science.

Later by some sixty years than Albategnius, another astronomer of great renown, Abu'l-Wafā', continued his work. Several modern scholars have thought they could see in the *Almagest* of this author the discovery of the third lunar inequality, which we call the 'variation', the first two being already known to the Greeks. A long discussion developed in the Académie des Sciences of Paris in which the most eminent scholars took part, Biot, Arago, Le Verrier, Joseph Bertrand, which lasted from 1836 till 1871. In the end it was not proved that the variation was really known to Abu'l-Wafā'. The Arab astronomers do not distinguish the first two lunar inequalities quite as we do; they break them up differently and this is what gave rise to some uncertainty.

But Abu'l-Wafā's services to trigonometry are indisputable. With him trigonometry becomes still more explicit and acquires the formula for the addition of the angles

$$\sin(a+b) = \frac{\sin a \cos b + \sin b \cos a}{R}$$

This formula, discovered at this time, did not, however, become known to the Latin world and Copernicus seems to have been unaware of it. Rhaeticus, the pupil and editor of Copernicus, rediscovered it very laboriously in his *Opus palatinum de triangulis*, after having given another formula much more complicated than Abu'l-Wafā's.[1] This is not the end of the services rendered by Abu'l-Wafā' to science. A geometer of great ingenuity, he dealt with a number of problems and studied the quadrature of the parabola and the volume of the paraboloid; in algebra he translated Diophantus.

During these two centuries in which the final form was given to these discoveries which are now at the foundations of all our modern civilization, a number of powerful minds were dealing with other problems relating to the philosophy of the sciences, and to physical and natural sciences. Without reaching final solutions, they trained the mind, elaborated ideas and prepared the way for future discoveries. Al-Kindī (*d.* 260 = 873), the

[1] We also find the secant in Abu'l-Wafā' which he calls 'the diameter of the shadow'; its introduction is usually credited to Copernicus.

first of the great scholastics, wrote on meteorology and optics. His treatise on the rains and winds and his improved version of the Optics of Euclid were translated into Latin. He also endeavoured to ascertain the laws that govern the fall of a body, a question with which the Arabs were not often concerned. Fārābī, 'the second master' after Aristotle, an eminent neo-Platonist with a profound knowledge of ancient philosophy, wrote a remarkable treatise on music, an art in which he excelled. In this treatise we find the germ of the idea of logarithms. We know how music is related to mathematics. As early as the time of Pythagoras the necessity for expressing by sections of chords the first musical intervals, the octave, the quarter, and the fifth, had given a stimulus to the study of fractions. All the musical theory of the Arabs is expressed in terms of fractions. It contains logarithms *in posse* because the addition of the intervals, fourths, tones, semitones, quarter-tones, &c., corresponds to the multiplication of the lengths of chords which define them and the subtraction of the intervals corresponds to the division of these terms; the notes on a stringed instrument are connected by a logarithmic law. Avicenna and Algazel discuss the question of infinite quantities, sometimes in connexion with religion and sometimes in connexion with physics. Is a past infinite series possible? Is there on a straight line a first point where it is met by another straight line inclined towards it?—and questions connected with atomism—a square being regularly divided into atoms, how can the diagonal contain more atoms than the side? How in a line of atoms can an atom remain indivisible when it is in contact on either side with two different atoms? Can movement, heat, and light be conceived in terms of atoms? These are problems of the same kind as the sophisms of Zeno of Elea. They represent the gropings of the human mind before the discovery of the differential calculus. Al-Bīrūnī, a scholar of exceptional erudition, a very keen critic, compiled a learned work on the chronology of the different nations. He travelled for a considerable period in India, tells us about the arithmetic of the Hindus, notes peculiarities connected with the game of chess, and deals with several questions of mathematical geography (projection, azimuths). He also did something to advance trigonometry.

We now come to a scholar who needs no introduction to our readers, for very few authors enjoy such fame; namely the celebrated Omar Khayyām ('Umar b. Ibrāhīm al-Khayyāmī), poet and mathematician (*d.* 517 = 1123). His skill as a geometer is equal to his literary erudition and reveals real logical power and penetration. His *Algebra* [1] is a book of the first rank and one which represents a much more advanced state of this science than that we see among the Greeks. Omar also marks a considerable advance on al-Khwārizmī: in the first place as regards the degree of the equations; the greater part of his book is actually devoted to cubic equations, while al-Khwārizmī only dealt with quadratics. Then as regards the discussion of the problems, possible and impossible solutions, and the limits of these solutions, it marks an enormous advance on the Greeks. Omar, however, is still under the influence of Diophantus, inasmuch as he endeavours to solve equations into whole numbers; he has therefore not completely freed himself from indeterminate algebra. He classifies equations of the third degree into 27 classes which are again divided into 4 categories, the last two of which consist of trinomial equations and of quadrinomial equations (with four terms). The fourth category contains the three classes: $x^3+bx^2=cx+d$; $x^3+cx=bx^2+d$; $x^3+d=bx^2+cx$. This gives us an idea of the difficulty of the problems conceived. The method used to deal with these problems is geometrical analysis, a kind of analytical geometry as it was conceived before Descartes at a period when the systems of co-ordinates and mathematical notations were not yet established. The last class, for example, is solved with the help of

[1] Edited and translated into French by F. Woepcke, Paris, 1857.

two hyperbolas, constructed according to the data of the problem, and according as *b*, the coefficient of the squares represented by a certain line, is equal to or less than the height of a parallelepiped constructed according to the isolated number and that of the roots, the conics intersect or do not intersect. 'There are different cases of this variety,' says Omar, 'some of them impossible. It has been solved by means of the properties of the two hyperbolas.' Such a method demanded a profound knowledge of the works of Apollonius and great skill in their application. Omar defends his originality as regards the Greeks and several Arab students who had preceded him. 'In this study', he says at the beginning of his treatise, 'we meet with propositions depending on certain very difficult kinds of preliminary theorems, in the solution of which most of those who have tried have failed. No work of the ancients dealing with them has come down to us.' This method of solving equations of the third degree is again found almost identically in the *Géométrie* of Descartes. As to the purely algebraical solution of the equation of the third degree, it did not see the light till the Renaissance when we find it in the writings of Scipione del Ferro, of Tartaglia, and of Cardan, but still in an obscure and uncertain form which gave rise to much disputation.

Omar's *Algebra* marks a stage in the advance of this branch of mathematics. Following on the excellent edition which he published in 1851, the learned editor Woepcke collected several other problems which were popular with Arab mathematicians and also presuppose a knowledge of conics, like the problem of the two proportional means, the trisection of an angle, the construction of regular polygons and especially of the enneagon. Several solutions of the problem of the trisection of an angle were known to the Arabs. An able geometer, Sijzī, gives one which includes all; it depends on the intersection of a hyperbola and of a circle. The construction of the regular polygon with nine sides, given by Ibn al-Laiṯh, depends on the intersection of a hyperbola and a parabola. A lemma not proved by Archimedes (*de Sphaera et Cylindro*, ii. 6–7) provoked research by Ibn al-Haiṯham and others. Al-Ḳūhī puts the problem in this form: to construct a segment of a sphere equal in volume to a segment of a given sphere and in surface to another segment of the given sphere. He solves it very cleverly with the help of two auxiliary cones and two conics: an equilateral hyperbola and a parabola, and he then discusses the limits.

In *arithmetic* the Arabs made several discoveries: about magic squares[1] and 'amicable' numbers. The invention of the proof by 'casting out the nines' is attributed to them, and the process known as the 'rule of the double false position' (*regula duorum falsorum*) which we again find in our arithmeticians of the seventeenth and eighteenth centuries. One of them enunciates the famous theorem of Fermat: the sum of two cubes is never a cube in whole numbers, but no proof is given. Al-Karḵẖī (*d. c.* 420 = 1029) gives by a very neat and simple geometrical process the sum of the third powers of the successive series $1^3+2^3+3^3 \ldots +n^3$ and later al-Kāshī, physician and astronomer to Ulūgh Beg in Samarḳand, gives the summation of the fourth powers, which suggests no mean degree of talent.

In the eleventh and twelfth centuries Arab *astronomy* was in a flourishing condition in Spain: it was for long afterwards studied in the East and continued to retain the interest of scholars of medieval Europe. In Spain al-Zarḳālī (Arzachel) who lived *c.* 420–80 (1029–1087) is famous as an instrument-maker. He invented an astrolabe, a *ṣafīḥa*, on which he wrote a treatise out of which a whole literature developed. A Jew of Montpellier translated it into Latin; King Alfonso of Castille

[1] Magic squares were used in talismans. I noticed recently in a treatise of the Arab occultist al-Būnī (d. 622 = 1225) a very ingenious general solution of the problem of magic squares. This solution enables one, when a square of side n is known, whether n be odd or even, to construct a square of side $n+2$.

made two translations of it into Romance (Spanish), and Regiomontanus in the fifteenth century published a collection of problems on the 'noble instrument of the safīḥa'. Copernicus quotes Arzachel along with Albategnius in his book *De Revolutionibus orbium coelestium.* Al-Biṭrūjī (Alpetragius), a pupil of the philosopher Ibn Ṭufail (twelfth century), had original ideas on the movements of the planets. He left a book which was translated into Hebrew by Moses ben Tibbon, then into Latin in the sixteenth century by Kalonymos ben David. The Alfonsine Tables compiled in the thirteenth century by Alfonso X the Wise are a development of Arab astronomy. The longitudes are referred to the meridian of Toledo.

These scholars had unfettered and inquiring minds; they do not hesitate to criticize Ptolemy, and with Averroes they declare themselves against the theory of the multiplicity and eccentricity of the spheres. They look for more simple and more 'natural' systems. Al-Bīrūnī had already admitted that astronomical hypotheses were all relative, that one could equally well, as Aristarchus of Samos and Seleucus of Babylon had proposed two thousand years before Copernicus, and, at a period not so remote, several Hindus attribute the diurnal movement to the earth and make it turn on its own axis and around the sun, while 'saving appearances', that is to say, explaining and calculating all the movements of the stars. The spirit of Arabian research at this period was not hampered by any fixed views or dogmatism.

In the East in the troubled period of the Mongol invasions there flourished a great scholar with a fine synthetic brain, Naṣīr al-Dīn Ṭūsī (*d.* 672 = 1274). He made observations at Marāgha in Asia Minor in an observatory founded by the munificence of the Mongol Khāns and drew up the astronomical tables called after the regal title of these conquerors 'The Īlkhānian Tables'. The instruments at Marāgha were much admired. The Arab astronomers devoted great attention to the perfecting of instruments. The most important was the armillary sphere, which was known to the ancients and represented in a general way the celestial sphere; it consisted of three rings corresponding to the meridian, the ecliptic, and the colure of the solstices, and of two rings of observation. The Arabs completed and perfected the sphere of Ptolemy and of the Alexandrians. They added to it two rings giving the co-ordinates of the stars with respect to the horizon, then a ring for the observation of the altitudes. They endeavoured to make their instruments as large as possible in order to minimize error; they then began to make special instruments, each being devoted to a special class of observations. In the observatory at Marāgha there were instruments made of rings for special purposes: ecliptical, solsticial, and equatorial armillaries. The ecliptical, which was very much used, had five rings, the largest of which was some twelve feet across. It was graduated in degrees and minutes. When Alfonso of Castille wanted to construct an armillary sphere, which would be the finest and best that had yet been made, it was to the Arabs that he turned for information. At the Renaissance, Regiomontanus, in order to reconstruct the ecliptical of Ptolemy, used Arabic books and it was from them that he became acquainted with the alidade, the name of which is Arabic.

Naṣīr al-Dīn is equally important as a geometer. He edited most of the mathematical works of antiquity to the number of sixteen, which, with four books of the Muslim period, practically constituted the whole scientific knowledge of the period. Among the books added was one by Naṣīr al-Dīn himself, namely the Treatise on the Quadrilateral,[1] a work on spherical trigonometry of the first rank. In it he expands this subject in a most orderly and lucid fashion, at first according to the method of Menelaus and Ptolemy and then according to new methods the advantages of which he points out. The rule which he calls

[1] Edited with a French translation by Caratheodory Pasha, Constantinople, 1891.

that of the 'supplementary figure', which dispenses with the use of Ptolemy's theorem of the quadrilateral, is simply the statement that the sines of angles are proportional to those of sides,

$$\frac{\sin a}{\sin A} = \frac{\sin b}{\sin B} = \frac{\sin c}{\sin C}.$$

To this rule he adds a 'method of the tangent' based on the relation $\sin b = \frac{\tan c}{\tan C}$. Trigonometry, plane and spherical, is now well established and finds in this book its first methodically developed and deliberate expression. In a short paragraph Naṣīr al-Dīn recalls his Arab predecessors who had had a share in its invention.

Lastly, we must mention the astronomers of Samarḳand, whose tables, prepared in 1437 for a prince of the family of Tamerlane under the title *Tables of Ulūgh Beg*, were highly esteemed in the West and published in part in England in the eighteenth century.[1]

Such then in its broad outlines was the scientific work of the Arabs. It came to an end when that of the Western genius began, that is to say in the fifteenth century. It is sometimes asked what were the causes of this cessation of intellectual activity in the Muslim world. Whence came this torpor after a period of such prolific activity? This, however, is a question which raises very obscure problems of general psychology about which no one has yet put forward any very definite theory and, as I have none to propound myself, I do not think I ought to attempt to discuss it.

CARRA DE VAUX.

[1] Edited by J. Greaves and T. Hyde, in Persian and Latin, London, 1650 and 1665. Sédillot translated into French the prolegomena to these Tables (Paris, 1846).

INDEX